# Freedom Burning

# Freedom Burning

## Anti-Slavery and Empire in Victorian Britain

RICHARD HUZZEY

CORNELL UNIVERSITY PRESS · ITHACA AND LONDON

First published 2012 by Cornell University Press

Printed in the United States of America

Library of Congress Cataloging-in-Publication Data

Huzzey, Richard, 1982–
    Freedom burning : anti-slavery and empire in Victorian Britain / Richard Huzzey.
        p. cm.
    Includes bibliographical references and index.
    ISBN 978-0-8014-5108-9 (cloth : alk. paper)
    1. Antislavery movements—Great Britain—History—19th century.   2. Abolitionists—
Great Britain—History—19th century.   3. Slave trade—Great Britain—Public opinion—
History—19th century.   4. Imperialism—Great Britain—Public opinion—History—19th
century.   5. Public opinion—Great Britain—History—19th century.   6. Politics
and culture—Great Britain—History—19th century.   7. Great Britain—Politics and
government—1837–1901.   I. Title.
    HT1163.H89 2012
    326'.8094109034—dc23          2012007352

Cornell University Press strives to use environmentally responsible suppliers and materials to the fullest extent possible in the publishing of its books. Such materials include vegetable-based, low-VOC inks and acid-free papers that are recycled, totally chlorine-free, or partly composed of nonwood fibers. For further information, visit our website at www.cornellpress.cornell.edu.

Cloth printing          10 9 8 7 6 5 4 3 2 1

*For my parents*

# Contents

———

# Illustrations

———

# Acknowledgments

——

I LIKE LIBRARIES. Much of this book was written in them. David Smith was a fantastic host at St. Anne's, Oxford, while John Pinfold and Lucy McCann helped me navigate Rhodes House Library. I also benefited from the advice of librarians and staff at the Bodleian libraries (in all their many locations), Yale University's libraries, the National Archives, the British Library, Columbia University's libraries, Anti-Slavery International, Cambridge University Library, the Gilder Lehrman Archive, the New-York Historical Society, the Harriet Beecher Stowe Center, Harvard University's libraries, Plymouth and West Devon Record Office, Durham University Library, and the Library of Congress. Special thanks must go to Ian Rayment at Plymouth University Library for letting me create images of nineteenth-century publications held there.

For permission to reproduce work first published in my article "Free Trade, Free Labour and Slave Sugar in Victorian Britain," *Historical Journal* 53, no. 2 (2010): 359–79, I thank Cambridge University Press and the journal's editors. I am also grateful to the Yates family for permission to quote from primary sources in their ownership. The rights to reproduce images throughout this book have been granted by Mary Evans Picture Library, the Bodleian Library, and the National Museum of the Royal Navy. The maps and graphs were created by Plymouth University's expert cartographers, though they have kindly assigned the copyright for them to me.

My footnotes acknowledge the rich historiography I have drawn upon, but I must use these few pages to thank the generous scholars who assisted me in my seven years as a postgraduate and postdoctoral researcher. Any errors or inadequacies are mine alone, but they are fewer in number thanks to the following individuals. David Brion Davis, Seymour Drescher, and

David Eltis have honored me with their interest in my work and with their extensive criticism of my ideas. Nick Draper, Catherine Hall, and Keith McClelland have made me feel a part of their "Legacies of British Slavery" project. Peter Jones was generous in sharing his work on Palmerston and Russell, while Heath Mitton and Joe Yanielli helped me articulate my arguments about ideology. Use of Michael Stenton's *Who's Who of British Members of Parliament,* 4 vols. (Hassocks, Sussex, 1976–81), helped identify Victorian MPs who turned up in the columns or division lists of *Hansard,* as did Seth Thevoz with his intimate knowledge of parliamentarians in this period.

For their excellent criticism and comments on all or part of the manuscript, I am immensely grateful to Cornell's anonymous readers, Bob Bonner, Kathryn Gleadle, Keith Hamilton, Philip Harling, Bob Harms, I. P. Xerxes Malki, Cai Marshall, Caleb McDaniel, Simon Morgan, Andrew J. Ratledge, David Rundle, Howard Temperley, and Joseph Yanielli, together with participants in seminars or conferences at Yale, Queen's University Belfast, Duke, Pittsburgh, Oxford, Bristol, Exeter, and Plymouth. My thesis examiners J. R. Oldfield and William Whyte were particularly helpful in suggesting what would make a good book. For encouragement and stimulating conversations about my work, I also thank Richard Anderson, Scott Anthony, Amanda Berlan, David Blight, Chris Brown, Robert Burroughs, Nandini Chatterjee, Haydon Cherry, Becky Conekin, Martin Crawford, Jan-Georg Deutsch, Lindsay Doulton, Stan Engerman, Bronwen Everill, Margot Finn, Peter Ghosh, Doug Hamilton, Alison Holmes, Anthony Howe, Paul Kennedy, Jane Landers, John McAleer, Clare Midgley, Robert Saunders, Sam Schaffer, Stuart Semmel, Simon Skinner, Nick Smart, Adam I. P. Smith, Adam Tooze, David Turley, Jim Walvin, and Mary Wills. My editor Roger Haydon has made the publication process a pleasure, helped by the skills of copyeditor John Raymond, indexer Victoria Baker, and production editor Susan Specter.

Amanda Behm, Justin DuRivage, Lucy Kaufman, S. Heath Mitton, Kenneth Owen, Jay Sexton, and Charles K. Smith all provided pivotal readings of my work alongside friendship and encouragement. Steve Pincus and Keith Wrightson gave me a brilliant opportunity to spend two years at Yale, which changed me as a historian, while a visiting fellowship at the Gilder Lehrman Center (GLC), hosted by David Blight, Melissa McGrath, Dana Schaffer, and Tom Thurston, allowed me push my thinking further.

I could not wish for more supportive (not to say enterprising) colleagues than those I have encountered in my first year with Plymouth University. Not only did they make it possible for me to take up the GLC fellowship, but the School of Humanities' research committee has paid for all this book's graphs, maps, and image rights, improving both the style and substance of my published research. I also received institutional support during my undergraduate and graduate education from scholarships and hardship bursaries at St. Anne's and St. Catherine's Colleges, Oxford, for which I will always remain grateful. During my doctoral work, the Gilder Lehrman Institute funded a research fellowship in New York that permitted me to use collections at Columbia and the New-York Historical Society. My thanks go to all of these patrons.

This project exists thanks to Lawrence Goldman and Richard Carwardine, who taught the undergraduate seminar where my research interests took root. Lawrence was an incisively honest and infectiously enthusiastic supervisor. Richard Carwardine adopted de jure the role of college advisor which he had long since performed de facto as a friend, persuading me to continue in the face of demoralizing financial challenges. Any merit that may be found in this book survives because of his encouragement and because of Lawrence's constructive and critical support.

I finished my doctoral work a few weeks after I met Irene Middleton and it is a pleasure to complete this manuscript a few weeks after marrying her, especially given that I have benefited from her intellectual insights, mean editing, and supportive love in the intervening period. I hope she will forgive me for waiting to dedicate a future book to her. Instead, I want to thank my family. Without my father's proofreading, there would have been many more references to "ant-slavery" or "Christ Brown," but it is not my parents' practical help that I have valued the most. My parents and grandparents have consistently put me—and especially my education—first, whatever challenges life brought. This work is a token of my appreciation to my mother and father. You laid all its foundations, in your kindness and your sacrifices.

# Freedom Burning

# Prologue

─────

## *Freedom Burning*

THE PAINTER captured the fire burning. It happened in West Africa, on the banks of the Gallinas River. On 4 February 1845 sailors advanced from their ships in small boats to reach the African settlement and burn it to the ground. The flags of the vessels and the flames of the fire reflected on the surface of the water, as the moment was recorded by an unknown artist. As the village burned, he captured the smoldering sky and the assembled vessels, the flaming houses and the raiding party.

The attackers were not slave traders or pirates but serving men of the British Royal Navy. So, was this part of some invasion force or some mission to colonize the area? No, they did not intend to stay. The sailors served on ships that formed part of the West Africa squadron, tasked with suppression of the Atlantic slave trade. A complex web of treaties between Britain and most other "civilized" governments required the flotilla's presence off the African coast. The navy was authorized to police most of the world's shipping, searching out illegal slave traders and delivering them to international justice. Beyond this surveillance of merchants, the squadron's officers were also instructed to secure treaties with African peoples for the suppression of the slave trade and the promotion of alternative forms of commerce.

More than a decade earlier the British had emancipated enslaved Africans in the West Indies and, twenty-five years before that, the British Parliament had banned a prosperous slave trade. Now the nation sacrificed millions of pounds and scores of sailors' lives each year to eradicate the slave trade that flourished illegally throughout the Atlantic. In doing so, Britain had reasserted its identity as a land of freedom, a friend of humanity, and a beacon of liberty. But in a distant part of West Africa, these noble

FIGURE 1. Detail of anonymous painting of African settlements being destroyed on the banks of the Gallinas River, 1845. By permission of the Museum of the Royal Navy, Portsmouth.

*Why does Britain want the end of slavery? And is that motive as benevolent as it seems?? Probably not...*

aspirations took the form of threats and intimidation against an African people.

The attack on the village was part of an operation against "the Chiefs and Head-men of the Native Tribes in the River Gallinas." These African leaders, living near the border between modern Sierra Leone and Liberia, had offended Commodore William Jones, commander of the West Africa squadron. The local rulers were accused of breaking their side of an 1840 treaty by "countenancing and encouraging foreign dealers in black men to live in your country, and to sell their slaves into captivity beyond the seas." But this was not all. Worse, they had taken their "contempt of the Treaty so far, as to enslave, and sell, the subjects of the Queen my mistress." Jones demanded "redress and reparation" for Great Britain and, more than a week before the attack, he bluntly requested that the chiefs of the Gallinas meet him for this purpose. He particularly requested the presence of Prince Manna, a leader who stood accused of personally trafficking into slavery black British subjects—free men and women residing in the Queen's Sierra Leone colony. From the start the commodore had threatened violence and, when Manna and his allies did not comply, he entered the river with a force of 286 men.[1]

*(margin note)* *note the continuance of slave trade*

The towns of Tindes, Taillah, and Minnah, aligned with these chiefs, were destroyed by fire. It is now impossible to know which of these three settlements was pictured by our artist. Commodore Jones, as part of his attempt to intimidate the rulers, had sent notice that women and children should vacate the villages, since he would soon "inflict a severe and summary punishment." When he made good on his threat, he found that the Africans had removed their property too, leading him to claim to his superiors with confidence that "the Chiefs will be the only sufferers from their wicked folly." The African families left homeless by the raid would probably have begged to differ; the chiefs' penalty was paid by their subjects.[2]

Elsewhere that same day, the commodore's men had destroyed the slave fort of an insolent Spanish slave dealer who regularly traded with Prince Manna. There had, however, been no reply from Manna himself, despite the reprisals against towns belonging to his allies. After being briefly distracted by duties at another point on the coast, the squadron returned to the area on 17 February. Approaching Guindemar, the key settlement in Manna's domain, Jones was ready to repeat the punishment he had inflicted upon the three Gallinas villages. His two hundred marines and sailors, some of the latter West Africans recruited to serve in the squadron, advanced on the town, encountering light resistance. The British force occupied Guindemar for two hours as a demonstration of the Queen's power, but Jones spared it from destruction as a demonstration of her mercy.

Manna saved the settlement by adopting a humble tone and providing evidence that his alleged offenses were overblown: while he admitted

selling slaves to the Spanish middleman, he produced the two Sierra Leonean women he had been accused of abducting. They convinced the officer
that, far from being abducted, they had chosen to marry men in Guindemar. Moreover, on closer examination, the evidence about selling other
British subjects into slavery fell apart; one eye-witness could not identify
Manna, so the chief helpfully promised to find the real offender and hand
him over to Jones. Broader complaints of supporting the slave trade, despite an 1840 treaty with Britain, stood, however, and the commodore demanded compliance.[3]

For Jones, these interventions were a vital part of his mission to intimidate coastal peoples into rejecting the European-stimulated traffic in slaves.
He had spared Guindemar, he claimed, so that "we leave the natives something to lose" if they defied Britain in the future. He was pleased to report
that he had advanced the nation's anti-slavery crusade: "We have evidently
impressed these people with a very wholesome terror, and they begin to
think resistance to our power is useless," he reported with satisfaction.[4] Although this incident did not expand the formal borders of British territory
of West Africa, it is clear with hindsight that the exercise of naval power
foreshadowed the following fifty years of colonial advance. Indeed, Jones's
ship, HMS *Penelope*, would take a leading part in the annexation of Lagos
six years later, which would mark the next stage of European penetration
of the continent.[5]

How did these events in West Africa fit into the wider history of anti-
slavery? The use of force to suppress the slave trade was not without controversy in Victorian Britain, but objectors were concerned more with the
principles of international law, pacifism, and free trade than the collat-
eral African victims of violence against slave-trading chiefs. Jones's actions
came as a colleague, Captain Joseph Denman, was being tried in the British
courts over a similar raid in 1840—but his trial was about his destruction
of a Spanish trader's nonslave merchandise, not his conduct toward local
Africans. For those very few Victorians who objected, the violence and suffering inflicted on the African families of these villages was, as it is for us,
a troubling version of anti-slavery morality.

The fires Jones and his fellow naval officers lit in West Africa sit uneas-
ily with modern expectations for what an anti-slavery policy should look
like. Was violence against Africans a betrayal of humanitarianism or a just
war for slave-trade suppression? Did the flames of the Gallinas villages help
kindle some new beacon of liberty or consume the spirit of freedom? Was
freedom burning brightly or was freedom burning down? The chapters
that follow uncover the complexities and contradictions of anti-slavery for
Victorian Britain and its empire. British emancipation cast shadows upon
many of the central questions of the age; there was a myriad of different
views on how the flames of freedom should burn on.

# I

# An Anti-Slavery Nation

*Dispel the blue haze,*
*Golden fountain of morn!*
*With meridian blaze*
*The wide ocean adorn!*
*The sunlight has touched thy glad shores, Caribee!*
*And day now illumines the Isles of the Free!*

D AWN ON the morning of 1 August 1834 brought a kind of freedom to the enslaved women, men, and children of the British West
Indies. As the sun rose, the Emancipation Act of the previous year
made them free—legally free, at least. Patriotic prose, images, and poetry
depicted the dawn of their freedom. Composed by the anti-slavery publisher Josiah Conder, the above lines are typical of the celebration and
self-satisfaction expressed by British abolitionists, politicians, and newspapermen. The "meridian blaze" of liberty had finally drenched the sugar
colonies in light and warmth equal to the midday sun, he believed.[1] Contemporaries understood emancipation as the climax of a spasmodic fifty-
year campaign by humanitarian reformers who had skillfully mobilized
popular support by means of petitions, consumer boycotts, and political
pressure on the House of Commons. In 1807 the slave trade had been abolished, but emancipation in the sugar colonies waited until the 1830s, following further public agitation.

What happened to Britain's enthusiasm for anti-slavery after this celebrated emancipation? This book argues that it did not collapse in the face
of Victorian racism, imperialism, or indifference, even if the contradictions, hypocrisies, and shortcomings of British anti-slavery became more

visible and so presented an image of decline. This chapter and the next will show how variety and diversity hid, in plain sight, the breadth of anti-slavery sentiment in Victorian culture. Within British society, anti-slavery could be claimed or rejected as a relevant precedent for particular reform movements depending on what individual Briton assumed "anti-slavery" to entail. Moreover, anti-slavery ideas shaped the use and abuse of British power by successive governments, who deployed unequalled force to establish a world free from slavery. Such a world was morally and materially desirable, though Britons disagreed enormously over how, when, and why their nation should act to promote anti-slavery. In the midst of these conflicts, anti-slavery policies favoring imperial expansion triumphed, and I shall explain why anti-slavery ideology failed to halt—and indeed encouraged—hardening attitudes toward Africans' racial capacity and political sovereignty. A basic consensus against slavery broke down on the particulars of almost any practical question; this being the case, why did certain answers triumph over others?

An attempt to understand and explain anti-slavery politics does not mean a simplistic search for moral condemnation or vindication. Rather, the relationship between anti-slavery and imperial power helps explain Victorian foreign and colonial policies as well as the context of domestic politics, revealing why particular interpretations of anti-slavery triumphed and others did not. The bulk of historical research on British anti-slavery concludes before Victoria's accession to the throne in 1837 and so ignores this question. Historians have pored over the popular and parliamentary campaigns that made this freedom possible and have begun to document the human experience of enslaved Africans in the middle passage. Scholars have also examined the realities of life for black freed people in the West Indies and the gross injustices they continued to suffer after the legal abolition of slavery. Africanists have recovered the history of a continent from the perspective of its indigenous peoples, slowly uncovering the human experiences that lie behind the silences and assumptions of Western sources.[2] A focus on the legacies of anti-slavery enthusiasm that framed British attitudes comes at a cost. The voices of Africans and the enslaved appear only fleetingly because they were largely excluded from British politics and policymaking—the notable exceptions being black abolitionists lecturing in Britain and those Africans whose actions disrupted the best-laid plans of the colonizers.

Linda Colley has suggested that "abolitionism became one of the vital underpinnings of British supremacy in the Victorian era" but historians have largely focused on explaining the motives for abolition and emancipation rather than the implications afterward.[3] *Freedom Burning* charts the political conflicts that emerged over what it meant to be an anti-slavery nation in a world where slavery still openly existed and investigates exactly what this "supremacy" meant (and whose supremacy it was). This uncertainty meant that there was more than a little "blue haze" over what was required for "the Isles of the Free" in the years after Conder's 1834 poem had heralded the "golden fountain of morn".

The era can be viewed as a period of anti-slavery decline—a decline indicated by the fading influence of anti-slavery societies, by the rise of racial thinking, by the stirrings of imperialism, and by the apathy of many Britons toward the cause of the North in the American Civil War. This has been the dominant view of historians, who have located the dotage and decline of British anti-slavery sentiment in the first decade of Victoria's reign, as fratricide replaced crusade.[4] However, judging the health of anti-slavery sympathies from the institutional survival of abolitionist organizations is a mistake. There was nothing as cohesive as an "anti-slavery movement" in Victorian Britain. A broader examination of society is reveals that organizations such as the British and Foreign Anti-Slavery Society (BFASS) represented only a portion of anti-slavery opinion.

Historical research has slowly begun to pick apart the complex network of interests and agendas that made up the "anti-slavery movement" before 1834 and to understand it as a shifting patchwork of alliances.[5] A focus on anti-slavery societies distorts the fate of anti-slavery ideas after West Indian emancipation; if the abolitionist societies were in decline, it does not follow that British anti-slavery sentiment was necessarily in decline too. To study the history of free trade after 1846 through the institutional fate of Britain's Anti-Corn Law League would strike historians as very curious. Doing the equivalent for the history of anti-slavery is looking for signs of life in all the wrong places.[6] A national abolitionist society was no longer the principal vehicle for anti-slavery ideas. Instead, it was an era of anti-slavery pluralism, and it was no longer obvious which policies best advanced the nation's opposition to slavery.

Unless, like Victorians, we wish to reserve the epithet "anti-slavery" for some favored methods and techniques, it makes sense to take seriously anti-slavery in all its chaotic and pluralist forms. As historian Howard Temperley notes, the epithet "abolitionist" could also apply to "a host of individuals and groups—for example those British Ministers, government officials and naval personnel who gave their energies (and sometimes their lives too) in the struggle against slavery." He is right to invoke a metaphor that the abolitionist Thomas Clarkson described in his 1808 history of slave-trade abolition. In his youth, Clarkson saw diverse campaigners as tributaries uniting in a great anti-slavery river, cascading toward a sea of freedom. Clarkson lived long enough to see British anti-slavery sentiment split, after 1833, from one river into numerous estuaries, streams, and puddles, muddily emptying into quite different destinations (although he would have found it too painful to adapt his metaphor to reflect this fact).[7] This diversity should not blind us to the continued influence of anti-slavery ideology in Victorian Britain.

"Ideology" is a key term here—and one that refers to the family of ideas regarding the wrongfulness of slavery. Describing anti-slavery as an ideology recognizes the variety of opinions, methods, and definitions that could be accommodated around a core set of beliefs. Before 1834, antipathy toward slavery had transformed into anti-slavery as a political idea pursued through legal intervention. Differences and nuances could be contained beneath the wider, unifying world view of opposing the ownership of human beings—an ideology of anti-slavery. Rather like a solar system or an atom, an ideology has a core orbited by different bodies of ideas and practices.[8] Ideologies are therefore "imaginative maps drawing together facts that themselves may be disputed. They are collectively produced and collectively consumed, though the latter happens in unpredictable ways, and that collective nature makes them public property."[9] This approach works well for Victorian anti-slavery, where opposition to the ownership of humans was the core of the ideology, but there could be disagreements over the racial equality or inequality of Africans to Europeans, the use of tariff barriers to promote free labor, or the morality of compensating slaveholders for emancipation. Groups of anti-slavery supporters, approaching the question of chattel bondage from varied perspectives, assumed different collections of beliefs. Anti-slavery was, however, a coherent ideology insofar as it saw the social norm of slavery as inimical to the national good (be that good defined by prosperity, godliness, or honor).[10] This "ideology" is therefore distinguished from both the rigor of a single political philosophy and the autonomy of a particular idea; it is instead a belief system for viewing the world.

If such scholarly theorizing seems foreign to the past we are considering, it should not do so. In 1872, Bartle Frere, a colonial official and anti-slavery advocate, used a similar metaphor when he regretted that "many atoms, and very influential atoms" would "tell you all these new fangled theories" of race. He remarked, however, that among the public a more generous, traditional attitude to anti-slavery remained.[11] Frere's model was a little simplistic, as many people—including himself—combined anti-slavery sentiment with racial prejudices, even when they did not subscribe to pessimistic scientific theories. Still, what matters here is his attention to the ways that issues such as race could cut across anti-slavery (as he defined it); he described society as clusters of beliefs. His atomic metaphor is useful, since it lends itself to understanding how Britons could find themselves allies in one anti-slavery controversy and enemies in another.

Therefore, "anti-slavery" can be defined as opposition to slavery rather than as the particular policy prescriptions or methods of any one faction.

Before August 1834, anti-slavery campaigners operated successfully despite a wide range of expectations, methods, and purposes. Without any clear agenda to unite strands of anti-slavery opinion in the Victorian period, differences became more obvious. A brief study of events between emancipation and Victoria's coronation on 28 June 1838 will help explain why.

## DIVISION AND DIVERSITY

On the day of West Indian emancipation, the London-based Anti-Slavery Society instructed the British public that "a day of such vast moment to the welfare of one part of the empire, and to the honour of the whole, ought not to pass unnoticed."[12] In the glow of victory it was possible for abolitionists to forget their internal disagreements over whether it was right that planters received £20 million in financial compensation and freed people suffered a period of compulsory work.[13] These disputes set aside, on the evening of emancipation day the anti-slavery elite gathered for a feast in Freemasons' Tavern to toast their success. Beyond self-satisfaction, neither the parliamentary leaders of the emancipation struggle nor the British public at large had any great sense of what an anti-slavery nation should do next; the Anti-Slavery Society had no plan to rally support for abolitionist movements in Europe or the Americas.

A group of radical campaigners calling themselves the Agency Society differed from their elders and betters on this, and they would become a leading force in the Victorian BFASS. Frustrated with the caution of parliamentary leaders such as Thomas Fowell Buxton, these men had declared independence from the Anti-Slavery Society in the summer of 1832, wanting to pursue more vigorous agitation against pro-slavery MPs seeking re-election.[14] It is debatable whether "an Antislavery House [was] returned by an Antislavery public for the first time" in the 1832 elections thanks to them, as some members claimed.[15] However, members of the Agency Society certainly were far more focused than their Anti-Slavery Society collaborators in seeking a new cause after the death of West Indian slavery. In February 1834, six months before the emancipation celebrations, they had reorganized themselves as the British and Foreign Society for the Universal Abolition of Negro Slavery and the Slave Trade. This new group intended to support abolitionist groups abroad and advance the cause of global emancipation. They were mostly campaigners who, unlike the anti-slavery establishment, rejected patience and compromise with the government's cautious ministers in the early 1830s.[16]

Differences over the speed or nature of anti-slavery policies originated in the abolition and emancipation campaigns. A majority vote for the 1833 Emancipation Act represented both more and less than it first seems. On the one hand, for all the measure's timidity and uncertainty, debate in

Parliament reflected a change in how slavery could be discussed by British politicians. Even those who opposed an act for immediate emancipation had grudgingly adopted the language of anti-slavery. The Tory Sir Robert Peel insisted, during the emancipation debate, that his gradualism was founded on a desire to avoid "the grave responsibility of having, by a precipitate attempt to ameliorate the condition of our own slaves, aggravated the hardships of those who were exposed to a more bitter fate in other parts of the world." Acting too quickly could lead to disaster, discrediting amelioration and emancipation, he suggested. Peel felt able to criticize the emancipation bill only in this guarded way; in a sense, everyone was an opponent of slavery now, even those who wanted a slower process of emancipation. Indeed, replying to Peel for the Whig government, Lord Althorp insisted that "the only difference between the course recommended by the right hon. Gentleman, and that proposed by the Government, was in the point of time."[17] Yet despite this language, there was no consensus behind emancipation. Both abolitionists and conservative MPs such as Peel resented the speed at which the Whigs moved and the package of compensation they offered to the sugar colonies: the former found the ministers too meek, the latter found them too harsh. The government sold emancipation as a careful, well-measured change; it was not a complete capitulation to the abolitionists' demands but a negotiated surrender to anti-slavery passions.

The nervous Whig government tried to ease the pain of the Emancipation Act for West Indian slaveholders by allowing an ameliorated, regulated kind of forced labor to continue for a few years under the new name of "apprenticeship"—despite howls of protest from many abolitionists. Loosely based on long-standing laws for apprentices in Great Britain, the Caribbean variant imposed physical punishment and compulsory, unpaid labor on the newly manumitted black population. Concerns about the treatment of apprentices emerged in the first year after emancipation but met with faltering official investigation. Both Lord Melbourne's Whig administration and the leaders of the Tory opposition were committed to the terms of the 1833 Emancipation as a solemn compact with the West Indian planters, and they would hear no talk of renegotiation. Buxton, William Wilberforce's successor as leader of the parliamentary anti-slavery faction, was hesitant to push the fragile ministry too hard. Parliamentary investigations of abuses of the system in 1836 and 1837 showed little appetite for action.[18]

Instead, Joseph Sturge, a Birmingham-based Quaker associated with the Agency group, emerged as the leader of a serious campaign against apprenticeship. He traveled to the West Indies with Thomas Harvey, William Lloyd, and John Scoble in 1837 to investigate. Emphasizing that their mission was "entirely independent of the Anti-Slavery Society," they sought to gather first-hand evidence of abuses under the system of apprenticeship.

Sturge and his compatriots acted on their own initiative, though they drew support from a subsection of the Universal Abolitionist Society's membership.[19] The death of King William IV in June 1837 triggered a general election, but it came too early for Sturge's group to make apprenticeship a key point of debate in the constituencies. Regardless, in the first few months of Victoria's reign, these abolitionists turned to the task of reviving anti-slavery pressure in the hopes of building a parliamentary majority that would end apprenticeship immediately.[20]

In the winter of 1837–38 Sturge published his own account of the horrors uncovered by the expedition and the narrative of James Williams, an abused Jamaican apprentice. "Apprentices get a great deal more punishment now than they did when they was slaves," asserted the eighteen-year-old Williams to his readers.[21] A "Central Emancipation Committee" was founded to mobilize the anti-slavery public, once more harassing government ministers and MPs. This "take-over by the provincial immediatists" caught the public mood. Sturge seemed likely to build a parliamentary majority to abolish this continuing form of forced labor. Behind the scenes, the colonial secretary, Lord Glenelg, encouraged the governors of the British West Indies to make a local termination of apprenticeship. He was motivated not only by public pressure on Parliament but also by fears that resistance to two more years of apprenticeship would provoke free people in Jamaica and other colonies to revolution.[22] Concerned to assert sovereignty over their own affairs and recognizing that the weak ministry was unlikely to withstand further pressure, the colonial assemblies chose to end apprenticeship themselves rather than wait for the inevitable.[23]

Though they were outvoted, both Whig and Tory MPs from English boroughs defied their party whips to vote for a premature end to apprenticeship in March 1838. Their constituencies were the kind where extra-parliamentary agitation could be intimidating; in small urban populations, anti-slavery sentiment could organize in favor of a rival candidate. West Indian planters surrendered the remaining two years of apprenticeship because they recognized that public outrage would ultimately sway a majority of MPs.[24] More fundamentally, the apprenticeship question was a taste of coming clashes between alternative models of anti-slavery. Glacially cautious attitudes did not die out after 1838; indeed, they became a politically accepted refuge for those who had previously opposed anti-slavery. Reluctance among politicians of both parties to curtail the period of apprenticeship shows that many remained committed to a gradual, conservative brand of anti-slavery, even after emancipation.

Still, on the morning of 1 August 1838, the sun rose over the Caribbean alongside another, slightly purer, kind of freedom for black Britons. In Britain, Sturge and his allies celebrated this new victory for radical

abolitionism. Daniel O'Connell, the Irish nationalist, was particularly keen
to launch a British crusade against global slavery off the back of the apprenticeship agitation. In the eyes of this democratic admirer of the United
States, slavery prevented America from being the perfect blueprint for British reform and Irish independence.[25] On the same day as these celebrations,
Buxton separately published a small private edition of a book he had been
working on throughout the tumult of the apprenticeship controversy. His
main concern after the emancipation act of 1834 had been Britain's plod-
ding efforts to suppress the transatlantic slave trade, and he wanted the
government to establish a model farm on the River Niger to diffuse Christianity, commerce, and free-labor farming across the continent.

These divergent concerns shaped two new abolitionist societies, the
BFASS and the African Civilization Society. The BFASS—which hoped
to be the national voice of anti-slavery concerns—was founded in 1839
as a result of Sturge's and O'Connell's ambition for Britain to attack foreign slavery. Its membership was drawn from among those campaigners
who had led the Negro Emancipation Committee's fight against apprenticeship.[26] Meanwhile, Buxton's plans found form in the African Civilization Society. He published his findings on the slave trade publicly and
used meetings at the venerable Exeter Hall—a famous rallying place for
charitable and religious causes—to spread his ideas.[27] However, his dream
perished in 1841 with a disastrous expedition up the Niger, just four years
before Buxton died. The BFASS proved longer lived, with its successor organization surviving to the present day. Still, the group occupied a different
role than its predecessor Anti-Slavery Society; despite its radical ambitions,
it was less successful in leading a popular national movement than it was
in providing information about foreign slavery to the British government.

By the late 1830s, newspapers had begun to discern the differences
among these bands of anti-slavery campaigners. Press judgments were
colored by broader concerns about religious denomination and political
partisanship. One article in the *Times* contrasted the African Civilization
Society, patronized by Prince Albert, Anglican churchmen, and Conservative leader Sir Robert Peel, with the "anti-slavery farce" of the BFASS.
The latter faction harbored "the inferior devotees of the anti-slavery pan-
theon," who were radicals, dissenters, or, worst of all, Irish. Good Angli-
cans and Methodists, the newspaper suggested, had become wise to "the
crafty dissenting objects for the promotion of which that great noble cause
had too often and too notoriously been desecrated."[28] As another reporter
put it in 1845, the BFASS was "a clique of great unknowns, a squadron of
busy-bodies who pursue great objects by small means."[29] Victorians increasingly distinguished between a universal opposition to slavery and the
prescriptions of particular abolitionists. This was in part due to the divisive

influence of American societies on their British counterparts. Transatlantic disputes over the role of women in anti-slavery societies were dismissed by some commentators as "one of the most paltry affairs which ever unsettled a great cause."[30] More fundamentally, alignment with radical Americans linked British activists with their allies' "bigotry" and "zealotry." When the *Spectator* argued in 1852 that "progress is made *in spite* of the party that unduly monopolizes that title" of "abolitionist," it was referring to Britain as well as America.[31] Another journal noted, five years later, that Britons had started "looking beyond the Faneuil Hall and Exeter Hall aspects of the anti-slavery cause" and thinking "beyond the narrow sphere of anti-slavery societies."[32]

Newspapermen ceased to identify any particular abolitionists as an "anti-slavery movement" with authority over what was, or what was not, good anti-slavery policy. To speak of anti-slavery was, for the *Times* of 1861, to speak of "England, for no 'Christian and philanthropic class' has any monopoly here of hatred for negro slavery."[33] Indeed, politicians, writers, and members of the public picked and chose which strategies they believed would best advance those goals. There was no great consistency in the contemporary language used to differentiate schools of anti-slavery policy, but there was an important conceptual divide. The *Spectator's* distinction between "abolitionists" and "anti-slavery" can be usefully adopted to distinguish between the surviving societies and the wider currency of anti-slavery sympathy in Victorian Britain. There were great varieties of opinion within these divisions. After 1838, contending factions struggled to define the meaning and to claim the mantle of anti-slavery. Some developed sufficient differences to become separate, rival species of anti-slavery despite sharing a common ancestor in their opposition to the ownership of human beings as property. Historians of the United States have understood anti-slavery ideas to exist on a spectrum, ranging from colonizers and moderate free soilers to radical abolitionists and racial egalitarians.[34] Alongside the well-studied failures of progressive abolitionists, it is critical to study the vibrant "moderate"—perhaps "conservative"—veins of anti-slavery opinion in Victorian Britain.

Although the abolitionist societies declined as a popular force, it would be wrong to dismiss their impact entirely, particularly on a local level. In many ways, it was the unity and national authority of a London leadership over a national movement that declined most markedly, while regional groups revived and declined periodically. The BFASS saw itself as the country's leading society but suffered from splits and divisions even with its own local auxiliaries. A wide variety of local institutions existed during the period, as well as abortive attempts to found rival national organizations. In Glasgow and Edinburgh, the abolitionist agitator George

Thompson established his own base of support aligned with William Lloyd Garrison's faction in America. The BFASS was, by contrast, allied to the Tappan brothers' American and Foreign Anti-Slavery Society.[35] Across the country, regional bastions of support would also emerge and survive under local leaders such as the Estlin family of Bristol and Wilson Armistead of Leeds.[36] Even so, early Victorian abolitionists largely found it hard to identify political issues they could unite about or on which to mobilize the public.

This problem of authority was sharply illustrated at the World Anti-Slavery conventions of 1840 and 1843. Called by the BFASS, the self-appointed head of the global anti-slavery cause, the conferences drew together a wide array of abolitionists. The impressive range of topics (encompassing Liberian colonization, Russian serfdom, "the slavery of Red Indians," the condition of British India and slaveholding in South America, the West Indies, the United States, Texas, the Ottoman Empire, and the Indian Ocean) illustrates a breadth of ambition but divided priorities. Indeed, the convention threw up signs that some strategies for spreading the anti-slavery cause were in direct conflict with others. The 1840 assembly rather lacked "that spirit of love, unanimity, and Christian charity" that Joseph Sturge urged delegates to show.[37] For example, the American radical George Bradburn antagonized many of the English clergymen present when he suggested that they were not forward enough in challenging pro-slavery attitudes on their visits to the United States.[38] Similarly, after the Oxford Baptist minister Benjamin Godwin gave a noncontentious lecture on the absolute sinfulness of slavery, an argument broke out over whether the convention should ask all churches to withdraw fellowship from slaveholders. Many delegates felt that the assembly should abstain from meddling in denominational questions of church discipline.[39]

The BFASS, influenced by Sturge and other Quakers, was committed entirely to pacifist methods of slave-trade suppression. When this was expressed in a motion suggesting that the government should employ only "religious" means, some British nonconformists were outraged that religion was invoked in relation to the state, thinking of their wider struggle for freedom of conscience.[40] Still, they at least did not object to the pacifism of the convention's stated principles, which excluded those who supported military suppression of the transatlantic slave trade. Charles Fitzgerald, a Royal Navy lieutenant, was in London recuperating from the damage to his health from a tour with the West Africa squadron. When this future governor of the Gambia and Western Australia rose to speak, Sturge "strongly and directly" chided him for being opposed to "the pacific principle" of the convention.[41] The dogma of the BFASS made its conference an exclusive rather than inclusive gathering.

Most notoriously, a large debate erupted when William Lloyd Garrison's female allies were denied seats on the floor of the first conference. Some American delegates insisted that the "customs and habits, not to say prejudices, of Englishmen" should not decide which representatives of world abolitionism should be admitted. The British organizers insisted on all-male debates and the women abolitionists ultimately sat with Garrison in a gallery as observers rather than as participants.[42] It is also worth noting that the delegates were not just exclusively male but almost exclusively white; though the British freedman William Beckford appeared during the opening session to give thanks for abolitionists' attention to his race, he was hardly treated as an equal during the convention, and the haughty John Scoble, secretary of the BFASS, objected passionately when Benjamin Haydon proposed painting him next to Beckford in a portrait of the gathering. Although they professed brotherhood with all races, abolitionists could be as condescending and contemptuous as other Britons.[43]

The 1840 meeting ended, as it had begun, mired in national and internecine squabbling, now over the location of any subsequent convention. Garrison's supporters suggested that any future event be held in the United States or France, where it would not be "under the shadow of any society" and, in particular, would not be closed to women. The delegates aligned with the BFASS defeated any such plan.[44] The promised 1843 convention was marred by problems similar to the first one, with any hope of unity overshadowed by the question whether anti-slavery was better served by free trade or protection.[45] A later convention, in November 1854, was intended to heal wounds between the BFASS and Garrisonians in Britain and America but ended in predictable bitterness.[46] In many ways, the anti-slavery conventions show how narrowly sectional the BFASS's positions were; they represented just one set of ideas, and a set of ideas that was not shared by other abolitionist sects, let alone the British public.

Moreover, the way in which anti-slavery ideas and sentiments impinged on British politics changed dramatically in the first years of Victoria's reign, in ways that removed abolitionist societies' role in marshalling or speaking for public opinion. Mass petitioning and the mobilizing of public opinion had been a sporadic but important part of the crusades against the slave trade and slavery since 1787.[47] The antiapprenticeship campaign suggested that Sturge's followers would continue this tradition, yet abolitionists failed to replicate such agitation. In an era when anti-slavery was the avowed policy of the government, it was not clear what should be petitioned for or who should be petitioned. The successes of 1807, 1833, and 1838 had abolished slave trading, slave-holding, and apprenticeship in the British Empire. All these were clear targets for legislative action by representative institutions, which might respond to popular agitation.

There was no direct reason after 1838 to petition the British government about a slave system it had completely expunged from the British
West Indies. Attacks on foreign slaveries encountered an additional problem, since foreign authorities were less likely to listen to the opinions of
the British public. In its early years, the BFASS attempted petitioning the
U.S. president and Congress, leading only to ridicule in the press.[48] Similarly, abolitionists stumbled over international etiquette if they tried to
address foreign governments directly, rather than working through their
own government.[49] The society, operating from offices in London's New
Broad Street, found that national borders interfered more often that they
would have liked in their international crusade. Anti-slavery auxiliaries
experimented with petitions from British towns to those locals who had
emigrated to the United States, an innovative but ineffective tactic.[50] Britons concerned with American slavery never discovered a way to apply the
pressure of petitioning to a foreign power. Besides the practical question of
whom to address, it was increasingly difficult to build a popular coalition
around a simple, moral objective. The legal status of slavery in the British
Empire was a fundamentally more straightforward question than—to take
examples—the relationship between free trade and slavery, how to create
an anti-slavery majority in the U.S. Congress, or the best method by which
to induce Brazilians to suppress their slave trade. Finally, the benefits of
petitioning were curbed after 1842, when public petitions ceased to trigger
a parliamentary debate and, instead, were simply delivered to an impotent
committee.[51]

The anti-slavery societies should not be forgotten in the period after
emancipation, but they have enjoyed too much attention relative to other
varieties of anti-slavery sentiment in Victorian Britain. The marginaliza-
tion of abolitionist societies did not mean, as has been argued, that "abolition had become, politically speaking, something of a marginal issue."[52]
Sir George Stephen, a prickly opponent of the BFASS, suggested in 1853
that "as a national movement, the stimulus was gone" but that he did not
doubt "the religious principle in which it had its source, or of the determi-
nation of the English character, when stimulated to action by the force of
conscience." If British feeling on the question, Stephen suggested, "may
appear wanting in energy or unanimity, it is simply because no point is immediately presented to be the view on which the feeling can be brought to
bear."[53] He was right.

## ABOLITIONISTS AND ANTI-SLAVERY

The division of abolitionist societies and the complexity of anti-slavery issues help explain why Victorian Britain has been mistaken for a place with

declining concern for slavery. Even if anti-slavery became an article of faith in Victorian Britain, hegemony did not dictate uniformity.[54] Although the wrongness of slave-holding and slave trading had become an unassailable truth, unacceptable to question publicly, there was a contest of ideologies and methodologies over what the country should do to eliminate them. It was easy for those who were disappointed in political or cultural endeavors to ascribe the failure of their projects to a decline in the nation's anti-slavery sympathy.

Every decade, someone declared that anti-slavery sympathy had recently evaporated and promised that only their cause or product would revive its status in Britain. The publication *Uncle Tom's Almanack* asserted that there had been a dismal decline of anti-slavery enthusiasm in order to promote the importance of zeal for Harriet Beecher Stowe's novel and its commercial spin-offs (such as itself, conveniently).[55] A decade later, Thomas Hodgkin expressed frustration that "public interest is reduced to zero," since Britons largely shunned his Aborigines' Protection Society (APS), which promoted the rights of nonwhite peoples in British colonies as the logical extension of anti-slavery policy.[56] After the playwright Dion Boucicault's *The Octoroon* bombed on the London stage in 1861, he blamed the embarrassment on a shameful swing away from sympathy with slaves. (Perhaps responses to Boucicault's play said more about the quality of his production or the theatrical taste of metropolitan audiences than it did about anti-slavery sentiment in Victorian Britain.)[57] Frederick Douglass answered his own complaint when he argued that "in all England the anti-slavery feeling lies dormant, as if it had nothing on which to vent itself." He said this when selling the idea of a new British society—the Garrisonian Anti-Slavery League—and he had a clear interest in presenting it as the vehicle that the British public had been waiting for.[58] However, by 1907, the centenary of slave-trade abolition, speakers once more claimed that anti-slavery concern had recently collapsed.[59] Such complaints should not, therefore, be taken at face value. Narratives of decline suited those with minority views who thought that their interpretation was the only legitimate one.

Those investigating literature and culture in this period have acknowledged the ubiquity of British anti-slavery sentiment much more readily than have historians of politics. Wherever there was money to be made in popular culture, slavery could be adopted as a theme. This happened as part of Britain's long-standing enthusiasm for black minstrelsy, which helped to make the slave lament "Lucy Neal" one of the nation's favorite tunes. Black minstrel groups such as the Ethiopian Serenaders played primarily for amusement, but they were actively marketed as an insight into American slavery and supported by abolitionists as such.[60] Drawing middle-class audiences, the minstrel shows must be counted as anti-slavery entertainment,

as curious as it now sounds.[61] Attractions such as the model of the captured
slave-ship *Semiramis,* with detachable decks to show the Africans imprisoned within, also provided visual representations of the middle passage for
a paying public.[62] By 1870, as the transatlantic slave trade drew to a close,
*Chambers's Journal* noted that "we have all been familiar" with its cruel-
ties "from our infancy."[63]

It would be surprising if this fascination with anti-slavery subjects coexisted with a total lack of interest in anti-slavery politics. The next chapter
looks at the problem of American slave-holding, contrasting—as contemporaries did—British enthusiasm for *Uncle Tom's Cabin* with the nation's
confusing and muted support for the Northern cause in the Civil War. In
the rest of this book I show how scholars have overlooked anti-slavery politics in other parts of Victorian Britain: at the heart of foreign policy and
diplomacy, in debates over domestic reform and society, in questions of
free trade and naval suppression, and in the shaping of imperial policy.
By shifting the emphasis from abolitionist radicals to broader anti-slavery
sentiment, it is possible to put the politics back into the story and to make
sense of British attitudes toward slavery.

In 1883 and 1933, anniversary celebrations would herald emancipation
as a national act of contrition and consensus, yet at the time of Victoria's
1837 coronation the proper course of anti-slavery policy was still in dispute.[64] Slavery had long been indefensible, but the terms of its destruction
were very much debatable. The novelist Anthony Trollope, writing more
than twenty years after the end of apprenticeship, declared:

> Slavery was a sin. From that sin we have cleansed ourselves. But the mere
> fact of doing so has not freed us from our difficulties. Nor was it to be
> expected that it should. The discontinuance of sin is always the commence-
> ment of a struggle.[65]

The sin of slavery continued to present difficulties to Britons long after the
expiation of their own slave-holding. Rather than endorse certain strategies or tactics as authentic anti-slavery and others as inauthentic, we must
examine the full range of contemporary opinion. Competing varieties of
anti-slavery ideology made it harder to agree on anti-slavery policies, at just
the time anti-slavery sentiment dominated public discussions.

This was because the "struggle" Trollope described had become visible only with the discontinuance of the national sin; existing inconsis-
tencies were no longer held together by the same objective. The best way
to imagine this is by borrowing a metaphor from the world of science,
familiar to photographers. Parallax is a visual trick of perspective; when
we move position, static items on the horizon seem to have stayed still,

but stationary objects near us will have apparently shifted a long way. Of course, neither has moved but, for us, their distance in relation to each other appears to have done so. That seems to be the case regarding anti-slavery's relationship to imperial or racial ideologies, where the Victorian age's choices and constraints might trick us into seeing a rise in colonialism and racism accompanying a distancing of anti-slavery values. Depth perception in human sight is based on the overlapping parallax views from our eyes, and astronomers use this to measure the distance of celestial objects. Historians might borrow it to describe how the same ideas were cast in new light in different periods of time.[66] The politics of the Victorians did not represent a fundamental break with the struggle for emancipation, but brought into view new aspects or conflicts within anti-slavery ideology as a "commencement of a struggle," to borrow Trollope's phrase. Events and individuals thrust some currents of anti-slavery thought into obscurity while others shaped national policy; those changes can be understood by decoupling our idea of anti-slavery from anachronistic expectations of antiracism, anticolonialism, or humanitarianism. Taking seriously the full spectrum of anti-slavery ideas allows us to perceive the depth of anti-slavery sentiment and, more importantly, the continuities or discontinuities with earlier enthusiasm.

If sentiment ran as deep as this book claims, should Britain in this period be considered some sort of "abolitionist nation"? The American abolitionist Ellis Gray Loring thought so. In a private letter to Lydia Maria Child, he wrote that "England, the most civilized, the most intellectual, the *freest* nation on the globe, is at the head of this [abolitionist] movement. To repair her wrongs to the negro, lies at the very heart of that great people."[67] Also in the early 1840s, considering British attitudes to fugitive blacks, Senator Thomas Hart Benton thought Britain was a land "where abolitionism is the policy of the government, the voice of law, and the spirit of the people."[68] He did not mean this as a compliment. He was referring, like Loring, to "a nation of abolitionists" in an American sense—meaning supporters of immediate emancipation around the globe. This was not quite right. Contemporary British distinctions between "abolitionist" campaigners and a broader "anti-slavery" sentiment, as noted earlier, are important. Victorian Britain was not a "nation of abolitionists" as these Americans hoped or feared, or in the ways promoted by British abolitionist societies. In the 1860s, British newspapers labeled their country "the leading anti-slavery nation of the world" and "a great anti-slavery nation."[69] This is a better fit. Don Fehrenbacher has described the antebellum United States as a slave-holding republic, given the way that slavery shaped its politics.[70] In a similar vein, Victorian Britain should be seen as an anti-slavery nation, with its institutions, policies, and people shaped by that identity.

   This book is not an encyclopedia of questions involving slavery between 1837 and 1901 but a study of the controversies that best explain the
varied descent of anti-slavery ideas and passions in this period. Different
aspects of British anti-slavery are examined with different lenses, bringing
into focus diverse debates and ideas within the public sphere, the Houses of
Parliament, and the offices of state. For many incidents it is possible only
to scratch the surface and show how they fit into the shape of anti-slavery
practices more generally. Taking the following chapters together, however,
it is possible to see how the tensions and dissent within Victorian anti-
slavery have hidden its ubiquity and significance. Throughout Victoria's
reign there was persistent difficulty in agreeing what it meant to be the first
anti-slavery empire.[71] However, as will become clear, anti-slavery shaped
the moral and material interests of the globe's first modern superpower.

# 2

## Uncle Tom's Britain

FIFTEEN YEARS into Victoria's reign, Britain was enthralled with "a remarkable and very exciting story by an American lady, whose purpose is to exhibit the evils of slavery."[1] Harriet Beecher Stowe's *Uncle Tom's Cabin* created a phenomenon that amazed contemporaries and has intrigued cultural historians. From 1852 the book racked up countless editions thanks to lax transatlantic copyright laws. Ten different editions came out in one October fortnight and forty were on offer by the end of 1853; the book sold 1,500,000 copies in Britain and her colonies.[2] One contemporary complained that the book's "title has been pirated to give currency to every drug in the literary market."[3] British society embraced hundreds of derivative books, theatrical adaptations, lectures about the novel, Staffordshire figurines of Stowe's characters, toy theaters, Uncle Tom wallpaper, and Topsy dolls.[4] The commercial frenzy around Stowe's novel spurred numerous new anti-slavery tracts and reinforced the crowds attending public meetings to hear fugitive slaves and other abolitionist lecturers.

In response to Stowe's book, the evangelical reformer Lord Shaftesbury prepared an "affectionate address," or petition, from women of all ranks, expressing solidarity with those female Americans who despised slavery. Alongside humbler hands, it attracted the support of the Duchess of Sutherland (a longtime friend of the Anglophile Stowe), Viscountess Palmerston, Mrs. Charles Dickens, and Lady Tennyson among its 562,448 signatories.[5] The novel's popularity spread across geographical and social divides. In his preface to a Routledge edition, former cabinet minister Lord Carlisle described "the violent outburst of tears which it has excited amongst some of the loftiest regions of our social life, and in the obscure

cottages of hard-working and unpolished labourers and miners."[6] Sympathy for Uncle Tom was equaled by rapturous celebrity for Stowe herself. As
she and her family set foot on the Liverpool docks on 10 April 1853, a passionate crowd greeted them.[7] The Duchess of Sutherland, one of Victoria's
ladies-in-waiting and close confidantes, introduced the American visitor to
high society.[8] The duchess gave Stowe a gold chain made of shackle links
inscribed with a series of anti-slavery dates but with room for new ones
to be added. She played host to a special reception for the author at her
Stafford House home on 7 May, with guests drawn from the cabinet, the
opposition, the clergy, and the nobility.[9]

Yet to Stowe—and to generations of historians since—it was puzzling
that just a decade after this frenzy Britain should respond so uncertainly
and ambiguously to the American Civil War. In the Union, one magazine
pictured John Bull, the personification of Britain, betraying past anti-slavery
pieties (fig. 2). Both British and American champions of the Northern cause
were astonished that a nation so enthused by abolitionist literature could
equivocate over a struggle for liberty.[10] How, they asked, could a country that so adored Uncle Tom turn its back on President Lincoln? Was
there really no political or moral commitment in the huge consumer response to Stowe's book? In 1863, the author herself asked if the answer
to those questions was a "decline of the noble anti-slavery fire" in Britain,
when she issued a belated public reply to the thousands of women who had
signed the affectionate address.[11]

Recent research has made it easier to navigate the complexities of British reactions to the American Civil War and appreciate the issues as contemporaries did. There was no direct pattern of support for North or South
based on social class or political party but rather a wide variety of responses. Those who agreed on other political questions found themselves
at odds over the rebellion.[12] British interpretations of the war were largely
formed by ideas of what the war was understood to be about. In part, this
was helped by antagonism over the Republicans' economic protectionism
and the *Trent* incident, where Southern diplomats were unlawfully seized
by the Union from a British ship.[13] Francis Power Cobbe replied on behalf
of British women to Stowe's complaint of inconsistency; she ascribed the
confusion to "the complicated motives which have blended in your war."[14]
As Douglas Lorimer concludes, British reaction to the American Civil War
confirmed rather than undermined "a continuing attachment to Britain's
anti-slavery tradition." Opinion could be mixed precisely because understandings of the war's relationship to slavery were mixed.[15] Even Stowe
herself accepted that confusion was the result of Confederate attempts to
"blind and bewilder the mind of England as to the real issues of the conflict
in America."[16]

FIGURE 2. A Union view of Britain's Civil War betrayal of anti-slavery tradition, embodied by the Exeter Hall venue for evangelical meetings. *Harper's Weekly*, 28 September 1861, 624. By permission of the Mary Evans Picture Library, ref. 10080884.

This was not entirely the product of Stowe's imagination. Southern agents were keen to raise support for their cause and in one of his earliest reports, William Yancey, the Southern commissioner to Europe, bemoaned the depth of anti-slavery feeling among the public. It was uncharacteristically good judgment on his part, not special pleading to his superiors, when he predicted that there would be no significant support for the Confederacy in Britain if it was identified with slavery.[17] Aware of the situation, most secessionist propagandists were concerned with neutralizing the slavery issue or even harnessing anti-slavery to the Southern cause. Typically, partisans of the Confederate States of America (CSA) warned that British anti-slavery traditions should not be "prostituted" in support of the North and argued that slavery would be sooner abolished in an independent Confederacy.[18]

Such claims were less ridiculous in the early 1860s than they appear to modern eyes. In the decades before the war, prejudice and segregation in the North struck some British visitors as equally gratuitous as the evils of Southern slavery.[19] Lincoln had put very little emphasis on the anti-slavery dimension of the conflict in the opening stages of the war.[20] These facts convinced the trade unionist T. J. Dunning, who promoted Confederate sympathy amongst British workers, to insist that "the trades of London are dead against slavery, but they have no confidence in Mr. Lincoln either as an opponent to slavery or a friend to the Negro."[21] More fundamentally, the armed conflict and forcible emancipation of Southerners' slaves was at odds with British views of the Civil War. Twenty-five years of public discussion of American slavery in literature, periodicals, and wider culture did create political sympathies, but they were often fairly cautious and gradualist in their approach. We can understand the apparent discontinuity between adulation of Uncle Tom and suspicion of Honest Abe not by extensively documenting those moments—because that has been done before— but by looking instead at the broader discussion of American slavery that had taken place in early Victorian Britain.

## GEOLOGIES OF EMANCIPATION

Britons' own experience of ending slavery in the West Indies fundamentally shaped popular attitudes toward the American South. Britain's Emancipation Act was not the dramatic measure of immediate freedom and racial equality that radical British abolitionists had dreamed of. Widespread suspicion of the Northern cause in the 1860s was perfectly consistent with some conservatives' reaction to *Uncle Tom's Cabin* and other anti-slavery culture in the preceding two decades. British abolitionists of all stripes had pointed to terrifying insurrections as one of the main evils of slavery, and emancipation had been framed by a desire to avoid them with an ordered, peaceful transition to freedom.[22] Such fears were further heightened after the British "trauma" of the Indian "mutiny" of 1857–58.[23] For Stowe, Lincoln's emancipation of southern slaves on 1 January 1863 should be proof of the anti-slavery sincerity of the North. Many British periodicals thought the opposite. Lincoln's proclamation did not provide for any period of apprenticeship or preparation and did not include any element of compensation for slave-owners. Most damningly of all, it only applied to the nation's rebels, not loyalist slaveholders. This seemed, to many British eyes, to be a desperate attempt by the North to incite a servile war, or slave revolt, as a last chance for victory.[24]

A year earlier, John Stuart Mill rightly noted the fix in which Lincoln found himself: his government was not anti-slavery enough for the British public, yet he would have been criticized all the more for embracing immediate abolitionism in a time of war.[25] Conservative British opinion sympathized with the containment of slavery but would never have any truck with radical abolitionism.[26] The *Times* review of *Uncle Tom's Cabin* in 1852 had emphasized this fear of revolutionary change. Patronizingly, it praised Stowe's ability to "excite the passions" but saw this as "the very worst mode of getting rid of a difficulty, which, whoever may be to blame for its existence, is part and parcel of the whole organization of a large proportion of the States, and cannot be forcibly removed without instant anarchy, and all its accompanying mischief." What they deprecated most of all was "a war of the races."[27] It is in this context that the same newspaper responded to the Emancipation Proclamation with a virulent attack on Harriet Beecher Stowe, suggesting that she could have helped end Southern slavery by writing a novel designed to convert rather than condemn planters. "As it is, she and her equally impassioned, but far less able and brilliant relatives and friends have done all they could to widen the chasm into which the whole American community, slave and all, appears to be falling headlong."[28]

Such reactions expressed sympathy with planters, mirroring conservative concern for compensation during the dismantling of West Indian slavery. These Britons still saw gradual emancipation as the logical and necessary direction of American politics, precisely because a slave war was to be deplored. Desire to avoid catastrophe cut both ways. Just a few months later, the same newspaper noted that Southerners "would tell with greater force against pressure from without if more movement could be observed within." Revolutionary change's "incalculable peril to blacks and whites alike" was best avoided by "some visible foundation for negro emancipation," even if distant.[29] A similar sentiment was expressed by the distinguished author Sir Arthur Helps in his review of Stowe's book. He feared "a great crash" (a sudden emancipation) might come to settle the question "with all the want of wisdom which there is in undue haste." For this reason he urged a gradual and moderate initiative should begin, drawing on Britain's experience of the Reform Bill, the repeal of the Corn Laws, and Catholic emancipation. These great changes would have "come still more abruptly than they did" if cooler heads had not embraced their gradual adoption.[30] In this view, wise men had to steer reform into the most peaceful and gradual channel. The "servile war of St. Domingo" (the Haitian Revolution) was seen as an example of why America needed a "bold application of the legislative knife" to Southern slavery.[31]

Such perspectives predated both Stowe's novel and the Civil War. In 1845, the eminent geologist Charles Lyell published well-read accounts of his travels in the United States. His views on slavery were pained. Lyell denied most slaves were kept "in a state of discomfort" but saw slavery as clearly "evil." He imagined himself in the role of a Southern planter, puzzling how he would deal with the predicament.[32] Lyell had spent most of his time in the South focusing on rock and fossil formations, the manufacture of millennia of geological pressure. In his reflections on slavery, he applied the same gradual approach to change that he advocated in geology. Just as he insisted that long-term pressures rather than occasional catastrophes had gradually shaped the earth, so Lyell was concerned for the stable, orderly formation of a free-labor society. His views formed part of a long tradition of finding sympathy for "the dreadful position" or the "Herculean task" facing slaveholders in ridding themselves of it.[33] Lyell ultimately decided that Southerners should allow education for slaves and voluntary manumissions by masters as the urgent first steps toward ending the institution. It could not be left to the euthanasia of economic inefficiency in fifty years or more.[34] In fearing a surge of pressure that would destroy Southern society Lyell and Helps were representative of an important section of British opinion.

Crucially, public debate was divided over whether the "social earthquake" of immediate emancipation was desirable, even when it was nonviolent.[35] This tension was revealed in the women's "affectionate address" to Stowe, which did not endorse radical social change. A rival immediatist women's petition was soon circulated in some areas alongside the more famous and more cautious address.[36] Although expressions of sympathy for planters can be seen as conservative apathy toward a "social earthquake," these gradualist anti-slavery prescriptions should be treated seriously, even if our sympathies clearly lie with marginalized radicals.

The widespread suspicion of immediate emancipation is better appreciated as part of a broad, cross-party tradition deriving from Whiggish conceptions of gradual reform.[37] Immediate abolition therefore seemed "absurd."[38] Explaining why, despite strong anti-slavery views, he had talked to planters during a visit to the South, Russell Lant Carpenter argued "if we wish to convince those in error, we must shew [sic] our comprehension of their point of view." His articles for the *Christian Reformer* reflected a similar tone to Lyell's, as he warned that "for Abolition I earnestly pray; but as to the degree in which slaveholders are guilty or abolitionists wise" he could not say.[39] With this emphasis on gradual reform, the language of Victorian social reform proved useful: in his 1856 novel *The Old Dominion,* one of the British author G. P. R. James's characters attacked an abolitionist as a "foolish fanatic" who would "attempt, in his vain self-conceit, to cause a violent change in the relations of the different classes of society without a consideration of all the consequences."[40]

More striking, though, was the antiabolitionists' ability to retain anti-slavery credentials as an intrinsic part of their Britishness. The same writers who criticized immediatism believed it was "incumbent on us to affect no disguise of our real and universal sentiment on the great question which agitates the country [America]."[41] Even the most cautious consideration of emancipation, such as Charles Dickens's jealous review of Stowe's novel, still looked forward to the end of American slavery and predicted that "England shall be foremost in the celebration of her triumph."[42] Lyell himself did not deny the need to be "pointing out the evil unreservedly."[43] Some of his reviewers praised the book for expressing "the true English, Christian abhorrence of slavery." His criticism of "the imprudent and fanatic crusade of the Abolitionists" was simply seen as good "judgement and temper."[44]

As British writers became acquainted with the political difficulties of ending the peculiar institution in America, they came to fear revolution and insurrection and to search for ways they might be avoided.[45] *Fraser's Magazine* believed that American abolitionists' "rabid attempts at freedom result in twisting the chains more closely and painfully." Slavery would have ended if it were not for their "injudicious attacks," which only made the slaves' position worse.[46] The *Morning Chronicle* doubted that abolitionist hectoring could make slaveholders' treatment of their slaves any worse, but it counseled that rousing further passion was less important than addressing the "terrible questions" of how emancipation could be practically effected.[47] Writing an introduction for Stowe's novel, the seventh Earl of Carlisle felt obliged to make excuses for the abolitionists, begging "due allowance for error, infirmity, and...intolerance" while they were engaged in the "Christian chivalry" of exterminating slavery.[48] The main charge cautious commentators laid against New England abolitionists was the revolutionary and dangerous nature of their program. The abolitionists appeared to want "manumission...at the point of the sword."[49] Under siege from vitriolic attacks, they argued, Southerners had been induced not only to reject any thought of amelioration but to actively defend the evils of slavery and ponder reopening the slave trade. Hence a counterproductive form of agitation had stymied and reversed moral progress on the slave question.[50] But the greatest fear of all was that abolitionists, and provocative British meddling in support of them, could stir up "a frightful calamity," a euphemism for servile insurrection.[51] Such "frantic projects" were no substitute for "plans devised on principles of common sense, peaceful suasion, and a reasonable allowance of time."[52]

Of course, there was a bolder vein of British anti-slavery sentiment that happily identified itself with Northern abolitionists. Some of Lyell's reviewers were appalled by his conservatism, seeing him as "the apologist of the slave-owners" when he should have praised "the northern missionaries of negro freedom."[53] Others regretted that Stowe did not explicitly incite slaves to run away in her book.[54] Many popular theatrical adaptations

of *Uncle Tom* rectified this with revolutionary endings, featuring mass
emancipation or perhaps a violent come-uppance for the tyrannical master
Simon Legree—precisely what more cautious columnists and correspondents feared.[55] And Stowe herself played to this market with an anti-slavery
sequel, *Dred*, that concerned black resistance.[56] This new radicalism was
not quite as antithetical to elites as we might expect; rather startlingly,
Queen Victoria preferred *Dred* to its predecessor.[57] Despite some negativ-
ity about the epithet, "abolitionist" was sufficiently acceptable to mass
consumers that *Uncle Tom's Almanack* was advertised as an "Abolitionist
Memento."[58] Britain was genuinely divided on whether the New England
radicals should be applauded or deplored. Indeed, if anything, the years immediately before the American Civil War saw an increase in sympathy for
the "ultra-abolitionists" in response to Southern politicians defending their
institution as an abstract good and talking of reopening the slave trade.[59]

What much of the British press demanded was a reforming political
movement that would begin a gradual amelioration and emancipation.[60]
This would require engagement with the proper political process, something that American abolitionists had eschewed. Dickens's *Household
Words* supported the "practicable-looking theory" of "more moderate abolitionists" who "without inflicting a class wrong" could achieve emancipation "gradually and slowly."[61] In a similar vein, Frances Trollope wished
that "the possibility of amelioration" was "taken into the consideration of
the legislature" so that "the negro population of the Union might cease to
be a terror."[62] The *Times*, declaring that it spoke "in the name of English
abolitionism," protested against Charles Sumner's and John Brown's respective attacks on the South. Rather than wrestling slaves from the hands
of planters, critics must convince masters that free labor was superior and
a peaceful transition was possible.[63] Hence, a British writer could demand
that Americans pay more attention to the slavery question and simultaneously denounce abolitionists as "puerile" for rejecting electoral politics.[64]
A *Chambers's Journal* article dismissed the New England movement as
"inconsiderable" but lectured residents of the free states that without "the
selfish compromises of the North, slavery must have long since have been
extinct." They should assert their anti-slavery objections more consistently.[65] It is a great irony, given later suspicion of Lincoln's motives, that
such commentators were delighted with the emergence of the Republican
Party, which pursued the reformist anti-slavery cause in electoral politics.[66]
The *Economist* cheered on the party's candidates for president in 1856 and
1860 despite their protectionism, in all other circumstances a dominant
concern for the paper.[67]

It should not be surprising that conservative and radical tempers for-
mulated different expectations of how slavery would be best removed.

Understanding these debates before 1860 shows how political sympathy with the North was not, by contemporary perspectives, the only course consistent with Britain's affection for *Uncle Tom's Cabin*. Sympathy for the South resulted not just from what John Stuart Mill called "inbred Toryism" but from twenty years of literary and cultural ruminations on American slave-holding.[68] A defense of the Civil War as an emancipatory purge grated with humanitarian horror at the massive loss of life incurred in the conflict.[69] Britons shuddered "to think that Abolition is destined to be achieved by such bloodshed."[70] Moreover, Confederate sympathizers revived old anxieties about the "radical" abolitionists and the free states. They drew on perceptions of slavery as a national, rather than a sectional, American crime in highlighting the North's complicity in antebellum slavery.[71] Before the war it had sometimes been argued that the North accepted slavery in exchange for the South swallowing protectionism. Republican support for protective tariffs, which the Confederate states sometimes presented as the cause of the war, predisposed some Britons against the Union.[72] Equally, Northern segregation and racism toward blacks were cited as evidence of its inhumane conduct, as was the section's complicity in the slave trade and shipping to England the fruits of slavery.[73]

Finally, supporters of the South could quote Garrison's antebellum predictions that disunion was the surest way to undermine Southern slavery.[74] They argued that Southerners would be able to effect an abolition of slavery when relieved from the siege undertaken by Northern abolitionists.[75] British newspapers often stated that the war would end slavery one way or the other; the system's fate was settled, whatever the result.[76] These claims went some way to neutralizing the best argument of Union propagandists, who loved to quote Confederate vice-president Alexander Stephen asserting that slavery was the "corner-stone" of his new nation.[77] The Tory Marquess of Lothian, writing in 1864, chastised "inflammatory" Northern abolitionism for not copying the British anti-slavery formula; they had denied compensation to slave-owners and disregarded the awful effects insurrection would have on both Southern planters and their slaves. He predicted that the border states would have freed their slaves before the war if not for the disruption of abolitionists, and he thought that the gulf states of the Confederacy would come to emancipation in their own time, once they had prepared slaves for freedom.[78] The marquess's gradualism—glacial gradualism—flirted with apology for slavery but took pains to condemn the "false philosophy" of Southerners who defended their institution as any kind of moral good.[79] Even pro-Union thinkers such as Mill accepted that an independent South would quickly emancipate its slaves.[80]

If explicit support for the institution of slavery was almost entirely absent from British debates on the Civil War, then we should not assume that it did not linger in private thoughts and writing. One of the few publications to defend slavery as a positive good was Robert Hardwicke's *The Slavery Quarrel*.[81] That others shared his views privately can be gleaned from the surviving letters of a family corresponding between Virginia and Cumbria, where an Englishwoman declared to her American cousin in 1861 that "slavery is perhaps not a very desirable institution for either masters or slaves" but "the darkies" were not "fit for freedom." Subsequent letters expressed her support for "you chivalrous Southerners" even though she was aware that the perpetuation of slavery lay at the core of the conflict.[82] Still, it is striking that it was impossible to be taken seriously in public debates if an author defended slavery, as opposed to explaining the South's tardiness in abolishing it. D. W. Mitchell, a British settler in the U.S. South, tried to explain to his former countrymen the pragmatic advantages of "abstractly unjust" slavery in a pro-Confederate tract. All he managed to do was provide reviewers with ammunition for the corrupting effects of a decade in a slave society.[83] Even James Hunt, the leading Anthropological Society racist, claimed in public to oppose the slave trade.[84] Outside of private prejudice, "*pro-slavery*" was "essentially *un*english [sic]," as one author apologized to readers, after using the word.[85]

If the conflicting and apparently baffling pattern of British responses to the American Civil War is explained by anything, it must be traced to the huge variety of plans and ideas that existed for dismantling Southern slavery in the decades before. Still, these were not perfect predictors of the attitude individuals would take to the war. Lyell, once the opponent of the abolitionists, praised Lincoln's reelection in 1864 and celebrated "the emancipation of the negroes in the South" as one good to come from the bitter fighting.[86] The one clear lesson we can take from public debates about American slavery before and during the Civil War is that by any sensible measure Britain had not lost its appetite for anti-slavery but retained traditional differences of taste over the best recipe to follow for its abolition.

## A GREAT, UNSEEN, GIGANTIC POWER

It is striking, after studying the varieties of British opinion over American slavery, how few of these disagreements translated into concrete political actions by Britons. The notable exception was the acute debate over whether to recognize or assist the Confederacy in the Civil War. In many other cases, there seemed to be no practical action behind anti-slavery ideas and rhetoric. The women's "affectionate address" was a rare example of channeling cultural enthusiasm for *Uncle Tom* into some political expression. Despite the wider inaction, contemporaries believed that Britain's reception of the book was laden with inherent significance; literary excitement was itself an act of meaningful solidarity. The *Examiner* asserted that the mere diffusion of Stowe's book would help peaceably expunge "this hideous plague of slavery."[87] The *Daily News* thought that "her fame is a protest on the part of the world against slavery."[88] This was hackneyed hyperbole from the press, in one sense, but it was a self-reinforcing declaration too. Before and after the book's publication, anti-slavery speakers had insisted that British condemnation of American slavery was an act of evangelism in itself. Stowe, corresponding with Sir Arthur Helps about his review of her book, spoke of how "this great unseen gigantic power the public sentiment of nations so hems in & encloses the slave holders"; Southerners were besieged by "the intolerable blaze of the contempt & indignation of civilized humanity."[89] In this sense, British cultural discussion of slavery could be a political pressure on pro-slavery Americans.

Stowe's hope was not new, as two incidents at the Great Exhibition of 1851, before the publication of *Uncle Tom's Cabin,* show. The United States had chosen Hiram Powers's sculpture of a Greek slave as an example of the country's artistic achievement, and the comical magazine *Punch* mocked this irony with a cartoon of a Virginian slave, suggesting it was a more honest choice for the slave republic (fig. 3).[90] A group of fugitive slaves and abolitionists took this cartoon with them to the exhibition's American section on 21 June 1851 and gathered by the *Greek Slave.* The group, which included the fugitive slave William Wells Brown, William and Ellen Craft (a couple who had escaped slavery in disguise), and the family of abolitionist George Thompson, loudly and publicly compared the cartoon with Powers's masterpiece. However, none of the American exhibitors or visitors reacted. Deciding that further provocation was required, Brown loudly proclaimed that he was a fugitive slave and that the *Punch* cartoon was a fitting comparison to the *Greek Slave* and placed it in the statue's enclosure. But still no one replied or challenged them. A further six or seven hours produced not one American or pro-slavery sympathizer who would openly disagree with the abolitionists. "The American citizens dared not come into court and plead to the indictment of American fugitive slaves, upon British soil, and before a British jury," reported Garrison's *Liberator.*[91] Pro-slavery politics could not be voiced in public.

In the Canadian section of the Crystal Palace, Josiah Henson, a minister and founder of an industrial community for his fellow runaway slaves, displayed finely polished walnut boards, the product of his workshop. In future decades, he would be better (but wrongly) known as the man on whom Stowe's Uncle Tom character was based. For the duration of the exhibition, however, he attracted more modest fame, including the attention of Queen Victoria during one of her tours. Because his lumber had been carried in

**FIGURE 3.** *Punch*, May 1851, 218. By permission of Plymouth University.

a ship with American wares, Henson was at first told he must display his work in their section. But he resisted this, insisting he was a British citizen. He embarrassed the American superintendent into allowing him to move his exhibit to the Canadian section by painting a sign above it: "This is the Product of the Industry of a Fugitive Slave from the United States, whose residence is Dawn, Canada." The protest meant that "English gentlemen began to gather around, chuckling with half-suppressed delight, to see the wrath of the Yankee" exhibitors.[92] Like the *Greek Slave* protestors, he had exploited the uneasiness of Americans in defending slavery to a British audience. These incidents chimed with the BFASS's hopes that the exhibition could be an opportunity to evangelize visiting foreigners on the subject of slavery.[93] At the end of an August 1851 meeting, William Wells Brown asked his audience, which included Alfred Tennyson and Thomas Babington Macaulay, to "expostulate with the Americans.…The moral and religious sentiment of mankind must be arrayed against slave-holding, to make it infamous."[94]

This emphasis on moral pressure through public discussion was not new in the 1850s. As early as 1839, Frances Trollope, in a fifth edition of her *Domestic Manners of the Americans,* noted Britain's new awareness of the evils of American slavery, explaining that "all truth on a theme so tremendously important should be uttered by every voice that can hope to make itself heard."[95] The American orator Henry B. Stanton asked British abolitionists to talk and write about his nation's sin because "the literature of Great Britain exercises so vast an influence over the public opinion of America."[96] Speaking in 1846, Frederick Douglass insisted that "discussion was its [slavery's] death." Douglass suggested, at different times, "a cordon of Anti-Slavery feeling" or "a wall of anti-slavery fire" that would bind slavery within its present limits and suffocate it.[97] A slave-holding American nation was too degraded to see its own sins; only the disdain of the world would force the United States to face the power of "the pulpit and press" and learn to repent.[98]

The booming Victorian newspaper and periodical press happily obliged, feasting on anti-slavery material for regular copy. Articles on slavery were frequently reprinted from American journals.[99] The *Times,* for example, featured details of slave auctions, to demonstrate how low whites were brought "by unlimited power to use human beings for gain."[100] Other papers and periodicals featured the chilling and gory tales of abuse that seemed to proliferate after the Fugitive Slave Act. Britons grew to pity escaped slaves, who killed their own children to spare them recapture, and to hate slave catchers, who imprisoned free people in cases of mistaken identity or willful kidnap.[101] Of course, the volume of coverage in the press is not in itself an accurate barometer of British opinion.[102] However, whatever their political attitudes toward abolitionists, newspapers tended to push an uncompromising censure of slavery. For example, the South's antebellum laws against free black seamen disembarking from British ships were reported in the *Times* as evidence of "the utterly indefensible nature of those institutions which this particular law was directed to maintain."[103]

British booksellers had a long pedigree in exhibiting the evils of American slavery too. Before British emancipation, writers had mocked the United States as a slave republic; after Britons had removed the mote from their own eye, their sense of moral superiority was even more pronounced.[104] We have already seen how the geologist Lyell was fascinated by slavery in his travel book and in the two decades after emancipation, the travelogues of Frances Trollope, Harriet Martineau, Frederick Marryat, and Charles Dickens had criticized American slave-holding.[105] Images of the United States were, by midcentury, invariably yoked to images of slavery, so common was the theme in newsprint and publishing.[106] In a children's book profiling the countries of the world and their peoples, Favell Lee Mortimer described the wickedness of American slavery, and the image chosen for its frontispiece showed Southerners abusing slaves, with one kneeling down in the pose of the British abolitionist cameo "Am I not a man and brother?" (fig. 4). From Americans, slaves received the lash, not freedom.[107]

Public meetings held by abolitionists such as Brown and Douglass formed part of a long tradition of speaking tours by African Americans who had liberated themselves from bondage. Richard Blackett has identified these campaigners as a "third force" for abolitionism in Victorian Britain, as they established their own authority and popularity independent of the warring sectarians in the Garrisonian and BFASS tribes. Most towns must have been visited by black abolitionists, often selling popular books about their experiences, before *Uncle Tom* hit Britain.[108] Scholars have been impressed by their influence on British readers. Audrey Fisch counts

FIGURE 4. A view of the United States, from a British children's geography book.
Favell Lee Mortimer, *Far Off; or Africa and America Described* (London, 1854, 2 vols.),
vol. 2, frontispiece. By permission of the Bodleian Library, copy held at 203 d. 306.

at least twenty slave narratives on sale by midcentury and Julia Sun-Joo Lee
suggests that their phenomenal popularity helped shape the conventions of
the mid-Victorian novel.[109] Douglass's book sold thirteen thousand copies
in 1845–47 and he calculated he had spoken three hundred times in his
nineteen-month visit to Britain.[110] Brown sold twelve thousand copies of
his book in 1850, and in five years on the stump he addressed a thousand
public meetings.[111] This black "third force" was part of a broader anti-
slavery culture that constituted a "third sector" of anti-slavery in the first
half of the Victorian period, beyond the institutions of abolitionist societies
and the state.

   Anti-slavery sentiment emerged in popular culture, as well as in the
worthy Town Hall lecture or the moralizing tome. Literature such as *Uncle
Tom's Cabin* was the dignified side of an enthusiasm and fascination that
also plumbed the depths of low culture. It seems more than a little odd, in
light of slaves' misery, to speak of "anti-slavery entertainments," but there
was such a thing in nineteenth-century Britain. One farcical play written
in 1853—"Chaff; or the Yankee and the Nigger at the Great Exhibition"—
imagined a mad American soldier killing a fugitive slave who rented the
same room in a boarding house. Alongside mockery of the racist American and an indictment of slavery were a plethora of jokes stereotyping
the former slave, "Gumbo-Jumbo." It was an odd mix, particularly when
the comic play both criticized racial hatred and mocked African American

speech patterns.[112] The following year, the music hall entertainer Henry Russell took "Negro Life! In Freedom and Slavery" as the material for a show that followed an African from the village "where the Free negro was born" to the cotton field "in which the worn-out slave ends his days." The ditties addressed a British cruiser capturing a slave ship and the depraved auction of freshly imported captives. Russell also composed a number of songs based on *Uncle Tom's Cabin* when the novel was at the height of its popularity.[113] In 1850, Brown offered the paying public a panorama of scenes of slavery, including the inspiring incident of slaves fleeing across the cracking ice of the Ohio.[114] Meanwhile, from the comfort of their own homes, Britons could enjoy ballad sheets of jolly musical entertainments on anti-slavery themes; one ditty celebrated the Northern Star guiding slaves to freedom and a flight from slavery in a shipping crate by a different William Brown.[115] "Box" Brown, as he was nicknamed, toured the country with a panorama of his own, which proved more controversial than William Wells Brown's. The *Wolverhampton and Staffordshire Herald* found "Box" Brown's images of human immolation and whipped female slaves indecent.[116] Many stories, lectures, or shows, besides his, appealed to Victorians' interest in foreign climes, exotic characters, heroes, and villains—in some cases even gore and sex.[117] Still, even if these elements titillated some consumers, the anti-slavery message was hard to ignore.

The growing American crisis of the 1850s attracted "an interest rarely felt in the domestic concerns of a distant country" among Britons. The Democrats' victory in 1856 left Britons "disappointed and disquieted" with the defeat of Republican presidential candidate John C. Frémont.[118] The battle over American slavery had captured the interest of the British public, meaning that, unusually, they had followed the bewildering "mazes of American politics."[119] One paper noted the coincidence that, with the exception of Iowa, every state that voted for the Republicans had bordered British land or British waters. It seemed that they alone had stood up to the slave-power.[120] The *Illustrated London News* showed its readers a South Carolina slave market with interesting commentary on the image. The artist had included a rusty old cannon, buried in the ground, which was explained to be symbolic of buried revolutionary enmity between Britain and her former colony. He hoped "in that spirit of true friendship we may be allowed to raise up our voice now and then against the curse of slavery."[121] Cassell's *Uncle Tom's Almanack* imagined that its readers, having read about the abuses of the slave system, would want to do something against it, but the best advice it could give its readers was to create a love of freedom and hatred of slavery throughout Britain. Given the number of poor Britons who emigrated to America, it reasoned, the anti-slavery climate in the old country would slowly diffuse, through immigrants, into the United

States.[122] *Wesleyan-Methodist Magazine,* reviewing Stowe's novel, gave Americans notice that "the withering indignation of Europe is directed to this institution."[123] And yet in substance, the most militant demand of these books, lectures, and newspaper pieces was that "we must have public meetings." There was an expectation that condemnation of slavery would reach across the ocean and spur action on the opposite shore.[124]

British publications were not merely adherents of this philosophy but were also understood to be the principal machinery through which cultural pressure could be effected. William Wells Brown believed that this "rapid increase in communication between the two sides of the Atlantic has brought them so close together" that the British public had contact with, and influence upon, the slaveholder.[125] The two countries had, "by the aid of steam and the power of science, been brought alongside each other, so that a word uttered to-day in opposition to the hateful system of slavery, may be heard fourteen days hence in the streets of Boston."[126] The British papers were assumed to hold this kind of cultural influence in the United States.[127] The idea of stirring up British anti-slavery disapproval was, then, principally a public relations campaign *within* Britain, whose moral disapproval would have a diffusive effect through Britain's press.

On the one hand, this may well have been because anti-slavery culture fed off itself, and Douglass and Garrison's idea of an "anti-slavery cordon" influenced wider circles of later speakers and derivative books. Yet it also arose from the fact that there were few alternatives to informal moral suasion. Indeed, besides preventing British intervention on behalf of the Confederacy (which, as Richard Blackett points out, was never very likely), many British supporters of the Union imagined sending Lincoln nothing beyond their good wishes. An anti-Southern partisan such as Mill admitted he was engaged in a contest only for "our moral attitude, for politically there was no other course open to us than neutrality."[128] Cairnes, a polemicist against the slave power who wrote a book of that name, was skeptical about the wisdom of any British interference in the Civil War, despite his moral sanction for the North.[129] In this, nothing had changed. Britons saw their role as sanctioning or condemning American practices.

From the perspective of a twenty-first century of grand international appeals and fearsome charitable fund-raisers, it seems remarkable how rarely antebellum British anti-slavery feeling was converted into practical resources for an attack on American slavery. We may be surprised that more was not done to bankroll abolitionist societies overseas.[130] Some Britons, particularly a few wealthy abolitionists with transatlantic friendships, did donate directly to anti-slavery organizations in the United States.[131] Some British anti-slavery women sent goods to be sold in America's East Coast bazaars. Up to fifteen boxes of British fancy goods were dispatched each year for the Boston sale from a variety of English, Scottish, and Irish towns.[132] Still, the vast majority of Britons who keenly consumed anti-slavery culture did not donate to the cause. Even in the case of the women supplying bazaars, it was not the monetary value of their gift that was valued, but rather, as Douglass put it, how "every stitch, every painting, embodied and shadowed forth a spirit of freedom and spoke of the power of English sympathy; and against that sympathy all opposition was fruitless."[133] Even such direct aid, undertaken by a minority, was understood primarily as a demonstration of the great British public's moral sanction. This might be dismissed as merely rhetorical were it not for the fact that sending items to America for sale was a fundamentally inefficient way of funding that country's abolition movement. Only in 1859 did supporters adopt the plan of holding a bazaar in Britain and sending the funds across the Atlantic in place of their donated goods. Whether this practice would have developed further if the Civil War had not settled the slave question forever, we cannot know.[134] It seems, however, that the moral force sending handmade goods was valued more than mere revenue.

Indeed, instead of raising funds in Britain, anti-slavery supporters focused on cultivating public opinion and seemed inclined only rarely to ask the public to convert its wrath into donations for American abolitionist societies. The failure to make financial sacrifices for American anti-slavery was caused by a number of factors. To begin with, it was far from obvious exactly to whom they should give money. Enthusiasm for American abolitionists lagged far behind broader British anti-slavery feeling. The apparent impotence, extremism, and petty factionalism of American anti-slavery societies, reinforced by their dogmatic vision for abolitionism, made it far from obvious that they were the best vehicles for striking down slavery. Instead, fugitive slaves, itinerant lecturers, and anti-slavery authors who cultivated the broader currents of anti-slavery enthusiasm fed (literally) off it. Many black fugitives lived off collections and sales of their narratives at these events. Giving money, on these occasions, was a way of keeping the lecturer—and their gospel—on the road, a motive in keeping with trust in the power of belief alone. A few lecturers were sent to Britain by American anti-slavery societies precisely in order to raise funds for their organizations—in 1856, for example, Douglass sent Julia Griffiths to secure money for his newspaper.[135] However, for most British audiences, supporting a lecturer was often the ultimate end of their fund-raising.[136] The point of paying speakers was to enable them to take their message to the next town.

The pattern was the same when Stowe visited Britain and found herself showered with gifts of cash. *Uncle Tom* led to public collections of money, but most were entrusted personally to Stowe. One plan envisaged every English reader donating a penny for a fund to be split between Stowe and the abolitionist cause in America.[137] Although participation was never broad, money for the "authoress" was collected in a fund she could dispose of as she wished. In April, two hundred women presented her with £130 and in Edinburgh she received £1,000. None of this went to American abolitionists, and it does not appear to have been intended for such a purpose. It was a private, almost commercial, appreciation of an individual advocate.[138]

An audience at a public lecture also expected to give a personal gift to the speaker. This extended to very specific fund-raising efforts, targeted at helping individual slaves or former slaves. It was not just regional groups of anti-slavery organizers who raised money for fugitives. For example, in May 1846 Douglass made an offhand remark to his white patrons that he would like to be joined in Britain by his family. They made an impromptu appeal to Douglass's Finsbury Chapel audience of over twenty-five hundred people, and had taken in £105 (worth about $500 at the time) by the next day.[139] These very specific appeals were the mainstay of anti-slavery culture, high and low, and formed an alternative to simply bankrolling the expenses of American anti-slavery societies. Quantifying the money generated by anti-slavery sympathy is difficult because of the diverse private and organizational uses to which it was put. It would be hard, too, to decide whether the cost of a ticket to watch the Ethiopian Serenaders or an *Uncle Tom* play was emotionally different from paying to hear Douglass or Moses Roper lecture. It seems doubtful that many Victorian consumers of this mass culture made distinctions when enjoying this popular theme.

Trust in "the force of public opinion" was tied not only to Britain's national duty but also to its role as a Christian country.[140] The common appeal to "testify against slavery" was no accident: anti-slavery lecturers and their lectures had much in common with the style of evangelical preachers and revival meetings making similar demands.[141] Addressing an audience at the Poultry Chapel in London, Samuel Ringgold Ward described escape from slavery "like a sort of resurrection, and the man becomes another being altogether." Slaves fleeing to Canada enjoyed, he thought, "the transforming power of the sacred aegis of British laws that said to the man who was a chattel, 'Be thou free—be a man!'"[142] But this culture did not simply share its rhetoric with religion; cultural passion was expected to function, like prayer, as a moral suasion.

Historian Edward Rugemar has argued that British anti-slavery provided a stream of abolitionist propaganda (and Southern reaction) that contributed to "the Caribbean roots of the American Civil War."[143] However, while cultural anti-slavery in the first half of Victoria's reign aimed to mobilize the British people, there were few plans offered for state action against slavery in the United States. Although it may seem weak to modern eyes, contemporary Americans—both pro- and anti-slavery—took this "soft power" seriously. If British readers seemed slow to connect their anti-slavery enthusiasm to any course of action by the state, this was because they were not asked to do so. American anti-slavery visitors showed little interest in mobilizing Britain's cruisers or consuls but rather appealed for the artillery of her presses and her pulpits. Any "physical or political interference" was explicitly rejected.[144] One African American lecturer warned in the 1830s that free blacks would defend the United States from any threat, even if the British waged a war on slavery as part of some future conflict with the United States.[145]

It would be a mistake to see the limited political implications of anti-slavery culture as simple amorality. Marcus Wood has suggested that English and American abolition merged by midcentury, becoming "a transatlantic propaganda that was homogenized and constituted a missionary and imperialist form."[146] This suggestion is problematic. Although abolitionist societies increasingly shared factional transatlantic alliances, British anti-slavery sympathy was heterodox and patriotic. British anti-slavery sentiment did not map onto America's politics of slavery very cleanly. Digesting *Uncle Tom's Cabin*, watching a freedman lecture, or reading about the wickedness of American slavery did not logically require support for Anglo-American abolitionist societies. A consensus against slavery contained plenty of variety, meaning that prescriptions for America—and hence responses to the Civil War—could follow different lines of anti-slavery logic. Indeed, as later chapters will show, the cultural dominance of anti-slavery sentiment was well hidden by political disagreements over how an anti-slavery nation should act.

# 3

## The Anti-Slavery State

ANTI-SLAVERY'S TRANSITION from reformist crusade to national policy was a curious and complicated process. After centuries of supporting the slave trade, the British state was transformed, in stages, from the patron of slavery to its determined enemy. How and why did international suppression of the slave trade become an objective for successive Victorian governments? Various strands of government policy responded to the challenge and the relationship between anti-slavery and the state was transformed as anti-slavery evolved from a question of imperial morality to a cause for moral imperialism.[1]

Anti-slavery action by the British state dated back to Sir William Dolben's act regulating the traffic in slaves in 1788. The abolition of the nation's slave trade in 1807 was accompanied by naval patrols to enforce the ban on British slave trading and, as gradually permitted by treaty and law, to stop foreign participation in the traffic too. Registration of slave ownership and ameliorative mandates preceded the Emancipation Act of 1833, controlling and then alienating private property. In order to compensate owners, the British government raised its duties on foreign sugar and spent £20 million on a compensation scheme that represented the largest financial transaction ever undertaken by the state.[2] The system of apprenticeship was supervised by London and looked set to be abolished by Parliament in 1838, although this was preempted by voluntary abolition by the colonial legislatures. In short, Britain had been developing anti-slavery state action for fifty years before Victoria's accession but her reign would see a further institutionalization.

When the question of British emancipation was settled in 1838, the "anti-slavery state" had passed through adolescence into its prime. As

Howard Temperley has suggested, the epithet "abolitionist" could apply to officials, sailors, and politicians as much as to members of the BFASS.[3] This does not mean that the British state adopted the form and practices that many anti-slavery activists would have wished. Among abolitionist campaigners, within the British public, and throughout government and the state, there remained great divisions over the best tactics—and sometimes over the right strategy too.[4] What united differing Victorian views was the presumption that the British state should give powerful consideration to the nation's impact on slavery and the slave trade abroad. However, British anti-slavery politics had never existed independently of imperial and foreign policy anxieties or of the perceived and suspected actions of other countries. After the Emancipation Act, Britons would discover that their interactions with other nations uncovered more and more anti-slavery problems; foreign and imperial policy hence became enveloped by these dilemmas.

For early Victorians, "the Empire" meant Britain's overseas territories and conquests: the sugar colonies of the Caribbean; the white settler colonies of Canada, Australia, New Zealand, and South Africa; the vast subempire of India; and various scattered territories. British power also "expanded overseas by means of 'informal empire' as much as by acquiring dominion in the strict constitutional sense," and focusing on occupied territories alone is "like judging the size and character of icebergs solely from the parts above the water-line."[5] Historians have recognized that Britain exerted a cultural and economic dominance over a vaster "informal empire" stretching from Brazil and Argentina, which were soaked in London finance, to Chinese, African, and Middle Eastern ports, which were opened to British merchants through violence and menace.[6]

This unwieldy, chaotic assortment of economic and military opportunities formed something greater than the sum of its parts, as they enriched and reinforced each other to create what John Darwin calls a "British system of world power." Thanks to "the chaotic pluralism of British interests at home and of their agents and allies abroad," this power sometimes led to full colonies carved from tiny "bridgeheads," sometimes to the preservation of these vulnerable outposts, and sometimes to compromise or retreat in the face of opposition.[7] As we shall see, foreign and colonial anti-slavery policies were part of a global assertion of imperial power, with British policies flexible, responsive, and opportunistic with different peoples in different circumstances. This book makes an arbitrary but necessary division, as many Victorians did, between relations with sovereign, or nominally sovereign, independent states (considered in this chapter) and countries over which Britain claimed ownership for at least part of our period (discussed in chapter 6). This practical distinction does not change the fact that British politicians and officials applied some common principles to both spheres of operation, though pragmatic discrimination led to inconsistent degrees of force being applied to other nations. Before anatomizing "the anti-slavery state," it is important to define what and who made up such a thing, how it related to the rest of the Victorian state, and what it did.

## ANTI-SLAVERS IN DISGUISE

The most visible manifestations of British anti-slavery policy were the squadrons of Royal Navy cruisers stationed in international waters to intercept slave traders. Although illegal trafficking by Britons was their initial target, after the 1807 Act it proved difficult to distinguish between foreign and British slavers. This problem—and a wider desire to spread anti-slave-trade values to other Christian countries—led British diplomats to embark on a long and frustrating project of enrolling other governments in Britain's crusade. A complex series of bilateral treaties authorized Britain and an individual partner country to intercept and detain slave traders from each other's country. The practical result was that Britain gained the right to search foreign nations' shipping, because other governments were unable to send naval squadrons to patrol the Atlantic.[8]

The ships assigned to suppression were not a quantitatively or qualitatively significant portion of Britain's total naval forces. Although the system directly cost hundreds of thousands of pounds each year, it absorbed, on average, less a twentieth of the naval budget and less than 0.05 percent of the national economic product.[9] Still, this represented, in a typical year, a third of one percent of the expenditure of central government, sometimes rising to as much as 1 percent (fig. 5).[10] Beyond the direct costs of fitting and crewing the cruisers, the British also paid crews prize money for every successful capture of a slave trader.[11] There were rarely fewer than one thousand men stationed off the West African coast and sometimes more than four thousand.[12]

Operationally, the campaign was directed from the Admiralty, which was often suspected of being halfhearted about the slave-trade mission. Lord John Russell, foreign secretary in 1861, wrote to a cabinet colleague that "the Sea Lords of the Admiralty endeavour to avoid this disagreeable duty. Palmerston says that in his time the Admiralty always sent their slowest and worst craft to catch the swift vessels used by the slave-traders."[13] It was a charge that the admirals tried to challenge, always insisting that governments (including those of Viscount Palmerston and Lord John Russell) did not give them sufficient funds to pay for the naval operations demanded of them.[14] Whatever the truth of such squabbles, the idiosyncratic crusade extended British maritime dominance into new spheres of influence and created innumerable challenges for British diplomats.

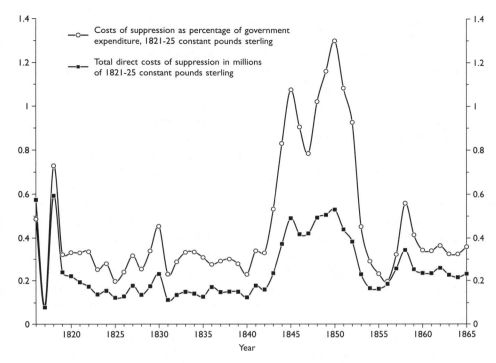

FIGURE 5. British expenditure on slave-trade suppression, 1816–65. The costs of suppression exclude indirect expenditure and are expressed as a percentage of government expenditure and in real terms. All values are converted to 1821–25 constant pounds sterling using the two price indices reprinted by Mitchell, calculating the ratio of the later to earlier series using an average of the ratio in overlapping years. The figures preceding 1854 capture calendar years ending 5 January, with subsequent dates for years ending 31 March; the first three months approximating expenditures of 1854 have been consequently excluded from these figures to avoid double counting and artificially inflating expenditures that year. *Sources:* Eltis, *Economic Growth,* 96; B. R. Mitchell, *British Historical Statistics,* 2nd ed. (Cambridge, 1988), 721–24, 587–95. Produced by Cartography Unit, Plymouth University.

The diplomatic and legal framework for this suppression system was, as Tory statesman Lord Aberdeen put it, "a new and vast branch of international relations." The Foreign Office's Slave Trade Department emerged in the 1820s when more than one clerk was required to manage these new challenges. The officials were placed, at first, on a temporary footing because, optimistically, the slave trade was expected to last only a few short years more.[15] Far from being a dry and obscure bureaucracy, the Department's paper pushing had hugely significant political and diplomatic implications. The Slave Trade Department's path to permanence came in steps between 1841, when it acquired its own staffing budget, and 1854, when it was finally recognized as a regular part of the Foreign Office establishment—a tacit acknowledgement that suppression was a gradual process, not an imminent revolution.[16] Although the Slave Trade Department enjoyed particular patronage from Lord Palmerston—foreign secretary in three governments—it survived in recognizable forms under the orders of a relatively small number of statesmen in various governments

The small size of the nineteenth-century Foreign Office meant that the secretary of state was in direct contact with the output of all departments and every dispatch arriving in London from overseas would cross his desk.[17] The four Slave Trade clerks working there in 1841 may seem an insignificant force to deploy against the international slave trade, but the entire Foreign Office, from the foreign secretary on down, consisted of a mere forty people (diplomats and consuls were administratively separate).[18] The Slave Trade clerks spent their days responding to the slave-trade dispatches from diplomats abroad, collating their findings, and publishing annual parliamentary papers on the progress of their campaign. As well as guiding ministers and consuls abroad on slave-trade matters, the Department provided them with news about treaties with other nations. The Foreign Office librarian compiled the bewildering and expanding collection of slave-trade treaties for the reference of government officials. During the most frantic periods of Atlantic suppression operations the Slave Trade Department sometimes accounted for almost a fifth of the dispatches received and sent by the Foreign Office, although this had been reduced to a twentieth by the end of the American Civil War.[19]

Although often jaded and weary from day-to-day contact with the problems of slave-trade suppression, the civil servants of the department generally became experts in their field. James Bandinel, the first Slave Trade Department superintendent, set a precedent for his successors when, in 1840, he became a de facto adviser to other government departments on African affairs, since he was the only one in government with direct knowledge of them. His "zealous and effective service" helped the Colonial Office to plan Sir Thomas Fowell Buxton's Niger expedition, although given its disastrous end, he was keen to have written absolution from "any responsibility whatever in respect to the Expedition...as it was to be, and was indeed finally executed."[20]

The strength he possessed in knowledge, Bandinel apparently lacked in other areas. He was a poor writer, venal (though not corrupt), and, in the words of his superior John Backhouse, "mean & tricky" over reorganization of the Foreign Office. Aberdeen praised his "friendly zeal" and willingness to pursue anti-slavery policy well beyond his "official duties," however, and Bandinel was happy, in retirement, to be involved in public inquiries into improving the suppression system.[21] He had spent twenty years as a Foreign Office clerk when, in 1819, he was first charged with administering the suppression system. He personally nurtured the growth of the department and his departure more than twenty-five years later left a void that was imperfectly filled by successive chief clerks Thomas Staveley, Thomas Ward, and Adolphus Oom. As Foreign Office historian Keith Hamilton has noted, Bandinel's influence over government anti-slavery policy would be matched only when his old job went to William Wylde, who succeeded Oom in 1859.[22]

Wylde was a statesman in disguise. Though a civil servant, he masterminded the campaign to suppress the East African slave trade in the 1870s and can be credited as one of the architects of the subsequent "scramble for Africa." He had risen from the ranks of the Slave Trade Department clerks and was briefly promoted out of the department, though he continued to advise on anti-slavery matters, before returning from 1876 as head of a larger division that included slave-trade suppression.[23] He was a keen activist for British attention to the "misery and ruin over a large portion of the African Continent" as a result of the east coast slave trade, and it is possible that he went so far as to leak the information that spurred a vital and hostile parliamentary motion against the government in 1871.[24] Corresponding regularly with British explorers, officials, and officers in Africa, he enjoyed collecting "African curiosities" sent by his friends.[25] On retiring from the Foreign Office, he pursued openly what he had quietly attempted as an official; he joined the committee of the BFASS and encouraged them to steer British policy in Africa toward his preferred brand of anti-slavery imperialism. In 1892, Edmund Sturge of the BFASS told Wylde that "you effected more for the cause than the whole Anti-Slavery Society put together."[26]

A second battalion of anti-slavers provided the global eyes and ears of the Slave Trade Department. A network of consuls abroad fed information from around the globe to the Foreign Office. Their duties, promoting commerce and representing British interests, included sending dispatches to the Slave Trade Department on developments in their local patch. In 1807, when Britain abolished its own trade, diplomats to other powers had immediately been instructed to lobby for permission to search their shipping; acting on the imperatives of slave-trade diplomacy would become a part of the duties of many consular postings. Indeed, anti-slavery policy could also require operating covertly. In Cuba, a consul's duty could extend to bribing foreigners for information and, in Brazil, to buying local politicians and newspapermen.[27] Alexander Dunlop, the British consul at Cadiz in the mid-1860s, was vexed that the Spanish authorities "don't care a farthing" about illegal slave trading, so he relied on informants among the port's boatmen and shipbuilders.[28] In Tehran, the British minister arranged for secret-service-fund payments over two decades for information from the Persian commissioner for the slave trade at Bushir. This "Secret Bribe" was deliberately hidden from Parliament by the Slave Trade Department, which did not want news of the arrangement to reach the shah.[29]

Together, a network of ambassadors, consuls, and commissary judges scattered across the globe fed information into the Slave Trade Department. At the most basic level, they observed the progress of anti-slavery sentiment and slave-trade suppression or collected statistical data as required by the Foreign Office.[30] Beyond this, dispatches filled with observations and suspicions would be sent to London. Where a host country was implicated, the British agent could make representations; when a third country was involved, the Foreign Office could coordinate a complaint to a third nation.[31] To some degree, British anti-slavery activity consisted of demands to other nations that they enforce their own laws better. On one occasion, for example, Palmerston chided the Greeks that they should "rescue the Greek name from the reproach attaching to the prevalence of the slave trade under the flag of Greece." He called for more than mere edicts, expecting tough enforcement and punishment of the perpetrators.[32] Such familiarity with other nations' failings helped reinforce contempt for foreigners' attitudes. Palmerston, prime minister in 1860, bemoaned that "it is as unreasonable to expect honesty in a Portuguese or a Frenchman" about slave trading "as it is to look for courage in a Neapolitan."[33]

Regardless of the many problems with suppressing international slave trading, the system initiated by Britain had some success. Of an estimated 7,750 Atlantic slave ships operating in the period 1808–67, about one in five were condemned by the courts or destroyed by naval interdiction, and all but 15 percent of such captures were the work of the Royal Navy (fig. 6). Ninety thousand enslaved Africans were freed in the three decades after 1836, just over 5 percent of the total slaves embarked for bondage in the New World.[34] The greatest challenges came in creating an international legal framework to prosecute and convict slave traders.

British naval power could be legally applied to subjects of other nations only when they ventured into British waters or when subject to treaties. In the latter case, these agreements were enforced through the system of courts established to try the cases of captured slave-trade suspects (fig. 7). In the Mixed Commission Courts planted around the Atlantic Ocean, a British judge sat alongside an appointed foreign counterpart to try suspects from both their nations. Although British foreign policy focused on the negotiated expansion of the Mixed Commission system, these courts made up a declining proportion of slave-trading convictions. The Vice-Admiralty Courts dealt with British subjects or foreigners detained under British law and delivered half of all such convictions; their activities made up the majority of successes in the period after 1837.[35] Each court was established according to individual bilateral treaties with other powers. If the commissary judges found a suspected vessel guilty of slave trading, then any Africans aboard would be liberated and the ship sold for the profit of the

FIGURE 6. East Africans liberated by HMS *Daphne*, 1 Nov. 1865. By permission of the Mary Evans Picture Library, ref. 10474557, under license from the National Archives, FO 84/1310/a.

two governments, but the crew members were not punished. An acquittal meant release and—should harm have been caused by the navy—potential legal claims for compensation against the capturing nation (in most cases Britain).[36] The commissary judges from Britain held an anomalous position outside the regular diplomatic and consular establishment, though the role could sometimes be combined with such appointments.[37]

FIGURE 7. Map of British and joint courts trying suspected slave traders in the Atlantic. Britain signed bilateral treaties establishing mixed commission courts at each location, with partner countries listed (in darker boxes) by date they consented. The Vice-Admiralty Courts most active in slave-trade trials after 1815 are shown (in lighter boxes) with dates where established during the nineteenth century. *Sources*: "Slave Voyages Database," http://www.Slaveyoyages.org; Eltis, *Economic Growth*, frontispiece; J. Eastoe Teall, *Slavery and the Slave Trade* (London, 1880). Produced by Cartography Unit, Plymouth University.

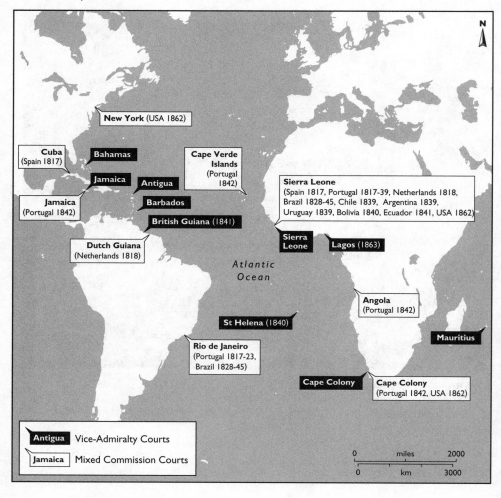

Although commissary judges of the Mixed Commission Courts were officially employed to decide cases that arose, they too could play a role in sharing information on the trade. They acted as an extension of the consular network in feeding information about the slave trade to the Foreign Office.[38] In 1848, a commissary report from Havana reported that "one vessel, if not more, has sailed from the City of Trinidad, two schooners from Santiago de Cuba, and several from the Island of Puerto Rico." However, the commissary judge, James Kennedy, realizing he was part of a wider intelligence system, suggested that "should these rumours be correct" then the foreign secretary "will no doubt have had fuller details respecting them, from Her Majesty's Consuls at the two last mentioned places."[39] The judges could themselves be forewarned by other agents of the anti-slavery state when illegally trafficked Africans were likely to be landed in their jurisdiction. Kennedy played detective among the island's slave population, on one occasion following some slaves he thought could have been recently (and therefore illegally) imported, because they had been speaking African languages. Even if his suspicions turned out to be unfounded, when he realized that their children could speak Spanish, the incident shows a personal zeal in tracking down illicit slave trading.[40] Finally, the commissioners in a slave-holding society such as Cuba's could report on the suppression system from the slavers' side: by 1849, Cuban planters believed that British cruisers were stationed only twenty miles from each other in a cordon around the coast.[41] In addition to their judicial functions, the Mixed Commission Courts were part of a global anti-slavery network.

That much is clear from the diaries of George Canning Backhouse. A clerk at the Foreign Office and son of its late permanent under-secretary, he complained of days when the bureaucrats were "very busy at the F.O. all day. No time for relaxation on the roof." Beyond his frustrations with days when work or inclement weather disrupted his afternoons smoking on the Foreign Office roof, the junior Backhouse was delighted to say "farewell to FO dreary drudgery" when he left London in 1853 to replace Kennedy as commissary judge in Havana.[42] He was dispatched with orders that "Govt. anxious *if necessary* to accumulate cases of misconduct of Spanish Authorities" and to work with the naval officers patrolling Cuba to document such evidence.[43] "No man keeps his word in this country," Backhouse quickly concluded after taking up residence on the island.[44] His frustration with the Spanish was confirmed by his early experiences of judging slave-trading cases that came before the court; when the commissioners from each nation could not agree on a verdict, lots would be drawn to decide which country's arbiter would break the deadlock. In many cases, this meant that a guilty verdict could be secured only when the British adjudicator was drawn.[45] Besides his role in suppressing the slave trade, the new judge also acted as a protector for the *"emancipados"*—liberated Africans—who worked in a tenuous condition of apprenticeship on the island's estates, bringing cases of unfair treatment to the attention of the colonial government.[46] Backhouse's Caribbean sojourn had a tragic end when he was murdered at his Havana home in 1855 during a break-in.[47]

The commissary judges, consuls, diplomats, and bureaucrats did not operate independently of other branches of the anti-slavery state. The Royal Navy's squadrons relied on information from the consuls to maximize their effectiveness. In one case, John Lindegreen, British consul at Puerto Rico, learnt of a slaver operating near the Rio Pongo through his web of informers. He passed this intelligence to the naval station at Barbados and subsequently heard, through news originating with the ship's owner, that the slaver had been destroyed. He knew this from his local contacts before the Foreign Office learnt of the naval interception.[48] At St. Paul de Loanda (in Portuguese West Africa, modern Angola) in the 1850s, Consul George Brand created a close working relationship with Rear Admiral Arthur Fanshawe, who commanded the naval squadron there. Fanshawe and other naval officers sent a letter of praise for Brand to the Foreign Office, testifying to "the advantage which the naval service derived from his intelligence and prompt attention to all matters connected with the suppression of the slave trade."[49] On these occasions, the different branches of the British state cooperated for anti-slavery purposes.

Beyond this, there is plenty of evidence to suggest that officials acted beyond the requirements of their political instructions. Many British agents abroad were committed anti-slavers and did not simply act on orders from the Foreign Office. A vibrant and enthusiastic culture of anti-slavery activism pushed them to doggedly pursue complaints, often before London had provided instruction. In this sense, "men on the spot" were often anti-slavers on the spot.[50] For example, in Athens, in 1840, Sir Edmund Lyons doggedly pursued action from his host government once he caught wind of Greek vessels indulging in slave trading off the Barbary Coast. When assured that a letter had previously been issued by the minister of marine against the trade, he checked and discovered it had not been circulated. He also engaged local lawyers to provide an opinion on the preexisting illegality of slave trading by Greek citizens. All of this was done by Lyons unilaterally and approved by the Foreign Office after the event.[51]

The most outstanding example of an anti-slavery man-on-the-spot is perhaps Sir Thomas Reade, a consul whose personal influence over the bey of Tunis was widely credited with the abolition of slavery in that country.[52] His first interview on the subject, in April 1841, elicited a promise from the bey to liberate all his own slaves and turn his attention to the suppression of the trade within his country—"the noblest acts possible," as Reade judged them. The meeting, held on Reade's initiative, was received with delight in London, where enquiries were made to arrange a gift for the bey.[53] The consul was proud to be "the humble instruct" of Great Britain and divine providence in advancing anti-slavery.[54] In other Tunisian cases he pursued anti-slavery as a vocation, on one occasion intervening to prevent the abuse of an enslaved Algerian boy and eventually buying his freedom.[55]

At the same time, the colorful Colonel Hanmer Warrington, Her Majesty's representative in Tripoli, was pursuing his own anti-slavery mission. As well as agitating to convince local rebels to make anti-slavery part of their cause against the area's Turkish rulers, he sent to the Foreign Office his ambitious schemes to civilize the interior of Africa and suppress the slave trade. He declared in one dispatch that "the civilization & emancipation of the poor & suffering slaves has created deep interest & reflection in my mind" and hailed "with prayers the present period when apparently the grand structure will be built on the foundations already laid."[56] He promised London that "if I can in the remotest way contribute to the Glorious cause it will give me infinite pleasure as I have no selfish feeling excepting doing good to my fellow creatures."[57]

In this way, some officials used their dispatches to emphasize their role as anti-slavery champions abroad. Career-minded or pious Britons in Queen Victoria's armed or civil services could rely on a broad culture of anti-slavery activism. Another consul, referring to the slave trade in 1846, insisted to Foreign Secretary Lord Aberdeen that "as an Englishman, I cannot but feel a just indignation at such a departure from a grand principle of humanity."[58] Beyond self-aggrandizement, the boasts of such consuls also suggest that anti-slavery was a national interest, holding glory for those who advanced its cause.

On the other hand, it is difficult to ascertain whether those agents who took less initiative were unconcerned and negligent or whether they lacked an opportunity to act. Certainly in some cases, such as in Spanish Puerto Rico, complicit local officials could run rings around gullible British officials.[59] However, there seems ample evidence that many British consuls often took pride in exercising their considerable discretionary powers to abolitionist ends. In this way, Britain's anti-slavery men-on-the-spot went beyond mere global omniscience and actually took the initiative in pursuing British interests as they saw fit. Through both policy and initiative, different limbs of the state pushed anti-slavery goals, but this raises questions about why politicians chose particular times or places to do so.

## BRITAIN'S ANTI-SLAVERY WORLD SYSTEM

It helps to think of a British "world system" of imperial power in the nineteenth century, varied in local tactics but united by strategic considerations and linked in subtle, myriad ways. Similarly, it is useful to see a British world system of anti-slavery, its "gravitational field" fluctuating in power depending on the terrain, atmosphere, and individuals involved.[60] On a practical level, we have already seen how the informants, commissioners, and agents of the Foreign Office shared information about slave trading across the world's oceans. There was no single set of uncontested policies, but the officials in the Slave Trade Department developed a narrow set of approaches. These assumptions designated the proper spheres of action and wisest goals for anti-slavery policy, constituting something close to an anti-slavery "official mind."[61] In making these assertions, the Foreign Office men clashed with foreign nations, ideological abolitionists, their own consuls, and other parts of the British government. Yet, by dissecting the anti-slavery lobe of the official mind, it is possible to understand how and when foreign policy pursued anti-slavery ends and exactly which disputes arose over its stewardship of Britain's identity as an anti-slavery nation.[62]

While the Foreign Office focused on the Atlantic slave trade, as it did before 1870, bilateral agreements were generally preferred. The nightmarish exchanges surrounding the Quintuple Treaty of 1841 between Britain, France, Russia, Austria, and Prussia, undermined by French Anglophobia at the point of ratification, had shown the difficulties of that approach.[63] When Palmerston ordered a renewed effort for all Christian countries to recognize the slave trade as piracy in 1851, he still expected this league to take the form of bilateral treaties with Britain.[64] The alternative—a multinational treaty recognizing the slave trade as piracy—was disfavored, as it opened British shipping to trial in foreign courts.[65]

Anti-slavery treaties generally permitted the parties a mutual right to search the other country's merchant ships for slaves or equipment used in the slave trade. This meant the establishment of Mixed Commission Courts with some countries (such as the Netherlands, Scandinavian nations, Brazil, and Spain), and the escalation of tensions with others. Some European nations insisted on the exclusive right to try their own subjects and expected British cruisers to hand over suspected slave traders to them. The United States (until 1862) and France (always) resisted conceding the right of search to perfidious Albion, preferring to maintain their own naval squadrons for the prohibition of slave trading by their citizens.[66] British diplomats gave all "civilized" nations, regardless of their power, the same courtesies and respectful language when contracting treaties. Their negotiations with African states stood in stark contrast; slave-trade-suppression negotiations created a lasting legal prejudice against acknowledging the statehood of "non-civilized" peoples.[67]

Beyond this, the simple divisions between "civilized" and African countries hid a wide variety of approaches to ensure compliance from other countries. The Foreign Office's anti-slavery worldview and the political realities of world power meant that different options seemed appropriate to different countries at different times. A brief review of British actions toward the United States, Brazil, and the Ottoman Empire illustrates these distinctions. These three countries were treated—in the repertoire of the Foreign Office—as advanced, civilized, and semicivilized states respectively, and their experiences are revealing and broadly representative of British policy toward nations possessing similar wealth and power.

The British state's anti-slavery policy toward the United States baffled and disappointed abolitionists in Britain and America. In ways the abolitionists disliked, British politicians balanced diplomacy with questions about the slave trade, slavery, and fugitive slaves across a range of different crises. For example, Britain struggled with the Republic of Texas, which flirted with the possibility of annexation to the United States following unilateral secession from Mexico in 1836.[68] Abolitionists had focused their energies on withholding recognition from the new republic so long as it remained a slave republic. BFASS president Thomas Clarkson had lobbied General Antonio López de Santa Anna of Mexico, Sam Houston of Texas, and the British government to make emancipation part of the settlement of the question.[69] Yet this question was not the principal problem in the eyes of the Foreign Office; Britain recognized Texas as a sovereign nation in 1840. Preventing American annexation and securing the permanent independence of the Republic of Texas seemed to offer better prospects for emancipation in official eyes. The price of recognition was a slave-trade treaty between the two countries, which made the recognition of a slave nation acceptable to the British public's anti-slavery sensibilities. As would so often be the case, the Foreign Office's priority was naval suppression rather than involvement in local emancipation projects.[70]

This was not what abolitionist societies on either side of the Atlantic wanted or what some Anglophobic Southern planters feared.[71] Writing back to Washington, President Tyler's private American agent in London, Duff Green, was certain that "England is stimulating the abolition of slavery in Texas."[72] He believed that a potential emancipation in Texas was being masterminded by the British chargé d'affaires, Captain Charles Elliot (recently transferred from China, where he had helped start the Opium War). "They exert themselves to abolish slavery everywhere else and will then press on us. Even war will not stop them," Green warned John C. Calhoun in the autumn of 1843.[73] He was completely mistaken in these assumptions, since the British government rejected a proposal from an abolitionist delegation for Britain to engineer Texan emancipation through the promise of national bonds. The foreign secretary, the Earl of Aberdeen, assured anti-slavery activists that he "felt the subject deeply" and that "the gov[ernment] would do all they could legitimately," but that did not include a bribe in bonds.[74] As Prime Minister Sir Robert Peel assured Green, "the government did not wish to interfere with the subject of slavery in the United States" even if the British public's "general sentiment against slavery was very strong."[75] Peel's Whig opponent, Lord John Russell, gave Green a similar promise regarding "non-interference in the domestic policy of other nations."[76]

These tensions over Texas underlined an important general rule. Britain's priority in anti-slavery diplomacy with other "civilized" nations was, as both political parties promised, not about interference with foreigners' internal laws.[77] However, the Foreign Office was disposed to fight more fiercely when enslaved Africans from abroad found refuge in British lands. Surrendering escapees to foreign slaveowners violated patriotic and romantic notions of national freedom. In the 1835 *Enterprize* case, an American ship engaged in the domestic slave trade entered a British harbor during a storm, leading local officials to free the enslaved people aboard it. The attorney general maintained that "a slave was as much free when he arrived in the Bahamas or at Bermuda as if he had reached Portsmouth or Plymouth." This judgment rendered void international agreements guaranteeing property in cases involving slaves.[78] Palmerston supported this view of Britain's anti-slavery sovereignty, believing that "there is no wrong, and there shall be no compensation."[79]

There was even greater acrimony after enslaved African Americans aboard the brig *Creole* had seized command during a voyage from Richmond, Virginia, to New Orleans, Louisiana, in 1841. They sailed the ship to Nassau, a colony of the British crown, where Governor Francis Cockburn told those slaves who wished to disembark (all but three) that they were free to do so.[80] The ministers of the United States furiously protested that this meddling had stolen the freed slaves from their owners, in contravention of maritime law, and demanded that the leading insurrectionists be extradited to America to stand trial for piratical theft of the vessel. However, the British law officers in London advised the Foreign Office that the rebels should not face charges or extradition, given that they had risen so that "they might obtain their freedom, and we think that the acts of slaves committed with such intent and object does not amount to piracy." Moreover, they maintained that Cockburn had not interfered to liberate the slaves but simply permitted them to "leave the vessel on board of which there was no legal power to detain them."[81] Taken with previous disputes, the *Creole* incident suggested that the two countries needed to find common principles in such cases.

To this end, in 1842 British diplomat Lord Ashburton and American secretary of state Daniel Webster constructed a treaty that would settle a number of outstanding tensions in transatlantic relations. Besides boundary disputes, the negotiations were dominated by the various ways in which British freedom and American slavery permeated each nation's borders. Webster, raising the *Creole* case, was assured by Ashburton that officials would seek "no officious interference" with the cargoes of American ships entering British waters. Still, he maintained that they had to uphold imperial laws permitting freedom to those on British soil: "On the part of Great Britain, there are certain great principles too deeply rooted in the consciences of the people for any minister to be able to overlook; and any engagement I might make in opposition to them would be instantly disavowed."[82] Cockburn's activist role in guaranteeing to slaves the right to go ashore—and hence to secure their freedom—meant that Britain ultimately accepted the need to compensate the Americans in 1853.[83] More broadly, however, British policy toward the United States sought to balance a rigorous application of British laws—not least, as Ashburton noted, because of his country's anti-slavery sensibilities—with recognition that transatlantic relations should not be too thinly frayed. Privately, Ashburton assured the BFASS that no "part of the Treaty lately concluded by me with the United States of America should tend to impair in any way the protection which fugitive slaves receive when they take refuge in any of our colonies."[84]

America's border with Canada created further tension over escaped slaves, since fugitives from the United States could escape to claim their freedom on British soil.[85] In 1837, for example, Britain had argued that a fugitive, Jesse Happy, had stolen a horse only in order to secure his personal liberty, which under British law he should not have been deprived of. The charge of horse stealing, it was reasoned, could not therefore be considered a crime under British law and therefore could not justify extradition to America.[86] The tenth clause of the Treaty of Washington, which emerged in 1842 from Ashburton's mission, addressed Webster's demand that Britain extradite escaped slaves such as Happy for trial in the United States, just like other fugitives from American justice. The BFASS was outraged that Great Britain had conceded the right, but the British Foreign Office was not worried. Lord Aberdeen, who as foreign secretary approved Ashburton's stance, was certain that Britain could appease American bluster and honor extradition rules in principle while ignoring them in practice. He made a private promise to concerned abolitionist opponents, in 1843, that if "the 10th article of that treaty would operate injuriously to the slave I would abolish it today."[87] Thomas Clarkson was overjoyed on receiving assurances from the governor general of Canada, Sir Charles Metcalfe, that he would "go to the utmost length that the late treaty will allow him to go to protect the unhappy fugitive against the claims of an enraged master, and he is quite aware of all the Tricks" they might employ.[88]

Aberdeen and Metcalfe had no need to break Webster and Ashburton's Washington Treaty. They showed cosmetic respect for international conventions and America's domestic institutions, while pursuing a strategy that freed the British government from any direct accommodation with the slave trade.[89] Far from conceding the right of extradition, the negotiations had respected American power at the same time as they permitted anti-slavery practice. The BFASS's initial response to these developments demonstrated their uncompromising and doctrinaire brand of anti-slavery. By contrast, the subtler British officials continued to apply their logic of 1839 in all cases; Canada never extradited a single fugitive slave to the United States.[90] In the final attempted extradition of a runaway slave, when John Anderson stood accused of murdering a white man, the Colonial Office was prepared to step in and overrule the verdict of his 1860–61 trial rather than see him returned. The case was dismissed on procedural grounds, but by this point London had instructed Ashburton, now Canada's governor general, not to surrender Anderson in order to give their own law officers time to assist in manufacturing a reason not to return him.[91]

The Webster-Ashburton Treaty also considered the question of suppression of the slave trade, though the United States still withheld from Britain the right to search its shipping—a sore point as it had been one of the causes of the War of 1812. Webster would not permit any measure that had "a tendency to place the police of the seas in the hands of a single power." The search of American vessels by British anti-slavery patrols thus remained unauthorized and the flag of the United States remained a safe choice for slavers of all nations.[92] The only concession to British concern was the U.S. Navy's deployment of an African squadron to enforce the 1808 American ban on slave trading. In the next two decades these ships caught an average of two ships per year. It was only when the U.S. government recalled its vessels from Africa during the Civil War that the State Department—now liberated from Southern opinion and recognizing the Union's inability to police the slave trade—gave Britain the right to search its merchant ships.[93]

British naval suppression was severely hampered by American obstinacy, but statesmen tended to be timid and pliant when dealing with the U.S. government. In 1860, for instance, the Duke of Somerset, first lord of the Admiralty, rejected instructions from Foreign Secretary Lord John Russell that cruisers should openly patrol off the coast of Cuba, fearing inevitable American opposition. Preferring not to elicit U.S. censure, he went so far as to request that a duplicate be sent without the order, so it could be omitted from the physical records of his department for parliamentary publication.[94] This delicacy in dealing with the United States had been a lesson of the ugly confrontation in 1858 over such British activities. Then, the American government had threatened war when the Royal Navy began to aggressively patrol all shipping near Cuba. The cruisers had visited American ships on the basis that they needed to check that they were not flying false flags. Although most British papers were jingoistic, the *Times*—and, it seems, British statesmen, on mature reflection—thought America's anti-slavery partnership was better secured by discretion and negotiation.[95] While Americans celebrated their victory, Aberdeen was "at a loss to understand what is given up" because "the zeal of our cruisers had converted into a rule that which was only intended to be an exception."[96] In these cases Britain attempted to tease greater support for slave-trade suppression out of Washington, but war would never have been a viable strategic choice. As a "civilized" and powerful nation, anti-slavery objectives could only be pushed tactically.

Foreign Office policy aimed to suffocate global slavery by strangling the slave trade rather than confronting foreign slave-holding by directly entering American politics as partisans. This partly explains why Britons could contemplate recognizing or even allying with the Confederacy during the American Civil War. In the midst of Southern secession, the anti-slavery state was most concerned that the Confederate flag would join the U.S. flag as a haven beneath which slave traders could hide.[97] The new nation included a ban on the importation of slaves in its constitution (despite some internal opposition).[98] Even if Jefferson Davis had been willing to concede to Britain the right to search Southern ships, a treaty would require recognition of the Confederate States of America as a sovereign nation. The British agonized long enough over whether to recognize the rebels as belligerents and recognition would have provoked war with the Union. Wily old Palmerston, now prime minister, saw the sectional struggle as a long-awaited excuse to extort the right of search from the Union. In this he succeeded, securing a (limited) right of search in 1862.[99]

Even if the Foreign Office was cautious in intervening in American politics, it maintained a robust stance on existing rights. There were still redlines beyond which anti-slavery policy could not be pushed or maneuvered. One of these was the liberty of British subjects. Just as the Royal Navy made special attempts to retrieve any Sierra Leonians abducted by slave traders in West Africa, so the Foreign Office doggedly hunted for abductees within America—though by rather different means. In March 1860, Mr. Archibald, the British consul at New York, informed British ambassador Lord Lyons about an "extraordinary & outrageous proceeding": news had reached Archibald of a black British subject, William Brodie, who had been kidnapped and sold into slavery by the people of Darien, Georgia. A Bahamian sailor, Brodie had been accused of encouraging American slaves to run away, and two years earlier he had been tried by the town's mayor in an impromptu informal "court."[100] The sailor was subsequently sold illegally into slavery and disappeared into America's massive internal slave trade between the upper and lower South. An urgent correspondence ensued between Lyons, Archibald, Foreign Secretary Lord John Russell and the British consul in Savannah, Edward Molyneux. Lyons insisted that "the object of paramount importance is the restoration of Brodie to freedom. To this, but to this only, the punishment of the offenders is secondary."[101]

Molyneux was sent £200 and authorized to spend any additional funds required to secure information and witnesses who could testify "to prosecute the perpetrators of the outrage" and to enable "the best counsel be employed to prosecute in every court before which the case can be brought the authors of this flagrant wrong"; moreover, Russell instructed him "that Her Majesty's Government will expect that every effort shall be made to discover whether William Brodie is living" and to "buy the freedom of Brodie, if it be impossible to rescue him from slavery in any other way." Despite the involvement of the federal government, the case was not resolved before the secession of Georgia from the union, and Brodie presumably found himself emancipated by President Lincoln in 1863 but stranded in Southern poverty for the rest of his life.[102] He was subsequently forgotten about by Britain's agents, who were apparently concerned about his reenslavement but not his ultimate fate. The episode was still a rather remarkable rescue attempt by the Foreign Secretary and his diplomatic agents. Even if they focused on the "outrage" caused to their country, they clearly also felt a moral obligation to recover the legal freedom of a victimized black Briton. There was no question of Britain's legal right to protect its subjects from arbitrary reenslavement, so the anti-slavery state was confident intervening in a local dispute. Such an effort still engaged with the sovereign legal processes of the United States, however, demonstrating a grudging deference to the republic. In West Africa, villages were burnt for similar offenses. The difference, of course, was that the United States was a crucial trading partner, an Anglophone cousin, a threat to Canadian security, and a pillar of the global balance of power that favored the empire's supremacy.[103]

Similarly, a greater disparity in military, economic, and geopolitical position meant that Britain was more willing to cajole, push, and bully an emerging South American nation such as Brazil than the United States. In Brazil, as with the United States, Britain focused on the slave trade and not on domestic slave-holding.[104] Under the Anglo-Brazilian Abolition Treaty of 1826, the Brazilian government had agreed to treat slave trading by its subjects as "piracy" after 1830. As a condition for British recognition of Brazil, the Brazilians assented that they would be bound by the agreement of 1817, made when they were Portuguese subjects. This agreement permitted the right of search and Mixed Commission Courts.[105] When the treaty of 1817 finally expired in 1845, the Brazilian government stalled renewal negotiations in hope of a better bargain.

The new nation had miscalculated, as Lord Aberdeen, then foreign secretary in Sir Robert Peel's Conservative government, sought a forcible solution from the repertoire of a political rival. His Whig predecessor, Palmerston, had passed an act in 1839 that unilaterally authorized the Royal Naval to search Portuguese vessels on the pretext that Britain was only enforcing an undertaking neglected by Portugal. The government's law officers had insisted that Parliament pass a bill because it was "expedient that before any steps are taken for detaining ships not now authorized to be detained express authority should be given by Act of Parliament so as to indemnify all parties concerned."[106] In exchange for the repeal of Lord Palmerston's Act, Portugal had grudgingly signed a new slave-trade treaty. Aberdeen's Act, six years later, found different legal trickery to justify a similar law in the case of Brazil, which he hoped would lead to a similarly speedy capitulation by the targeted nation.[107]

Embarrassingly, the Conservatives had previously criticized Palmerston's approach to slave-trade diplomacy, promising to secure suppression while respecting "the framework of international law, and without taking any action which might endanger amicable relations with other states whose goodwill and co-operation were essential to the attainment of Britain's object."[108] Their own repeat performance was no less controversial. Parliamentary opponents attacked Aberdeen's Act as "a colourable pretext" and "subterfuge" to get around international law and regularly lobbied for its repeal.[109] Aberdeen in private admitted to Peel that it was "certainly a great stretch of power and open to many objections on principle."[110] After he returned to the Foreign Office the following year, Palmerston conceded that the new law had angered the Brazilians, but he denied that the antagonism would ultimately be counterproductive. Although British highhandedness might retard the development of domestic anti-slavery feeling in Brazil in the short term, the act would help attack the slave trade and drive up the price of imported slaves; only this would permit local abolitionism to take root. In 1850, in the midst of a political storm over whether to adopt softer tactics, Palmerston violated Brazilian territorial waters to attack slave traders. Brazil promptly accepted the enforcement of abolition, but Aberdeen's Act would remain on the statute books until 1869, underlining Britain's contemptuous distrust of the country. Palmerston argued that "if you were to repeal it, depend upon it from that moment the Brazilian slave trade would recommence with all its attendant evils."[111] The Palmerston and Aberdeen laws, as unilateral assertions of British power, led to more captured suspected slavers being tried by the Vice-Admiralty Courts, which operated on the basis of British law alone.[112]

With a young South American nation, Britain was willing to indulge in what the explorer Richard Burton would remember as "one of the greatest insults which a strong ever offered to a weak people."[113] Britain knew from experience that a similar violation of American sovereignty would have led to a bloody nose. Further pressure would follow in the early 1860s, when British officials pursued the condition of *emancipados* who were rescued from slave ships only to be forced to work in conditions akin to slavery.[114]

Commercial links ensured that the British government had no desire to cause a war or revolution in Brazil. Compared to the United States, however, Brazil was less able to resist British bullying and force. For this reason even the Conservatives were willing to use national law and imperial power to override the Brazilian government's obstinacy. British diplomacy was the art of the possible with the archness of the powerful.

Abolitionist critics of British policy, such as the BFASS, put their efforts into policing the business affairs of British subjects in a slave-holding country such as Brazil. Their main concern, expressed at the 1840 convention and after, was to attack the use of British goods and capital in the slave industries of Brazil.[115] It was not just pacifism that led the BFASS to focus on domestic emancipation rather than international slave-trade suppression. It also reflected a fundamental difference between "abolitionist" and "official" brands of anti-slavery over how global slavery would most likely be throttled. Although both options required British imperial power to direct the development of other countries, the Foreign Office's methods stayed closer to the spirit of international law and permitted greater flexibility depending on the strength and circumstances of individual countries.

This streak of government pragmatism is particularly evident in British relations with the Ottoman Empire. It was commonly accepted that the existence of slavery "amongst the degraded tribes that people the continent of Africa is not surprising," but it was unclear whether such pessimism should apply to the Ottoman domain.[116] The Turks' slavery posed particular problems: should their empire and its client states be held to the standards Britain expected from Christian and "civilized" societies, such as Brazil or the United States, or be permitted to behave as "degraded" peoples, with domestic slavery as a natural phase they were going through?[117] The fact that Ottoman slavery relied on importing non-Muslim slaves pointed toward the former approach, but the Foreign Office had difficulty formulating a consistent policy toward a non-Christian people. Turkish reliance on the protection of Britain during the Crimean War produced early fruits, with laws proscribing the Black Sea slave trade in 1854 and the African slave trade in 1857.[118] However, enforcing these legal concessions was a much trickier matter.

These comparisons of foreign policy risk suggesting that Britain had a single-minded approach to anti-slavery. The "anti-slavery state" was not a homogeneous organism; there was plenty of disagreement between officials. For example, many consuls on the spot found diplomatic caution about Ottoman slavery to be perplexing and frustrating. The consul in Tripoli, Drummond Hay, caused consternation for his heavy-handed approach with local officials over slave-trade matters in 1870. He was berated for failing to appreciate "the necessity of great prudence in tampering with slavery in Mohammedan countries." The chargé d'affaires in Constantinople warned

Foreign Secretary Lord Clarendon that "I have deemed it necessary to ex-hort Mr. Consul General Hay to a more conciliatory attitude."[119]

Britain's consul in Smyrna, Mr. Henry A. Cumberbatch, had to be simi-larly restrained after he took an abrasive approach. His abuse of Turkish officials turned out to have been prompted by his mistaken impression that the internal sale of slaves within the empire was illegal; in fact, only the im-portation of new African slaves had been banned.[120] His superior, Sir Henry Elliot, the ambassador in Constantinople, stressed to Cumberbatch that too outspoken an approach could retard rather than advance the state of public opinion in the country.[121] Having sent seven reports about suspected slave trading in May 1872 alone, the Foreign Office warned Cumberbatch that while Clarendon gave "you full credit for the zeal which you display in this matter, His Lordship suggests that you should make as minute enqui-ries as possible."[122] Cumberbatch was also ordered not to allow his consul-ate to become a refuge for runaway slaves and to "confine himself, except in extreme cases, to notifying local authorities of any fresh importation or instances of slave dealing."[123] This mirrored practice in Egypt, where the Foreign Office encouraged officials to attack the slave trade rather than dabbling in helping slaves who had escaped to the consulate.[124] For the senior echelons of the anti-slavery state, the day-to-day realities of Otto-man governance seemed to prove that anti-slavery could only be advanced through a more cautious and pragmatic approach.[125]

Sir Henry Elliot, who would within a decade earn notoriety for his amoral reaction to the 1876 massacre of thousands of Bulgarians by their Ottoman overlords, stated his position that

> the slave trade's most revolting features and the demoralizing publicity of sale may be said to have nearly ceased already, and the vigilance of Her Majesty's Consuls may well be exercised in seeing that they do not revive, but for anything more, we must, I believe, wait for the development of the higher moral tone of feeling.

Elliot, advocating such restraint in 1869, was naturally keen to preface such pragmatism with a disclaimer that "I trust not to be taken as an apolo-gist for this detestable institution."[126] The clash with Cumberbatch's anti-slavery zeal could be seen as simple, apologetic Turkophilia on the part of Elliot, but there was a point of policy at stake too. Elliot argued that emancipation was impractical in the short term because "even if the [Otto-man] Government was willing to attempt it (which it certainly would not be) it would find itself powerless to carry out such a reform contrary to the general feeling of the country."[127]

In this regard he shared a realism that had been broadly applied by British policy makers for fifty years. Yusuf Erdem, a historian of Turkey, has argued that British anti-slavery policy in the Ottoman Empire was split between these two models: an idealist vision of destroying demand for the trade by attacking the institution and a more pragmatic one that regarded this as impossible and preferred to restrict operations to the trade.[128] These differences stretched back to 1840, when the General Anti-Slavery Convention lobbied Palmerston to act for Ottoman emancipation. He had responded with a campaign to suppress the slave trade and yet to resist interfering in domestic institutions.[129] As late as 1883, when Wylde and Henry Layard succeeded in forcing an Anglo-Ottoman slave-trade convention upon the Porte, the same distinction was made. During their negotiations, Layard agreed with Wylde that "it would be very unwise to ask the Turks at the present time to take any measures, or to give any pledges, as to the abolition of the status of slavery. No Turkish Government could do anything of the kind. It would be to create a social revolution" since "domestic slavery is interwoven into all the domestic institutions of this country... to abolish it at one swoop would be to irritate them beyond measure."[130] By the end of the nineteenth century, British officials still rehearsed many of the same fears about meddling with "Islamic slavery" in another region, the Persian Gulf, where Britons struggled to balance realpolitik and slave-trade suppression.[131]

This caution mirrored that shown in the Ottoman Empire, where foreign secretaries' priority, following the official view, was to retain Britain's leverage on larger anti-slavery questions and to prop up the sultan's regime. This explains why they took an ambivalent approach, preferring to apply pressure in subtle ways. The Foreign Office seems to have shown a remarkable indulgence for officials acting beyond their authority for anti-slavery ends. Although official action focused on the slave trade itself, local agents were still encouraged to informally explore progress toward emancipation. Even Hay, one of the more exuberant consuls, was encouraged to use his "discretion to make such unofficial friendly representations as you may deem expedient."[132] The Foreign Office did not like to allow British consulates to become refuges for runaway slaves, but in cases where there was clear abuse local consuls had considerable latitude.[133]

The strength of Britain's anti-slavery network across the Ottoman Empire's shaky dominions proved invaluable in coordinating slave-trade policy. Consuls around the Mediterranean exchanged intelligence on slaving regularly. In practical terms, while British diplomats had little success in undermining the status of slavery, they did act as an unofficial watchdog on the enforcement of the 1857 ban on public auctions of imported slaves. For example, when the governor general of Tripoli told Hay that he doubted the Porte would wish for him to interfere with the conduct of the local slave trade, Britain's ambassador in Constantinople swiftly ensured that the governor was disabused of this notion by his masters.[134] Equally, when it emerged in 1870 that the authorities in Roustchouk (in modern Bulgaria) had never been given instructions to act on the 1857 order, the Foreign Office ensured that they were furnished with some.[135] On one level, then, the British anti-slavery network provided an unwanted augmentation or assumption of governance functions that the sickly Ottoman Empire would not perform, reflecting a more general evisceration of the sultan's political and economic independence by Britain and other European powers.

Local circumstances and geopolitical considerations clearly dictated how the anti-slavery world system would respond to opportunities and dilemmas.[136] The weakness of the Ottoman regime and the strength of the United States both caused British governments to avoid the kind of aggression they showed toward Brazil, because the alternatives seemed less attractive for the long-term advancement of anti-slavery and British imperial power. As foreign secretary in the mid-1820s, George Canning—Palmerston's mentor—had held back from demanding immediate abolition of the slave trade from newly independent Brazil, fearing that it would only destabilize that government and undermine a pliant partner.[137] The calculus had changed by Victoria's reign, when suppression policy could be pursued much more forcefully. Such judgments were, naturally, an art rather than a science; while Palmerston and most Britons thought that pressure and violence had defeated Brazilian obduracy, recent research suggests domestic factors persuaded the ministry in Rio to abolish the slave trade.[138]

More generally, though, these calculations show that anti-slavery could be a serious objective of British foreign policy while being balanced with other considerations. Frequently, statesmen saw broader interests melding with anti-slave-trade policy, rather than conflicting with it. In August 1869, for example, the Foreign Office counseled Clarendon not to pursue a new suppression treaty with Turkey as it might endanger the informal anti-slavery work of British consuls, currently tolerated, and expose Britain to reciprocal search arrangements in the sensitive Mediterranean. Annotating the memorandum, Clarendon summed up the overriding pragmatism behind Britain's pursuit of any foreign-policy objective: "the object is of great importance, but it may be purchased at too high a price."[139] Similarly, in exchange for Tunisian anti-slavery efforts in the 1840s, Palmerston was happy to guarantee protection against the bey's local enemies—"as long as he pursues the wise and prudent course which he has hitherto followed." The anti-slavery mission happily dovetailed with other interests in this case, as support for the bey helped undermine French influence within his court.[140]

Paul Michael Kielstra, examining Anglo-French diplomacy over suppression, judges that "without the dexterity of the statesmen involved, a worthy ideal might have sparked a war on more than one occasion"; it was precisely such dexterity that the Foreign Office prided itself on.[141] As in other spheres of influence, British anti-slavery policy aimed to get away with as much as possible without sparking war or permanent damage to Britain's local or global standing; the whole point was to guide a world system that advanced the causes of Christian civilization and British dominance at the same time, not to purchase one at the price of the other.

In 1965, Roger Anstey observed that "the notion that action against the slave trade on both humanitarian and commercial grounds was a good and proper concern of policy became the received conviction of the Office, something which did not require to be argued afresh as one generation of officials succeeded another, as one Foreign Secretary gave place to his successor."[142] Since his untimely death, there has been little attention given to this "received conviction" in the Foreign Office.[143] Historians and nineteenth-century rivals were right to see a crafty national interest at work in Britain's policies, but wrong to assume, invariably, that this rendered humanitarian intentions false. The anti-slavery state sought to spread anti-slave-trade laws around the globe, using whatever methods appeared expedient. This meant the vigorous pursuit of the right of search or other arrangements with Christian sovereign nations and some others such as the Ottoman Empire; this informal legal imperialism extorted a concession of maritime sovereignty, to greater or lesser degrees. For Brazil and Portugal, Britain used a formal legal imperialism, with Palmerston's and Aberdeen's acts manufacturing a right to search suspected slavers.[144]

As flexible as these practices were, there was a discernable shape to the anti-slavery mentality, which linked trade, Christianity, and civilization to the ending of the slave trade. The historical works of Sir Arthur Helps, a future clerk to the Privy Council, offer an insight into the view of one British official. Fascinated by the history of slavery in the New World, he undertook a study of its origins in the Spanish conquest of America. He mused that other planets in the galaxy might be very similar to Earth in their histories and developments, but that any visitors from those worlds would sadly discover that the most unusual thing "in the records of our Earth, may be its commercial slavery and its slave trade." Helps claimed there was a "natural" phase of slavery in ancient societies, such as Greece or Rome, which was "gradually modified by Christianity and advancing civilization." The European slave trade created "a new branch of commerce" in human beings, resurrecting slave-holding in civilized societies where it was otherwise dead or dying.[145]

Helps's "science" of slavery understood slave-holding and slave trading by modern, "civilized" communities to be a diversion from historical laws of progress. The same year he published the final volume of his account, the jurist Henry Maine completed his tome on ancient law, counting as the characteristic of civilized progress a transition from status (such as slavery) to contract (such as wage labor).[146] Both authors reflected a common "civilizational" approach to human societies, putting the British at the front of a historic march of progress.[147] Beyond these intellectual theories, Joseph Denman, an officer in the West Africa squadron, was repeating official doctrine when he argued that "much as we may deplore and condemn the Slavery of other states, we have no right to interfere....The views of this country should be confined to those cases in which the Slavery is supported by Slave Trade."[148] As the *Times* rightly observed in 1876, Britain had never looked to overthrow slave-holding governments; it had looked to attack the slave trade, on the basis that "the foreign supply of slaves being once cut off, domestic slavery must rapidly perish."[149] More sardonically, Foreign Office official Sir Villiers Lister observed that "it is like permitting the consumption of meat while punishing butchers," but such a diet was one that successive governments stuck to none the less.[150]

As strange as this distinction seems, there was a reason for it. Whereas slavery was seen as a natural stage that less-developed societies would grow out of, the international slave trade clogged and reversed the motors of civilization. As a writer argued in the conservative *Fraser's Magazine*, "the evils of slavery are deepened and darkened by the difference of race...[causing] the utmost cruelty of which human nature is capable."[151] Interracial slave trading and slave-holding seemed to create particularly unnatural evils and would retard the development of civilization. Officials and the public largely accepted the suppression of the slave trade as a moral and material national interest, just as they "saw Britain's fate as tied up with its overseas interests."[152] This is why slave-trade suppression became a foreign-policy objective, alongside other ways that British leaders hoped to shape the world economic system.

## CONSENSUS, CONFLICT, AND PARTISANSHIP

Although politicians shared anti-slavery objectives, they differed dramatically in the way to obtain them. It is abundantly clear that while the Foreign Office followed certain theories in anti-slavery policy, officials were besieged by critics and skeptics within Britain, as well as the considerations of realpolitik and real-world events. Anti-slavery rows erupted more often over management rather than purpose, but the differences could be stark. Opposition to particular anti-slavery actions came from other branches of the British state, abolitionist societies, and partisan politics. Examining these can help identify the areas of dispute and the relative power of each in curbing or redirecting anti-slavery foreign policy.

It is already clear that anti-slavery could run up against other national interests pursued by branches of the British state. When Commodore

A. P. E. Wilmot tried to work with the Slave Trade Department to develop economic and political means for suppression, he was offended when told by one of the "gentlemen at the admiralty" that "I think you sometimes forget that you are employed as a naval officer & not a diplomatic one." Wilmot was advised that "your well-intentioned desire to benefit Africa" did not "belong to your province or fall within the scope of Admiralty business."[153] Although the Foreign Office regularly suspected the Admiralty of harboring institutional resentment toward the dictates of anti-slavery policy, naval officers varied in their enthusiasm for assignments in Africa or the Americas, where deaths from disease were common. Wilmot was one of the keener ones. Although some sailors were surely sincere in their enthusiasm, there are hints at the edges of surviving sources that others were not. In 1877, William Houghton, a British subject enjoying the bar of the Shepheard Hotel in Cairo, overheard a fellow drinker attacking the foreign secretary, Lord Derby, as a "b[lood]y old fool." "If he thinks *I* am going nigger hunting he makes a damnation error," ranted Henry McKillop, a former naval officer now serving the khedive of Egypt. His new employer, under British pressure, had asked McKillop to catch slave traders. Foreign Office officials heard of this outburst thanks to a report Houghton made to the BFASS but would not take action on the basis of hearsay, even if it was likely to have been true.[154] This unusual case, however, implies that some British sailors disliked slave-trade-suppression duties.

Even among the Foreign Office's own network of judges and consuls, information and cooperation did not always flow smoothly and collegially. For example, George Canning Backhouse, commissary judge at Havana, quickly fell out with the British consul, Joseph Crawford, over the latter's reluctance to share intelligence about slave-trade operations in Cuba; he suspected his colleague of being "jealous no doubt" of his successes. The two engaged in a bitter turf war in the year before Backhouse's death, with Crawford posing to the Foreign Office as a zealous abolitionist while taking little action over cases of liberated Africans reported to have been abused.[155] Backhouse's clash was just the latest episode in a long-running series of melodramatic clashes between Britain's diplomatic and judicial personnel in Cuba.[156] Even more seriously, the previous commissioner and other staff of his court had been implicated in (and in some cases proven to be) holding slaves themselves. Moreover, despite its strict attitude toward other countries, the Foreign Office was not above false economies and oversights in its own operations, such as not sending a replacement arbitrator to the Mixed Commission Court at Havana for several years after 1847.[157]

The anti-slavery state was not in practice the perfect, homogeneous organism that Foreign Secretaries might have wished it to be. Yet for all the incompetence and evasion that doubtless arose in the privacy of consulates and courts abroad, anti-slavery had become a routine part of the British interests promoted and defended overseas. Some officials could be lazy or duplicitous in their duties; what is more surprising is that so many took the responsibility so seriously, eagerly talking up their part in the world anti-slavery system to the Foreign Office.[158] Outside the confines of the state, however, there were two main impulses for public discussion of whether this system was working well and whether it was the right way to develop a free-labor world. The first was pressure from surviving, marginalized factions of abolitionist activists, and the second was from partisan political opponents of whoever the foreign secretary was at a particular point in time.

Popular abolitionism had succeeded, between 1807 and 1833, in seeding anti-slavery sentiment within government, where it had rooted itself in the apparatus of the state. To the frustration of groups such as the BFASS, "what happened to the Atlantic slave trade had gone beyond the control of the abolitionists and into the hands of government officials," as Duncan Rice puts it pithily.[159] Early foreign overtures by the BFASS met opposition from supporters on the basis that "it is quite understood that the only means of one government communicating with another is through the diplomatic agent at the court of that government."[160] Moreover, relations with the campaigners' own government were rocky. The BFASS found itself frustrated on a wide variety of questions besides Texas annexation, the Webster-Ashburton Treaty, or violence against Brazil. Successive British governments were "anxiously desirous to see the Slave Trade put down and the condition of slavery abolished in every part of the world," as Palmerston typically declared.[161] Still, this did not mean that they could tackle these two objectives simultaneously and instantly. British and American abolitionists often hoped to confront slave-holding in any country and to pursue tactics "of a MORAL, RELIGIOUS, AND PACIFIC NATURE" to promote emancipation in foreign lands.[162] This provided relatively little common ground for radical influence on state anti-slavery policies.

Sir Thomas Fowell Buxton argued that his Civilization Society's focus on spreading commerce and Christianity in Africa could complement the BFASS program. He suggested that the BFASS and African Civilization Society were

> not rivals; your first blow is aimed at slavery, ours at the slave-trade; you wish to extinguish the demand, we desire to crush the supply; your operations are in one hemisphere, ours in another. There is no possibility of interference; on the contrary, success cannot attend the one without its also attending the other.[163]

Yet, there was an important difference between the two approaches. Buxton's project was funded by the government, as part of its crusade against the slave trade; the BFASS worked at cross-purposes with the state, hoping to interfere in foreign countries' political affairs. So long as this strategic gulf existed between the BFASS and the state the influence of the former would be limited. Buxton might have been right that the approaches of the two voluntary societies were complementary, but his rivals' methods were incompatible with state anti-slavery.

These ideological differences were reflected in clashes of style and procedure, too, which limited radical influences on policymaking. From the founding of the BFASS in 1839, the society's members gained a reputation in some quarters as irresponsible idealists.[164] Sturge's abolitionist followers had not endeared themselves to the Whigs during the apprenticeship crisis of 1838. The radical MP Sir Eardley Wilmot had managed to pass a nonbinding resolution in favor of the immediate abolition of apprenticeship in May, due to the incompetence of the government's whips. Wilmot refused Lord John Russell's requests that he follow etiquette and introduce a bill proposing immediate abolition of apprenticeship (which properly whipped government MPs would have defeated). This was because Wilmot and Sturge wanted news of the first vote to reach the West Indies and create confusion about whether abolition had taken place. Although their campaign succeeded, the Sturgeites' willingness to threaten ministers with the risk of a violent colonial rebellion in the sugar colonies helps explain the later coolness toward them from some civil servants and politicians, particularly Russell.[165] By contrast, Buxton had shared with his friends in government the content of his critical speeches in advance so they could prepare informed and compliant answers to his probing public interrogation; this cozy relationship would have been anathema to the early BFASS activists.[166] Even a man such as Sir James Stephen, under-secretary of state at the Colonial Office and son of a leading abolitionist, did not show particular deference or respect to BFASS lobbying.[167] Only the advice of men such as William Wylde from the 1870s onward would transform the society into a more effective lobbying group. Before this time, they lacked both the popular support and the bureaucratic influence to regularly shape government action.

Despite their early Victorian disadvantages, however, the BFASS did succeed to some degree in shaping anti-slavery policy in particular areas where they had the potential to raise public anger. As much as the BFASS struggled to dictate policy, it could erratically perform the function of an auxiliary to the anti-slavery state; without its lobbying, politicians might have been even more cautious or conservative. One of the society's lasting victories was to ensure that officials abroad were prohibited from profiting from slavery. In 1841, Palmerston responded to pressure from the General Anti-Slavery Convention when he banned all British agents from associating with slave-holding. A circular demanded that all British ministers, consuls, and agents avoid the taint of owning or dealing in slaves and asked for representations to be made to all host governments for them to replicate the instruction with their employees.[168] When a case arose that year involving Sir Thomas Reade's agent in Tunis, the Foreign Office was quick to demand his dismissal.[169]

Parliament eventually moved beyond the regulation of British government employees abroad and in 1843 banned British subjects owning slaves anywhere in the world (the inadequacies of this law are discussed elsewhere).[170] How much this directive to officials was honored in public and broken in secret is hard to know. William Hamilton, a zealous minister to Brazil during Palmerston's and Aberdeen's anti-slavery escapades, explained in an 1837 personal letter that "it would be anomalous for the English" minister to buy slaves, but "the hire of slaves from their owner, which we are obliged to do to supply ourselves with under servants, is enormous. £24 sterling a year are the least."[171] In 1841, he would complain that Palmerston's new ban "has magnified our difficulties a hundred fold, by giving in to the request of the Anti Slavery [sic] Society folks at home. We are not allowed to hire slaves. As if our depriving ourselves of the service of half a dozen of these people, and giving them comfortable good places, could, or would, suppress the trade!"[172] Historian Michelle Anders Kerney has revealed that consul Edward Molyneux of Savannah had extensive hidden interests in slaves after the 1841 ban. When caught for a small part of his dealings, he successfully convinced the Foreign Office that he was engaged in a humanitarian scheme to evacuate inherited slaves to the British West Indies.[173] Consuls found their own accommodations with the rules. Backhouse's own son would find himself in a dilemma in 1852 "as to [the] propriety of my having the slave of my landlord living at my house & working in my garden without wages." The consul in Cuba, Crawford, advised him that "he did not see any obstacle; [he] said there was not a washerwoman in this place who was not a slave."[174]

Some other successes of abolitionist lobbying on the government were equally uncertain and transitory. A victory in 1839 banning the indentured migration of "coolie" Indian laborers to the West Indies was overturned in 1842. Although it had seemed, initially, that the recruitment of emigrants for the colonies was incompatible with Britain's diplomatic campaign for slave-trade suppression, the declining economy of the West Indies led to a reopening of the partially regulated trade.[175] In fact, the abolitionist societies retained greatest power when they acted as an unofficial branch of the anti-slavery state, harvesting and sharing intelligence for the Foreign Office to act on. For example, the African Civilization Society's evidence of Egyptian slave hunts in 1843 led Aberdeen to warn the pasha of the consequences of "practices the most revolting to human nature and inconsistent with the sentiments he professes."[176] In the same year, the BFASS asked for Aberdeen to arrange for an abolitionist from Malta to meet the sultan of Morocco about abolishing slavery; while he could not do so officially, Aberdeen was happy to instruct the British consul at Tangiers "to assist Mr. Richardson unofficially, so far as it may be within his power."[177] The previous year, informants in Liverpool had suggested a ship was being fitted out for the slave trade and the BFASS worked closely with government solicitors to see if a case could be built for prosecution.[178]

It was in these ways that the BFASS carved out a role uncomfortably alongside or within the anti-slavery state. Palmerston responded generously to a memorial in 1842 from the Society, thanking him, despite their disagreements, for his shared enthusiasm for anti-slavery. Yet, in an early draft of his reply, he spoke his mind when he declared that "we must not strain theoretical doctrines to a degree of inapplicable refinement so as to prevent us from taking measures best calculated to accomplish the great & human purpose we have in view." Even if he decided to withhold his criticism from the final draft, Palmerston's thoughts summed up the differences between the anti-slavery activists and the anti-slavery state.[179]

Besides the efforts of the abolitionists, the second major force for criticizing and reshaping anti-slavery policy was Britain's partisan parliamentary system. Although a broad strategy for slave-trade suppression emerged and survived largely unscathed through regular changes of government, politicians were quick to make political capital out of anti-slavery issues where their policies disagreed. Hence Palmerston, with a crafty eye on public opinion, was eager to paint his Tory opponents as weak on slave-trade questions whenever he could.[180] His extensive period in office as foreign secretary and then prime minister might lend credence to the idea that the anti-slavery state was his personal fiefdom and the result of his personal patronage rather than national politics. However, distinctions between the two can be overemphasized. There were differences of manner and method between Palmerston and Aberdeen—his Conservative opponent in the 1840s—but not differences of commitment. Palmerston showed characteristic disregard for Spain when he appointed the fiery Scottish abolitionist David Turnbull as British consul and superintendent of liberated Africans in Cuba. Turnbull was expelled by the Spanish in 1842. Aberdeen subsequently made him commissioner of the Mixed Commission Court in Jamaica, which would require zeal but not diplomacy, and opted to send a more tactful consul as his replacement to Havana. The difference in style reflected a more consensual, less confrontational, approach on the part of Aberdeen.[181]

Their dissimilarities were grounded in part in personality, but also in political ideology. Aberdeen's greater regard for international law and respectful diplomacy reflected his broader foreign policy differences with Palmerston. The latter, encountering legal objections to his policy in 1845, declared, "it is the duty of the British govt...to set [slaves] free despight [sic] all the Queens Advocates in the world."[182] Aberdeen never shared his temper. For this reason, many Britons believed that the failure of the French to sign the Quintuple Treaty in 1846 would have led to war had Palmerston been in the Foreign Office.[183] Indeed, French public opinion turned against the Quintuple Treaty—undermining its conclusion—at least in part because of Palmerston's aggressive attacks on the unrelated question of French policy in the Middle East.[184] Paul Michael Kielstra's close study of Aberdeen's and Palmerston's diplomacy with France rightly concludes that both British ministers had a genuine desire to crush the trade.[185] Aberdeen was actually more willing to use (or abuse) British power in the case of the slave trade than in other areas of policy. His Act of 1845 targeted against Brazil was no less confrontational than Palmerston's law against the Portuguese in 1839. He preferred different methods, but pursued the same objectives.[186] Indeed, in some contexts he could test the limits of anti-slavery policy further than his Whig rival: Aberdeen "had a more activist approach to antislavery than Palmerston," in so far as he briefly considered negotiating for an end to slave-holding in Brazil rather than limiting his objectives to the intercontinental slave trade.[187]

In opposition, an opportunistic attitude toward anti-slavery crises paid dividends; in government, therefore, a defensive posture was essential. On matters of slave-trade diplomacy, Palmerston considered his vulnerability to Tory criticism when making government decisions.[188] Public outcries about slavery also haunted and rewarded his successors during periods in government or opposition. During William Gladstone's temporary sabbatical from the Liberals' leadership in 1875–76, his party found political capital in opposing the Fugitive Slave Circular. The previous year, Benjamin Disraeli's ministry had instructed the navy, in the Fugitive Slave Circular, not to provide refuge for individual slaves who might stow away on British ships in the ports of slave-holding nations. It was a policy designed to end the ambiguity and discretion afforded to British officers off the east coast of Africa. A maritime convention allowed that sailors in foreign ports were not subject to the host country's laws when aboard ship—only when they set foot on land. Wylde noted that "I do not much like laying down hard and fast rules in these matters," but he accepted that the alternative would be an unwarrantable extension of British anti-slavery laws within another country. However, when news of the Conservative measure became public the following year, local Liberal groups led a political and popular outcry.[189] BFASS grandees, such as Rev. Horace Waller, did not want to miss out on a chance to publicize their cause. However, he despaired to see "a mean-spirited partisan" tone to meetings, complaining that there was "1 word for the slave and 20 for the Radicals vilifying

the Govt. in all ways." With his colleagues, he accepted speaking invita-
tions reluctantly and appreciated the enthusiasm but not the temper of the
Liberals' agitation.[190] After a series of false starts and a royal commission,
the instructions were speedily reversed in August 1876. Besides mocking the Tories' desperate reversals in the face of public outrage, *Punch*
caught the national mood by depicting John Bull as a stout Jack Tar declaring he would as soon lower the Union flag as follow orders to betray
his country's anti-slavery traditions (fig. 8). With the rough-spoken English of a common man, the sailor showed patriotic honor in the face of
elite indecency.[191] As one newspaper warned Disraeli, on matters such as
slavery Britons "are capable of being raised to a white heat of anger that
burns up sooner or later the object of their hate." Ironically, in office the
Liberals had pursued a similar course but were cowed by their own grass-
roots' hostility to the policy.[192]

The demands of principle repealed an act of pragmatism thanks to the
insistence that, as one clergyman in Glasgow put it, "if the Circular were
issued in consequence of international law and foreign policy, then international law and foreign policy must square itself with the conscience of the
country." Theoretical discretion (and practical indifference) to the fugitive
slaves' requests hence returned to the sailors-on-the-spot.[193] Wylde's friend
and colleague Clement Hill observed that the difficulties this caused for
slave-trade diplomacy in East Africa were "another of the things for wh[ich]
we have to thank the meddlesome press & British public."[194] In making an
adjustment, the government tacked toward the opinions of creative lawyers
such as Robert Phillimore and Henry Maine, who had advised them that
law, even international law, "varies with the progress of opinion and the
growth of usage, and there is no subject on which so great a change of
opinion has taken place as slavery and the slave trade."[195] Because the issue
concerned pearl divers in the Persian Gulf, rather than slaves in a powerful
Western nation, the British government could permit a fudge that snubbed
another country's sovereignty.

They may have been the opportunistic champions of partisan anti-
slavery in 1876, but the Liberals were not invulnerable to such pressure
themselves. Gladstone unenthusiastically supported the expansion of British suppression efforts off the east coast of Africa under pressure from
the popularity of David Livingstone's and Bartle Frere's propaganda.[196]
Paradoxically, though, the decline of abolitionist popular mobilization did
not end politicians' fear of public rebuke over anti-slavery issues. Now,
however, it was their electoral rivals that roused the specter of national
condemnation as much as abolitionists pursuing a radical agenda. British
anti-slavery policy was not exactly the product of a consensus; rather, it
was the product of a limited consensus and the invasive probing of political

FIGURE 8. "The 'Flag of Freedom,'" *Punch*, 2 Oct. 1875, 331. First Lord of the Admiralty: "A runaway slave, John! You'll have to give him up, you know! See our circular of 31st of July." John Bull: "Give 'im up, yer honour!! As well order me to haul down that there flag at once, sir!!!" By permission of Plymouth University.

opponents, always seeking evidence of incompetence or indifference.[197] It is surprising that ideological clashes over the limits, methods, and expense of anti-slavery policy were as rare as they were—confined primarily to the free-trade struggles of 1841–50 and the scandals of the 1870s.

Ironically, at the same time that politicians presented themselves to the British public as lonely guardians of the torch of liberty, they emphasized national consensus in their dealings with other countries. Just as abolitionist campaigners sought to speak as the voice of national consensus (successfully before 1838 and unsuccessfully after that point), so the British government spoke for "the people" when it lobbied foreign powers over the slave trade. In 1840, Palmerston reminded the Ottoman Empire that British support for the sultan's regime was contingent on the sanction of the British public, whose foremost desire was to see the slave trade ended.[198] Appeals to the will of the "British government and nation" became part of the vocabulary of anti-slavery diplomacy under different foreign secretaries.[199] This tactic was handy in negotiations. In communications with François Guizot, his French opposite as foreign secretary, Aberdeen confided in 1843 that slave-trade suppression was one of those issues "on which my country is not tractable, and I not as free as I would wish" since the British people were "all saints on these questions." Whether or not this weariness reflected a touch of cynicism on his part, it strengthened his hand in diplomacy and verifiably reflected public expectations.[200]

Therefore, depending on the circumstances, British statesmen were happy to paint slave-trade suppression as national purpose or partisan struggle. Both interpretations were correct, to a point. Despite attempts to monopolize slave-trade suppression for one party or the other, contemporaries such as Charles and David Livingstone suggested that

> instead of viewing our leading politicians as eager only for place and power, the efforts of Liberals and Conservatives in this one direction [slave-trade suppression] would tend to prove them, in the widest sense, promoters of peace and good-will among men.[201]

This does not mean disputes between parties were free from ideological conflict. It was politically unacceptable to deny that British policy should oppose slavery around the world; still, there were massive differences over whether that meant interfering in the internal laws of other nations (most politicians thought not) and how exactly Britain could lead the eradication of the transoceanic slave trade (on which question there were hundreds of different opinions). The remainder of this book will show how a theoretical consensus and practical conflict played itself out in other debates: in the implications of anti-slavery ideology for domestic reform, in the balance between the roles of the state and the market, and in the strange career of anti-slavery imperialism. In all these spheres, the British and their politicians struggled over what being an anti-slavery nation dictated for an anti-slavery state.

# 4

## Britons' Unreal Freedom

G IVEN THE political struggles over anti-slavery in Victorian foreign policy, it would be surprising if anti-slavery did not cast long shadows over domestic policy. Having looked at the politics of anti-slavery abroad, we now turn to the ways anti-slavery sentiment affected domestic Britain. Although Britons had broadly agreed that slavery was incompatible with national freedom, they struggled over which rights and protections should subsequently be advanced or rejected. The splintering of abolitionist societies did not diminish a strong anti-slavery influence on public debates about social, moral, political, and economic reform within Britain. Of course, every authorial reference to slavery was not a direct comment on chattel slavery, since slave-related metaphors had long been common in Christian theology and secular rhetoric. Indeed, in Victorian Britain these extended to the alcoholic "guzzling slave" pitied by temperance campaigners or "the slavery of ignorance" targeted by advocates of education.[1] In this chapter, however, I look at the various ways that chattel slavery and anti-slavery identities and ideas were directly employed in arguments about how Britons exercised British freedoms within Britain. This helps to highlight the broader contest over what being an anti-slavery nation should mean.

It is clear that the abolitionist campaigns served as a template for Victorian reform societies. Anti-slavery provided a powerful institutional model for the Anti–Corn Law League and missionary societies. Yet the legacies of earlier crusades and a continuing identification with anti-slavery influenced Britons in other ways, beyond the boundaries of these respectable organizations. Victorian debates over democracy, labor, and poverty contested the meaning of anti-slavery ideas. Which other freedoms required redemption and exactly how should they be redeemed? As this chapter will examine, Britain's anti-slavery tradition was invoked in discussions of domestic reform, in the context of women's rights, democracy, labor, and the suffering of the poor. Before turning to those, however, it is worth noting the ways anti-slavery interfered with other reform causes.

A bewildering array of religious and moral causes sought to borrow credibility from anti-slavery because it commanded widespread goodwill.[2] These comparisons were doubtless assisted by the fact that those women and men who tried (and, more often that not, failed) to revive national anti-slavery societies labored on many other causes connected with philanthropy or religious dissent. For example, G. W. Alexander was treasurer of the BFASS and the Voluntary Schools Association.[3] Louis Chamerovzow, the secretary of the BFASS, had served in that capacity for the Aborigines' Protection Society (APS) and was succeeded in the latter role by his friend Frederick Chesson, an abolitionist acolyte of William Lloyd Garrison.[4] Since being founded in 1816, the British Peace Society had shared many nonconformist personnel with the abolitionist movement, not least Thomas Clarkson.[5] Joseph Sturge and his fellow Quakers, who had insisted on the BFASS's pacifism, aimed to follow in his footsteps in both movements.[6] Indeed, Sturge was perhaps the most promiscuous reformer, championing a range of different philanthropies and founding the National Complete Suffrage Union for universal male enfranchisement.[7] He sought to broker an alliance between the bourgeois Anti–Corn Law League and the workers' Chartist movement.[8] Given these diffuse and overlapping enthusiasms, it is hardly surprising that anti-slavery ideology permeated many other parts of the Victorian "middle-class reform complex."[9]

Of course, given the links between British and American organizations, the slavery issue caused problems for international cooperation. Sturge threatened to withdraw his sizeable donation to an international temperance conference if slaveholders were admitted to it. When the event did take place, Douglass caused acute embarrassment for the American delegates by speaking not only against drink but also against the neutrality many of them showed toward that other great tyrant—slavery—which he saw as a related social evil.[10] Daniel O'Connell, the champion of repealing the union between Ireland and Great Britain, refused donations from slaveholding sympathizers in the United States, putting his abolitionism above his nationalism.[11]

Links between anti-slavery and other reform causes were regularly constructive rather than divisive, however. Visiting anti-slavery celebrities often spoke under the banner of groups other than abolitionists. Samuel Ringgold Ward, a fugitive slave touring Britain in the mid-1850s, found that within a month of arriving "I had been upon the platforms of the Bible

Tract, Sunday School, Missionary, Temperance, and Peace, as well as the Anti-Slavery, Societies."[12] During her visit to Britain, Stowe was invited to the British and Foreign Bible Society's annual meeting;[13] her husband Calvin Stowe and her brother Charles Beecher regularly addressed temperance groups.[14] In his Civil War tour of Britain, the fugitive slave William Andrew Jackson made a habit of lecturing to Sunday schools, addressing upward of three thousand youngsters all told.[15] Liberated slaves and visiting abolitionists offered ways to bolster support for these disparate reform causes.

The growing transatlantic communities of denominations and churches meant that religious associations were prime targets for stigmatizing proslavers. Successive lecturers saw it as a tangible benefit to foreign abolitionism if slaveholders were made to feel uncomfortable in Britain. Fugitive slave William Wells Brown imagined that such pressure would leave slaveholders' brows spiritually branded with infamy.[16] In the early 1840s, the newly formed Free Church of Scotland became a test case when it was embroiled in a campaign by Edinburgh and Glasgow abolitionists to "give back the money" it had taken from Southern slave owners.[17] The Scottish ministers were accused of "bowing down to the Moloch of Slavery, and worshipping before its blood-stained altar" because they had "BETRAYED CHRIST—SOLD YOUR SAVIOUR—BARTERED HIM WHO IS GOD OVER ALL, BLESSED FOR EVER—for £3000."[18] The approach can be said to have been broadly successful, and after the middle of the century Britons could congratulate themselves that their churches refused communion with slaveholders. International religious conferences made public their anti-slavery credentials and swiftly rebutted suggestions to the contrary. Bitter controversy over the slavery question meant that the Evangelical Alliance only ever operated in a highly decentralized fashion, thwarting its principal objective.[19]

## SLAVERY AND BRITISH SOCIETY

Unfolding debates over the proper role of women and working people were the product of individuals' initiative and many social and cultural forces within British society. These issues would have emerged within Victorian politics without the Abolition Act of 1807 or the Emancipation Act of 1833. An examination of the relationship between these social questions and anti-slavery ideas cannot, therefore, explain why democratic and gender questions took on new urgency for the Victorians. However, such an exercise does reveal the ideological differences over what anti-slavery should mean and what future responsibilities or consequences it should dictate. Given how much anti-slavery sentiment had penetrated and dominated public debate, the language of anti-slavery could be fruitfully borrowed and molded to these ends. Sympathy for slaves was so widespread that comparisons with slavery offered a potent moral and rhetorical strategy for the advocates of women and the poor.[20] This contrasted with those other understandings of anti-slavery that reinforced "middle-class definitions of freedom based around the promotion of male waged labour and female domesticity."[21]

There is much to learn from Victorian arguments over the appropriateness of comparisons between domestic traditions and chattel slavery. These debates tell us a lot about the contours of these reform causes as well as about the contest over what Britain, as an anti-slavery nation, opposed. A good example is the struggle for male universal suffrage, where working men's political disabilities were compared to slavery. The radical MP Joseph Hume said Britain's unenfranchised workers were "like slaves" so long as elites could arbitrarily and unanswerably rule over them with the full power of the law and the violence of the state.[22]

In the Victorian era, the question of popular representation sparked interest in how to understand the triumph of humanitarian politics in the recent past. The successful passage of the 1833 Emancipation Act was, by one reading, the result of conservative influence on parliamentary reform. Linda Colley, in *Britons*, has argued that the majority vote for West Indian freedom demonstrated that Parliament was responsive to public opinion and heeded the wishes of the nation. In this view, the triumph of abolitionism reinforced the mainstream Whig and Tory view that no further extension of the franchise was required after the 1832 Great Reform Act. Anti-slavery sentiment "became an important part of the Victorian culture of complacency in which matters of domestic reform were allowed to slide," she writes.[23] In fact, anti-slavery ideas played a complex role in a wider debate about popular sovereignty and the quality of government. There were as many views of the implications of anti-slavery virtue for electoral representation as there were opinions about political reform. Given the scale and importance of abolitionist mobilization, the triumph of anti-slavery was also "a message of long-term popular power," not a benevolent concession by elite legislators.[24] If anti-slavery was remembered as a success for popular piety and public virtue over privileged interests and entrenched evil, then it could suggest that the masses were better arbiters of national policy than the ruling classes. This question of interpretation had a crucial resonance after 1834, when the worker-led Chartist movement embarked on an unprecedented reformist campaign for universal male suffrage.[25] London's Working Men's Association believed that MPs had "yielded to public opinion what in safety and in justice they could no longer withhold" when they approved the Reform Act and the Emancipation Act.[26] At a radical meeting in Bath, in 1837, Whig caution over the Emancipation Act was likened to their conservative approach to franchise reform.[27] Proponents of popular sovereignty were thus able to draw radical lessons from anti-slavery.

However, this interpretation was contested. While viewing emancipation as a good thing, conservative commentators looked back with contempt on the pressure that the Agency Society exerted on politicians in the early 1830s. In 1833, the Society's youthful radicals had, when the Whig ministry seemed intransigent, declared that "the people must emancipate the slaves for the Government never will."[28] The group's outspoken tactics in the final years of the emancipation struggle were controversial many decades later. From the Society's point of view, the abolitionist victory had been seized by virtuous public pressure in a new era of popular sovereignty. That was the view of Sir George Stephen, who, despite falling out with his former compatriots, was happy to publish his memoirs about the Agency Society in 1859. The details he provided in the book about public agitation in constituency elections outraged the conservative *Fraser's Magazine*. The paper suggested that Sir George Stephen and his collaborators had been exposed as "an electioneering instrument, to enable themselves to influence elections, and if not exactly to nominate members, to domineer over candidates." "Has political freedom receded?" the writer in *Fraser's* asked, concerned that the disproportionate influence of electoral pressure groups had corrupted Parliament's role as a deliberative assembly.[29]

In a different vein, the derivative cash-in novel *Uncle Tom in England* drew equally conservative lessons from the experience of anti-slavery campaigning. Rather than censoring radical agitation before 1833, the book saw anti-slavery campaigns as a lesson in patience for British workers. The author claimed that the redemption of the democratic, egalitarian United States from the sin and shame of slavery was a prerequisite to spreading democracy and equality to Britain. The book therefore sought to teach "physical force" Chartists that they should abandon violence as a means to secure concessions from elites in favor of "moral force."[30] Here, anti-slavery pieties could be used to denigrate domestic radicalism. Moreover, the struggle over slavery in America seemed to offer just as many lessons for the British political system as the crusade against West Indian bondage.

The slave system of the United States cast powerful shadows on early Victorian debates concerning political reform. Until the American Civil War, Southern slavery was a painful problem for British democrats because tolerance of slavery in a democracy was a strong argument against the expansion of the franchise.[31] A letter to the workers of the United States in 1837 from the Working Men's Association of London ventured "to enquire of men who for more than half a century have had the power of government in their hands, why the last and blackest remnant of kingly dominion has not been uprooted from republican America?"[32] So long as American democracy upheld slave-holding, it fed conservative fears of the tyrannous potential of democracy. The *Times* in 1852 asked why Americans had been willing, ninety years earlier, to reject British government, an institution "more ancient and more universal than that of slavery," but had tolerated slavery in their republic.[33] Despite having completely different political views, Frances Trollope and Harriet Martineau both sniffed in their travel writing at "the mocking words 'All men are born free and equal'."[34]

There was, we must note, more than a hint of jingoism when British crowds were assured by an American such as Frederick Douglass that their influence on the rest of the world, including his homeland, came by virtue of being "free and brave England, a country to which the nations look up as the paragon of Christian purity and freedom."[35] American abolitionists often helped inflate British pride, perhaps to the detriment of their cause in the United States, by explaining how their republican institutions were undermined by slave-holding. Henry B. Stanton—who had brought his new wife to the 1840 Anti-Slavery Convention for their honeymoon—was one visitor who took pride in quoting to Britons a relevant stanza by John Greenleaf Whittier:

> *While every flap of England's flag*
> *Proclaim that all around are free,*
> *From farthest Ind' to each blue crag*
> *That beetles o'er the Western Sea;*
> *And yet, we scoff at Europe's kings,*
> *While Freedom's fire is dim with us,*
> *And round our country's altar clings*
> *The damning shade of Slavery's curse.*[36]

Similarly, the physical closeness of Canada to the United States meant that Britain's flag was inserted—climactically—into the standard story of fugitive-slave escapes. Britons were well aware of Canada's mythological status for runaway slaves, as an inspiration and a destination. Hence theatrical stagings of *Uncle Tom's Cabin* specifically took liberation on British soil as their triumphal endpoint, with emancipation beneath the folds of Britain's Union flag.[37] Reinforcing these feelings, one stereotype of fugitive-slave narratives was the experience of feeling like a free man for the first time on setting foot in Britain.[38]

These motifs allowed politicians and journalists to theorize generally from the peculiar circumstances of the United States. For the *Economist,* "the absolute right of a strong race to oppress all feebler races, and the right of crowds to tyrannise over all smaller groups of men" was "the characteristic sin and peril of democratic institutions."[39] The Marquess of Lothian,

in a pamphlet defending gradual emancipation and the Confederacy during the Civil War, wrote that slavery existed upon a scale "which mounts
up from the lowest barbarism to the highest privileges of civilisation." He
used a comparison with nonenfranchised British workers to argue that,
while the civilized should help raise up their inferiors, "both with regard to
the electoral franchise and to slave emancipation, it may be possible to
advance too hurriedly; and in that case, our philanthropy does more harm
than good." In both cases, he explained, a gradual development was better
than a sharp shock.[40] Robert W. Russell's 1849 book *America Compared
With England* tried to rebut the idea that slavery survived because, not in
spite of, the American political system.[41]

Far from providing decisive evidence for either democrats or oligarchs,
anti-slavery was more often a generic form of ammunition in battles of at-
trition whose combatants would seize upon any weapon to hand. It is more
interesting to observe that anti-slavery was such an important example of
popular opinion influencing government policy that political reformers and
their opponents all needed to account for it as a positive influence in their
narratives.

Parliamentary reform was not the only cause to claim anti-slavery as a
precedent for social change. A similarly complex picture emerges regarding "woman slavery." British women's vulnerability to the arbitrary rule
of husbands, fathers, and other men offered parallels with the situation
of slaves. Early feminists attacked both social and political constraints
on women as forms of slavery; an article in the *Monthly Repository* suggested that "a marriage contract" was similar to American slavery since a
wife "*is* property, while she cannot possess property."[42] William Linton, an
early male feminist, suggested that "the woman-slave has not yet learned to
think; because she is too fallen to feel her wrongs." Therefore, he argued, a
woman did not realize that she could and should assert her potential as an
independent subject.[43] It is rather hard to know whether the more general
uses of "slavery" metaphors were inspired by literary or biblical traditions
or whether they directly evoked chattel slavery and abolitionism for the author or audience. Historian Kathryn Gleadle warns scholars that the radical Unitarians she studies thought about slavery in the ancient world more
often than slavery in the New World. Still, she also suggests that it was a
narrative of slavery that laid the foundations for the organized women's
movement.[44]

Abolitionist organizing, abstaining from slave-grown sugar, and buying anti-slavery products offered an unprecedented chance for women to
participate in a public debate. Abolitionism allowed many women, for the
first time, to seek to directly influence government policy.[45] From the 1820s,

women such as Lucy Townsend and Mary Lloyd in Birmingham, Anne Knight in Chelmsford, and Ann Taylor Gilbert in Nottingham took the lead in creating separate female societies.[46] There were British women authors whose work addressed anti-slavery themes, such as Harriet Martineau, who drew inspiration from feminist abolitionists in America such as Angelina Grimké.[47] In 1833, on the eve of British emancipation, a Methodist petition saw significant numbers of women signing for themselves—one hundred thousand by estimates.[48] Anti-slavery, with its religious ends, was an ideal cause for pioneering female political activity, subverting rather than destroying traditional gender roles. Women were central to the culture and politics of anti-slavery, but it is less clear that anti-slavery was central to the culture and politics of women's rights.

For some women, their experiences protesting before 1833 or campaigning afterward may have been transformative, but for many this activity existed within cultural assumptions that women were sentimental, empathetic, and devout in character. After the victory of slave emancipation, very few campaigned for women's democratic or cultural emancipation within British society. In America, female participation and leadership in the abolitionist movement had met with controversy and the first public discussion of women's changing roles, while French women had artfully used anti-slavery as a weapon in feminist radicalism.[49] By the time Victoria acceded to the throne of Great Britain in 1837, two generations of British women had taken active roles in anti-slavery agitation, yet this activism had curiously little impact on any movement for women's rights. Unlike American abolitionism, British campaigns against slavery did not see women accepted in positions of authority and leadership. Women's separate anti-slavery societies tended to be treated as female subcommittees of a local branch, supporting the work of male leaders.[50]

The Duchess of Sutherland's "affectionate address" from the women of Britain to Stowe showed the ambiguous gender politics of a socially diverse petition from female campaigners. In addressing American women directly, the 1852–53 campaign reinforced traditional assumptions about feminine sensitivity, spirituality, and emotion. Critics in the British press complained that the "ladies had no authority to assemble in any corporate capacity. They had no power to act" and were naive to assume there could be a transnational feminine diplomacy over slave-holding.[51] On the other side of the Atlantic, pro-slavery Southern women issued their own rebuttals.[52] *Punch* found the idea of quarrelling British and American ladies both comic and arousing, offering to act as an intermediary for a kiss-and-make-up between the warring women.[53] The address to Stowe highlights not only the problems for voluntary groups engaging in public diplomacy but also the patronizing response to women organizing politically.

The "woman question" was imported into British anti-slavery in 1840, at the World Anti-Slavery Convention. Garrisonian female abolitionists had been refused full participation by the BFASS, which expected women to be seen but not heard. The early omens were poor for Garrison's prediction that the protest had done more "for the rights of women, than could have been accomplished in any other manner." At a private meeting, the Garrisonians found the British women abolitionists "had little to tell us" and feared "they might get 'out of their sphere' should they speak aloud even in a social circle."[54] Although anti-slavery proved a less direct route to women's rights for Britons than Americans, Clare Midgley's deft research offers many examples of female abolitionists who became the first generation of suffrage campaigners. Anne Knight formed the Sheffield Female Reform Association a decade later, campaigning for women's suffrage after hearing once too often "the puny cry of *custom*" from male abolitionists.[55] She also argued for male championship of female political emancipation on the basis that just as black slaves could not free themselves without abolitionist help, so "domestic slaves cannot organise themselves—each one owns a master," directly drawing parallels with the experience of anti-slavery.[56] Josephine Butler, who led the campaign against the misogynistic Contagious Diseases (CD) Acts, had her first taste of activism through fund-raising for American freed people after the Civil War. Many other campaigners against the CD Acts of the 1870s saw direct parallels with anti-slavery, dubbing themselves "abolitionists." Given the important role of this campaign in organized British feminism, anti-slavery might be considered a grandparent of women's rights activism.[57] In sum, not all women abolitionists became feminists but many early feminists had been women abolitionists.

The route from anti-slavery to women's suffrage was clearly a crooked one, but Midgley concludes that it was still "central to the development of an extra-Parliamentary but public female political culture." However, some women abolitionists accepted male anti-slavery leaders' gradualist and conservative attitudes on their proper role. Anti-slavery activism provided opportunities for women who wanted to challenge political hierarchies, but it did not instill a radical view of gender relations in all female campaigners.[58] That view chimes with comparisons of British society to France and the United States. In the United States, fear of a multiracial free society and the democratic majority in favor of slave-holding meant that "antislavery activity constituted a far greater challenge to the social, political, and economic status quo," therefore promoting a greater ideological radicalism from abolitionists.[59] In France, anti-slavery was closely associated with the revolutionary fervor of 1789 and 1848 and so lent itself to other egalitarian radicalisms. However, this is less impressive than it first sounds, given that both feminism and anti-slavery enjoyed marginal popularity in France.[60]

British anti-slavery activism was a less-fertile laboratory for women's advocacy because it could be advanced alongside establishment values and because campaigning alliances were forged through existing political structures such as Parliament and the churches.[61]

In the cases of men's voting rights or women's political and legal emancipation, anti-slavery ideas did not necessarily support either radical or conservative positions. However, widespread acceptance of anti-slavery as a national tradition provided the opportunity to question how legal prejudices against other groups might be considered a form of slavery. The political moral of British anti-slavery was therefore open to debate and ripe for appropriation by either side. Emancipation was plainly invoked as useful evidence for deeply held views, rather than being a clinching argument for winning converts. Views about democracy and women's rights, however, helped frame arguments over the meaning and implications of anti-slavery. While the experience of campaigning against slavery encouraged some petitioners and campaigners to join the campaign for extension of the franchise, mobilization did not guarantee radicalization and democratization.[62]

## WAGE SLAVERY

So far we have looked at the ways in which anti-slavery ideas could be deployed to attack political "slaveries." However, the most visceral attempts to draw parallels between African enslavement and British society came in the realm of labor relations, in disputes over whether industrial society had created hidden economic "slaveries."[63] David Turley has rightly cautioned his fellow historians about the difficulty of making any direct connection between British abolitionism and the sociopolitical advancement of working people. Anti-slavery sentiment was a house of many mansions; some campaigners emerged from the emancipation campaigns in sympathy with social reforms while others were violently hostile.[64] A controversy raged among historians throughout the 1990s over whether or not anti-slavery was an expression of liberal, bourgeois "cultural hegemony," a Marxist explanation for working-class support for capitalist culture despite "natural" class interests. Some critics thought David Brion Davis's early scholarship promoted "hegemony" as an explanation for the origins of abolitionism, but he has argued against this interpretation of both his work and British history. Instead, he believes that anti-slavery's consistency with the dominant fetishization of wage labor made it easier for elites to embrace abolition than they would have done otherwise.[65] This caution chimes with the diverse views we find in the decades after emancipation.

How, then, did anti-slavery feed into growing anxieties over the material conditions of British workers? Old debates over the differences between

*[handwritten margin note: Is wage slavery as bad as "chattel slavery"?]*

tropical slavery and domestic working conditions continued in Victorian Britain. From the 1780s to the 1830s, West Indian defenders of slavery had commonly complained that white workers suffered more than enslaved Africans, that ordinary Britons were being tricked into campaigning on behalf of those whose lives were much better than their own.[66] After British emancipation, some Americans continued to argue that the conditions of slavery were preferable to the "wage slavery" of northern England, hoping to counter abolitionism at home and British criticism abroad. In 1860, the pro-slavery author John C. Cobden published *The White Slaves of England* to prove this point from Britain's own "official documents."[67] Governor James Henry Hammond of South Carolina told his British critics that their complaints about the punishment of a man who had assisted a runaway slave were absurd; in America, he argued, it was the British class system that looked more like slavery: "Can you tell me what *freedom* is—who possess it, and how much of it is requisite for human happiness? Is your operative... who is not cheered by the slightest hope of ever improving his lot... is *he* free—*sufficiently* free?"[68]

Among Americans, it was not only supporters of slavery who made the connection; the analogy was made by Stowe in *Uncle Tom's Cabin.* Reviewers from publications opposed to factory legislation, such as the *Leeds Mercury,* rejected this suggestion, despite liking the rest of the book.[69] Sir Arthur Helps's views on the clear differences between "manhood and brutehood," published in *Fraser's,* prompted a volte-face from Stowe. She wrote to him privately, apologizing for the negative impression she had gained about British industry from Charles Dickens and other English authors, and she suggested that his points would do much to counter pro-slavery Southern propaganda.[70] Stowe made this case publicly in *The Key to Uncle Tom's Cabin,* arguing that slavery helped to reduce poor whites' wages in the Southern states.[71] In his article, Helps suggested that she ought to visit a few British workers' cottages herself. She later did so, following in the footsteps of other visiting abolitionists, including fugitive slaves such as William Wells Brown, whose English patrons took him on a tour of how the British poor actually lived.[72] Seduced by the reception she received in Britain from aristocratic friends such as the duchess of Sutherland, Stowe abandoned her early censure of British manufacturing as the moral equivalent of American slavery.

Stowe's association with Sutherland opened her to criticism directed toward the duchess's family, who had ruthlessly cleared traditional tenants of their highland estates in Scotland to maximize revenues.[73] In the *People's Paper,* Karl Marx declared "the enemy of British Wages-Slavery has a right to condemn Negro-Slavery; a Duchess of Sutherland, a Duke of Atholl, a Manchester Cotton Lord—never!"[74] More generally, the correspondent for *Reynold's Newspaper* said that, while he could not defend American slavery, he thought that the female petition organized by the duchess was ridiculous and pompous given English workers' suffering.[75] A pro-slavery response from President John Tyler's wife and other female signatories in the United States made this point more aggressively. More than a decade later, Charles Dickens's *All The Year Round* suggested that "a good deal might be said upon both sides" in the transatlantic quarrel over the evils of American slavery and British industry.[76]

The controversy over the women's petition was also reflected in a division within British thinking about slavery. *Punch* was happy to mock the well-to-do philanthropists who seemed to think "dark skins must now take precedence of white," but also lectured American critics of industrialization: "Slaves for *want of legislation* / Are not quite like *slaves by Law*."[77] In this vein, the abolitionist George Thompson had insisted that the definition of slavery was properly limited, because "labour is not slavery, for freemen labour. Poverty is not slavery, for freemen are poor. Suffering is not slavery, for freemen suffer. Slavery is the deprivation of human liberty."[78]

The propriety of such distinctions mattered a great deal to debates over domestic legislation in Britain. Emancipation could be seen either as the removal of an unjust institution under law or as a positive act of state.[79] From the former—negative—viewpoint, slaves and free laborers were completely distinct. This separation of the legal conditions of slavery from the social conditions of wage laborers was natural to liberal political economy. In this spirit, the workhouse of the new poor law and a free labor market were liberating measures. From the second—positive—view, however, abolitionism might be the prelude to further interventions in the labor market to reduce poverty and misery. This was Richard Oastler's argument, when he championed the Factory Act of 1833 as a blow against "Yorkshire slavery."[80] Divisions between the two models persisted long after West Indian emancipation. It is hard to sustain the claim that "antislavery appeared entirely consistent with laissez-faire principles." Parliamentary supporters of emancipation held very mixed views toward labor legislation and the new poor law in the 1830s.[81] For many workers, British master-and-servant laws criminalized lateness, slowness, or absenteeism in ways that rendered contract labor distinct from free labor.[82] By contrast, as early as 1788, the *Times* had tried to assert that "slavery does not consist in what a man suffers,—but in a power existing in another man to encrease [sic] or decrease those sufferings at pleasure."[83] For more than two centuries afterward, British politicians would debate which aspects of industrial society qualified, by such a definition, for abolition.

For the most part, transatlantic abolitionist networks often distinguished tactfully between the struggle for global abolition and questions of domestic politics. Whenever the subject was raised with him, Frederick Douglass explicitly rejected a link between "slavery" and any working practices in Britain, however much sympathy he had with workers.[84] In an account of his visit to Britain from 1851 to 1853 largely aimed at British readers, the African American abolitionist Samuel Ringgold Ward was eager to record his surprise at the good conditions of English workers and their superior standard of living compared to slaves.[85] By contrast, Garrison and many of his followers, despite being cool to labor activists in the United States, embraced Chartism as a vehicle to advance their cause within Britain. Garrison benefited from a takeover of the committee of the Glasgow Emancipation Society by his Chartist ally Patrick Brewster in 1841 and, five years later, recruited William Lovett and other Chartists to his new Anti-Slavery League, based in the north of England.[86] His ally John Anderson Collins believed that abolitionists could join forces with British Chartists against their respective enemies in the capitalist and slave-owning classes.[87] Such a strategy had the practical problem of limiting his influence to supporters of Chartism, a consideration that presumably shaped the position taken by Douglass, Ward, and, after her conversion, Stowe.

Equating slave ownership with the exploitation of wage labor was popularized by Marxist thought; the workers of the world would lose their chains, according to *The Communist Manifesto*. Karl Marx and his later disciples saw slave labor as part of the historical progression toward wage labor, finding both to be manifestations of class exploitation: "Modern nations have been able only to disguise slavery in their own countries, but they have imposed it without disguise upon the New World."[88] Like his collaborator Friedrich Engels, Marx's own ideas were heavily influenced by noncommunist thinkers.[89] Impressed by John Elliot Cairnes's *Slave Power* and other abolitionist tracts, Marx saw Abraham Lincoln as a champion of the proletariat against a Southern slave system that degraded white labor as well as African Americans.[90]

Marx's idea of human development, from slavery to feudalism and then wage labor, is remarkably similar to the opinion of Sir Arthur Helps. We have already seen how Helps understood the transatlantic slave trade and colonial slavery to be aberrant backsliding from a general march of progress in Christian countries. As James Wilson, founder of the *Economist*, put it, "looking back to the history of the world, it would be impossible to deny that there had been any nation, which in the course of its rise from barbarianism to civilisation, had not passed through a condition of things, wherein a great mass of her population were exposed to slavery."[91] John Stuart Mill concurred in his 1848 *Principles of Political Economy*.[92] Yet Helps, Wilson, and Mill would have parted company with Marx over the

differences between chattel slavery and wage labor. Where Marx saw a
free labor market as a new form of an old evil, liberal economists saw it as
incomparable to forced servitude.[93] Mill argued that a free laborer should
never be allowed to voluntarily enter a contract of slavery. However, while
he criticized some restrictions on workers' freedom to bargain for wages, he
never acknowledged the impact of penal sanctions for British wage laborers
withdrawing from or violating long labor contracts.[94]

Therefore, if they shared an evolutionary view of slavery's transformation of free labor, Marx and Engels differed from liberals over the relevance
of anti-slavery pretensions to British treatment of workers. The evocative
phrase "wage slavery" reached them from earlier critics of Victorian industry. Tory and radical critiques of the conditions of British laborers had both
compared industrial workplaces to slave colonies: like plantations, factories
seemed to impose strict supervision, threaten physical punishment, and destroy families by consuming the work of wives and children.[95] The Tory
radical Oastler swapped his abolitionist work for the cause of "Yorkshire
Slavery" in 1830.[96] Thinking of the pamphlets and leaflets distributed in
support of emancipation, he expressed his frustration that "the very streets
which receive the droppings of an 'Anti-Slavery Society' are every morning
wet with the tears of innocent victims at the accursed shrine of avarice."[97]
The powerful metaphor of "wage slavery" did not mean, though, that reformers such as Oastler had ceased to support anti-slavery—they merely
questioned the selective philanthropy of abolitionists.[98]

Rather than defending slavery in any way, most British critics of poverty
used anti-slavery rhetoric to draw attention to their concerns. Such appeals
tried to argue that by removing suffering at home, Britons could actively
help anti-slavery causes abroad. In *Bleak House,* Dickens used the character
of Mrs. Jellyby to satirize the philanthropy of the middle classes who worried about foreign suffering without caring for the poor at home. Of grand
schemes for the civilization of Africa, Dickens urged that "the work at home
must be completed thoroughly, or there is no hope abroad."[99] In the midst
of the mania for *Uncle Tom's Cabin* and its offshoots in the 1850s, an article
on the plight of British needle-workers argued that the "surest way of testifying sympathy and one-heartedness with the noble strugglers for emancipation, and of proving the practical good which has been done in this country
by 'Uncle Tom's Cabin,' will be to labour for home-emancipation." Doing so
would remove the planters' taunts about "white slavery."[100] This followed a
tradition established by some plans to celebrate West Indian emancipation
in 1834, including the construction of a new school for the poor by a Baptist
congregation and the distribution of bread to "poor industrious families."[101]
This was an astute strategy, hoping to harness widespread anti-slavery sentiment to aid Britain's poor.

On other occasions, representations of black slavery could be much more ambiguous. There was a fine line between attacking the hypocrisy of anti-slavery activists and excusing slavery. The best-known example of the latter tendency is Thomas Carlyle's "Occasional Discourse on the Negro Question," which first appeared in *Fraser's Magazine* in 1849 and was revised and reprinted in 1853—with the more incendiary word "Nigger" in the title—as a pamphlet to savage the "tom-foolery" of the popularity of *Uncle Tom's Cabin*.[102] Carlyle's racist attack on free West Indian blacks has led later scholars to judge him a "pro-slavery propagandist."[103] He raised contemporary ire for similar reasons, as he idly played down the suffering of slaves in order to promote his ideal of a feudal, paternal hierarchy rather than wage labor.[104] *Punch* scoffed that Virginia planters would embrace the writer as a hero and desire little statues of him for their mantelpiece.[105] William Wells Brown, previously an admirer of Carlyle's *Past and Present,* resented that he found himself sharing a London omnibus one day with the author of a "laborious article in favour of the re-establishment of the lash and slavery."[106]

Brown's insult of "laborious" was more incisive here than he realized. For Carlyle, if not for his audience, the principal point of the "Occasional Discourse" had been to show "you cannot abolish slavery by act of Parliament, but can only abolish the *name* of it, which is very little!"[107] By denying the particular evil of chattel slavery, Carlyle undoubtedly belittled the peculiar suffering of Africans' bondage. But his purpose was to show that enslavement was barely worse than other hardships that the philanthropic "Exeter Hallery" tolerated. His targets were the sentimental reaction to *Uncle Tom's Cabin,* the other miseries of the world, and the discipline of work.[108] Slavery, as the pariah of the Victorian world, was employed to illustrate the Carlylean view of wage labor in the most shocking possible terms.[109] Rather than idealizing chattel slavery as no worse than wage labor, he condemned wage slavery and the modern industrial system as the equal of chattel slavery. Virulently racist, he wished to see black West Indians and African Americans as nature's servants, properly held in "mastership and obedience."[110]

In his spiteful racial hatred, Carlyle's views went beyond polite opinion. However, he did not call for a restitution of West Indian slavery, preferring to see former slaves forced into his paternal model of human labor.[111] In this respect, Carlyle's ideal for black workers was not so different from that of mainstream politicians as they or he imagined. Although he differed from Russell, for example, on the superiority of wage labor, they both hoped to keep black people in servile labor. Although Carlyle's apathy about the unique evils of chattel slavery drew controversy, it was in his attitude toward British—not West Indian—labor where he really differed from mainstream opinion. At home he hoped to restore feudal obligations; by his reckoning, this kind of hierarchy would emerge from an enlightened slave society more readily than a free-labor community.[112]

Most Chartists were far more careful than Carlyle in invoking black slavery to highlight their critique of political economy and industrial manufacturing. William Lovett, the leading light of the London Working Men's Association, embraced anti-slavery as an extension of his Chartist principles.[113] Among the more radical Chartists in the country's capital was the tailor William Cuffay, son of a West Indian slave, and certainly no apologist for black slavery.[114] In Glasgow, the Rev. Patrick Brewster led his fellow moral force Chartists to stand for election and win a majority of seats on the local Emancipation Society's committee.[115] Still, there were striking exceptions—Chartist leader Bronterre O'Brien was hostile to emancipation because it pretended that "outside of the blacks there was no slave under British rule."[116]

For the most part, though, Chartists focused "their hostility squarely on the hypocrisy of abolitionists rather than on abolitionism," as one scholar neatly puts it.[117] This was even the case when, like Carlyle, they denied the unique status of chattel slavery as a condition of exploitation. The anti-slavery campaign against West Indian apprenticeship was a particular target because it coincided with the economic downturn of 1838. Northampton Chartists, for example, agitated for an end to *their* slavery too.[118] In 1840, a meeting in Norfolk to attack foreign slavery, attended by the local bishop and other dignitaries, was hijacked by Chartists who demanded that it debate "the despotic slavery now increasing at home." Thomas Fowell Buxton, the main speaker at this event, cast the workingmen as selfish and self-absorbed, stating that "for the purpose of gratifying your own passions" they had "interrupted the cause of humanity and Christian charity."[119] In 1841, Peter McDouall, editor of *McDouall's Chartist and Republican Journal,* claimed that he would prefer to be "the slave of the West Indies and possess all the physical benefits of real slavery, than be the white factory slave of England, and possess all the hardships of an unreal freedom."[120] Although such statements could be misconstrued as defending slavery, they were founded more on jealousy of the money expended on compensation for West Indian planters. An address pressing the need for better-funded education of working people complained, among other wasteful spending, that "twenty millions were paid to compensate the owners of slaves for relinquishing their unjust traffic." The author expressed outrage that money had been paid; like radical abolitionists, advocates of the poor wished that emancipation had been enforced without reparation.[121]

The power of direct comparisons between enslaved Africans and British laborers declined after American emancipation. As we have already seen,

British views of the relationship between the Civil War and slavery are difficult to judge, for working people as much as any other group. Some workers' newspapers supported the Confederacy and many textile jobs were hit by the lack of cotton, but we know many still "detested slavery of every kind whether among the white factory operatives at home or among the negroes of America."[122] The Civil War saw a revival of such comparisons, but by the 1870s Britain had begun to focus on the slavery of African or Arab societies, whose practices were less easily compared to England's dark satanic mills than the British colonies or the American South.

Still, the use of parallels did not disappear entirely. The journalist Robert Harborough Sherard published articles and then a book, in 1895, on *The White Slaves of England*. He followed this with *The Child Slaves of Britain* a few years into the next century.[123] He admitted, of the former book, that "the title has been used over and over again" but made no excuse for re-presenting a familiar critique of industrial suffering. In words that could have been uttered by Wilberforce or Clarkson, he insisted that "silence is felony" and "the evil must be shouted from the house-tops till not a man or woman in the British Isles can plead ignorance as an excuse for indifference of the abominations in our midst which should make one ashamed of the name of Englishman." Although the chain-makers of Cradley Heath, who he visited, did not make chains for slaves, he observed that their "hunger can bind tighter than any iron links."[124] In 1898 Joseph Arch, the organizer of the National Agricultural Labourer's Union, wrote that, as a child entering work in the fields, his position had been "not a whit better than that of a plantation nigger boy."[125] Although industrial work was the more common comparison, this late Victorian memoir is a reminder that parallels were sometimes drawn between rural labor and black slavery too.

The phrase "white slavery" would find an entirely new life in the Edwardian period as a term to describe the international trafficking of women for prostitution.[126] Meanwhile, the use of "slavery" as a euphemism for the experience of the poorest British laborers continued to provoke controversy beyond the end of our period. The playwright Arthur Shirley insisted in 1904 that the title of his play *The White Slaves of London* was a metaphor for the sweated labor it portrayed—but the lord chamberlain banned its performance on the grounds that there were no slaves in London.[127] National pride in British anti-slavery values made these recurring comparisons a sure way of attracting attention. Although these conflicts seem, on one level, purely semantic—contesting the definition of slavery—they represented more substantial disagreements over the meaning of anti-slavery. For one group, anti-slavery was a political movement only to protect Africans from abusive ownership under the sanction of law; for others, it opened up broader questions about the development of meaningful freedoms, individual potential, and human capabilities.

It is much easier, of course, to catalog the thoughts of the authors, reformers, and leaders who spoke for working people than to reconstruct the experiences of poorer Britons themselves. It is still possible, though, to gain an impression by looking at their eager consumption of popular anti-slavery culture. For decades, metropolitan and provincial lectures by escaped American slaves and abolitionists drew a wide cross-section of British society, including significant numbers of workers.[128] Such events also attracted large numbers of working women—and even children such as the little girl in Croydon who gave one lecturer a farthing "for the slaves."[129]

Poor families were similarly involved in the warm reception of *Uncle Tom's Cabin*, its associated merchandise, and its author when she visited Britain. Jonathan Rose has unearthed a number of striking insights into the views of Victorian workers who read Stowe's book and were deeply moved by its "beautiful contrasts" and "the sense of sin—never to be quite expiated." In a Welsh mining village, a dramatization of the story led one distressed woman to be escorted out "sobbing and crying" while among her peers who stayed "there was not a dry eye in the Pavilion."[130] Stowe was astonished when the maid at one of her British residences turned out to be an avid fan of the novel and fetched her copy of *Uncle Tom's Cabin* from her room for the author to sign.[131] In public, Stowe found herself mobbed by crowds of the respectable and the rabble: "One little chap seemed too impetuous and was seized by the shoulder by the police and pitched out. 'I say I will see Mrs. Stowe!' he shouted, and back he came and dove headfirst into the crowd."[132]

Samuel Ringgold Ward was impressed with anti-slavery sentiment all over Britain, but particularly in Scotland, where, although he did not like bagpipes, haggis, or oatcakes, he welcomed the greater involvement from working people. He attributed this to more church-going north of the border, but it may also reflect wider participation in the Edinburgh and Glasgow abolitionist societies organized by George Thompson.[133] Certainly, Ward's implications about the middle-class nature of anti-slavery might reflect his unusual perspective as a guest of abolitionist elites, given workers' interest in anti-slavery culture. Anti-slavery meant different things to different sections of British society and could be honored in different or contradictory ways.

Seymour Drescher has argued that the campaign for West Indian emancipation, far from distracting attention from domestic reform, provided working people of the 1830s with new language and tactics to pursue their goals.[134] This seems to be broadly true, too, of the Victorian period, when conflict over the meanings of slavery and freedom sharpened, rather than blunted, contemporaries' debates over domestic reform. Many "respectable" abolitionists doubtlessly despised radical appropriation of their cause, but they could assert no patent over it. Where working people were aggressive toward or derogatory about anti-slavery, their target was the hypocrisy of its middle-class or upper-class proponents rather than the cause itself. Some British workers probably shared with Carlyle an antipathy toward enslaved Africans and a jealousy that colonial others sometimes received more sympathy than poor whites at home. Yet, so far as it is possible to generalize, domestic reformers seem to have seen abolitionism as a form of leverage for their concerns, rather than an impediment to them.

## SWEETENING THE CONDITION OF ENGLAND

Anti-slavery contributed to broad debates over the meanings of slavery and freedom within British society. However, there were occasions when chattel slavery was more than a metaphor or parallel for questions of political reform; it was in at least one instance the center of a particular domestic problem. The starkest confrontation between the economic interests of white workers and black Britons came over the price of sugar.[135] The MP William Ewart pointed out that sugar was almost twice as expensive in Britain as it was abroad because of tariff barriers protecting West Indian free labor by excluding cheap slave-grown sources.[136]

This problem was acute because sugar "had now become a necessary of life."[137] It was "the only little luxury that many families can enjoy; it renders palatable their rice, their crout [cabbage], their gruel, their indifferent tea or coffee."[138] Anxieties over the material welfare of working people had taken on a new prominence by 1840. Carlyle had dubbed rising awareness of the human suffering within Britain's dark, satanic mills as the "condition of England" question.[139] Sir Benjamin Hawes MP compared it to "a direct law, prohibiting nine-tenths of the people of England from tasting sugar and coffee."[140] Sugar was a vital component in the poor's transition from alcoholic drink to coffee. Such a switch—refining as it did the character of poorer Britons—could only be sustained by access to cheap sugar, since coffee and tea were considered unpalatable without it.[141] Public dismay at sugar prices motivated politicians to attack the duties as "an artificial system of legislation inflicted on the people" and "adverse to the interests of the people of the country."[142]

How did this controversy over workers' diets bear on anti-slavery? Many people—including distinguished abolitionists—feared that free trade would harm "the population of those colonies which had been so recently manumitted." In 1841 the MP Stephen Lushington "went so far as to say, in scriptural language, that they [the people of England] would prefer a dinner of herbs to the stalled ox of slavery." Ewart countered that "the rich, who could pay, would still have the stalled ox. The dinner of herbs would be the lot of the poor only."[143] On similar lines, Lord Ashburton argued that he still considered sugar a luxury, which was hardly a popular view.[144] Only the most inept or courageous proponents of protection followed Lushington and Ashburton in denying that the price of sugar was a problem requiring a solution.

The defenders of the tariff had more success questioning whether there would be any benefit for workers, mocking, as Lord Egerton did, that "there was no denomination of coin sufficiently small to measure the advantage to be obtained by the poor customer of the grocer."[145] Five years later, Lord George Bentinck was willing to admit "the question was, whether or not the people of England would have slavery and sugar...cheaper by 6s. per cwt., or two-thirds of a penny per pound more for sugar grown by the free hand of British industry?"[146] When he attempted, in 1848, to save the sugar duties and retain discriminating duties a while longer, the jockey-turned-politician found the most audacious tactic of all. In a numerical table presented to the House he tried to demonstrate that the greater protection he proposed could deliver cheaper sugar and trumpeted his plan as "the poor man's bill."[147]

Free traders contrasted the freedman's alleged plenty with the British laborer's desperate need. This juxtaposition was used by Lord John Russell when, in May 1841, as Leader of the House of Commons, he introduced the Whigs' proposals to narrow the difference in sugar duties. Russell reported on the happiness of the free people and their widespread ownership of small-holdings (small farms). He declared that "I do not think that we should be justified in giving our attention exclusively to their [freed blacks'] interests...whilst the people of this country were suffering from want of the common comforts of life." Moved to describe the misery of the town of Bolton, he described ruined shopkeepers and impoverished customers, their possessions sold to pay debts. Russell asserted that the lowly British worker, whose suffering was induced by the protection of the West Indian laborer, would gladly switch places with them. Reaching his crescendo, the MP asked:

> Is the poor man to go into the grocer's shop (a case which I have heard occurred last year) and, after hearing the price of sugar, turn away in sorrow and despondence because the article is placed beyond his reach? That has been the case under your present law—that has been the effect under your present duty.[148]

Plain as day, the British worker had replaced the West Indian slave or apprentice in Russell's conscience. The freed Briton was a slave no more, but a free laborer who must compete in a free-trade world. As allegations of black idleness and luxury circulated, free-trader politicians and journalists asked whether "a little of that feeling which was so redundant in favour of negro labourers might overflow in behalf of our white brethren at home."[149] Bentinck asked whether the British people had intended "that those slaves should be raised to a condition far beyond their own."[150] It became common to speak of the happy black West Indian who earned extortionate wages for little work and "carried silk umbrellas" and "may drink at his ease his Madeira or Champagne."[151] James Ritchie, an abolitionist free trader, equated people who cared only for West Indian blacks to those who wept at tragedy on the stage but ignored the miseries of the real world.[152]

Former slaves had rapidly moved from being effective figures of sympathy to being seen as idle exploiters of privilege at the cost of the poor in Britain. In 1846 Lord Clarendon boasted of the Whig government's regard for "the British producer, to the wants of the people, and the exigencies of the revenue, without, as I trust I shall be able to show, the flagrant violation of such morality as we can lay claim to." The black freed people were absent from the list of concerns.[153] So far as the fate of the sugar colonies was admitted to be an anti-slavery question, it was a question of proving the superiority of free labor, not black welfare. The latter increasingly came to be portrayed as the main impediment to the former.[154]

The freeing of black West Indians had ironically removed one of the principal reasons they had evoked sympathy in the British Isles. Few Britons seemed to see a link between their recent anti-slavery enthusiasm and any future concern for those emancipated. As late as 1840, in a private letter, Russell made clear that sugar production was a secondary priority to the relief and development of the ex-slaves in the West Indies.[155] And yet a year later, as we have seen, he was attacking the "lazy" freedman. He was not the only one to abandon a concern for black Britons.[156] G. R. Porter defined the new orthodoxy when he stated plainly that

> the only fund from which the negroes must be supported is the produce of their labour.... When Parliament voted, and the nation so willingly gave, twenty millions of money to bring about this blessed change in their condition, it was not proposed to give to these our fellow-citizens greater privileges and immunities than are enjoyed by other labourers; but to argue that a higher price is needed for the products of their labour than the price at which the same products are yielded elsewhere and by others, is to affirm that something more than freedom was designed for them by the generosity of the nation.[157]

As they were now regular British subjects, Porter concluded that "it is neither wise, reasonable, nor just, that the people of England should, under any circumstances, be this heavily taxed for the benefit of any class of our fellow subjects, however respectable."[158] Such comparisons stung, given that in the early 1840s labor-contract laws in the West Indies were more generous to workers than the domestic British equivalents. This fueled resentment, though it was a paper distinction given the harsher treatment that colonial magistrates meted out to black defendants. By 1846, the Whigs abandoned this approach, encouraging harsher prosecution to compel colonial workers back to the sugar plantations.[159]

In the 1840 debate, Charles Villiers defended his vote for free trade as a "vote for the community" against the interests of a privileged section. For him, the issue at hand was no longer a question of anti-slavery but a question of some free British subjects being supported by the state at the expense of others.[160] After apprenticeship ended, abolitionists who cared about the social and racial equality of black West Indians were few and dwindling. When a commentator such as Herman Merivale expressed concern for the moral development of blacks after emancipation, it was in fear that their alleged luxury was debasing them and undermining West Indian productivity.[161] Catherine Hall is correct to observe that by the 1850s "Britons might indeed hate slavery, but their enthusiasm for the racialised others was strictly limited." But it should be underlined that while "some abolitionists had lost faith," it was their faith and interest in blacks or their faith in free trade that had waned, not their faith in anti-slavery.[162] Indeed, J. B. Estlin, a Bristol abolitionist aligned with Garrison, complained that the BFASS's work now had "nothing anti-slavery in it" and wished the London society "would concentrate their energies more upon American slavery until the negroes there are as well off as those in the W. Indies."[163]

Any connection between the welfare of blacks and the success of the "great experiment" in the West Indies, or indeed freed people's connection with the fate of anti-slavery, had been eroded. The "virulent racist counterattack" on the emancipated black population was not only consistent with anti-slavery but, in the view of many, had been caused by the failure of freed people to perform the role assigned to them by anti-slavery expectations.[164] The irony was that emancipation had stripped black West Indians of the status that invited pity and sympathy from the home nation; now they were exposed to the same potential contempt as poor whites at home. Indeed, the post-emancipation decline in sugar production strengthened preexisting prejudices about the industry and habits of black Britons. The sudden attack on former slaves was not a reversal from British anti-slavery sentiment of the 1830s; rather, it showed how little most supporters of anti-slavery cared about racial equality.

We have already seen how Victorian Britons disagreed virulently over whether British industrial labor reduced white workers to the level of slaves. Yet the sugar duties debate clearly revealed that, for all but a minority of protectionist abolitionists, Britons overwhelmingly rejected the notion that freed people should get compensation, assistance, or support for their years of suffering; the emancipated population was reduced to the level of white workers, entitled to no special sympathy for being slaves and deserving few avenues for ambition. For free traders, continuing to support West Indians through the sugar duties would have been to value the liberty of former slaves over the pleasures of poor consumers in Great Britain. This controversy therefore hung on a question of whether freedom for trade would require a betrayal of Britain's commitment to freedom for slaves. The next chapter explores precisely how Britons held diverse expectations as to how anti-slavery principles could be best combined with the national pursuit of power and wealth, not least in these debates over free trade.

# 5

## Power, Prosperity, and Liberty

I T WAS a painful truth for Victorian Britons, as the Earl of Clarendon observed in 1846, that "for our necessaries and luxuries of life, for the employment of our people, for our revenue, for our very position in the world as a nation, we are indebted to the production of slave labour."[1] As an anti-slavery pioneer, it was not clear how much Britain could or should isolate itself from other countries' surviving (and often thriving) slave systems. Debates over economic sanctions for the importation of slave-grown products and the use of violence to suppress the international slave trade burned brightly in the years before the American Civil War. The British puzzled how morality (in the form of anti-slavery) was best married with prosperity (in the form of trade). It was not clear how they could be advanced together. Both sides of the sugar contest claimed to be the authentic standard-bearers of anti-slavery and prosperity; they assumed different moral economies of how the two would interact. For protectionists, free trade might lower prices in the short-term, but at the long-term cost of destroying the wealth of Britain's West Indian colonies and encouraging slavery. By contrast, the free traders thought protection was a delusion or trick that would hurt the poor at home and halt the spread of anti-slavery around the globe: "Commerce was the great emancipator."[2]

This chapter examines the particular debates over sugar and violence and then analyzes how Britain's economic interests related to her policies toward slave labor and free labor. The fundamental question linking these themes is how Britons imagined anti-slavery to interact with national interest, world power, and economic growth. Was anti-slavery good for British prosperity and, if so, how? Revisiting the issue of sugar protection will demonstrate differing expectations for whether free production could compete with slavery in the world marketplace. It also reveals whether free trade required Britons to choose between morality and prosperity. Before British emancipation, slaveholders and monopolists were one and the same; protective tariffs for the West Indies subsidized the evil of slave cultivation and made Britons pay more for their sugar. However, the adoption of free labor in the sugar colonies created questions about whether enemies of slavery should embrace or continue to oppose duties that taxed foreign sugar (much of it produced by slaves) at a higher rate than that produced by Britain's newly freed peoples. The needs of working people, as we have seen, formed a key part of the resulting debate, but that is only part of the story. There were broader ideological questions at stake too.

## CHEAP SUGAR MEANS CHEAP SLAVES?

Victorians had to decide whether an anti-slavery nation could or should wean itself off such an addiction to the fruits of slavery. Sugar created a particular dilemma because "all considerations mingle in it; not merely commercial, but imperial, philanthropic, religious; confounding and crossing each other, and confusing the legislature and the nation lost in a maze of conflicting interests and contending emotions."[3] So declared Benjamin Disraeli, future prime minister and long-standing opponent of free trade, in 1852, after he had spent more than a decade fighting unsuccessfully to keep the tariff. The politics of sugar, as he suggested, rested on so complex a cocktail of ideological judgments that partisans on a particular side of the debate could have quite different reasons for choosing it. As an old observation goes, political disputes over economics quickly become passionate rather than rational.[4] But, more profoundly, the debate was one about how economic ideas could be applied to a political question: a passionate contest to define rationality. This is why sugar divided loyalties, defeated governments, and soured party ties.

The Emancipation Act of 1833 had increased the sugar duties in order to pay compensation to West Indian slaveholders. Radical abolitionists had at the time opposed compensation on principle, but found the tax on buyers of sugar a particularly odious way to fund it. The attack on sugar protection after 1838 came as part of the broader movement for free trade, which believed that the country's taxation system was rigged to reward a parasitic aristocracy and dull the energies of entrepreneurial industrialists and their armies of workers. The Anti–Corn Law League, as its name announced, focused its wrath on the taxes that, they argued, kept the price of bread high and padded the purses of British landowners at the expense of working people and their employers. Immediately after the repeal of the Corn Laws in 1846, Parliament voted to phase out the discrimination in the sugar duties over the next five years. After a slight delay, equalization came in 1854.[5]

Laissez-faire doctrine held that the nation would prosper more, not less, from a greater exchange of goods between Britain and other countries of the world. It is not enough to establish "free trade" as an independent historical force, functioning to explain why Britain abandoned protection of the free-labor experiment in the West Indies. We must explore the interaction between free trade and anti-slavery ideas, how they fitted together, and whether the repeal was really a victory of the former over the latter, as has often been suggested. The extensive parliamentary debates, furious pamphlet skirmishes, and bitter newspaper coverage all reveal the principles that the contending parties offered to the public. The storm over the sugar duties would have been a great deal simpler if it had merely mirrored the divisions that existed over the protection of corn and other commodities. Sugar fractured existing divides because some free traders thought that Britain's anti-slavery struggle required a special case to be made for the emancipated West Indies.[6] James Deacon Hume, a Board of Trade expert, made this case. His testimony to an 1840 select committee dismissed the application of free trade to sugar. Even after he died, his judgment was quoted frequently by defenders of the sugar duties, precisely because he was such an unlikely ally.[7]

Support for free trade in sugar grew gradually but inexorably. A motion removing West Indian protection was first introduced in 1833 and attempted annually from then onward. At the forefront of these efforts was the free trader William Ewart.[8] In 1840, his bill was defeated by a resounding 122–27 vote with opposition from both Whigs and Tories.[9] From the next year, however, the Whigs supported only a moderate preference for West Indian sugar, not the existing gulf in duties. A bill to reduce the foreign tariff was defeated and led to the fall of Lord Melbourne's Whig government in 1841.[10] Having been brought to power in this way, it was ironic that Sir Robert Peel's Tory cabinet came to embrace limited reform in 1844. The ministers still resisted attempts from radical free traders to abolish preference altogether and from the Whigs to reduce it. Rather than treating all foreign sugar equally, the Tories experimented with discrimination in favor of free-labor sugar from abroad, but found this unworkable given Britain's commercial treaty obligations.[11] The death knell for West Indian protection arrived, however, when Peel's own party disintegrated on the question of the Corn Laws and brought the Whigs back to power. The end of West Indian protection can be dated precisely to July 1846, when Peel and Melbourne's successor, Lord John Russell, shared a division lobby to vote for reform. How had the two both changed their opinion in six short years?

The growing tide of conversions to free trade meant that staunch defenders of protection in one debate appear as free-trade advocates in another. One such politician, frequently derided for his change of heart, was Lord Sandon, who had introduced the amendment that defeated Melbourne in 1841. Five years later he voted with the Whigs against an almost identical amendment from Lord George Bentinck.[12] Sandon's conversion was typical of some Tories and most Whigs. While Peel had been brought to power by his support for protection, he voted for equalization in 1846 on the basis—so he claimed—of a desire to see the matter finally settled rather than sourness toward the Tory rebels who had ousted him.[13] For men such as Peel, concerns about "the condition of England" doubtlessly weighed more heavily than the meaning of freedom for black colonial subjects. Yet, even so, it would have been politically unacceptable for parliamentarians to ignore the anti-slavery aspect of the free-trade question; rather than letting cheap sugar trump humanitarianism, the enemies of protection had to show how their policies could advance both at once.

Even if the West Indian freedman was now so much a man and brother that he did not require any special care, suppression of the Atlantic slave trade was still an established objective of British foreign policy. For protectionists, an increase in British consumption of slave-grown sugar would mean an increased demand for slaves on the foreign plantations supplying that sugar.[14] Their moral economy therefore demanded higher sugar prices, rather than taking the risk of stimulating the illegal slave trade to Cuba or Brazil. Conservative John Colquhoun set out the logic behind such claims in 1841. He explained that cheap sugar was cheapened "at the price of blood, and by the sacrifice of human life" because a greater supply of sugar for Britons would require more slaves to be taken to Brazil and Cuba.[15] Lord Brougham warned Parliament in 1846 that a man who voted for freer trade in sugar "must see that he held up his hand not only for slavery, but for the extension of the execrable crime, and that most revolting of crimes, the African Slave Trade."[16]

Lord Stanley offered some calculations about the encouragement that a free trade in sugar would give to the slave trade. He estimated that the new imports of sugar would provide £735,000 a year directly to slaveholders, while stimulating the passage of at least ten thousand new slaves in the transatlantic slave trade.[17] The calculations by Samuel Wilberforce—bishop of Oxford and son of the abolitionist—were even more dramatic: he predicted one new slave would be needed for every additional ton consumed in Britain.[18] The possibility of admitting foreign free-grown sugar, but not that made by slaves, would have divided the protectionists. Some would have doubtless defended complete protection as the best means to promote the success of the West Indian "Great Experiment" in free labor. As it was, the attempts by Peel's administration in 1844–45 to apply such a principle had already been proved unworkable.[19]

The free traders were quick to point out that it was only sugar their opponents proposed to abstain from importing from slave-holding countries. This principle could also exclude slave sources of cotton, which was credited with employing a million and a half British artisans, or tobacco, which produced a revenue of three and a half million pounds to the exchequer.[20] The logic behind protecting free-grown sugar implied "a total non-intercourse with the slave-grown countries." Russell teased in 1841, "where is the philanthropist who will tell me, 'I have a cup of slave-grown coffee, and by putting a lump of free-labour sugar into it I shall make the potation quite innoxious'."[21] This inconsistency was a font of Whig humor. Lord Lansdowne mocked the protectionists for using a peculiar moral thermometer that "rose to boiling point on Cuba sugar, but sank to a most agreeable temperature on Carolina cotton."[22] John Bright argued that "the idea of enquiring into the moral condition of every people with whom we trade seems to me most irrational—hitherto no result but injury to our own people has followed."[23] Behind their derision lay a serious objection to the protectionists' high-minded anti-slavery claims: it was difficult to speak of absolute morality when principle operated on a single commodity alone. In rebuttal, protectionists ridiculed their opponents' logic for the suggestion that "because they did wrong in admitting one article of slave produce, they were justified in admitting others." Was it to be a free trade in morals, they asked?[24]

Yet the sheer impossibility of imagining a British economy without any slave-grown imports was perhaps the greatest single impediment to excluding slave sugar on anti-slavery grounds.[25] In 1841, Sandon (then still a protectionist) accepted that total abstinence from slave-grown produce would be utterly impractical and confessed that "he had never heard the warmest abolitionist profess it."[26] The problem for the BFASS was that they increasingly came to hold just such a position. Sturge and others in the organization held that the state should act against all slave produce consumed in Britain.[27] Their alliance with the sugar protectionists tainted the cause with the stigma of utopianism. Lord Brougham, in particular, found himself derided for giving a speech defending protection of West Indian sugar as a special case when he had just presented an Anti-Slavery Society petition demanding abstention from all slave goods.[28]

The *Economist* mocked the idea that a British tax on sugar could suppress the slave trade. They attacked the anti-slavery protectionists for looking to "the state to do that [anti-slavery work] at once by a tax which can only be done by the gradual progress of knowledge and humanity."[29] On the contrary, Russell argued in 1841, "the more free and unrestricted is intercourse, the more the nations of the world are mingled together by the ties of peaceful commerce," the more civilization and Christianity were spread. Increasing British trade with Brazil would provide greater influence and leverage than would refusing commerce, he hoped.[30] In 1846, he branded as "insanity" any principle that concluded anti-slavery in America would be best served by British abstention from cotton.[31] The *Morning Chronicle* berated protectionist abolitionists for not seeing the link between free trade and anti-slavery: American emancipation would rely on a better market for free-labor exports, like Northern corn, meaning that "our corn-law is the main prop of the accursed slave-owning interest in that country"[32] Free trade seemed to offer closer relationships and foster cooperation; slave-holding nations would be peaceably convinced they were mistaken.[33] One pamphleteer saw abstention from slave-grown produce as "pharisaical" and warned that to "do a man good, we must teach him to look upon us as friends, and not foes. We have no right to shut up a man in his guilt.... we [should] speak in friendship to our fellow-man, however degraded he may be, and win him over to the adoption of that which is just and true."[34]

The difference of opinion over the sugar duties mirrored a smaller conflagration in 1840, when the BFASS saw a commercial treaty with the slave republic of Texas as "a fearful impulse given to slavery and the slave-trade" while Palmerston insisted that "the greater intercourse between Great Britain and Texas, which will probably result from the treaty, may have the effect of mitigating, rather than aggravating, the evils arising out of the legal existence of slavery in that republic."[35] These conflicting interpretations divided Britons at the time of the sugar debates. A convert to free trade in sugar, supporting it for the first time in 1846, explained his realization that "for this country to attempt to control the social state of other countries by our fiscal arrangements was a complete mistake."[36] For the free traders, the special status of commerce in civilizing the world made total abstinence from slave produce short-sighted; they held that freedom of trade was an absolute good that was ordained to produce moral results.

Although protectionists denounced the importation of slave produce as the acceptance of stolen goods, such a metaphor, their opponents argued, broke down in practice. A normal shopkeeper could return stolen goods to their rightful owner, but slave sugar excluded from the British market would just be sold elsewhere.[37] "Every hundred-weight of free-labour sugar we consume, must be replaced by an equal amount of slave-labour sugar," so the logic went.[38] Free traders also questioned the inconsistency of British ships distributing slave-grown sugar to foreign ports when it was banned for home consumption. One estimate suggested that 23,889 tons of Brazilian sugar had been carried by the British in 1845 alone.[39] These facts seemed to indicate that, while individuals could choose to abstain from slave-grown sugar if they felt obliged, it was difficult to impose such a regime nationally.

The slave-trade element of the debate ultimately came down to how far an individual was willing to trust laissez-faire. Free traders could not simply promise cheap sugar; they had to demonstrate that their reforms would not assist the slave trade and would, rather, combat it. At the same time, a key part of the protectionist argument was showing how free trade would stimulate the demand for slaves and increase the traffic of the middle passage. As much as the pains of the domestic consumer were played upon, therefore, the anti-slave-trade angle could not be ignored entirely. Both sides needed to address the effect an admission of slave sugar would have on the slave trade. Where they differed was on whether a free market would produce moral outcomes or whether the state could and should step in to use protection as a coercive measure.

Proponents and opponents of the sugar duties, unsurprisingly, held just as polarized views on the best action for the West Indies as they did on the suppression of the slave trade. Debates regarding the stimulation of slave trading rested, as we have observed, on the question of whether Britain, as a free-labor nation, was right or wrong to open its markets to products derived from the labor of trafficked slaves. But the other side of the question was over how Britain best served its free-labor sugar colonies.[40] It was clear by the 1840s that sugar production in the British colonies had declined since emancipation and the end of apprenticeship.[41] Would British free labor thrive or decline without protection?[42] Many of the free traders drew on older arguments for the superiority of wage labor, claiming that fair competition between sugars, slave and free, would produce anti-slavery results. From the start, free traders expressed "the fullest confidence that the power of free labour was equal, nay superior, to slave labour." The success of free-labor sugar in Siam, China, Manila, and Java on the open market pointed to the old adage that "the labour of one free man is equal to that of two slaves," and that slavery could be routed from the market.[43] Clarendon claimed in 1846 that "the advocates of abolition previous to emancipation of the West Indian negroes" had been correct to say that "the work of free men is more profitable than that of slaves, and that they can compete with and drive slave labour out of the market."[44] On these lines, free traders argued that "monopoly was a misfortune to commerce, and to the sugar growers themselves."[45] The interference of the state insulated the sugar colonies from economic reality and deterred them from the changes they needed to succeed.[46]

James Ewing Ritchie, a free trader, quit the BFASS over the issue. He warned that by keeping monopoly, Britain effectively conceded that emancipation had been a mistake, not an example to the world. Ritchie confidently predicted that "slavery can only be destroyed by freedom"; when given "the right to buy in the cheapest market and sell in the dearest" then "the employer of free men will soon be left alone in the field."[47] Monopoly was bad for the consumer and deadened the innovation of the producer.[48]

Protectionists argued the opposite; that, far from saving the West Indies, free trade would "throw a vast number of estates out of cultivation" and drive free labor from the marketplace.[49] For them, it was important to respect traditional and recent national duties to the West Indian planters, whose economic interests were expected to be ruined by abolition of the duties.[50] According to reports, the possibility of the 1846 bill passing led many planters to cease investing in improvements to their estates.[51] Protectionists therefore argued that Britain's free-labor experiment was being watched by the world and should not be undermined by unfair competition with slave labor.[52] Crucially, they maintained that a cheap and reliable supply of sugar for the British masses was secured only with "the maintenance of cultivation in the West Indies," and described it as "a national object."[53] The West India lobby crowed that they had been right; Bentinck proclaimed that those who promised free labor would lead to a doubling of sugar production had been bitterly disappointed.[54] Gladstone, the son of a planter, denied there was any example where "the produce of free labour, could or did compete with the produce of slave labour."[55]

It proved more difficult for abolitionists to explain why they wished to give planters further advantages. Stephen Lushington tied himself in knots when he argued that reducing the duties would express "utter hopelessness that free labour was able to compete with slave labour" and "abandon that great experiment as an utter failure." He maintained that black people could not be expected to work as hard immediately after emancipation as before, but that they would return to the fields in good time. Meanwhile, "it was their duty to extend every indulgence towards that experiment and towards the colonies in which it was made."[56] Similarly, Samuel Wilberforce denigrated the power of wage labor in order to defend the duties.[57] The bishop argued that "it is not true then that free labour is cheaper than that of slaves, in the sense of a more immediate production of wealth. It is altogether untrue." The sanction of God on free labor was hence only demonstrated by the fact that slave wealth "brings a curse, not alone on the individual, but on the nation that so obtains it; and thus we see that slave labour, while it produces more immediate riches, produces also evils which are the sure witness of God against it."[58]

Arguments for the marketplace superiority of free labor had been advanced before 1833, in the context of anti-slavery campaigns. Such beliefs

had been far from universal, but that did not stop free traders from claiming that their faith in free labor made them the real abolitionists.[59] As Joseph Beldam, an anti-slavery veteran, noted, "monopoly was considered
by abolitionists generally as one of the principal obstacles to agricultural
improvement, to colonial prosperity, and to the general interests of freedom."[60] Charles Villiers took pleasure in 1840 in taunting protectionist
abolitionists that, in denigrating free labor, they were peddling on behalf
of "the great array of colonial proprietors opposite" the "very arguments
which, for a quarter of a century, have been urged against themselves [abo-
litionists] when pleading for freedom for the negro."[61]

For their part, protectionists maintained that a longer transition would
be required to give emancipation a fair chance. As one MP put the case,
"there could be no competition between a racehorse and a steam-engine."[62]
This was a particularly strong argument with those who were generally
free-trade supporters but had come to see sugar as an exceptional case.
General proponents of free trade found themselves on both sides of the
sugar question, depending on their confidence in the doctrine's applicability in the case of free and slave labor. More generally, both sides of the debate mustered evidence to suggest the other was unfaithful to anti-slavery,
depending on their assumptions about *how* slave labor would reveal its
inferiority to free production. Although the welfare of freed people was
largely ignored, improving the chances of global emancipation and the suppression of the slave trade remained priorities for many in both camps.

## MORAL ECONOMIES

The ethics of marketized economies are cultural constructions. Every society has a set of competing "moral economies" that see particular economic
practices as legitimate or illegitimate. Even unbridled market capitalism,
with its typical focus on maximizing economic growth as the ultimate public good, assumes a moral economy of which behaviors should be rewarded
or punished as beyond acceptable practices.[63] This approach has important
implications for the relationship between British anti-slavery and selfish
material interests.

Of course, contemporary rhetoric rarely portrayed the debate as ideological, preferring to question the morality and intentions of their rivals.[64]
Lord Brougham and Earl Grey, one opposing and the other proposing
free trade, squabbled over which of them, when they had served together
in the government of 1833, had done more to push for emancipation.[65]
Bishop Wilberforce, arguing against equalization, was unusual in his conciliatory note that "I mean by no covert insinuation to suggest that noble
Lords who support this measure, are one whit less humane, one whit less

sincere and earnest in their desire to prevent slavery and the slave trade than myself."[66]

The coherence of the protectionist case was weakened by the odd marriage of radical abolitionists and conservatives sympathetic to the West Indian planters. Many of the latter group had been hostile to emancipation, but were now required to veil their criticisms in the language of reform rather than opposition. Henry Barkly, not only a West Indian but a future colonial governor, confessed that emancipation was "the best reparation this country could make for having shared so deeply in the profits and guilt of the Slave Trade," but he would "hold the people of this country to be responsible, not for having abolished slavery, but for having abolished it badly."[67]

With memories of recent public mobilization against slavery, politicians were keen to present their side of the argument as the anti-slavery side. As part of these attempts to shape public debate and define public opinion, parliamentarians seized upon the vaguest evidence to prove public support. Lushington tried to argue that the thousands of abolitionist petitions over the years had vastly outnumbered those few that had protested the price of sugar.[68] Bishop Wilberforce similarly predicted that "the people will insist upon morality and honour; they will dash at once from their lips the chalice you offer to them, tinged as it is with the blood of fellow-creatures sacrificed to the economy."[69] And yet the public outcry against the repeal of the duties did not appear. Provincial BFASS societies generated as many petitions in favor of free trade as against.[70] The arch-free-trader Richard Cobden, William Wilberforce's successor as a representative for Yorkshire, boasted that those of his constituents who had vigorously supported Wilberforce when he was their MP were the ones against the sugar monopoly.[71] His ally John Bright warned Sturge that he was in league with "the supporters of monopoly" and "could not affect any election in any Borough of England" on such a principle.[72] As the vote on the 1846 bill approached, the *Economist* judged too that the Tory protectionists could not win an election triggered on the question of sugar protection. The paper suggested that the slavery issue, not protection itself, would be the only aspect on which the public could be moved to oppose free trade. And, in their estimation, urban constituencies were those where anti-slavery concerns decided how votes were cast, yet among such electors the anti-slavery case for protection could not be made credibly.[73] Although heavily partisan, this analysis rings true. Anti-slavery protectionism never had a grip in the firmest anti-slavery constituencies.

Free trade promised to let the British public have their conscience, their sugar, and eat it too. The crucial advantage of the free traders was that they offered a model where the cause of anti-slavery and the condition of England could be improved at the same time. It is wrong to dismiss "the windy generalities of Cobden and others about commerce being the great emancipator, which no one who gave the matter a moment's thought could believe."[74] The free traders held their convictions honestly and passionately. If the economic system of the world was moral, then immoral behavior would find its own punishment without the need to inflict painful taxes on British consumers. Earl Grey "firmly believed that a wise and gracious Providence had so constituted human nature, that that which was not morally right was never really profitable." "Justice to Africa," John Bright insisted, was not done by "injustice to England."[75] This was the moral economy of free trade.

Laissez-faire anti-slavery was not, therefore, an oxymoron. Although zeal for the Anti–Corn Law League doubtlessly distracted some middle-class reformers from broader abolitionist causes, charges of ideological fratricide cannot stand. It was not "just that the cheap sugar cry was drowning the anti-slavery cry" but that two anti-slavery traditions, which had happily coexisted until emancipation, were now set in conflict.[76] The historian Eric Williams famously suggested that abolitionism was "a part of the general attack on monopoly and imperialism which characterized the transition of the English economy from mercantilism to laissez-faire."[77] Although evidence of abolitionist protectionism, not least from the BFASS, proves Williams wrong, it is mistaken for historians to take the opposite view and see free trade as incompatible with sincere anti-slavery. Like other aspects of Victorian society, faith in laissez-faire doctrine cut across other loyalties and issues.[78] The 1841 defeat of free trade in sugar was not "the last unalloyed victory of abolitionism over countervailing economic pressures," but it was the last unalloyed victory of protectionist anti-slavery over free-trade anti-slavery.[79]

In seeing protection of the West Indies as axiomatic of sincere anti-slavery in this period, historians have taken their cue from the defeated anti-slavery protectionists who believed that "the philanthropy of 1834 was sacrificed, with the freedom of Africa, in 1846" (when the sugar duties were repealed).[80] Indeed, the BFASS declared that this free-trade measure represented "a crisis…in the history of the Anti-slavery cause."[81] The public, however, disagreed, and by the 1850s protectionist abolitionists focused on encouraging voluntary abstention from slave-grown sugar. Indeed, they expanded the principle to promote free-labor sources of other imported goods, particularly cotton. The African American abolitionist John Brown told British consumers that "so long as there is a good market for slave-grown cotton, so long will it pay slave-holders to produce it."[82]

In form, this tactic revived the consumer protest tactics used with great success in 1789–92 and 1824–33.[83] The American abolitionist Elihu Burritt wrote a pamphlet to promote the practice in Britain and emphasized that, where the "anti-saccharites" of the 1790s had abandoned sugar altogether, modern families need pay only a little more for theirs.[84] The tactic had a large following among American abolitionists and had been debated as long ago as the 1840 World Anti-Slavery Convention, when divisions over free trade in sugar had first loomed large.[85] A new generation of Quaker networks and transatlantic abolitionist exchanges attempted to exclude the fruits of slavery through consumer choice now that the country's tariffs did not.[86] However, this nineteenth-century revival of consumer abolitionism never had the same impact. Estimates of around three hundred thousand people boycotting West Indian sugar in the late eighteenth century are questionable, but contemporary references to this practice underline its real popularity.[87] Although some local anti-slavery groups promoted free-labor stores, there was nothing like the public response enjoyed by the first generation of boycotters. Whereas earlier efforts had used abstention to pressure the Parliament and British planters to remedy a national sin, the 1850s initiative requested a broader lifestyle change to combat, in a very general way, an international evil.

The 1846 measure appears to have reflected enthusiasm for free trade and its moral economics, rather than for trampling over popular opinion. Sturge convinced Stowe and her family to support the free-produce campaign when they stayed with him during their 1854 visit to Britain, but they quickly discovered its unpopularity in some quarters.[88] After Stowe's husband, Calvin, backed it publicly, the *Times* chided him that it was the zeal of immediate abolitionists that impeded U.S. emancipation, not the strength of slave-grown cotton exports to Britain.[89]

A decade earlier, the free trader William Ewart had suggested that concern about slave labor in the production of British imports was "a principle for individual agency. The international commerce of the world should go on, whatever might be the nature of individual opinions."[90] Concerned with state prohibition rather than personal choice, free-trade radicals responded to the free-produce movement with puzzlement rather than hostility. At a breakfast with Sturge and the Stowes' party, Richard Cobden vowed not to attack them publicly. However, he thought abstinence entirely impractical. One of the American breakfasters recorded in his diary that "Sturge is for *principle*. Cobden is for practice."[91] Still, even if he thought it fruitless, Cobden welcomed the attention that public debate of the plan would bring to the urgency of anti-slavery: "I say to those who have a different opinion—*agitate for the* exclusion of slave grown produce. Let the subject be incessantly discussed." Remarkably, Cobden went so far as to declare to the Quaker Charles Gilpin that "I am so much more an anti-slavery man than a free trader that I should...very likely convert to your...prohibitions against slave grown produce, if such measures were practicable."[92] This private declaration from the high priest of free trade underlines the fact that free-trade abolitionism was the child of anti-slavery ideology, not a cuckoo in the nest. The principles of laissez-faire anti-slavery were summed up by Cobden's insistence that "from my observation of anti-slavery movements, I believe that everything you have ever done, or attempted to do, *through the Government,* has retarded your sublime mission"; "you will be wrong if you call upon the Government, as a Government, to aid you in any way."[93]

The post-emancipation clash between schools of anti-slavery thought was much more sophisticated than a mere division between protectionist and free-trade forms of abolitionism. On some matters, the advocates of laissez-faire sympathized with the complaints of West Indian monopolists. One planter, writing anonymously in 1840, had already accepted that free trade in sugar was inevitable and the real struggle was to ensure access to cheap new labor in return. He argued that "free, unrestricted immigration from all parts of the world, can alone save this fine colony from impending ruin" and "affords the only chance of rendering slave labour unprofitable," whatever the "efforts, however praiseworthy, of Christian missionaries and Anti-slavery societies."[94] Restrictions on immigration to the sugar colonies were targeted alongside protectionism; "in both cases a restrictive policy has been found to be fraught with inevitable ill. It were time that they should both retire," one author wrote.[95] Another former slaveholder described how his peers had been "thwarted by the fancy legislation resulting from the unpractical philanthropy of Exeter Hall, and the weakness and imbecility of the Colonial Office, in all our efforts to recruit our stock of labour."[96] West Indian sympathizer Henry Barkly (and future colonial governor of Jamaica) similarly traced the history of government regulation in the sugar islands, culminating in restrictions on labor migration. His critique ingeniously dressed the issue of cheap labor in the clothing of free trade, complaining that the interference by the government in West Indian affairs had given a monopoly position to those few freedmen who chose to remain working the plantations.[97]

Regulation of indentured migration had quickly followed the first attempts to recruit Indian laborers, just before apprenticeship ended in 1838. Still, it was not long before select committees on West Africa and the West Indies both endorsed further emigration and recommended state support. Officials were sincere, if patronizing and prejudiced, when they claimed that it was in the best interests of Africans to live in the British sugar colonies rather than anywhere else in the globe.[98] A fuller pool of labor in the West Indies seemed to be precisely what the great experiment needed to succeed against the slave owners of Cuba and Brazil. In his lectures as professor of political economy at Oxford, Herman Merivale argued that a greater supply of cheap employees would allow the free-labor colonies to triumph over slave sugar producers. This would, he believed, enable "the ultimate destruction of slavery, and the redemption of the children of Ham from their age of captivity."[99]

A consensus in favor of greater emigration among both protectionists and free traders had been one of the most significant fruits of the sugar duties debate. Those who disagreed over equalization shared a vilification of black workers and a desire for new sources of labor to reduce planters' costs.[100] Their logic was that "the mass of the population when freed from coercion will only labour to supply real or artificial wants" and that wages hence needed to be lower to make freed people work longer hours.[101] Merivale argued that wage labor would display its superiority to slavery only when an oversupply of labor depressed wages.[102] Special protection for free laborers in the West Indies ran counter to an ideal that "all persons of age in any part of the United Kingdom may bind themselves to work in any other part."[103] In the 1846 debate, Russell admitted that the planters had tried without success "to offer wages instead of compulsion" and therefore that "they are somewhat justified" in demanding fewer controls on indentured migration.[104] The *Economist* was initially skeptical as to whether the promotion of immigration was a wise use of West Indians' capital, but heartily defended their civil right to employ whom they chose; the paper came to argue that "the West Indian most justly demands that, with the abolition of protectionism *in their favour,* shall cease all protections and restrictions which *exist against them*" because immigration was "the most likely means of improving the condition of the African race, and of finally abolishing the slave trade itself."[105] In 1848, Russell responded to evidence of West Indian planter distress after free trade by promising tighter laws on vagrancy and £500,000 to underwrite the cost of new emigration to the sugar colonies. The prime minister explicitly mentioned that restrictions on labor in the sugar colonies had too often reflected the quixotic concerns of the BFASS.[106]

More than a decade later, Anthony Trollope offered a similar prescription to readers of his *West Indies and the Spanish Main.* With a critique that bore the marks of Carlyle, he suggested that the freed man "*is* a man; and, if you will a brother; but he is the very idlest brother with which a hardworking workman was ever cursed."[107] Could black Britons be free, he asked, but also compelled "as is the Englishman, to eat his bread in the sweat of his brow?" His solution was more immigration by cheap laborers.[108] When the islands declined in the decade after sugar equalization, Trollope and the majority of Britons did not abandon their anti-slavery, but they did question the racial capacity of black people and the probability of free labor triumphing in the West Indies.[109]

Until 1917, questions remained over how much the state should promote and regulate migration rather than leaving it in private hands, yet the pendulum had decisively swung from a humanitarian position. The question of indentured labor and "free" emigration created a new cleavage over what a moral economy looked like. For a majority of both free traders and protectionists, a moral economy was one in which individuals worked hard and played a full part in maximizing the wealth of the wider community. For a rump of faithful abolitionists, national sacrifice was required for the welfare and development of former slaves. Abolitionists believed that planters wanted to revive a slave trade through "emigration," but they were left largely isolated with the exception of some unlikely allies.[110] With his own perverse logic, Thomas Carlyle saw indentured migration as a market solution, so he preferred to coerce the existing black population into cheaper wages on the estates.[111] More compassionately, a few zealous free traders such as George Thompson and John Bright thought that state help in reducing wages was unfair to freed people.[112] The radical MP and *Lancet* editor Thomas Wakley expressed concern that this would be open to abuse and obtained clarification from Russell that new labor would be procured only from British African settlements, "for fear that anything approaching slavery should take place." He also feared "the introduction of crowds of labourers into those Colonies would swamp the West India labourers, at present living in comfort; and the enormous importation of men would revive slavery there in its worst form."[113] The migrants were, of course, meant to "swamp" the freed workers. That was the point.

However, supporters of free trade were as likely as the planters and protectionists to embrace indentured labor for the emancipated colonies. By 1848, Lord George Bentinck, still opposing the abolition of the sugar duties, had secured a committee to investigate Britain's struggling sugar and coffee production. He and his fellow MPs took particular interest in the planters' cries for more labor and succeeded in delaying, but not stopping, the equalization of the duties.[114]

At the same time, another committee—examining Britain's naval suppression of the slave trade—was also considering the question of migration and West Indian labor. Set up by the free trader William Hutt, MP for Gateshead, the slave-trade inquiry wrestled with the question of whether military force was the best to way to end slavery. Because the prosperity of the free West Indies was so closely tied to the fate of global slavery and the transatlantic slave trade, Hutt also focused on the question of immigration.[115] African witnesses were invariably quizzed on whether they thought others would want to work in the sugar colonies, while merchants testified about various ways of encouraging migration.[116] The Whig leadership was sympathetic to this view, as we have seen, but Hutt was using the emigration issue as part of a wider attack by his select committee on a cause sacred to Russell and Palmerston—naval suppression. One of the most common objections to new emigration was the fear that it would look like a thinly disguised slave trade and undermine Britain's international efforts to stop the Atlantic traffic.[117]

Twisting this argument around, Hutt suggested that it would be wise to scrap the expensive suppression system altogether. Although he had been a keen opponent of the sugar duties, he was able to use the promise of emigration to convince some protectionists that the suppression system should go. British violence against illegal slave traders did less to undermine global slavery than a free-labor migration from West Africa to the sugar colonies would, he argued.[118] Some supporters of naval force feared that widespread hunger for African "free" labor would drain public support for the suppression system and legitimize something very close to the slave trade.[119] Yet "anti-coercionists" won support from protectionists and free traders alike with the promise that if the British

> withdrew our cruisers from the coast of Africa, and permitted free trade in labour, we should not only benefit our own colonies, but, by emancipating our commerce with the African coast from the restrictions which at present crippled its energies, that we should, ere long, give a death blow to the slave trade by showing the African chiefs that it would be more profitable to employ Africans in raising produce, to be exchanged for British manufactures, than to sell them for slaves.[120]

Still disorientated from the agonizing battles over free trade, British politicians and the public were immediately pitched into another battle over the proper limits of state intervention in international slavery. What began as a personal crusade for Hutt would, in the years after 1846, slowly grow in stature and come very close to bringing down the Whig government.

## THE BENEVOLENT CROTCHET

Britain had committed a squadron of ships off West Africa to suppress the slave trade since 1808, policing first British and then foreign traders. After thirty years during which anti-slavery politics had focused on West Indian slave-holding, attention swung back to the transatlantic slave trade. A critique of forcible naval suppression was developing by the late 1830s, even among prominent abolitionists. Quaker influences meant that Sturge and the BFASS had always supported exclusively pacific policies. Sir Thomas

Fowell Buxton's *The Slave Trade* (1839) suggested that the number of Africans trafficked across the Atlantic was actually increasing, but he did not call for military suppression to end (although after his death he would often be misquoted as thinking that). Rather, he condemned the current operation as ineffective and likely to increase the sufferings of the middle passage.[121] The 1842 Select Committee on West Africa had become "in reality an inquiry into the slave trade." By the middle of the decade, criticism of the naval cruisers appeared frequently, focusing on the power of trade as a superior alternative to the power of violence.[122] The touch paper was finally lit by Hutt, a radical advocate of free trade, on 24 June 1845 when he introduced a parliamentary motion. The session ended before Foreign Secretary Lord Palmerston could respond, but the issue was clearly not going to disappear.[123] Both the sugar controversy and the subsequent enthusiasm for indentured labor gave opportunities for further attacks.[124]

In February 1848 Hutt won approval for a select committee to investigate the cruiser system and made no secret of the fact he considered it illegal, ineffective, and immoral.[125] His investigation spilled from one parliamentary session into the next, as the MPs heard evidence from a variety of witnesses—naval officers, missionaries, planters, Africans, traders, members of Parliament, and Palmerston himself.[126] After more than two years of hearings, on 19 March 1850 Hutt proposed a motion to sever all British treaty obligations that prevented the withdrawal of Britain's cruisers.[127] The cruisers, one writer noted, "were no longer seen as the executors of sound policy, but simply as the auxiliaries of the Anti-Slavery party"— which was to say, the cruisers seemed symbolic of the mindless activism attributed to abolitionist societies.[128] This association of suppression with impractical philanthropy was painfully ironic, given that the pacifist BFASS was opposed to the coercive system.

Prime Minister Palmerston and Foreign Secretary Russell robustly defended the coercive system against its critics (the "anti-coercionists"). They would contemplate improvements to the suppression system but not an end to it. Samuel Wilberforce initiated a separate House of Lords inquiry on this question designed to highlight the evidence that it could be modified successfully. James Bandinel, the recently retired head of the Slave Trade Department, expressed Britain's dilemma by suggesting that "the time has arrived at which it is desirable to consider whether any means, whether of force in addition to those that have been used, or whether gentler means in addition to force, or gentler means instead of force, should be used."[129] The report of two commissary judges posed the dilemma more starkly: "if the present system is not altered, this country has no alternative but retiring at once from the contest she has so long waged, baffled, beaten, and insulted by a set of lawless smugglers."[130]

At the most basic level, some experts thought that the ships of the naval squadron were not adequate for the task. This was sometimes expressed simply in a demand for a larger squadron; at other times there were more sophisticated suggestions to use new steamships.[131] Crucially, there was also debate over the policies and regulations governing suppression. Some critics, such as the abolitionist David Turnbull, thought that mercenary officers waited until slave ships were at sea to capture them because they got paid more for nautical rather than coastal interceptions.[132] There was also new interest in an international treaty between world powers to outlaw the slave trade. Piracy on the high seas was an offense under international law, but it did not include slave trading within its definition.[133] Moreover, the committees considered whether British ships should be distributed at the points of departure or arrival or both. Palmerston unsurprisingly defended the current strategy of stationing cruisers on both sides of the Atlantic but others differed.[134] Skeptics thought it was more disruptive to legitimate trade.[135]

The most eye-catching suggestion for new tactics was proposed, however, by Joseph Denman, a young naval officer who had served in the West Africa squadron. Like his father, the law lord Baron Denman, the sailor saw suppression as a national moral duty. Joseph Denman believed that the deployment of the cruisers miles off the coast of West Africa was a flaw in the whole operation.[136] While the ships sat at sea scouring the waves for their quarry, slave traders could load their cargoes and operate at the barracoons (slave forts) with impunity.[137] He hoped to secure permission from African chiefs to destroy the barracoons and strangle the slave trade at its point of origin rather than trying to intercept slavers on the open seas. Although Denman rejected accusations that officers deliberately allowed slaves to be embarked because of the bounties paid by Britain ("head money"), he admitted that the payment system should be reformed to prevent such an impression.[138] In order to provide the necessary ships, he proposed redeploying all the cruisers off Brazil to West Africa. As he explained in an 1843 memorandum, a coastal blockade to prevent slaves from being loaded aboard ships would be more effective and cause less suffering to them.[139]

Denman's manifesto for aggression was not merely theory; he had tried it in 1840, in the Gallinas River. Commanding a naval expedition hoping to rescue two British subjects, he had forced King Siacca and his son Prince Manna to sign an agreement banning the slave trade throughout their Gallinas demesne. With this legal necessity having been obtained (albeit under coercion), Denman burned down the barracoons of the Spanish slave-dealer John Buron. His business ruined, the Spaniard begged Denman for passage to London and was given it.[140] If the story seems slightly familiar, it should be. Five years later, in 1845, Commodore Jones burned down the homes of Manna's subjects in retribution for the violation of Denman's

treaty and the alleged abduction, once more, of British Sierra Leoneans
by slave traders. It is that attack that was captured by the painting on
this book's cover and in the prologue. Yet the two incidents had very different conclusions. Whereas Jones's actions were perfectly legal, Denman
found his policy—and himself—on trial in the intervening period. The immediate response to Denman's actions was positive: he was promoted, Parliament approved the payment of £4,000 to him and his men as a reward,
and he was praised by Palmerston. Despite this, Buron sued the young officer for destruction of his nonslave property in the barracoon.[141] Aberdeen, who had succeeded Palmerston at the Foreign Office, was advised
by the queen's advocate that Denman's actions "cannot be considered as
sanctioned by the law of nations or by the provisions of any existing treaties" that concerned Buron as a Spanish citizen.[142] The case was eventually
settled in 1848, when the judge in the case ruled that Denman could not be
sued personally for an act he undertook on behalf of Queen Victoria, which
the approval of Palmerston suggested he had.[143]

The ongoing trial did not stop officers such as Jones from attacking African communities—as he did in 1845—but they took care not to damage
the nonslave property stored in Europeans' barracoons.[144] Soon, Denman's
tactics were revived by Sir Charles Hotham, the squadron commander, but
James Bandinel, the Slave Trade Department's old chief, expressed skepticism that these tactics had led to a diminution in the slave trade from 1840–
41.[145] Denman claimed that legitimate commerce had briefly emerged after
he burned the slave factories, only to die with the revival of the slave trade
when news of the legal setback arrived in Africa.[146] For the Foreign Office,
Bandinel argued that the fluctuations in the slave trade were controlled
by numerous causes; he pointed to the welcome efforts of the Brazilians
in the same period to disrupt slaving operations. He disapproved of Denman's aggression within Africans' territory because it relied on the extor-
tion of permission to burn the slavers' forts on their land. This seemed to
be unduly antagonistic to a potential set of allies. Bandinel contemplated a
reformed role for the cruisers, as he had previously set out a decade earlier
in a Foreign Office memorandum. The old man's critique touched on two
of the main alternatives to force alone (or any force at all): his questions
about diplomacy and persuasion were at the heart of arguments to remove
the cruisers entirely.[147]

More broadly, anti-coercionists argued that the slave trade could only
be eliminated by slave-holding nations themselves.[148] The squadron assumed unilateral responsibility to police merchant shipping of all nations
under treaties that had often been conceded to Britain reluctantly. To Hutt
the current system was perfectly designed to promote the slave trade by
"enlisting the passions and prejudices, and even the national pride and

honour of all slave-trading countries in its defence." Lecturing other nations on morality and "interference out of our legitimate sphere of action"
would be a problem in itself, he maintained, but Britain with her cruisers
and treaty network did far worse.[149] Bright denounced coercion as Palmerston's "benevolent crotchet" because it was antagonistic to the emerging
laws of nations and hopes for international peace.[150] The cruisers, others
suggested, could take Britain to or beyond the brink of war.[151] It was often
said that Brazil and Cuba resisted acting against their own slave trade because the cruisers promoted the idea that abolition was a British economic
interest, not a humanitarian good.[152] Hutt suggested that any increase in
the importation of slaves would soon help those countries realize that the
slave trade was a danger to them. By this, he meant that fear of a slave rebellion on the lines of Haiti's would convince Brazilians and Cubans that
it was in their own interest to end their illegal slave trade.[153] Hutt bluntly
told the Commons in 1848 that "effeminate as they [Cubans] were, and
ignorant, the mere brutal instinct of self-preservation would warn them to
shun the fate of St. Domingo in 1795."[154]

These contending predictions of what would happen without the cruisers were accompanied by vigorous debate about how to measure the impact of the coercive system. At their most generous, critics suggested that
it merely displaced the trade from established ports to slaving dens, rather
than preventing it.[155] More brutally, some suggested it "aggravates the horrors it is intended to prevent."[156] Reduced space and reduced provision of
water for slaves in the middle passage were all seen as side-effects of the
furtive, underground slave trade.[157] Worst of all, there were suggestions
that cargoes of enslaved Africans were thrown overboard when a British
cruiser was sighted.[158] Skeptics even suggested that a higher mortality rate
stimulated a greater consumption of slaves, meaning that suppression of the
slave trade increased the number of enslaving wars within Africa.[159] Anti-
coercionists deployed these horrific stories using a rhetoric of sensibility
and empathy developed by the abolitionist campaigns before 1838.[160] Hutt
declared that "the shores and seas of Africa...were pouring forth human
blood like water, for an object which it was impossible for us to attain."[161]
He told MPs that all those who voted against withdrawal would become
"participators in the perpetration of the crime....Humanity never taught
such a system as this, and still less the Christian religion!"[162] The orthodox Foreign Office policy of anti-slavery through slave-trade suppression
found itself under attack with precisely the same emotive, humanitarian
language that had championed the destruction of British slave trading and
slavery.

Palmerston mounted a robust defence of the Royal Navy, denying that
mortality in the middle passage had grown and asserting that "the avarice

and covetousness of man was about the same at all times, and that there was the same disposition to crowd as many as possible within the space" as there had ever been.[163] Other defenders of the system argued, somewhat unconvincingly, that any such privations were mitigated by a shorter sailing time in smaller, faster boats that slave traders were increasingly adopting.[164] Yet these squabbles over facts stood beside a larger debate over the moral calculus of suppression. Lord Denman held that any such sufferings "flow from the master evil itself and are, for the most part, inseparable from it."[165] Speaking in 1846, Palmerston insisted that the cruisers brought "not only a great diminution in the number of the victims of the Slave Trade carried over to America; but also the condition of the slaves in the Brazils had been essentially improved."[166] His proposition was that fewer slaves were embarked and those that reached slavery in the New World were better treated on account of the higher price paid for them. In his view the "aggregate amount of human suffering" clearly had been diminished, and the cruisers had ameliorated the slave trade and slavery, even if they had not stopped them.[167]

Aside from the human costs, others questioned whether violence worked. The survival of the suppression policy depended on whether the British Parliament and people believed it could succeed. The core of the anti-coercionist case was that "there were not ten men out of Bedlam" who believed the policy could be effective in reducing or eliminating the slave trade.[168] A few defenders of the cruisers tried to claim that victory was just around the corner, but even Palmerston grew sanguine as the debate dragged on. He and other supporters of coercion felt surer arguing that the squadron had never been intended to destroy the trade entirely; the suppression of even more trafficking was a victory in itself.[169] The cruisers might not exterminate the slave trade alone, but by trying, with the right tactics, they would assist the spread of legitimate commerce and diplomacy with African peoples.[170] However, such promises did not impress anti-coercionists, who felt the cruisers had had their "fair trial." The *Daily News* compared all excuses to utopian Robert Owen's defense of his experimental, failed socialist communities.[171] For Richard Cobden, "the signal failure of the *diabolical* means resorted to for putting down the slave trade abroad" proved "the great principles of peace, & the supremacy of moral over material forces."[172]

The national suppression project aroused such passion because of the costs both sides associated with its maintenance or destruction. Service in the West Africa squadron was one of the navy's most deadly tours.[173] The level of national expenditure was highly controversial at a time of domestic social anxiety and state retrenchment. Commentators doubted that Russell could wrestle with both the budget deficit and the transatlantic slave trade at once.[174] However, Palmerston maintained it would be a crime to let "the mean calculation of a temporary saving" prevent Britain from confining the trade to "infinitely narrower limits than those within which it is presently contained."[175] Here was a moral economy of sacrifice: a painful price was required (in money and blood) to honor Britain's duty and secure future glory.

This was no simple party struggle. Disagreement over the value of naval coercion stemmed from two very different understandings of what drove demand in the Atlantic slave trade. For the coercionists, the supply could be effectively choked off by the cruisers; it followed that withdrawal would lead to many slave voyages and a huge expansion of slave labor in Brazil.[176] As Britain possessed no viable means to attack slave-holding within foreign countries, only the Atlantic sources of supply could be attacked.[177] Anti-coercionists imagined a very different model of demand behind the slave trade. They argued that "the demand for slaves will always create a supply" and that the goal of stopping trafficking was hopeless as long as the market for slaves existed.[178] If the slave trade was inevitable, it seemed most logical to permit the trade to resume unimpeded and startle Brazilians and Cubans into terror at the resulting likelihood of servile war.[179] This was the moral economy of laissez-faire, which trusted that moral outcomes would follow from the uninterrupted operation of markets. These two theories, implicit in the arguments of the most extreme partisans of each side, were the axis on which the question of coercion turned.

The debate over slave-trade suppression saw more attention given to Britain's relationship with African peoples. Men such as William Smith, a former commissary judge at Sierra Leone, thought that African leaders could be bribed with subsidies and the promise of more valuable "legitimate" trade with Britain to stop supplying Europeans with slaves. This would require only a small fleet to protect the new commerce, it would save much of the cost of the cruiser system, and it would develop new markets for British traders.[180] However, the promise of greater trade with the indigenous societies of Africa was not an aspiration for anti-coercionists alone. Both sides could agree that the slave trade and trade in nonslave goods were natural enemies, the one increasing at the expense of the other.[181] Trade would give economic value to the free labor of Africans who otherwise would be sold as slaves. Where the two sides differed is in how they saw the cruisers interacting with legitimate trade in Africa.

Proponents of pacifism thought that the slave trade could be quickly routed "if the government of this country would go hand in hand with the mercantile enterprise of this country."[182] Palmerston agreed with the premise but differed on the method, believing that "as legitimate commerce spreads and increases, you will find the disposition to slave trade to diminish, especially if the legitimate commerce is protected, and if the slave trade is impeded by the means which are now in force." Removing the cruisers entirely would mean "an end to security for legitimate trade."[183] Witnesses to the select committees differed on how many of the warships would be required simply to protect commerce. The same number of cruisers would be required to protect British traders as were needed by the current suppression system, its defenders argued.[184]

By this logic, military suppression of the slave trade was the first step; the cruisers were a tourniquet without which commerce could not stanch the trade in slaves.[185] By contrast, anti-coercionists thought suppression a false remedy proposed by quacks. They claimed that the cruisers' violence actually retarded the growth of free commerce with Africa. Witnesses to Hutt's committee testified that Denman's barracoon-burning antics had led to chaos in the Gallinas region, disrupting legitimate trade more than the slave trade.[186] Some, such as Tory parliamentarian Bingham Baring, argued that a predictable, regular export market of slaves would establish a consistent price, free of fluctuations, and thus leave the value of other goods in Africa more stable. From his point of view, coercion was creating chaos in an otherwise ordered market and helping disrupt the natural death of slaving.[187] More commonly, British traders objected violently to the difficulties they had trading when they were liable to regular detection and inspection by suspicious naval patrols.[188]

Palmerston and Russell, defending coercion to their own party as well as to Parliament and the nation, adopted the promotion of trade as their main argument.[189] At a meeting of the Whig Liberals in Downing Street, Palmerston and Russell—who made Hutt's motion a question of confidence in his premiership—said that only commerce could suppress the slave trade but that coercion would give it the opportunity to do so.[190] This was a canny move by the ministry: they swapped their weakest suit for their opponents' trump. Such concerns had been Slave Trade Department policy since at least 1838 but they were rarely emphasized in defending the cruisers' specific role. One of the main outcomes of the suppression crisis was a renewed focus on commerce as an instrument of anti-slavery and civilization in Africa.

Because he coordinated the campaign, it was closely linked to Hutt's radical free-trade and commercial interests. In fact, the anti-coercionists represented a broad range of opinion.[191] Some supporters of the Whig government probably suppressed their preference for withdrawal in the interest of political tactics. In the crucial March 1850 vote—the high point of "anti-coercionism"—the anti-coercionists registered 154 votes to the government's 263.[192] Some, like Hutt, Cobden, and Bright, were true apostles of laissez-faire, but only a minority of free-trade Liberals and Peelites supported withdrawal of the cruisers in the decisive 1850 vote.

Hutt's motion of 1850 was seconded by Henry Baillie, a Tory protectionist whose speech emphasized the loss of the sugar duties.[193] More than half of the votes for withdrawal of the cruisers came from Tory protectionists.[194] Traditional champions of the West Indian interest, like Grantley Berkeley, thought that Britain was supporting a white elephant when protection offered "the most effectual, the most religious, the most moral way for putting an end to the slave trade."[195] The laissez-faire leaders of anti-coercion, often the greatest proponents of the free trade in sugar in 1846, were happy to set aside such antipathies if it brought them allies against the cruiser system.[196] A significant number of Tory protectionists saw political advantage in defeating Russell's ministry on an issue that he had declared to be a matter of confidence and on a policy he promoted as a necessary complement to a free trade in sugar.[197]

The relationship between political views on coercion and protection was complex, as demonstrated during an unsuccessful attempt to reinstate preferential duties for British sugar just two months after Hutt's motion failed. Only a handful of MPs accepted the most extreme laissez-faire combination of free trade and pacifism. Of those who repealed protection for sugar, a large majority endorsed naval coercion.[198] Although these figures are somewhat deceptive, given that the cruiser vote became one of confidence in the ministry, they nevertheless show that liberal orthodoxy refused to trust that global emancipation would be the result of a free trade in slaves as well as a free trade in sugar. The question of military suppression reinforced the messy balkanization of anti-slavery politics that had unfolded during the sugar debates.

The BFASS petitioned Parliament in 1845, stating that "it is felt, not only by those who object by principle to the use of an armed force, but by the public generally, to be impracticable to suppress it [the slave trade] by such means."[199] By contrast, George Stephen, an abolitionist supporter of coercion, complained that "the Peace Society rules paramount in the councils of the self-styled champions of the Negro."[200] The increasingly fractious nature of the issue led the BFASS to distance itself from Hutt. Ironically, this meant that an anti-slavery free trader such as Cobden complained "that the Anti Slavery peace party do not sufficiently disavow such unholy measures" as naval suppression; they should repudiate "the *devils* [sic] instruments over the world."[201]

Ideology divided not just abolitionists but the planters of the West Indian colonies too. Commissary judge David Turnbull and the bishop of Jamaica coordinated a series of public meetings in Spanish Town to support the suppression system. This "Jamaica Movement" publicly lobbied for more effective enforcement of the treaty network, with petitions presented to the upper and lower houses of Parliament by Samuel Wilberforce and

Palmerston, respectively.[202] Although the colonists grumbled that protection should be restored, they had no desire to see the navy withdrawn from its campaign, as they expected suppression to undermine their slave-buying competitors.[203] Many of those West Indians who supported the cruisers reserved their greatest venom for anti-coercionists, such as Milner Gibson and Cobden, who had also been so keen on removing protection.[204] In his 1850 speech supporting the Whigs over the squadron, Tory evangelical MP Sir Robert Inglis did not refrain from censuring "their unhappy measure" of 1846 and supporting the Jamaica Movement in their hopes to revive the duties as well as the coercive system.[205]

In contradiction to this, Baillie and other protectionists believed that without the duties suppression served only as the façade of morality when, in reality, the nation had become a receiver of stolen goods. He said, with some malice, that consistency required Britain to "announce and declare to the nations of the world that in England free trade was at length triumphant and that the slave trade must proceed."[206] A reporter for the *Christian Reformer* chided free traders' "faith in their favourite principle, that if they will have patience with it, it will pay them all," while agreeing that "the ill success of our crusade against slave-ships confirms the truth, that Satan cannot cast out Satan, and that cruelty cannot be put down by violence."[207] *Punch* was similarly cynical of the Whigs' free-trade-and-suppression policy in a mocking poem about the slave trade:

> *If I mean that it should cease, I must renounce my toothsome sin,*
> *Resolv'd from this time forth to take no slave-grown sugar in.*
> *But I can't resign cheap sugar; so I'll keep up my blockade,*
> *For appearance sake—by way of demonstration and parade.*[208]

Despite this vitriol and the disquiet of many of their own MPs, Russell and Palmerston won their gamble and saved both their careers and the cruiser system. By threatening resignation, the pair bludgeoned their supporters, but by emphasizing a greater role for commerce Palmerston gave MPs a reason to claim they had won concessions and had not put party loyalty over humanitarian concern. Hutt's defeat marked the high watermark of anti-coercionism. Afterward, some newspapers predicted that a fatal wound had been inflicted and that the cruisers would be withdrawn yet.[209] But just three years later a new select committee concluded that the suppression system was working and, in 1858, another anti-coercionist motion was defeated by a vote of 223 to 24. The change cannot simply be explained by partisan tactical voting in 1850. In Parliament and among the public, opinion had clearly shifted.

The intervening factor in those years had been the collapse of the slave trade to Brazil. In the midst of the 1850 crisis of coercion, Russell's ministry had begun to plot a new offensive against Brazil, one of the last significant destinations for the Atlantic slave trade.[210] Shortly after the 1850 vote, British cruisers were authorized to enter Brazilian territorial waters in order to suppress the slavers.[211] Brazil's government, affronted by this violation of national sovereignty, reacted with new measures to enforce, for the first time, their own abolition of the slave trade—which had been a dead letter since it passed in November 1831. By the end of the year British aggression had, seemingly, secured Rio's own assumption of responsibility.[212] The motives for Brazilian enforcement of abolition were much more complex, including disparate domestic political questions, but, in Britain, this was reported as a triumph for Palmerston's cruiser system.[213] However mistaken the causal connection, Brazilian abolition saw the number of enslaved Africans taken across the Atlantic halved by the end of 1850. Beyond the political ruminations in Great Britain, policy over sugar or diplomacy over suppression could unleash or restrain untold misery for thousands of Africans.[214]

Opposition to the cruisers almost vanished as these results became clear, suggesting that it was faith in methods—rather than a broader suspicion of anti-slavery sacrifice—that had been tested by the parliamentary wrangling. The Whigs, in the intervening period, looked like free-trader patrons of the slave-sugar industry. For a brief period around 1850, champions of free trade, protection, pacifism, pessimism, and sensibility had found common cause in Hutt's opposition to the cruisers. As one contemporary observed, "Whigs and Conservatives, West Indians and Abolitionists, Free-traders and Protectionists, have all become jumbled and jolted together."[215] This unholy coalition did not last. A number of those who voted with Hutt in 1850 could not sustain their hostility after Palmerston's Brazilian escapades, seeing events as "the most complete vindication" for the government position. The twenty-four MPs who voted for withdrawal in 1858 were a lonely rump of laissez-faire ideologues, unmoved by events.[216]

Nonetheless, the midcentury crisis of suppression can be interpreted as proof that anti-slavery sentiment was waning or at least in conflict with newer pressures. Historians have largely sided with the Whig leadership, seeing interventionism to be the only authentic voice of "antislave-trade policy" rather than a particular brand of it.[217] At the most extreme, one saw Hutt's crusade against the cruisers as part of a new "crypto-fascist" Victorian racism.[218] However, as the anti-coercionist *Manchester Examiner* maintained at the time, "there is nothing in dispute amongst us, but the question as to the most effective way of attaining the desired end."[219]

Similarly, the *Leeds Mercury* declared that "there are good, philanthropic, and very able men on both sides" of the conflict.[220] Alongside the dramatic abuse hurled in this debate, both sides offered coherent claims to being the champions of anti-slavery.

Advocates of withdrawal could only prosper by selling their policy as a surer scourge of global slavery than Palmerston's quackery. Hutt protested that he and his allies would "not...conceive that if the use of force is to be abandoned, it therefore follows that Great Britain is to become neutral or indifferent with respect to the slave trade."[221] In the heat of the 1850 debate, Palmerston accused Hutt of wishing to see Britain sanction and support a regulated slave trade to Brazil during a private discussion between the men at the Foreign Office. It seems likely that Hutt discussed schemes such as this, but he was adamant in the House of Commons that he had never contemplated accommodation with the slave trade.[222] Whereas indentured emigration from West Africa to British colonies, Brazil, and Cuba was politically acceptable, Hutt knew his cause would be fatally undermined by accusations of reviving the slave trade. Although advocates and opponents of such plans squabbled over which schemes were cloaks for the slave trade, the binary distinction between contract labor and forced labor stood largely unchallenged.[223]

Hutt may well have been indifferent to the evils of the slave trade, but if he was then it is telling that he would never admit this in open debate.[224] In 1845, he attacked expenditure on Africans in general, rather than the cruisers in particular; he dropped this theme in later debates. Yet even at his most reactionary, he said that "I am no apologist for the Slave Trade. I regard it as an appalling crime.... But I contend that we cannot, without culpable neglect of nearer and higher duties, assume the task of extirpating the crime from among all other people, or patrolling the world to put it down."[225] As in the sugar debates, British politicians could debate the realities and methods of anti-slavery policy, but they had to do so by selling their solutions as the most likely means of opposing global slavery.

## FREE LABOR AND WORLD POWER

By the 1850s Great Britain had partially resolved these debates over the limits to which laissez-faire could be applied to anti-slavery. Skepticism about the effects of state intervention, tariff barriers, violence, and government expenditure were entirely in keeping with the currents of midcentury social thought. National enmity to slavery expressed itself in varieties pacifist, interventionist, passionate, pretended, protectionist, and free trade. As David Eltis observes, "it was not that the British commitment to abolition was weakening, but rather that abolitionism itself was much less focused than it had been."[226] Different interpretations of economic morality—founded in very different systems of belief—divided anti-slavery Britain over the course it should pursue. By 1850, Palmerston and Russell's desperate faith in naval suppression reflected their fear that free trade had, indeed, spurred the theft of Africans by slave traders; modern research confirms that this was the case in Brazil but not in Cuba.[227] Exactly how much free trade intensified the decline of British sugar production is a matter for debate among economic historians today; Philip Curtin suggests that the old duties would not have insulated planters from the long-term collapse in the price of their crop.[228] At the time, impressions of the policies' results tended to reflect assumptions within the debates.

Moreover, the clashes over free trade and slave-trade suppression may have split opinion along laissez-faire or interventionist lines, but, more subtly, they created new orthodoxies. Politicians on both sides of the sugar debate embraced derogatory stereotypes of West Indian blacks and the consequent need for indentured labor to create wage competition. Similarly, Hutt's challenge to the cruiser system focused new attention on the promotion of British commerce in Africa—whether as an augmentation or replacement for naval force. It was not inevitable that indentured labor emigration and the economic "improvement" of Africa would be adopted by mainstream British opinion as pillars of anti-slavery policy. Russell, Palmerston, and the Whigs chose to embrace and adopt elements of their opponents' attack in order to help them win the immediate conflict. Forged in the heat of battle, these newly shared assumptions would shape the future of anti-slavery politics, the expansion of the British Empire, and the fate of the African continent. There was still plenty of room for conflict over the best way of moving a colonial workforce within the British colonies or the best way to "civilize" and develop trade with Africa, but critics were muted.

Despite differences over method, did Victorian Britons expect their country to gain or lose from its enmity to slavery? The answer to this question must lie in attitudes toward free labor and its connection to British world power. The British West Indies embarrassingly declined in economic output in the decades following the abolitions of first slavery and then the sugar monopoly. Yet this did not necessarily shake British faith that slavery was wrong and—on some level—unrewarding. By 1859 Anthony Trollope had adopted an ambiguous, resigned attitude to the state of the Caribbean colonies. What had happened to the British sugar plantations was tragic, but he could not bring himself to criticize either emancipation or the end of protection.[229] "Abolition of slavery is good, and free trade is good. Such little insight as a plain man may have into the affairs around him seem to me to suffice for the expression of such opinion." Trollope thought that,

like the hand-loom weavers, the planters had sadly found that their interests stood in the way of national progress and they were hence ruined.[230]

Historian Seymour Drescher is right to write of an abandoned faith in
the West Indian experiment of free labor by the 1860s, but even as hopes for
the prosperity of the sugar colonies dwindled, faith in Britain's anti-slavery
principles did not. New variables were admitted to explain how slave labor
could enjoy superior production when the labor supply was restricted and
there was a limitless supply of fresh soil.[231] This was a bastardized form of
free-labor ideology, locating the material superiority of wage labor beyond
productive output. For many thinkers, the risk of slave insurrections, the
way slavery corrupted an entire nation's values, and slave monocultures'
inevitable exhaustion of soil all still pointed to the wisdom of Britain's
example in making a peaceful transition away from slave-holding. Anti-
slavery was still identified with the historical forces of progress, morality,
and civilization, but not necessarily with immediate economic gratification.
The protectionists were defeated over the sugar duties, but it was a Pyrrhic
victory for them: free-trading liberals came to adopt their view that free
labor could outperform slave labor only if there was a sufficient supply of
low-paid workers. In other words, faith in the universal, consistent superiority of wage labor was tempered and refined.[232] The free trader James
Stirling struggled to square the example of Jamaica with his predictions
for the United States. Looking to the West Indies, he accepted that there
was "less sugar and rum produced than before; and if the end of human
existence were the production of rum and molasses the argument would
be triumphant. But this is not a question of rum, but right and wrong."
Although the "indolence of the free negroes of the British Colonies is to be
regretted," he believed that "no ruin...could cloud the glory of that great
act of national justice." He therefore grasped for economic signs that free
labor would turn out better in the long run.[233]

The triumph of free labor and the demise of global slavery were still
understood as inevitable. Providence, in the form of social externalities and
divine mission, was co-opted by political economists to square the circle of
free trade and slave labor. John Stuart Mill believed that slavery may sometimes be more profitable for individual planters, but it stifled innovation
and moral sentiment in the longer term.[234] More than a decade after the
sugar duties act, his acolyte John Elliott Cairnes accepted that the sugar
colonies' transition to freedom had largely failed economically in the West
Indies, but he was still certain that Britain had set a good example for any
society. Indeed, he saw the short-term superiority of slave labor as self-
defeating because its productivity was based on exhaustion of the soil.
"Wherever a few staples are raised on large plantations by gangs of slaves
for the export market," he argued, "there the cheap labour of Africa has

always been found to be economically profitable; and, where it has not been artificially excluded, has always, in fact, been employed."[235] When an economic thinker such as Cairnes came to abandon traditional free-labor ideology and to abandon hope of the West Indies' productivity returning, he did not regret emancipation or ascribe it to the end of protection. He accepted West Indian decline as a sad inevitability, but one that invalidated neither anti-slavery virtue nor free-trade ideology.[236] Thomas Ellison, a statistician and economist who worked closely with the cotton industry, espoused similar views in his 1861 *Slavery and Secession in America*. He argued that slavery was artificially more productive than free labor in certain circumstances, but that it was unsustainable given its vulnerability to slave insurrection and soil exhaustion.[237] Mill, Cairnes, and Ellison located the advantages of free labor in other places than eternal market superiority, and they still believed a free world could be happier and more prosperous than global systems of slavery.

In his speech rejecting Hutt's motion of 1850, Russell showed that his own views about slavery, morality, and economics had evolved since the Sugar Duties Act four years earlier. Predicting that withdrawal of the cruisers would ensure that "we have no longer a right to expect a continuance of those blessings which, by God's favour, we have so long enjoyed," Russell ultimately relied on providential duty—and the violent blockade of slave trading—to prove free labor superior. He argued that the expense of the West Africa cruisers was justified because "the high, the moral, and the Christian character of this nation, is the main source and secret of its strength." The Whig prime minister saw the suppression of the slave trade as a national interest that trumped any financial interests; withdrawing the cruisers would be ungodly and hence a false economy.[238] On this occasion, Russell was a pugilist in an ideological conflict, using providential language to defend his anti-slavery policies. But his opponents, who expected that the slave trade would be ended only through completely contrary means to those supported by Russell, would have at least shared his presumption that British interests and anti-slavery were interwoven. Regardless of whether anti-slavery required state intervention or state abstinence in global commerce or the illegal slave trade, the British people and the wider world would benefit from the collapse of slavery.

One MP, who supported free trade, maintained that it was "unjust to say, that because in a certain state of civilisation slavery was improper, we should not hold any intercourse with countries which under other circumstances were compelled to admit the continuance of such a state of society." This argument in favor of commerce with slave-holding countries was naturally contested. However, even opponents would have agreed with his assertion that in "the history of the world, it would be impossible to deny that there had been any nation, which in the course of its rise from barbarianism to civilisation, had not passed through a condition of things, wherein a great mass of her population were exposed to slavery."[239] Victorian Britons divided on the question of *how* other nations would best be encouraged to make this destined transition, not on whether it would or should come.[240]

Britain's eager importation of sugar and cotton from the slave plantations of the New World seemed, to American slaveholders, like a repudiation of faith in free labor. They and we may wonder whether Britons' enthusiasm for anti-slavery abroad might have waned thanks to this dependency. On the contrary, addiction to slave-grown Southern cotton made Britain more, not less, anxious to see emancipation in the United States. Slavery might have proven profitable, but it would not prove stable. The cotton industry and the Foreign Office therefore sought to find new, free-labor sources of cotton.[241] Anxieties were born from fears about the sustainability of slave cultivation: "The Englishman's hopes are mortgaged. He stands or falls by—cotton!" Although one journalist denied in 1851 that American emancipation would happen any time soon, he still predicted that "assuredly the day will come when this dismal system will terminate. A sudden conjecture of circumstances might instantly shatter it to pieces." He did not think the "failure in the free labour of the West Indian negroes" contradicted his analysis; rather, it made the search for sufficient free-labor supplies of cotton more desirable, since America's exports would suddenly be reduced when (not if) slavery was disrupted or dissolved.[242] In 1857, Viscount Goderich, a radical Liberal, was given an identical interpretation by his American informant, the journalist William Henry Hulbert. Precisely because the British economy relied on Southern cotton, Hulbert argued, it had to hope for emancipation in the United States.[243]

Mill thought there was "disinterestedness," not "selfish purpose," in British emancipation, even if, when working "to procure the abandonment of some national crime and scandal to humanity, such as the slave-trade," foreigners "believe that we have always other objects than those we avow." He noted that "when we taxed ourselves twenty millions…to get rid of negro slavery, and for the same object periled, as everybody thought,—destroyed, as many thought,—the very existence of our West-Indian colonies, it was, and still is, believed [by foreigners], that our fine professions were but to delude the world; and that by this self-sacrificing behaviour we were endeavouring to gain some hidden object, which could neither be conceived nor described, in the way of pulling down other nations." In order to demonstrate the nature of Britain's commitment to free labour, Mill deployed a fable: "The fox who had lost his tail had an intelligible interest in persuading his neighbours to rid themselves of theirs; but we, it is thought by our neighbours, cut off our own magnificent brush, the largest and finest of all, in hopes of reaping some inexplicable advantage from inducing others to do the same."[244] He denied that anti-slavery would mean "pulling down other nations" even if he characterized emancipation as "self-sacrificing behaviour." The paradox was resolved by the fact that there *was* "some hidden object," but one Mill expected to enrich the whole of mankind, rather than to "pull down" rival empires and economies. He believed that Britain, in foreign affairs, bore the costs of upholding civilization, but "the fruits it shares in fraternal equality with the whole human race."[245] On one level, this was self-satisfied patriotism. Yet Mill was hoping to shape domestic opinion in a contentious debate over foreign policy, so his real purpose was to harness this example to his more contentious claims about British meddling in other cases.[246]

Economists, politicians, and journalists doubtlessly differed on the exact mechanics or means through which slavery would reveal its inferiority. In many cases, not least Mill's, they accepted that anti-slavery would require sacrifices and create immediate difficulties. Whether through market laws or providential judgment, they believed that free labor would prove superior to slavery, not only for souls judged in the next world but for nations tested in this one. This assumption was broadly shared, so debates pivoted on the reasons and methods by which free labor would prove itself better than slavery. Curiously, British faith in the morality *and* prosperity of anti-slavery policy survived orthodox faith in free labor's productivity. The superiority of free labor could be relocated outside of the marketplace, permitting the broader belief to survive the disenchantment of a particular tenet. Hence, as one British statesman put it in 1848, "slave labour, in spite of its apparent cheapness, was really less efficient and more costly than free labour."[247]

Attempts to break Britain's addiction to slave-grown cotton would meet with success only during America's Civil War, when Southern cotton briefly disappeared from the market. Although the exact circumstances of that conflict and Lincoln's wartime emancipation of Southern slaves could not have been predicted, the war was the kind of violent conflagration that Britons had long feared.[248] Britain's anti-slavery mission, despite faltering faith in the productive superiority of free labor, took new urgency from the nation's dependency on the products of slavery. Modern parallels might be drawn with Western reliance on oil from politically unstable regions or the dangers of running nuclear power stations in unsafe conditions, where short-term productivity gains may be reckless given the likelihood of future catastrophe. Although dependency on slave cotton created concerns for a peaceful and gradual end to slavery, it remained impossible to defend slavery as a positive good simply on the basis of this dependency.[249]

Although Britons argued over how much and how the state could undermine foreign slavery, they broadly agreed that British prosperity was ultimately aligned with anti-slavery. Conversely, the empire's championship of anti-slavery civilization meant that the prosperity of Britain and the progress of the world were bound tightly together. In 1858, Palmerston defended the pressure that had been put upon the Brazilian people in the past two decades, believing that British policy promoting suppression, "so far from injuring the people of that country, has conferred upon them invaluable benefits" and economic development.[250] Although there were fierce political debates about the right sort of trade policy, Palmerston was not alone in believing that British economic development would benefit the rest of the world morally and economically.

His triumphant defence of his cruisers policy in 1858 drew on providential promises of reward for these ends. He admitted that MPs should not lecture each other on "religious questions" because "our sphere is politics—our sphere is commerce—our sphere embraces simply matters of national interest." Yet, Palmerston said,

> there are occasions on which higher considerations than those ought to be impressed on the minds of the Members of this House and the country...it is a curious coincidence—though there may be no real connection between the two—that from the time when this country first began to abolish the slave trade, followed up by abolishing slavery within the dominions of the Crown, and to use its influence for the suppression of the slave trade elsewhere,—from that period this country has prospered in a degree which it never experienced before.

He went on to predict that "if the English nation were now to recede from its high position...I think it is not assuming too much of the functions of a prophet to say that the crime would be visited on the people of this country in a manner which would lead them to repent."[251] Despite his reluctance to debate theology in the House of Commons, Palmerston was happy to yoke providentialism to his expectations that national interest and national commerce were intimately connected to slave-trade suppression.[252] Indeed, he had used very similar terms in a private memorandum of 1844 to the French foreign minister François Guizot: providence may mean that by conceding the right of search Britain and France "would not find themselves less well off, even with Respect to their most worldly Interests."[253]

By defending the naval system in these terms, Palmerston was happy to present the expansion of British trade and the suppression policy as actions of national interest as well as national duty.[254] An 1872 article in the *Quarterly Review* offered an important development of this view. The author argued that, having suppressed the transatlantic slave trade in the past decade, Britain should repeat its success in East Africa, where an Indian Ocean slave trade was flourishing. If the British Empire did not use its immense power for good then it would decline, like the decadent Roman Empire of Gibbon's history. This precedent showed that "the peculiar danger of a high and general civilization is, that selfishness should eat out the cement of society, whilst luxury, like some wasting rot, saps the strength of its foundation-stones." Redemption, he explained, required "the noble warfare of bringing moral force to bear upon nations who are below us in religion, morality, and civilization." This meant British commerce, naval suppression, and forceful diplomacy with the peoples of East Africa.[255] The author did not speak for all Britons in his specific prescription, but his faith in anti-slavery as a mark and guarantee of British civilization would have surprised few readers. Neither they nor he knew, in 1872, that the next three decades would see "the noble warfare" of "moral force" take shape in an anti-slavery imperialism of physical force. There would be little that was noble or moral about the results.

# 6

## Africa Burning

THE RELATIONSHIP between anti-slavery and British imperial power was complex.[1] Before 1838, anti-slavery campaigning promoted imperial morality, reforming governance in the empire. After West Indian emancipation, this impulse contributed to a moral imperialism, a forceful quest that pried into societies across the globe.[2] With British slave-trade suppression on the west and east coasts of Africa came racial contempt and massive territorial expansion across the continent in the last quarter of the nineteenth century. Victorian sentiment against slavery could be used to fuel both expansionist and anti-expansionist politics, but the former proved to be a dominant interpretation of anti-slavery and the latter recessive.

British territorial ambitions in Africa developed after the abolition of slavery in the empire, not before, and this may seem counterintuitive. However, Britain's role in the "scramble for Africa" at the end of the nineteenth century was strongly influenced by anti-slavery traditions, not by a straightforward rejection or betrayal of them. The story of British imperialism would be much simpler if anti-slavery arguments provided convenient propaganda for domestic audiences or cultural capital for racist paternalism. Instead, imperialists used anti-slavery ideas not as a humanitarian shield but as the core basis of their greed. In the complex judgments behind empire, politicians, capitalists, and the public favoring expansion into Africa formed their expectations, ideas, and assumptions from anti-slavery traditions. Many of the economic and political calculations for expansion drew on anti-slavery ideologies, and many of the opportunities or crises prompting expansion arose thanks to anti-slavery commitments.[3] Indeed, free-labor expectations were one of the few impulses that could override the powerful case for the British ignoring

West Africa in the first three quarters of the nineteenth century.[4] Anti-slavery traditions helped to translate private interest and personal ambitions into national interest and patriotic duty—the latter were vital in deciding when military or political intervention should assist missionary or commercial ambitions.[5] Anti-slavery was by no means the sole ingredient of British imperial expansion, but without it the directions and consequences of economic or strategic designs would have been unimaginably different. In Africa, the Victorians' "aggressively interventionist ideology" can best be explained by understanding the "obsessional hostility to the slave trade."[6] This "moral imperialism" drew British attention to the continent during a period when the decline of the slave trade had destabilized traditional social and governance systems, creating opportunities and motives for European acquisition.[7]

Most Britons would not have imagined anti-slavery as a purely colonial issue, given its wider connection with foreign affairs, but that makes the moral ambiguities of this heritage all the more fascinating.[8] Contemporaries were afraid that anti-slavery designs in Africa would rouse "the jealousy of all the other nations of the world" who would doubt "that we go there principally for the purpose of suppressing the slave trade."[9] It is easy for historians to dismiss that purpose too. However, anti-slavery was nothing as simple as an *excuse* for the rise of British formal imperialism in Africa.[10] British anti-slavery was not simply "an integral part of an ideological package which justified the subjugation of colonial peoples and the reorganization of their social, economic, and religious structures," as historian Suzanne Miers terms it, but the motive for those interventions.[11]

Anti-slavery sentiment did not operate as some sort of monolith, succeeding or failing to curb the territorial expansion of empire. Britons overseas did not simply encounter different circumstances; they did so with very varied expectations of how anti-slavery should be advanced in practice. The diverse cultures of African societies, not to mention Africans' diverse political reactions and choices, created challenges or opportunities for any Briton advancing anti-slavery interests, even if there had been full agreement on what those interests were. Just as "missionary enterprise" encompassed a range of theological perspectives, local circumstances, political situations, and African reactions, so did "anti-slavery enterprise." Sincere anti-slavery politics acted as "agent, scribe and moral alibi" for British imperial aggression, while performing the same services for anti-imperialist critics of expansion or exploitation.[12] It is a mistake to deny that anti-slavery created and defined imperial as well as anti-imperial interests, just as it is to deny that humanitarianism often combined with self-interest in prestige, wealth, or salvation.

Britain's role as international policeman took on different forms of imperial exertion, forcibly attempting to set right the conscience of the world.

Anti-slavery ideas directly influenced the nature and shape of the British Empire, often in surprising ways. This can be traced in the suppression of the transatlantic slave trade, which framed British policy toward Africa in the period before 1874. We can then examine British participation in the European invasion of African territory in the last quarter of the century to understand why territorial expansion proved quite compatible with anti-slavery politics. (British attitudes toward coercion, race, and labor within imperial territories are treated in the following chapter.) To study these episodes, however, means starting with an analysis of British ideas about "the land of bondage," as one children's book called it in 1854, and why it stood for "ignorance, darkness, and slavery" in contrast to Europe's "learning, and light, and liberty."[13]

## IMPROVEMENT AND THE SLAVE TRADE

The slave trade and slavery defined British contact with African peoples in the crucial decades after 1830. As historian Philip Curtin suggests, "endless negotiations" over slave trade suppression were "the only source of sustained interest keeping West Africa before the British public and parliament" until 1860.[14] Suppression of the slave trade was commonly seen as intimately connected with the development of trade and civilization, though politicians differed over the order they would come in. Bureaucratic arrangements within the state further underlined the relationship between anti-slavery and African policy. Before 1884, all sub-Saharan African affairs were handled by the Slave Trade Department. African and anti-slavery matters were also treated as identical by various select committee inquiries during this period. The 1842 inquiry into possessions on the west coast of Africa was spurred by panic over alleged British complicity in the slave trade and how it might be stopped. A central object of the subsequent 1865 committee was to assess the West African colonies' functions in suppressing the slave trade. In 1848–50, 1853, and 1863, select committees on the suppression of the slave trade assumed that all questions of African policy were pertinent to their remit. They were understood by one contemporary to have covered "the moral and physical character of the various African nations; the progress of Sierra Leone as a colony; the relative slave mortality of the former and the present system of Slave-trading; the nature and value of African produce; *cum multis aliis*."[15] The same pattern would be repeated for the east coast from the 1870s onward.

A tradition of anti-slavery plans for the "improvement" of the continent shaped understandings of African politics, economics, and society.[16] Abolitionist interest in Africa dated back to the earliest criticism of the slave trade itself; the improvement of Africa was expected to overlap with the solution to slave trading since legitimate trade would replace slave dealing in local economies.[17] When Thomas Fowell Buxton developed his plan for a Niger expedition in the wake of West Indian emancipation, he drew on these older schemes.[18] Having privately detailed his plans to the Whig cabinet in 1838, he revised them for publication as *The African Slave Trade* and *The Remedy* in 1839–40 (subsequently republished together in one-volume editions).[19] Buxton stated the connection between the expansion of "legitimate" commerce and the slave trade simply: "Is it not possible for us to undersell the slave-dealer, and to drive him out of the market, by offering more for the productions of the soil than he ever gave for the bodies of the inhabitants?"[20] Like others, he quoted Edmund Burke's assertion that "to deal and traffic—not in the labour of men, but in men themselves—is to devour the root, instead of enjoying the fruit of human diligence."[21] However, "improvers" differed over how Africa could be weaned off the root and onto the fruit. For Buxton, trade with Africa was the great medicine that could put down the slave trade and allow African civilization to spring forth.[22]

For others, such as missionary David Livingstone and trader Macgregor Laird, the slave traffic had to be suppressed by other means before the development of Africa could begin.[23] There were important differences between models of development that can be explored by examining, in turn, attitudes toward religion, trade, and the role of the state. The disagreements among various authors and authorities were reflected in political debates.

Buxton shared with many other writers an assumption that the slave trade had artificially stopped normal historical progress in Africa, creating chaos and tumult unsuitable to civilization and development. Different plans for improvement shared this diagnosis of Africans' problems without agreeing on the relationship between slavery, "barbarity," and "heathenism."[24] Buxton's own faith doubtlessly guided him in his work, but his cultivation of missionary enthusiasm for his expedition was largely pragmatic; his actual plans did not reflect his rhetorical focus on the need for Christianity to "shed her light upon the tenfold darkness of Africa."[25] The advance of Christianity might be a positive side-effect of civilizing measures, such as the suppression of the slave trade, rather than being itself an engine of historical change.[26]

Missionaries varied wildly in their response to imperial power and commercial expansion in Africa. Enthusiasm for the rhetorical pairing of "Christianity and commerce" left open the question of which would be the cause and which the effect. The attitude of missionaries toward particular improvement plans was therefore rather mixed, even if they shared an interest in slave-trade suppression.[27] In 1842, John Beecham, a missionary enthusiast, praised Buxton's zeal but insisted that the Christian faith would be more effective than trade and farming as a force for civilization.[28] However, others, such as minister William Tait, writing a decade later, thought that spreading the Gospel was utterly dependent on the suppression of the slave trade.[29] Horace Waller, who had come to anti-slavery through his missionary work with Livingstone, thought that the Gospel required civilization, civilization required the end of the slave trade, and that missionaries should therefore "break down its influence."[30] Even if support for particular development schemes was conditional, anti-slavery objectives offered a bridge between missionary and state attention to Africa.[31] In her 1844 history of British anti-slavery, Esther Copley advised British women that "evangelizing Africa" was the next step and promoted involvement in African, as well as West Indian, missionary societies.[32] The popularity of slave-trade questions was ideal for missions' promotional efforts, particularly in the second half of the century. In 1897, the Universities' Mission to Central Africa promoted Livingstone's slave-trade revelations as their founding concern.[33] A journal such as *Central Africa,* the organization's magazine, traded on this fascination with frequent reports of slave-hunting atrocities and their disruptive effects on the opportunities for evangelization.[34]

There was a strong religious dimension to all theories of development as feelings of guilt mixed with ambitions of civilizing Africa. Whether morality led to prosperity eventually or prosperity eventually promoted morality, the dynamic between the two objectives was clear. The trick was to get the right formula for both to flourish over time. We have already seen how readily popular constructions of providence could unite British national interest with altruistic aspirations in anti-slavery foreign policy. Opening up the resources of Africa would be similarly good for its native peoples and the "one great family" of the Earth.[35] Britain's sin as the leading slave-trade nation before 1807 was part of this argument. Macgregor Laird argued that Britain's empire would decline and fall if the nation did not atone for its guilt by repairing the evil it had done so much to promote. He saw the recent decline of the authoritarian and immoral Spanish Empire as a warning to his country.[36] By this reasoning, the British would assist Africans in escaping their degradation, to the profit of both. At the same time, Britain would happily enjoy the rightful profits from the burden it had taken up, but not from any special privilege.[37] The 1842 Select Committee on West Africa expressed this purpose in its remarkable conclusion that "in all we are attempting in Africa, we are only endeavouring to provide a feast of which all may equally partake; and seeking, as the reward of our exertions, no advantage to ourselves, save that which may fairly fall to our lot from a proportionate share of a more abundant table, spread out for the common benefit of all."[38] Such a vision was part of a wider conception of industry and trade as a moral project that brought forth the fruits of the earth for human utility.[39] The sheer economic irrationality of Africa remaining enslaved by the slave trade was a direct challenge to "civilized" peoples, and particularly to the British as the most civilized nation. Inaction was offensive.[40]

Such lofty goals directed both godliness and greed toward what one scholar calls a "development plan for Africa," or, more precisely, a series of development plans for Africa.[41] Improvement plans sought to rationally demonstrate to Africans that their own interests were better served by legitimate commerce than by a trade in slaves.[42] In this view, improvement was as much about spurring Africans to perceive and pursue their own financial advantage as it was about awakening a moral repugnance of the slave trade. If the slave trade was presently the principal source for Western goods, it would be critical to demonstrate they could be procured more easily through other, less destructive, forms of trade. Thus, enlightened self-interest would reveal to Africans that there were better ways of doing business with Europeans.[43] This was a project of moral and social education (or, as we might now recognize it, cultural imperialism) to spread the benefits of a free-labor society. Every slave stolen was not only a lost producer of goods for export but also a lost consumer of goods from countries such as Britain.[44]

For more than thirty years after the Niger expedition's failure, similar ideas of anti-slavery civilization would recur, not only in the books of "improvers" but in government doctrine and public debate.[45] William Hutt's 1850 motion to end suppression never articulated a clear alternative but simply rehearsed the commercial principles that had informed Buxton's project.[46] In 1864, Livingstone described the combination of commerce and Christianity as "the Palmerston policy" against the slave trade.[47] It went unnoticed that only the operation of the cruisers distinguished such a policy from that of Palmerston's old foe Hutt. However, defending the record of the West Africa squadron in an 1857 letter to the *Times,* Livingstone emphasized that the cultivation "of the raw materials of our manufactures and the influence of Christian civilization alone will effect a permanent suppression of the slave-trade."[48] Two years later, an editorial in that newspaper proposed that "British philanthropy, science, and capital put their heads together" to achieve such results.[49] Commerce held common currency even among those who disagreed on the role of the cruisers.

Despite the improvers' promises of lucrative future trade when the slave trade was put down, the actual significance of sub-Saharan Africa for British trade was minimal. The first half of the nineteenth century saw a consistent decline in the continent's proportional significance to British trade from a peak in the slave-trading 1780s that would not be matched again until the 1970s. Even if it was on the rise from the midcentury, trade with the whole of Africa constituted less than 2.6 percent of British trade in the period from 1794 to 1856.[50] Still, as Palmerston argued, "the commercial resources of Africa are of vast importance" for Britain's future, even if they did not make up a large proportion of current trade.[51]

Economic interest in Africa was founded on public interest in exports that could emerge after the suppression of slave trading. In 1852, the foreign secretary, Lord Granville, suggested that security for British trade was a priority for his Office, "considering the great natural advantages of our Foreign Commerce, and the powerful means of civilization it affords."[52] As early as 1854, *Chambers's Journal* celebrated the early fruits of such a policy in West Africa, as British importation of stearic acid (extracted from palm oil for making candles) was directly undermining the slave trade.[53] In 1865, William Wylde, then the Slave Trade Department's superintendent, advocated "striking the slave trade at its root" by promoting trade in cotton, palm oil, shea butter, and indigo around the Niger region in his testimony to the Select Committee on West Africa.[54] Private schemes of the period took up the challenge, such as the mission of William Craft, a former American slave. After raising half his initial target of £1,000 from anti-slavery and missionary supporters, he planned an expedition to the kingdom of Dahomey. There, he would attempt "to civilize and Christianize the people, and to destroy the wicked slave trade." His initial expedition in 1862 aimed to show that the cultivation of cotton provided better profits than the slave trade, which he thought was the cause of the king's human sacrifices.[55] The black emigrationists Martin Delany and Robert Campbell hoped their Niger Valley Exploring Party, active from 1859, would cultivate the growth of free-labor exports with support from the Manchester cotton magnate Thomas Clegg.[56]

Old ideas of forming partnerships with Africans to end the slave trade were easily assimilated by most anti-slavery schools of thought.[57] Prevailing anxieties about the supply of free-labor cotton made its cultivation in Africa particularly attractive in the years before the American Civil War.[58] A state project to import cotton- and sugar-processing machinery had been attempted in Fernando Po, during Britain's brief naval lease there.[59] Cooperation between the government and the Manchester Cotton Supply Association in the cultivation of cotton on the Gold Coast and in Lagos proved a modest success. Imported from Alabama, gins were deployed in Lagos to help with efforts to cultivate cotton there. By midcentury, the Slave Trade Department had begun to act as an economic development agency as well as remaining a watchdog for anti-slavery policy.[60] As Archbishop Whately put it, it would be "better for all parties that cotton and sugar should be grown there [West Africa]...than to carry away the negroes to cultivate them 1,000 miles off."[61]

Although commerce might seem to aid anti-slavery policy, the relationship with state action was fraught. The government often expressed concern over the conduct of British traders in West Africa, particularly their coercive systems of credit and monopolistic practices.[62] One of the most serious challenges to a comfortable relationship between anti-slavery and commerce came when the Irish abolitionist R. R. Madden was sent to investigate the complicity of Gold Coast officials and British merchants in the slave trade in 1840. He penned a devastating report, suggesting that foreign slave traders purchased captured Africans with cheap Western goods largely manufactured in Britain.[63] These materials had long been dubbed "slave goods," as their poor quality marked them out for export to Africa or to slave societies where they could be used as barter for all manner of goods, legitimate and illegitimate. Madden argued that any Britons selling to slave dealers were complicit in human trafficking, and he questioned why any British traders were permitted to do business with ports in which slaving occurred, as they became part of its supply chain. The report criticized Governor George Maclean of the Gold Coast for allowing this to continue.[64] Maclean protested his innocence, insisting that he had no power to interfere with friendly ships conducting themselves lawfully in British waters. He was subsequently exonerated and demoted, as is so often the way with political scandals.[65]

Madden's investigation had little long-term impact. A select committee convened to consider his findings was convinced that, without legitimate trade as an alternative, Africans would resort to slave trading to meet their desire for Western goods.[66] Legally, traders could be charged with abetting the slave trade only if they were aware how their merchandise would be used, which was hard to prove. Additionally, the committee was convinced by evidence that the mere presence of British citizens—even as private merchants—was anathema to slave trading, citing examples where the navy had gained valuable intelligence from traders. Legitimate traders were exonerated and again hailed as allies, not traitors, in the national crusade against the slave trade.[67] The 1842 inquiry resulted only in greater state control of the Gold Coast colony, not in a retreat from faith in the civilizing effects of trade.[68] Traders and merchants proved great propagandists for their supposed role in advancing civilization.[69] The committee sided with the views of the merchant and MP William Forster, who, in an indignant letter to Madden, insisted that "the only progress which had been made in the civilisation on the coast has been through the medium of trade." He declared that he had done more to end the slave trade in twenty-five years of business there "than Government has done in all its wasteful expenditure."[70]

It is clear that merchants picked and chose when they wanted anti-slavery intervention by the state and when they disavowed it depending on their own interests. Opposition to Buxton's expedition in 1841 had been led by Robert Jamieson, a merchant invested in trade around the River Niger who resented government support for a rival venture that might break his monopoly.[71] Palmerston, as prime minister, gave considerable assistance to Laird's steamship company, launched in 1852. This was hugely unpopular with those Liverpool merchants who exercised control over the African coast given that the steamer's cargo haul from Britain gave openings to competitors.[72] Although the promotion of legitimate trade in Africa was seen as synonymous with efforts to suppress the slave trade, this did not leave politicians blind to the selfish interests of some merchants.

Despite a widely held faith in the power of commerce to "civilize" and develop Africa, such questions were very rarely matters of public concern in the period before 1865.[73] The Niger expedition was exceptional in the degree of government involvement and the fanfare that surrounded its departure.[74] Both parties had supported state involvement in Buxton's plan, but the expedition's staggering cost of £79,143 was borne by taxpayers largely because the Whig prime minister, Viscount Melbourne, wanted to associate his faltering ministry with a popular anti-slavery project.[75] The Niger expedition was commissioned in the final gasp of public anxiety over slaveholding in Britain's own West Indian colonies and as a desperate attempt to revive the current ministers' anti-slavery credentials.[76] These circumstances were unique; future expeditions would rely on private finance or receive significantly less state support. Still, it is remarkable how little Buxton's failure dented faith in the possibilities for improvement, even if popular interest was largely dormant until Livingstone's crusade two decades later.[77] In the year after the disastrous 1841 expedition, a select committee reendorsed legitimate trade, protected by state establishments and the navy, as the long-term salvation for Africa.[78]

This undented faith does not suggest that there was any kind of consensus in favor of the British "civilization" of Africa. Charles Dickens had loathed Buxton's scheme, attacking it as the work of "telescopic philanthropists" who should focus on the misery around them in Britain.[79] Similarly, the Times criticized the expedition, with one of its editors denouncing Buxton's plans at a meeting of the Civilization Society. He objected to spending more money after Britain had paid £20,000,000 compensation to the West Indian planters, suffered a 30 percent cut in sugar production, and experienced a doubling of the price of sugar. The newspaperman claimed to support anti-slavery policies, but he ridiculed the false promises of Buxton's scheme and Whig economics.[80] More fundamentally, the Times denied that Africans were "improvable," making rational appeals to economic interest and the cultivation of savage morals a hopeless exercise.[81]

This 1840s pessimism contrasts with the newspaper's later enthusiasm for Livingstone's plans in Central Africa and Eastern Africa.[82] Regardless, critics continued to doubt the effectiveness of the well-meaning but expensive efforts of the Victorian state.

In this opinion they had an ally in James Stephen, the long-serving under-secretary of state at the Colonial Office. He thought that the West African colonies' value for commerce and slave-trade suppression was "enormously exaggerated" and "in fact they are nothing else than factories kept up at the expense of the Nation at large for the profit of half a dozen inconsiderable merchants."[83] He did not doubt that Britain should oppose the slave trade—his family included prominent abolitionists and he had drafted the Emancipation Act—but he doubted that the promotion of British commerce in Africa would help. These sentiments were not alien to those with more commercial interests in Africa. During one of his occasional periods of pessimism about Africa, Laird insisted that Britain's free-labor colonies were "the only channels through which we can affect the demand for slaves." He mocked the idea "of civilizing a continent, by sending two or three expeditions, or 50 expeditions up any of the rivers," saying it was "perfectly ridiculous." Instead, he suggested that "moral power on the coast of Africa means a 24-pounder, and British seamen behind it." Because this large-scale use of physical force was impractical, he argued that the civilization of Africa would be wrought in the West Indies, through the short-term emigration of free labor there.[84]

By midcentury, improvers and their pessimistic detractors could at least agree that Africans had failed to play the role assigned for them in the suppression of the slave trade. Blunt bigotry and frustration at African slave dealing led the *Spectator,* in 1853, to moan that "British lives are lavished on the African coasts to negotiate and treat with the Black babies who can't keep from selling each other and cheating us." The paper concluded that it was impossible to educate West Africans as "moral observers of the Anti-Slavery faith."[85] Such anger about the slow progress of "educating" Africans in the economic irrationality of selling their own people was an emotion that gelled with the rise of racial thinking. However, this frustration could stir in some a desire for stronger formal involvement by the British state rather than despair.[86] As historian David Eltis observed, "the refusal of Africans to behave as a European elite expected in the wake of suppression" moved Britain to kindle freedom with force.[87]

## ANTI-SLAVERY IMPERIALISM

British suppression of the slave trade kept the Royal Navy on the coast of West Africa in the decades after the Abolition Act of 1807, but the crusade also fostered early prejudices against African nations. In 1839, during preparations for the Niger expedition, Palmerston insisted that undertakings with Britain by "barbarous or semi-barbarous tribes" for slave-trade suppression should be categorized as agreements, without the full status of international treaties, and the distinction stuck.[88] Instructions to British naval officers had separate procedures for "uncivilized African states," against which force "may be exercised upon shore as well as at sea, and irrespectively of the consent of the native government."[89] Palmerston continued to promote the idea, following the early exploits of Denman and Jones, that traditional rights under international law could be suspended when dealing with African nations on matters concerning the slave trade.[90] After Denman's trial, the navy struck at more slave traders, burning barracoons. By the middle of the century, British audiences were familiar with images of burning slave forts from the Solyman River (fig. 9) in Sierra Leone to the shores of Mozambique (fig. 10) on the east coast.[91] When Commodore Jones burned the villages of the Gallinas in the course of his gunboat diplomacy with Prince Manna, he acted to punish and intimidate an African sovereign. This went a step further than destroying barracoons, where slaves were kept for embarkation. Jones's actions were an escalation of violence, targeting a community rather than just a slave-trading post. In the following years, British slave-trade suppression moved toward even greater coercion of African nations.

This did not reflect a calculated desire for territorial control. Although Britons at midcentury entertained robust differences over how or whether they could speed Africans' salvation from the slave trade, they saved even more passion for questions about the size and scale of state expenditure on colonies in West Africa. The conquest of African societies was hardly considered.[92] Empire on the smallest imaginable scale was a model for an "imperialism of free trade," where officials sought to secure national influence and commerce rather than occupation.[93] Early Victorian concerns about climate and the problems of governance led to debates about formal imperial commitments that were small or smaller.[94]

Visions for improvement differed less over the scale than over the form that state activity should assume. Besides familiar contests over the upkeep of naval cruisers, there were various disputes over whether to occupy forts along the coast or to strategically acquire territory.[95] Buxton looked to revive Britain's use of Fernando Po and also flirted with the idea of acquiring Mombass on the east coast.[96] New commitments were, unsurprisingly, given extensive scrutiny. Still, as a direct result of concerns about the slave trade, the 1842 Select Committee on the West Coast of Africa paved the way for direct rule at Cape Coast Castle by the crown rather than a merchants' committee.[97] Anti-slavery interests could justify formal colonies at a time when they were least favored in Parliament. In July 1850,

FIGURE 9. British attack on slave barracoons on the Solyman River, Sierra Leone. *ILN*, 14 April 1849, 237. By permission of Mary Evans Picture Library, ref. 10012261.

FIGURE 10. British attack on slave barracoons in Mozambique. *ILN*, 18 Jan. 1851, 44. By permission of Mary Evans Picture Library, ref. 10015377.

Cobden opposed the acquisition of the Danish forts along the Gold Coast (at a cost of £10,000), but he was heavily defeated in the House of Commons.[98] British interest in West Africa outstripped the volume of trade in the area. It seems unlikely that British involvement would have been so extensive on the basis of trade policy alone.[99] Moreover, greedy expectations about the future development of legitimate trade were predicated on anti-slavery ideas.[100]

Anti-slavery policies locked an unwilling state into obligations toward African colonies. Charles Adderley, the chairman of the 1865 Select Committee on Africa, believed that Britain would never have undertaken any settlements in Africa or made entangling treaties of protection with West African chiefs if it had not been for first the promotion and later the suppression of the slave trade. His committee's report mourned the need to maintain such commitments and suggested preparations for British withdrawal. However, any such departure was conditional on an end to the slave trade.[101] The case for maintaining a British presence on the Gold Coast (modern Ghana) was largely based on fear that the Ashanti would otherwise reestablish slave trading as they asserted their domination over the region.[102] Adderley's analysis on this point was surely correct. This was hardly a retreat from anti-slavery policy, even if the committee wished that more had been done by trade alone so that so many formal commitments in West Africa had not been made.[103]

When Britain did add to its formal empire in Africa in the period before the "new imperialism" of the 1880s, it came through the entangling logic of anti-slavery ideologies. For example, Britain's kidnapping of the rebellious Bonny priest Awanta in 1848 was primarily spurred by merchants' complaints about his disruption of their trade.[104] Similarly, King Pepple of the Bonny was deposed in 1854 after Consul John Beecroft had spent years denouncing him as a supporter of the slave trade. Their enmity was in fact rooted in more mundane economic disputes, but slave trading helped justify national intervention.[105] In these cases, intervention and the protection of legitimate commerce were intimately bound up with anti-slavery ideologies. Commercial concerns were easily connected with abolitionist goals.[106]

African or European defiance of British power was usually conflated with a zeal for slave trading; civilization and cooperation with Britain were assumed to chime with abolitionist piety.[107] Back in 1840, Buxton predicted that anyone profiting from the slave trade would aim to stop native chiefs working with Britain.[108] Africans' disruption of trade or resistance to the authority of British officials were construed as pro-slavery activities.[109] The Ashanti, for example, were dismissed in 1865 as "a great slave-hunting despotism."[110] Moreover, treaties with existing African powers offered the

British a cheap way to secure cooperation against the slave trade and for legitimate trade. By 1857, there were forty-five anti-slavery treaties on the west coast and these easily provoked entangling alliances.[111]

The security of Abeokuta, a West African town allied with Britain and embracing Christianity, became a recurring concern, in part thanks to missionary propaganda.[112] It was identified as a bridgehead for Christianity, anti-slavery, and British civilization, while the hostile kingdom of Dahomey was portrayed as a hotbed of war, savagery, and slavery.[113] This provided the backdrop to the most famous example of British gunboat diplomacy in Africa before the European scramble for colonies. King Kosoko of Lagos was condemned as a rogue supporter of the slave trade. Britain had, by default, taken up the cause of his rival Akitoye, who had been deposed years earlier and claimed to be the legitimate ruler of Lagos. Far more relevant to British support was Akitoye's pledge to assist efforts against the slave trade.[114] A sour mood toward his rival had set in at the Foreign Office by 1851. The occasion for Kosoko's removal was heralded by missionary reports that the king of Dahomey was working with this "usurper at Lagos" to conquer Abeokuta and reopen it to slave dealers.[115] Rumors of a raid to capture slaves and murder all whites and freedmen stirred action.

In September 1851, Palmerston wrote indignantly to the Lords of the Admiralty that the "great purpose" of the British government and people in suppressing the slave trade could no longer be thwarted by "the minimal and piratical resistance of two barbarous African chiefs." The foreign secretary ordered that Whydah be blockaded and new action taken against Kosoko at Lagos.[116] Prime Minister Russell was content to "wink at any violation of Vattel" (referring to the scholar of international law Emerich de Vattel) where slave trading was involved.[117] Palmerston predicted:

> If Lagos, instead of being a nest for Slave Traders, were to become a Port for Lawful Trade, it would in connection with the Navigable River which there discharges itself into the Sea, become an important outlet for the commerce of a large Range of Country in the Interior, and instead of being a Den of Barbarians, would be a diffusing Centre of Civilization.[118]

Encouraged by this, the British consul and naval commanders attacked Lagos and deposed Kosoko in December 1851.[119] Akitoye subsequently signed a treaty banning the slave trade as well as human sacrifice.[120] The British public received news of Kosoko's defeat as just punishment for "persistence in carrying on the inhuman traffic."[121]

Attempts by the British consul at Lagos to rule through Akitoye and later his son Docemo did not proceed smoothly, however. The new dynasty did not enjoy popular support in Lagos, precipitating further British intervention, again for anti-slavery reasons, a decade later. By 1861, Doc-emo's allies found him unable to prevent slave trading in the area sur-rounding Lagos.[122] Russell, now serving as Palmerston's foreign secretary, promised that

> the permanent occupation of this point in the Bight of Benin is indispens-able to the complete suppression of the slave trade in the Bight, whilst it will give great aid and support to the development of lawful commerce, and will check the aggressive spirit of the King of Dahomey, whose barba-rous wars & encouragement to slave trading are the chief cause of disorder in that part of Africa.[123]

The anti-slavery intent of this annexation was underlined by instructions from the Duke of Newcastle to Lagos's new governor insisting that no fur-ther territory should be claimed for Britain beyond that absolutely neces-sary to suppress the port's slave trade.[124] Anti-slavery and the failures of informal rule—wrapped up, of course, in other concerns—overcame of-ficial reluctance for formal rule.[125] The main justification for British med-dling and then formal rule was abolitionist. Dissenters such as Sir Francis Baring opposed such high-handed treatment of African rulers in the hope that self-determination would be more successful in permanently under-mining the slave trade and advancing civilization. A lonely voice, Baring's example serves to demonstrate that even opponents of anti-slavery annexa-tion rested their logic on anti-slavery concerns.[126]

Deepening commercial involvement and frustrations over the sup-pression of the slave trade created apparent crises in Africa.[127] Historian Michael Craton's assessment—that "complacency led British statesmen into gunboat adventures and even the acquisition of colonies, whenever their concept of progress seemed unjustly blocked"—holds true.[128] That "concept of progress" was invariably focused on anti-slavery concerns and formed the basis of imperial interventions (such as King Pepple being de-posed) and formal empire (such as the annexation of Lagos). Although a formal colony such as Lagos technically became the responsibility of the Colonial Office, the Foreign Office's responsibility for the slave trade gave it the lead in imperial expansion and influence. As one governor put it in 1864, "Lagos is the child of the FO" and so needed its parent's help in dealing with the Colonial Office, even after Britain had formally annexed the colony.[129]

As part of the intervention of 1851, the Royal Navy had shelled Lagos. Among the ships participating in the attack was HMS *Penelope,* the flag-ship of Commodore Jones when he attacked the villages of the Gallinas in 1845. British experiments in burning down African barracoons or

FIGURE 11. "The Destruction of Lagos," 1851. *ILN,* 13 March 1852, 224. By permission of Mary Evans Picture Library, ref. 10472512.

settlements in the Gallinas region had reached a new maturity or, rather, a new boldness in Lagos, first destroying and then annexing the city in 1851 and 1861. Domestic newspaper readers had previously seen images of burning barracoons or read about Jones's revenge on Manna, and so the scenes would have seemed somewhat familiar when they read about the "destruction of Lagos" in the early months of 1852. Heavy bombardment from the *Penelope* and the other ships had struck Kosoko's arsenal, creating a series of explosions in his capital. The *Illustrated London News* offered readers a striking engraving of the attack on "the nest of the slave trade" with an account from one of *Penelope*'s sailors (fig. 11). He described how a rocket attack meant "the whole town was soon in a blaze" and "the town burnt famously all night."[130] Although the stirring account of British naval adventures in West Africa looked similar to the familiar scenes of burning barracoons or settlements, intervention at Lagos marked a shift from commerce and slave-trade diplomacy toward British occupation. It was a pattern that became more familiar in the following decades.

## DECOY ELEPHANTS

In 1877 Frederic Elton, the British consul in Mozambique, told his friend William Wylde that in East Africa "what is needed are decoy elephants." These elephants were not metaphorical. Elton suggested that a team of Indian elephants and "a staff of elephant catchers from Ceylon" could put down the slave trade in the region around Lake Malawi. Because of the

tsetse fly, horses and cattle were not feasible beasts of burden. Great caravans of slaves hauled goods to the coast for sale, where they themselves
were also sold. In order to undermine this thriving slave trade, operated by
Arab merchants, Elton hoped that elephants would provide an alternative
way to transport the produce of the African interior. The most efficient
way, he suggested, was to use trained "decoy" elephants to trick local, wild
African elephants into following them. Since the creatures were social and
prone to traveling in lines, the wild elephants could then be loaded with
merchandise and led to the coast.[131] Although the East African context was
exotic, Elton's ploy drew on a familiar technique from British India, described by one storybook in circulation during his childhood: "The female
is used in this work, and exhibits much ingenuity . . . being sent out amongst
a troop of wild elephants . . . to entangle the affections of one of the male
species . . . intently gazing on the charms of his mistress, he disregards the
approach of his enemies."[132] In his letter, Elton sounded a little desperate in
his plea that "I am by no means dreaming dreams or advocating impossible
measures."[133] As unlikely as it may sound, the business ventures of King
Leopold of the Belgians and Scottish investor William Mackinnon would
later experiment with imported elephants for just such purposes.[134]

Elton's significance does not lie in his unrealized ambitions to civilize
African elephants as abolitionist agents in Malawi, though. His hope of
disciplining a local population with techniques and skills developed in
other parts of the British Empire reflected a developing taste for intervention in East Africa. Anti-slavery sentiment can be seen as a decoy elephant, tempting the British public to support colonizers bent on their own
economic interests. Historian Marcus Wood thinks that "abolition as a
propaganda movement justified white expansion into Africa."[135] Examining the relationship between slavery and imperialism in the period of the
"scramble for Africa" provides a chance to test this proposition. By looking
at British imperial policies it will be possible to decide whether anti-slavery
functioned as a "propaganda movement" and a justification for British
actions—effectively, as a decoy.

Because of his role in Portuguese East Africa, Elton plays a part in
these case studies, even if his imported elephants do not. From the 1860s
on, the division of African territories between South Africa and Sudan was
uncertain, with Portugal and Britain, later joined by Germany, concerned
to protect and advance national interests. In the case of the British, this
included a new crusade against slave trading off the east coast of Africa.[136]
The intensification of British slave-trade suppression there hinged on two
groups: the first was a small elite network of men with an activist vision
for anti-slavery, and the second was a receptive public with an appetite
for anti-slavery. Elton became, in later years, a peripheral associate of the

former group and his letter, mentioned above, is a useful device to explore it. His 1877 missive was sent from the Livingstonia mission at the south of Lake Malawi to Wylde in England. He sent a copy to Sir Bartle Frere and—toward the end of the message—asked Wylde to pass on his good wishes and his news to Horace Waller. These three men were preeminent architects of Britain's early interventions in East African affairs, along with a missionary who was dead by the time Elton was working in the region of the lake (see map, fig. 12).[137]

FIGURE 12. British colonies, protectorates, and other possessions in Africa, 1901. Produced by Cartography Unit, Plymouth University.

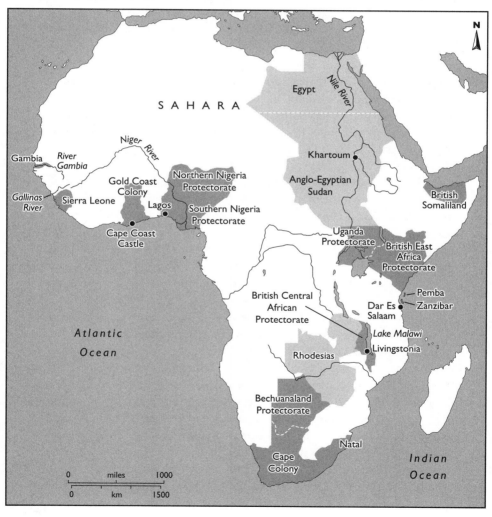

The Livingstonia mission was, of course, named for the late Scottish missionary and explorer David Livingstone. That was appropriate as El-ton's eccentric plan was forged in the mold of Livingstone's ambitions for Christianity, commerce, and the suppression of the slave trade in Africa. Quite separate from any direct relationship with slavery, the godly sections of Victorian Britain had long embraced missionary activities for peoples overseas. When Buxton promoted his expedition to missionary organiza-tions, he expected them to gratefully follow in the wake of his anti-slavery objectives. In Livingstone, the mission movement developed its own abo-litionist; ironically, he shared with Buxton the priority of suppressing the disruptive slave trades of Africa, but as a missionary he was better placed to argue that evangelism was dependent upon anti-slavery. In 1865, Living-stone confidently invoked the success of Palmerston's policy in the Atlantic as he called for it to be repeated "on the opposite side of the continent." He argued that "no reasonable expense, that preserves us from contamination, should be esteemed a sacrifice."[138] His private publications and the fund-raising literature of the Church Missionary Society embraced the cruisers-and-trade formula once more.[139]

Livingstone's work along the course of the Zambesi River deliberately used anti-slavery to attract public interest, money, and support for his mis-sions and expeditions.[140] Dedicated to Palmerston (as patron saint of West African slave-trade suppression), Livingstone's *Narrative of an Expedition to the Zambesi* featured slaves prominently in its illustrations. Fascinated with the interior of the continent, Livingstone publicized the existence of a second slave trade in Africa. The western slave trade had been an aberrant European disruption of African development; now, an Arab slave trade from Central Africa to the coast and then to the Middle East appeared as a second blight. Livingstone's talent for self-publicity and promotion of a new evil within the unexplored interior of the continent prepared the ground for political developments in the years immediately before and after his 1873 demise.[141]

Thanks to the activities of a network of anti-slavery men seeking Brit-ish initiatives in East Africa, Livingstone's missions and death spurred state action. Dissatisfied with the inadequate legal apparatus for suppression of the slave trade around Zanzibar, officials from the Foreign and Colonial offices and the government of India had desperately sought to find a way forward starting in 1870.[142] However, when they agreed to bribe the sultan to get him to concede greater anti-slavery measures, the plan foundered on the opposition of a new sultan in Zanzibar, Barghash, and the chancellor of the exchequer's horror at the expense to British taxpayers. Scrutiny by the Select Committee on the Slave Trade in eastern Africa drew attention to the fact that, in 1822, Britain had signed a treaty that simply limited the export of slaves from Zanzibar and Pemba across a narrow strip of sea.[143]

Foreign Office officials mourned that the sultan, under his agreements with the British, had a "reserved privilege of transporting slaves by sea for the home market," which "has always been...a cloak" for external slave trafficking.[144] Moreover, when privately consulted on the measure, abolitionists such as Sir Fowell Buxton (son of the anti-slavery MP) were appalled that Zanzibar would still be permitted to operate a regulated trade; he had been wholly ignorant that they were presently entitled to do so.[145] These concerns were aired angrily in public after a hostile parliamentary motion was tabled in 1872. One historian suggests that these events were sparked by an official leak. If so, Wylde's close friendship with the ringleaders of the subsequent outcry, not to mention his activism on policy matters, would make him a likely suspect, though there is no proof.[146]

In the first few months of 1872, the British press had become more agitated about the "Polynesian slave trade" of the South Seas, but in the longer term the East Africa inquiry had a greater effect than government measures brought forward to prosecute Australian abductors.[147] The Select Committee on Africa was concerned that there had been no concrete actions to stop de facto slave trading.[148] However, their cry would have largely been ignored without agitation in favor of direct action. From February 1872 onward, with reports of Samuel Baker's "anti-slave trade war" in Sudan and Livingstone's disappearance in East Africa as a backdrop, political pressure grew.[149] While public meetings pressed humanitarian duty, some speakers, such as Russell Gurney, did offer "one word, in conclusion, as to their interest in putting down the slave trade" since, on the west coast, Britons "were being repaid every year for the expenditure in putting down the slave trade there, and that the same results would ensue on the East Coast." Similarly, provincial newspapers described "a new world of production and consumption" if the slave trade could be suppressed.[150] Such commercial promises took second place, however, to moral diatribes. Widely reprinted letters from the hitherto-lost Livingstone arrived with perfect timing, condemning "the open sore in the world."[151] The Liberal government under Gladstone—a longstanding skeptic of anti-slavery violence—reluctantly sanctioned a mission to Zanzibar.[152] In August, his ministry declared war on the East African slave trade in Queen Victoria's speech opening a new session of Parliament. The cabinet approved negotiations for concessions that would allow the Royal Navy to suppress the slave trade effectually.[153]

The man Gladstone sent to deliver action from Zanzibar was Sir Bartle Frere. A keen student of non-Western peoples, Frere had had a distinguished career as a civil servant in the East India Company and its successor regime, the Raj. Having secured western India for Britain during the Sepoy Mutiny, Frere was promoted to governor of Bombay in 1862. By 1872 he had returned to London and become a candidate for special missions from the government.[154] The public meetings of that year, which he orchestrated, led to his appointment as the government's envoy to Zanzibar.[155] Frere had "smelt blood," as one historian puts it, during the select committee hearings and saw an opportunity to encourage a more aggressive policy in East Africa. Through association with the provincial networks of the BFASS, a speaking tour of Britain in the spring and summer of 1872, and shrewd lobbying, Frere ensured that substantial numbers of MPs felt under pressure from their constituents. One measure of his success was that much of the press had converted from supreme skepticism to enthusiastic support for British attention to Zanzibar's slave trade.[156]

Frere's principal collaborator in formenting public agitation was the Reverend Horace Waller, another of Elton's associates. Waller was a disciple of Livingstone and, like his mentor, saw the suppression of the slave trade as the foremost task for Christians who wished to spread the Gospel. He took this work forward after news of Livingstone's death reached Britain in 1874. In life, Livingstone had directed an enthusiastic public and a reluctant government toward focusing on the East African slave trade. In death, he would continue to do so, not least thanks to the careful work of his literary executor, Waller, who carefully edited Livingstone's last journals to highlight the martyr's attention to anti-slavery (fig. 13) and to omit an embarrassing reliance on the help of Arab slave traders or the problems controlling liberated African employees.[157] This complemented the press's response to the explorer's grand public funeral, with obituaries praising Livingstone's mission to open Africa "to the light of religion and civilisation, and extirpating the slave trade, which is the main hindrance to that beneficent consummation." The time was at hand, one newspaper predicted, when the "traffic in flesh and blood" would be ended, and then (and only then) would Africa be open to "Christianity, civilisation and commerce."[158] More broadly, British influence and interest in East Africa had been seeded. The press again celebrated British naval heroes hunting down vicious slavers (fig. 14).[159] Livingstone's anti-slavery legacy, so carefully cultivated after his death, would form the basis of an imperial interest in the region.[160]

In this goal, Frere, Waller, and Elton shared an ally in Wylde. A frequent correspondent of them all, this anti-slavery civil servant sat at the heart of an official and unofficial web of humanitarians, imperialists, missionaries, and businessmen with interests in East Africa. By 1876, for example, Wylde had taken a keen interest in Elton's work, confiding in him his delight that "we are every day assuming a more active Policy on the East Coast... and from this Policy we can scarcely withdraw, even if we wished, considering the interest taken by the Public in African Affairs."[161] As his enthusiasm suggests, Wylde wished to push the anti-slavery state in particular directions, and he largely succeeded in shaping African policy. His Foreign Office colleague Clement Hill praised Wylde's achievements,

FIGURE 13. "East African Slave Trade, by Johann Baptist Zwecker," after David Livingstone, *Livingstone's Last Journals*, ed. Horace Waller (2 vols., London, 1874), 1:56. By permission of Mary Evans Picture Library, ref. 10448300.

FIGURE 14. Boats from HMS *London* chase a slave dhow near Zanzibar. *ILN*, 17 Dec. 1881, 586. By permission of Mary Evans Picture Library, ref. 10015376.

remarking that "so much has been done of late years" in anti-slavery policy "almost in spite of the Gov[ernmen]t."[162] Wylde's experience and expertise gave him remarkable autonomy, and he wielded executive power typical of a much later generation of civil servants.[163]

Frere's mission to Zanzibar, which Wylde had encouraged despite the Liberal cabinet's concerns, was a prime example of the civil servant's agency. Arriving on the island in 1873, Frere found Sultan Barghash intransigent. The diplomat's subsequent gunboat diplomacy would have made Palmerston proud: Frere ordered the commander of the Royal Navy's squadron on the east coast to begin illegally intercepting all slave traffic. Reluctantly, the Liberal cabinet endorsed his stance and authorized him to declare war on Zanzibar if the sultan did not submit to a treaty. The ruler capitulated to British terms.[164] Even though it did not lead immediately to formal occupation, such an assertion of British power laid the bridgeheads for future control of the kingdom and parts of continental Africa.[165] John Kirk, the British consul at Zanzibar and an old companion of Livingstone's, had assisted Frere's mission, and in years to come he would rule the island through his puppet sultan. The slow disembowelment of Zanzibari sovereignty, begun in 1822 when a consul was appointed to the island under a slave-trade treaty, approached its conclusion.[166] Frere himself celebrated that his work meant that Britain "had succeeded without seeking it and almost without knowing it, to a dominant position in commercial interests in East Africa" and a "tempting opening for an Empire," though his countrymen should not, he thought, covet "the coarse material reward of extended dominion" from a "Philanthropic enterprise."[167] Still, even if he did not wish to see "extended dominion," Frere welcomed the benefits of commerce to both philanthropy and Britain.

If the links between the state, anti-slavery philanthropy, and private commerce were fertile and incestuous, they were not simple. Frere's "tempting opening" unleashed a host of subsequent intrigues. By 1877 shipping mogul William Mackinnon and Sir Thomas Fowell Buxton, grandson of the anti-slavery hero, were in the advance stages of planning a European trading company in East Africa. Like Elton, they saw roads as being key to commercial access to the interior and to the suppression of the slave trade.[168] Kirk had no doubts that "schemes for the good of Africa must be financially successful to the promoters" and that Mackinnon "has a good eye to business in all these concessions" he proposed.[169] He was willing to champion the project, which was partly orchestrated by Waller, with whom he was related through marriage. Wylde, who privately agreed to prepare a favorable report on the venture, was also keen to see it happen, as was Frere, who was a strong supporter of Mackinnon's previous ventures in running steamships to southern Africa.[170]

The Colonial Office insisted that ventures such as the one that Mackinnon and Buxton proposed be undertaken by a British company rather than by a subsidiary of the International African Association, which was masterminded by Belgium's King Leopold. Elton's advice to Lord Carnarvon, colonial secretary in the Tory government, helped shape a view that it was imprudent for British energies to be directed to an *international* scheme, just as it was imprudent to involve the Prince of Wales—a friend of Frere's who had agreed to be honorific head of the venture.[171] Ironically, Elton's xenophobia scuppered the plan his collaborators had hatched.

The alternative, a purely British venture led by Mackinnon, collapsed because of the sudden opposition of two critical government actors. Sultan Barghash, whose territory on the East African coast would be ceded to Mackinnon's company, decisively swung against the scheme. Lord Salisbury, the new Conservative foreign secretary in 1878, may have deliberately undermined negotiations between the company and the sultan. For whatever reason, the negotiations stumbled, frustrating the network of supporters within the Foreign Office and outside it. R. B. D. Morier, the British minister to Portugal, warned Wylde in 1879 that "if the usual procrastination which prevails in everything which has to be done with or through the C[olonial] O[ffice] is allowed to prevail we shall lose one for all [sic] the only chance we may ever have of... dealing a final blow at the Slave Trade on the coast & our last chance of future measures... in the interior."[172] In a preface to the late Elton's journals published in 1879, Frere pleaded that "the Foreign Office will but permit another 'oscillation' from the dead indifference of the last twelve months" in order to stop the slave trade reviving in East Africa.[173] It was not Foreign Office civil servants such as Wylde he needed to convince, but ministers.

Despite unmoving political skepticism, Kirk still nurtured hopes for British commercial opportunities and used his consular influence at Zanzibar to promote them. He successfully argued in 1882–83 for a realignment of anti-slavery expenditures that would establish consuls in the sultan's coastal possessions to promote trade, supervise his weak administrators, and report on slave trading. His victories suggested that British policy had turned its focus to the interior of East Africa in order to preserve strategic dominance and advance anti-slavery operations. The moves could be presented to other government departments as economical and pleased the Foreign Office by centralizing anti-slavery operations within their control.[174]

However, Kirk's plans were assisted by favorable political pressures. Negotiations between Britain and Portugal to allow the latter to access the Congo precipitated an international crisis in 1884 and spurred the Berlin Conference. There, Britain accepted the domination of the Congo region by Leopold's International African Association. Beyond promoting free trade in that part of Africa, British diplomats used the conference to secure an international declaration against the slave trade on sea and land by the great powers of Europe. The idea for this resolution seems to have been a somewhat idle suggestion from civil servants to Foreign Secretary Lord Granville, and one official, Clement Hill, admitted that the subsequent declaration was "sadly milk and watery." It still secured the government something to take pride in at home and abroad.[175]

Significantly for future European expansion, though, the Berlin declaration promised that the powers would "watch over the preservation of the native tribes of Africa" to assist "their moral and material well-being, and to help in suppressing slavery, and especially the slave trade."[176] The combined promotion of anti-slavery, civilization, and commercial development in Africa was nothing new, but the Berlin Conference augured both the division (and ultimate annexation) of the continent alongside traditional anti-slavery measures to promote trade and suppress maritime slave trading.[177] In 1885, Germany annexed the region to the north of Lake Malawi, including the route of Elton's putative elephant train. Challenging the sultan of Zanzibar's ineffective sovereignty over the region, German chancellor Otto von Bismarck successfully seized the inland territory from Britain's informal orbit. Gladstone, again prime minister, was happy to concede this. His successor, Salisbury, inherited British-occupied Egypt and was similarly happy to purchase German acquiescence to that annexation with Sultan Barghash's possessions.[178]

Paradoxically, this development made William Mackinnon's ambitions more palatable to the two men who had undermined them in 1878. Salisbury was willing to support a British East Africa Company exploiting the area to the north of the new German sphere of influence. Barghash, humiliated by the Germans, turned to British private finance in 1887 to secure what was left of his continental possessions. The sticking point remained whether Foreign Office support for Mackinnon's venture would be moral and unofficial or political and official.[179] Salisbury, like Gladstone, remained reluctant to pursue the latter course. The state certainly feared direct action, and in 1887 the British government had avoided these sorts of entanglements for another anti-slavery mission devised by Mackinnon. Henry Morgan Stanley, the journalist who had "found" Livingstone and helped publicize his work, led an expedition to relieve Emin Pasha, a German-born general in Charles George Gordon's Sudanese regime. Emin governed the province of Equitoria, where, in the eyes of Stanley and supporters such as Mackinnon, he was preserving British civilization and anti-slavery rule in a land forgotten by the government. Salisbury refused to sanction Stanley's expedition, though Belgian king Leopold did. Given the venture's farcical end, which involved the evacuation of Emin and Leopold's diversion of the mission to support his commercial opportunities, government doubts were probably justified.[180]

Fortunately for Mackinnon, he got the state approval he needed for a new company in September 1888, long before news of this embarrassment reached London. His new Imperial British East Africa Company (IBEAC) was more to the government's taste, because it used private initiative and capital rather than state support. The investors ranged from financial speculators, such as Royal Niger Company president James Hutton, to philanthropists, such as Buxton. Many of the humanitarians involved, such as Lady Burdett-Coutts, had also been supporters of the Emin Pasha Relief Expedition alongside Mackinnon.[181] John Kirk, still British consul, was a private investor in the scheme and handled the Company's negotiations with the Sultan.[182] The Foreign Office continued to provide informal support to Mackinnon's venture, even if Salisbury emphasized the private nature of the scheme.[183] The Foreign Office encouraged the IBEAC to pursue anti-slavery objectives and to assert its sphere of influence in the interior, although this would turn out to be harmful to the Company's profitability. By 1890, when Stanley returned to London to publicize his account of the Emin Pasha mission, the IBEAC had embarked on a fateful expedition.[184] The consequences of their move into Uganda, for the anti-slavery state, the IBEAC, and the peoples of East Africa, will be explored later. For now, it is worth considering how closely anti-slavery was woven into the commercial and diplomatic warp of the men pursuing these schemes to draw Britain into African territories.

The question remains whether economic interests drove British policy in East Africa. Herbert Rhodes buried Elton after he had succumbed to disease while seeking a route for trade—whether by elephants or free porters—to reach the coast.[185] When, if ever, did greed bury philanthropy in the calculations of East African policy? Was anti-slavery a seductive decoy to cover the rapacious advance of Rhodes and his ilk? Men such as Elton, Kirk, Waller, Wylde, and Frere, who became governor of the Cape and high commissioner in South Africa just months before Elton's death, combined sincere anti-slavery zeal with enthusiasm for African trade and wealth, brokered in British hands. It is naïve to see them as greedy liars or fools believing their pieties. The psychology of imperial penetration was far more complex.[186]

Mackinnon was being too simplistic when he insisted that IBEAC investors would "take their dividends in philanthropy" alone. Still, it is significant that African speculators emphasized their Christian mission to the public and to the state. His ally Kirk insisted that "my doctrine has always been that no philanthropic scheme can do good to Africa or to ourselves unless it has in it the elements of commercial success."[187] Harry Johnston, a British explorer who had befriended Kirk, similarly told members of the Royal Colonial Institute in 1889 that "no philanthropy is sound and lasting that is not based on self interest" and that, thankfully, Africans would enjoy the benefits of civilization alongside British traders.[188] Men such as Herbert Rhodes—and Cecil, who saw the IBEAC as a potential vehicle for the future ambitions of his South Africa Company—doubtlessly did focus on the profits. However, the IBEAC and similar schemes relied to a significant degree on philanthropists whose anti-slavery work predated their economic interests in Africa.[189] Commercial ambitions were hijacked by anti-slavery zeal, as well as the other way around.[190] British foreign policy had always promoted the country's strategic and economic interests alongside higher-minded concerns; there was little new in looking to Africa for riches.[191] One historian of East Africa condemns British policy as "the humanitarianism of self-interest"; it was, but anti-slavery assumptions also created the promise of self-interest where there was none.[192]

British imperial policy was not controlled by any particular cabal in London, to be manipulated easily for private reward. Within the state, the Slave Trade Department often operated at odds with other parts of the Foreign Office, and the Foreign Office as a whole often despised the policy instincts of the Colonial Office; Wylde's agency had limits. Besides this institutional jostling, groups of missionary, humanitarian, and commercial interests could dictate different lines of action. Mackinnon's 1870s scheme with Leopold was undermined by a suspicion of international, rather than British, agency, even though business interests—and sincere anti-slavery intentions—aligned in favor of the scheme. By contrast, Frere's mission to Zanzibar succeeded, despite muted cabinet enthusiasm, without any capital at stake. South African employers seized the opportunity to recruit free-labor emigrants from the suppression operations, but this was a local initiative rather than a goal of officials, the cabinet, or the prime minister.[193] As a final example, in West Africa merchants became more active supporters of state involvement thanks to better lobbying, not to any fundamental shift in economic interests.[194] In sum, the fluid, pluralist politics of imperialism were not hatched by some unipolar conspiracy.

Although figures such as Salisbury held back from official sanction, his differences with Foreign Office officials or entrepreneurs were actually quite slight. As the British political agent in Zanzibar, Frederic Holmwood, observed in 1878, "every one interested in Africa has an ideal scheme for its regeneration, yet among those who would see England enter the field, few hold exactly the same views as to what should be the extent of our action, or where it should reach its limits, though all agree that an undertaking intimately connected with the development of trade should be a leading feature."[195] Debates over the role of the state were still limited in scope, even if strategic concerns about Egypt, the Suez Canal, and India loomed larger than before. For all his activism, Frere himself judged that "Alfreds and Charlemagnes are not to be got by official indent, but they are sure to appear when men trained as members of great civilized communities are brought in contact with masses of uncivilized men, tractable, teachable, and strong to labour, under any other conditions than those of the slave and his driver." Despite welcoming British commerce in East Africa, Frere insisted that "the men required will be found when they are attracted, not by merely worldly motives, by love of gain or adventure, but by the religious zeal" of Christian faith.[196] Applying the distinctions made by modern historians, Frere advocated imperial power but not formal colonies. He thought influence was best created by informal agents rather than by state engineering.

Suzanne Miers suggests that the reorganization of the Foreign Office in 1884, which saw the Slave Trade Department become the Africa Department, demonstrated that "the suppression of the slave trade might...well become a pawn in the game of power politics."[197] British policy in Africa undoubtedly became more intricate at the end of the nineteenth century, but anti-slavery could take on the role of a knight, bishop, or queen as readily as a pawn. Anti-slavery sentiment constrained the actions of statesmen, who could be pushed into actions such as Frere's expedition to Zanzibar. More fundamentally, and less deceptively than this, the assumptions of future wealth in Africa were founded upon old traditions of legitimate commerce developed by anti-slavery campaigners over more than a century. To this end, Holmwood could expect support for the view that "we shall find our reward not only in the benefits" to Africans but "also in the revival of our trade," an idea shared by everyone from the Church Missionary Society's Edward Hutchinson to the Anti-Slavery Society's Sir Thomas Fowell Buxton.[198] After Wylde's departure, the new Consular and African Department pursued a similar course. His successor, Percy Anderson, shared the view that commerce would be the key means through which the slave trade would be suppressed and wider British civilization spread in Africa.[199]

In explaining Britain's turn toward East Africa in the 1880s, historians have long examined a memorandum composed by the African Department's Clement Hill in 1884.[200] Far from focusing only on the Egyptian-Indian strategic dimensions, Hill outlined the commercial prospects for future exports from the interior regions.[201] This was likely influenced by his active desire to show that British influence in the area could be economically sustainable as well as morally advantageous. It also reflected a broader concern to avoid British commerce being squeezed out of East Africa by rival powers.[202] Yet Hill's ideas and the wider activism of the Africa Department can be illuminated by his and his department's past. Hill had seen Zanzibar for himself in 1873–74 when he accompanied Frere's special mission. He was a correspondent of Wylde who had, in 1876, been convinced to stay at the Foreign Office because of his interest in the slave-trade question, and it was Hill who had praised the Office's achievements "in spite of the Gov[ernmen]t."[203] As an old Slave Trade Department man, Hill understood that the slave trade remained a prominent obstacle to political stability and commercial prosperity in Africa.[204] The rechristening of his department as the Africa Department did not reflect the absorption of anti-slavery affairs by expansionist concerns. Rather, it reflected the extent to which anti-slavery ambitions had expanded the scope of British objectives in Africa.

## ANTI-SLAVERY AND THE SCRAMBLE FOR AFRICA

If anti-slavery was more than a decoy in the early politicking around the east coast, then its role in the later development of formal rule needs to be considered too. This can be traced through case studies of British imperial policy in Sudan, at the Brussels Conference, and in Uganda, Central Africa, and Nigeria. Among this list, slavery in Sudan may seem conceptually and geographically detached from questions of anti-slavery expansionism in Africa, but for the Victorians Sudan was politically and intellectually intertwined with East Africa as much as with Egypt. The salience of slavery questions in the region merits its inclusion on the list and it is a good place to begin our studies.

From the 1860s, British explorers had presented their involvement in the region as an anti-slavery mission. Samuel Baker had been appointed by the khedive of Egypt to lead an expedition into Sudan in 1869. The BFASS criticized Baker as a pawn in selfish Egyptian designs for expansion, but he won plaudits as an anti-slavery hero from the Prince of Wales, among others.[205] Although encouraged initially, the Society found Baker's successor, Charles Gordon, equally troublesome. Declaring a monopoly on the ivory trade as an anti-slavery measure, Gordon insisted that civilization would precede the emancipation of Sudanese slaves.[206] In a hectoring letter to Waller, the army officer compared utopian pressure for immediate emancipation in Sudan with the care Britain showed toward West Indian planters in compensating them. Gordon wrote furiously that he would do "what I like, and what God may in his mercy direct me, to do about domestic slaves," arguing that suppression of slave trading required the tolerance of existing slave labor within Egyptian and Sudanese society. "I will buy slaves, for my army, for this purpose.... I will do it in the light of day, and defy your resolutions and your actions," he ranted. There was some accuracy in his complaint that the BFASS and the British public "speak & pass resolutions, on matters of great import, without understanding the whole question. Every man who does not agree with you, you brand as conniving at slavery." However, this was not just sensitivity to local traditions; Gordon saw himself as a martyr and a man of action, hoping for glory from his practical results.[207]

A more active policy of stopping the slave trade from the Sudan and a nominal system of slave registration thawed his relationship with the BFASS after 1878. Gordon returned to Britain in 1879 and used the Society to aid his campaigns against the khedive, with whom he had fallen out, and in favor of a European-managed regime in the Sudan.[208] Until this point, the British government had not taken a formal role in Egypt's Sudanese subimperialism, only granting Baker or Gordon leave to serve the khedive. Things changed after Britain's "temporary" occupation of Egypt from 1882, though this action had little to do with slavery directly. Gladstone's invasion was the product of financial and strategic interests alongside "the late-century view that economic and social progress was too urgent to be obstructed by Afro-Asian regimes" such as the Egyptian rebels under Colonel Ahmed Aribi.[209] The Mahdist supporters of Aribi had partly objected to the anti-slavery measures foisted on the Egyptian regime. This was not the only cause for their revolt against Western influence, but its indirect consequences would have a long-term impact on the course of British policy towards slavery.[210]

On retaking Khartoum in 1884, Gordon had bought local support by disavowing the abolition of slave-holding, which was planned for 1889 under the Anglo-Egyptian Convention of 1877. His attempts to co-opt Al-Zubair Rahman Mansur as a local ally were vetoed by the British government, because it was politically unacceptable for a known slave trader to be given power over Sudan.[211] Gordon's policy enjoyed the support of such an inauspicious champion as the bishop of Lincoln, who pleaded in March 1884 that Saint Paul would have approved of the general's pragmatic approach.[212] Meanwhile, journalists openly mocked the Prince of Wales's recent praise for Gordon's abolitionism, given the officer's "revival of slavery in the Soudan."[213] In the last few months of his life, therefore, Gordon found himself widely vilified for his un-English compromise with slavery.

Death redeemed him. Gordon lost his life in January 1885 defending Khartoum during his disastrous attempt to suppress the Mahdist conquest of Sudan.[214] Following news of his demise, he was canonized as an abolitionist saint, his Sudanese soldiering resanctified as a crusade.[215] In the House of Commons, one MP mourned Britain's loss of both the general and Sudan as the greatest possible victory for slave trading; he praised Gordon's lieutenant Emin Pasha for flying the flag for civilization and anti-slavery in East Africa.[216] Having been ignored three years earlier, Gordon's book about slavery in the Sudan became a bestseller.[217] Like Livingstone's

death in 1874, unprecedented national grief and outrage at Gordon's demise provided an impulse for new imperial ventures and anti-slavery sentiment.[218] Baroness Burdett-Coutts, "England's greatest philanthropist,"
advocated a railway to civilize Sudan and to prevent it falling back into the
hands of slave dealers.[219] Verney Cameron, a British officer and African
explorer, hoped to raise money for a Central African expedition through
the auspices of a "Livingstone-Gordon Society" in 1888, jointly honoring
the anti-slavery martyrs with a new mission to suppress the slave trade.[220]
However, the scheme that first carried forward Gordon's imagined anti-
slavery crusade was the Emin Pasha Relief Expedition, backed by Burdett-
Coutts and others to rekindle his legacy. Despite high hopes at its departure
and smart propagandizing by Stanley on his return, the mission was an
embarrassing disaster.[221]

By the time Stanley and the few survivors had limped back to European territory, anti-slavery attention had turned to a new initiative involving his ally, King Leopold. The Brussels Conference of 1889–90 was
one of the single most important meetings in the European scramble to
divide Africans' lands among themselves. Unlike the Berlin Conference,
where slavery had been an afterthought, Brussels was ostensibly stimulated
by anti-slavery considerations. Since 1888, Cardinal Charles Lavigerie, with
the sanction of the pope, had sought to lead a new crusade against the African slave trades not just in his native France but throughout Europe. His donation of nearly £2,000 to the BFASS, alongside the Society's recruitment
of men such as Wylde and James Hutton, helped revive the group as allies in
his quest.[222] Although appreciating the "peculiar gallic flavour" of his pronouncements, some sections of the British press were skeptical of Lavigerie's
proposed alliance under Catholic leadership. One paper, lecturing foreigners on their Johnny-come-lately conversion to anti-slavery, observed that
"an allied crusade into the interior of Africa" would raise fears that "professed motives are not always their ulterior motives. Compassion for Sambo
is quite compatible with earth-hunger for tropical possession, and with the
desire of an energetic Church to extend its spiritual dominion."[223] In other
words, foreigners might use anti-slavery as a "decoy" for imperial, commercial, or evangelical ambitions; modern suspicion of British motives parallels
Victorian doubts about their continental cousins.

Public cynicism toward foreign powers was mirrored in the Foreign Office. Clement Hill suggested that the Berlin Conference powers undertake a
new compact against the slave trade in Africa, yet he admitted that it would
be more effective for the government's popularity than for its practical effect. His doubts did not reflect personal antipathy to anti-slavery politics
but pessimism toward Britain's European rivals.[224] A parliamentary debate
on the slave trade in 1889 reinforced the consensus on the importance of

British anti-slavery policies and, simultaneously, the disagreement over what they should be. Speakers looked from the west to the east coast of Africa and differed wildly on whether other European powers were allies or enemies in Britain's efforts to suppress the slave trade.[225] The previous year, Salisbury—against the advice of officials such as Hill and Kirk—had connived with Bismarck in a blockade of the rebellious East African coast. Germany's pretensions to suppress the slave trade were widely seen as a mask for the suppression of African resistance to their brutal occupation policies. Incidents such as this helped Britons scoff that Germany's "invasion of the Dark Continent" was not "primarily due to a desire to put an end to slavery."[226]

Despite this hostility, Britain did secure a conference on the slave trade, though without full control of the agenda. Salisbury was aghast to discover that the host, Leopold, intended to discuss only slave hunting in the interior of Africa. The British successfully kept the conference open to maritime slave trading, which still interested the Foreign Office. Britain's representatives were Kirk and Sir Hussey Vivian, a Foreign Office clerk who had risen to become Her Majesty's ambassador to Belgium. They did not secure an international right of search, as the French still bitterly resented anything of the kind, but an alternative compact was agreed on, policing the transport of Africans and using national flags. Although this meant giving up searches outside of acknowledged slave-trading zones, it was a more practical outcome than Hill had dared to imagine.[227] Other powers were more concerned about slave-holding within Africa. Zanzibar had banned the introduction of new slaves or the enslavement of newborn children from 1890, and the Brussels Conference considered ways of replicating this formula in other parts of the continent. Despite grand pronouncements from Persia, Tunis, and the Ottoman Empire, little of substance was achieved in deterring slave trading within delegates' own countries. Similarly fruitless was the establishment of an international anti-slavery bureau in Zanzibar; its supervision and information-sharing powers matched the long-standing habits of the British Foreign Office, but without the same vigor in execution.[228]

Thanks to King Leopold, the most significant outcome of the conference was a declaration in favor of the European civilization of Africa. The powers committed themselves to building arterial railways and roads throughout the interior and to promoting missionary and commercial activities, though with no definite timescale. There is little doubt from the proposals that Leopold sought material advantage for his personal empire, the Congo Free State. However, even if the Conference crudely permitted him to extend his dominion, not all signatories saw the resolutions in the same light. Britain was keen to avoid commitments to territorial expansion, which Salisbury saw as expensive.[229] Therefore, it is hard to see anti-slavery leadership as a cynical ploy. While the British government welcomed their advantage from the conference in domestic politics, slave-trade suppression was so integral to expectations of developing African trade that anti-slavery was its own material motive, not needing to cloak any other.

Indeed, Salisbury supported the suspension of free-trade principles for the cause of anti-slavery, permitting tariffs to be levied on trade in the Congo to fund slave-trade-suppression efforts. As ever, anti-slavery interests ran alongside tactical concerns, though. The prime minister's enthusiasm to check Portuguese challenges in the Great Lakes region temporarily aligned his interests with those of King Leopold.[230] At the same time, the IBEAC and Cecil Rhodes's South Africa Company were keen to win concessions from the Congo Free State that would allow a Cape to Cairo railway to be built through East Africa. These Mackinnon won, during the Brussels Conference, in exchange for Leopold's access to the upper Nile, where he hoped to recruit laborers.[231] When it came into force two years later, the Brussels Act would have a more momentous impact on the IBEAC and British imperial policy than anything that came from such dreams. Rather, the undertakings from Brussels helped create a nightmare in Uganda for IBEAC investors and the British government, not to mention for Ugandans themselves.

With gentle support from Salisbury and the Conservative government, the Company had looked north from their Zanzibari concession. Lying between the IBEAC's existing zone of influence and the lost lands of Sudan, Uganda seemed to hold strategic value in defending British Egypt. In preparation for his railroad, Mackinnon authorized an expedition under Frederick Lugard, an adventurous former army officer. Waller and Kirk had introduced Lugard to Mackinnon, just as they had previously wooed Gordon, almost successfully, to work for the IBEAC.[232] Arriving in Uganda in 1890, Lugard found a raging civil war between Protestant and Catholic converts. As one MP would later argue, missionaries had turned Uganda into "the Belfast of Africa."[233] Far from ending this unstable chaos, Lugard joined the fighting against African Catholics and divided local chiefs against each other.[234] By 1891, the Company could not finance the escalating mission and told the Church Missionary Society that a withdrawal was imminent unless the Society could provide a subsidy. Controversially, Alfred Tucker, the bishop of Uganda, helped raise donations of more than £15,000 to support Lugard's operations, but this only bought one more year of the Company's presence.[235] By the time the company issued a final ultimatum in 1892, requiring state support to avert withdrawal, Lugard was recalled to Britain to lobby for his nation's continued involvement in the region.[236]

The IBEAC had been financially unstable when Mackinnon was dispatched on his expedition; after it, he looked to the government to save the venture from impoverishment. Far from saving the Company with a new branch of commerce, the Uganda debacle had been an expensive failure. Hope lay in the construction of a state-financed railway into Central Africa. The IBEAC, still burnishing its philanthropic motives, insisted that it "has done its share of public duty ungrudgingly" but felt that commerce could not shoulder the full burden of the next steps. Salisbury, surprisingly, was willing to provide a subsidy, reasoning that the Brussels Act required such activity by the government and that the IBEAC seemed to offer a cheaper long-term solution than further naval suppression.[237] As the *Pall Mall Gazette* noted, in public he made great "stage-play" of his victory to convince the Treasury to fund the railway, seeking popular recognition for wishing "to pursue this evil to its home and kill it at its root."[238] After losing power in the general election later that year, his press supporters boasted that Salisbury's "party, at all events, will leave no stone unturned to utilise this opportunity of dealing a death-blow to the slave trade and at the same time of developing the industrial sources of Central Africa."[239]

In opposition, the Liberals had condemned the payment of £25,000 to assist with building a railway, seeing it as unjustified state support for a private venture. Lugard was asked by the IBEAC to ensure "that public opinion may be stirred up."[240] With support from Lugard, humanitarians and missionaries objected to the evacuation of Uganda and "excited more interest throughout the country than any question which has been raised for a considerable period," as one newspaper judged it.[241] Public agitation in favor of further subsidy emphasized that the consequent "introduction of British trade into Africa would get rid of the slave traffic in a more efficacious manner" than the £200,000 a year currently spent on east coast naval suppression. Local chapters of the Church Missionary Society (CMS) took a keen interest. Missionaries believed the railway would suppress the slave trade and create conditions for the spread of the Gospel.[242] More than a hundred local meetings, including Anglican and Conservative Party groups, sent resolutions to the Foreign Office. While local Liberal associations tended not to act as corporate entities, party men such as John Cowan, chairman of Gladstone's Midlothian election committee, formed regional organizations in support of the railway and in defiance of their government's policy.[243]

The BFASS lobbied Lord Rosebery, the new foreign secretary, over the importance of a railway between Victoria-Nyassa and Mombassa; the abolitionists suggested that this would suppress the slave trade, meet Britain's obligations under the Brussels Treaty, and "avoid an indefinite extension of Imperial responsibility."[244] The *Birmingham Daily Post* published a pro-intervention letter from a reader signed as "A Voice from Sturge's Monument," evoking the late, local founder of the BFASS, Joseph Sturge.[245] The CMS, desperate to see support for their mission, insisted to Rosebery that though they were "not an anti-slavery society...they had always heartily supported the national policy of suppression of the slave trade."[246] For both business and missionary interests, anti-slavery remained the politically relevant way of converting private interest into national interest. Rosebery, maintaining public neutrality while he championed intervention behind the scenes, helpfully coached the CMS delegation; he told them that they should focus on slavery more because it "was a great element in the case, and if it could be shown that the cause of anti-slavery was largely interested in their contention, that would be a further element of consideration" in their favor.[247]

For some supporters of imperial expansion, "the continuity of England's moral policy is of far more importance than the success of a commercial enterprise, than the addition of another country to the markets of Europe."[248] BFASS supporter Reginald Bosworth Smith coined the phrase a "continuity of the moral policy" during his delegation's meeting with Rosebery. The foreign secretary seized upon it and agreed that this "continuity of moral policy is the moral force by which, in my opinion, this country has to be judged." British imperial policy must pursue "a higher and purer spirit," embodied by anti-slavery, rather than "selfish, grasping and greedy motives."[249] Responding to the BFASS, Rosebery insisted that while other questions, not least finance, influenced the Ugandan question, "the great cause of suppressing slavery must occupy a commanding place."[250] George Mackenzie, chief executive of the IBEAC, certainly realized this, emphasizing anti-slavery interests over those of missionaries in his public defence of the company.[251] At town hall speeches in Kensington and Birmingham, Lugard insisted that "that large portion of the British people" would ensure that their sphere of influence did not become "the sphere of influence of the slave trader & slave stealer."[252]

However, this emphasis on national duty complemented arguments, made by Stanley among others, that Ugandan annexation was wrapped up in a broader national interest as a future market for British exports.[253] Not all commentators, however, were so optimistic about the benefits of intervention for Britain. *Punch* ran a series of cartoons expressing weary obligation rather than eager desire. In one from 1892 (fig. 15), Uganda was a "white elephant"—an expensive liability—sold to the public under duress.[254] This image was not strictly incompatible with Stanley's promise of African trade flourishing and, ultimately, manufacturing jobs for workingmen, but it certainly showed less confidence in the financial rewards of the venture.

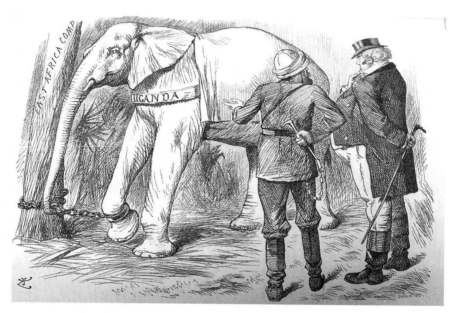

FIGURE 15. "The White Elephant," *Punch*, 22 Oct. 1892, 187. Present proprietor: "See here, Governor! He's a likely-looking animal—but I can't manage him! If you won't take him, I'll have to let him go!" By permission of Plymouth University.

Material and moral concerns for East Africa blended together seamlessly in different proportions depending on the audience. Whether it was cast as an ally or an alternative to material interest, Britain's anti-slavery honor dominated public debate about the annexation.[255] As Lugard publicly admitted, Uganda was not "the hot-bed" of slave wars. However, the opportunity to block a slave route to the coast provided a sufficient basis for anti-slavery campaigning.[256] However, the IBEAC's emotive calculations, to "maintain the public and sentimental interest in Uganda," were not only about profit motives. In a private letter to Lugard, Mackenzie also insisted that "we can show satisfactory results" from "the view of Philanthropy," which was what Mackinnon and his friends cared about; the Company's survival, though, depended on "the investing public of the country" and that was why the railway was required.[257]

Lugard had drafted much of his promotional book on Ugandan intervention in the sleepy rectory of the BFASS's influential Horace Waller.[258] The officer did not subscribe to the Society's brand of abolitionism, but neither did he use anti-slavery as an excuse for commercial interests. Rather, Lugard had his own vision of British anti-slavery policy. Whereas the BFASS had tended to be idealistic, he saw himself offering a practical anti-slavery imperialism. After his success agitating action from leading politicians, he boasted to his brother that "when I came home the Slavery subject was on a footing with the CMS or the Anti-opiumists." "It was a *fad*" championed in Parliament as "the hobbies of small cliques," and "the House emptied" when they spoke. Lugard may have exaggerated his own importance, but his contempt for "a small set of Quaker faddists" was revealing.[259] These humanitarian traditionalists certainly lacked his success in lobbying statesmen, priming the press, and rallying crowds, but their brand of anti-slavery faced a tougher audience. When anti-slavery issues broke into public debate, the BFASS tended to follow the lead of partisan campaigns or imperial interests, championing less radical anti-slaveries. One of the Society's leading members, Waller, tried to reassure Lugard that it was "a piece of machinery, useful for collecting facts" and attracting public opinion to crises. Still, he admitted that "left to itself, and allowed to ride its Quaker hobby, it is also capable of infinite harm," but he hoped "to make it useful & to correct some of its tendencies."[260] That he did. Under Waller's influence, the BFASS enjoyed new success, promoting particular imperial policies rather than opposing imperial expansion per se.[261]

The Uganda agitation was one of their greatest successes. Favoring British influence in Uganda despite the opposition of his Liberal colleagues, Rosebery extended IBEAC occupation by renewing their subsidy.[262] He did so by suppressing negative reports from Sir Gerald Portal, the special emissary on Ugandan matters. Portal had been supportive of an imperial policy in the area until he arrived and found the IBEAC's conduct had "brought disgrace to the British name." The foreign secretary's colleagues saw no national interest in assisting the company or expanding the British Empire. Still, by the end of 1892, cabinet ministers, deceived by Rosebery, felt powerless in the face of the anti-slavery "violent jingo fever" of the country. After becoming prime minister in March 1894, Rosebery moved swiftly to annex the IBEAC's territory as a formal colony. Mackinnon and the IBEAC had sought public subsidy but secured the nationalization of their failed venture.[263]

Behind the scenes, Lugard had tried to pressure the Liberals, while "going quietly to [the Conservative Joseph] Chamberlain to coach him how to embarrass the Govt. if they don't run on my lines."[264] In the 1894 debate on annexation, he was delighted to see the "intimate knowledge" deployed on "technical subjects" by the other MPs he had coached.[265] BFASS supporter Joseph Pease endorsed Portal's view that "to efficiently check the Slave Trade, there is but one course open. The only means of effectively doing this is by making a railway."[266] Sir John Kennaway, an evangelical MP representing the views of the Church Missionary Society, argued that "while the British flag floated over Uganda, slave caravans did not go through...Withdraw from that country, and the traffic would be

resumed." Kennaway's plea for British involvement was particularly surprising as British missionaries had originally opposed government intervention in Uganda, but now they found themselves reliant on imperial
protection given the insecurity and instability stimulated by IBEAC and
government meddling.[267] In the press, proannexation journalists gleefully
quoted Portal's useful pronouncement that control meant "a preponderance
of influence and of commerce" while withdrawal meant "a renunciation on
the part of England of any important participation in the present work of
development, in the suppression of slavery, and in the future commerce of
East and Central Africa."[268] Commerce, civilization, and Christianity once
again featured as assisting the suppression of the slave trade or as benefits
deriving from suppression.

Some MPs did resist the idea that anti-slavery required imperial expansion. Sir Wilfrid Lawson was one of the MPs who opposed the expense assumed by the British government in ruling Uganda. He suspected that only
firmer action from Zanzibar would end East African slavery and accused
the Ugandan enterprise of being "a filibustering expedition"; with unsettling accuracy he predicted that "formerly we stole Africans from Africa,
and now we stole Africa from Africans."[269] Lawson did not question Britain's interest in promoting anti-slavery, only whether that interest was relevant to Uganda. By contrast, many Liberals stomached annexation without
much appetite, accepting that popular anti-slavery demanded it even if it
was economically wasteful. Sir William Harcourt expressed a weary skepticism "as to whether we are going to establish a flourishing colony where
white men are to cultivate the ground under the Equator. I still doubt the
probability of that event."[270]

D. A. Low's study of British colonization in Uganda helps explain the
different levels of imperial policy at play in territorial expansion. The crucial stages of British intervention and consolidation in the area were shaped
by a small number of men on the spot who used their own initiative to
respond to African peoples. Government policy and metropolitan politics
intervened rarely, though crucially, in the process. There is no doubt that a
host of factors, besides anti-slavery, contributed to both these "small-scale"
and "large-scale" imperialisms.[271] However, the future economic value of
African territories that drove many individual imperialists was founded on
anti-slavery assumptions about post-slave-trade wealth. This would have
remained a private ambition without the national popular politics of anti-
slavery, which nationalized responsibility for imperial interests at crucial
junctures through deft appeals to existing sentiments.[272]

Two further examples bear out this pattern. The first comes from Central Africa where, since 1878, the African Lakes Company waged a private

war funded by humanitarian appeals against slave traders in the area.[273]
The venture was supported by missions including the Free Church of Scotland's.[274] After Livingstone's death, the church, "in obedience with his dying
wishes," launched their mission and the Lakes Company around Blantyre
and Livingstonia, on the south shore of Lake Nyassa (now Malawi). To
spread the Gospel and encourage industry, the Scottish missionaries aimed
to destroy the slave trade in the region, causing inevitable friction. Conflict
with groups living around the lake had complex causes, but to British colo-
nists writing home the conflict was simple.[275] After an attack in 1888 on his
party, Rev. Robert Laws insisted hostility "is part of a concerted scheme
for resuscitating the slave trade to more than its previous vigour. The slave
trade and this alone, is the mainspring of the whole."[276] A "Nyassa Anti-
Slavery and Defence Fund" back in Britain looked to the "proper action of
the enthusiasm of her individual citizens" to defeat "a slave force which was
a collection of all the scum of humanity."[277]

Still, much activity was focused on promoting ways the British state
could aid this struggle. Some parts of the metropolitan press suggested that
the government should force the Portuguese to remove tariff barriers on
trade heading up the Zambesi.[278] At public meetings in Manchester, missionaries and manufacturers combined to condemn "the Arab invasion,"
while the dean of Manchester chaired a gathering of the Universities' Mission Society to express solidarity with the pioneers in the Lakes region.[279]
A young Frederick Lugard led the Company's military efforts in the region,
and he used the same talent for publicity that he would deploy two years
later in Uganda. Writing to the press, he welcomed Lord Salisbury's parliamentary support for "the British community on Lake Nyassa" and the
Conservatives' promise of diplomatic assistance. However, Lugard tartly
reported that the British consul had told Arab slave traders "that this fighting had nothing to do with the British Government, and that it was solely
undertaken by this little party here."[280] Such politicking aimed to shame
the state into more active support for the bridgehead of commerce, Christianity, and civilization.

Another partisan for the Lakes Company possessed an equally keen
eye for publicity. Harry Johnston mixed literary efforts and adventuring
achievements in Africa, advertising the moral purpose of British penetration. In 1888, he published his sketch of a Central African slave raid in
the *Graphic* (fig. 16). In starker terms than Victorian audiences had seen
before, he showed the mayhem, murder, and disruption caused in a village when Arab slave traders raided. In an accompanying article, Johnston insisted that Britain and other European powers should use territorial
power over areas of Africa to suppress this alien slave trade.[281] He followed
this with the graphically illustrated *History of a Slave* in 1889, a fictional

narrative of an African's ordeals that drew on stories Johnston had heard from ex-slaves in the western Sudan. Having captured other Africans to sell to an Arab slave trader, the imagined narrator found his own village invaded to satisfy the same trader's greed. Johnston's brother later recalled that Sir Harry had no sooner "finished fighting slavery with his pen and still more eloquent brush when he was called upon to combat it with the sword" by becoming, later that year, consul to Portuguese East Africa (the duty Elton had once undertaken).[282]

Johnston was exactly the supportive British consul that suited Rev. Laws, the Lakes Company, and Lugard (who now left Nyassa for his IBEAC employments). It also suited Cecil Rhodes, who provided Johnston with funds to purchase the support of Nyassa's local peoples, hoping that this would secure the British sovereignty required for a Cape-to-Cairo railroad.[283] As part of his treaty-making, Johnston issued Union flags to the Makololo people of Katangas so they could display their friendship and proclaim the British sphere of influence.[284] However, while he was busy "pacifying" the Arabs based at the north of Lake Nyassa, the Portuguese entered Britain's presumed territory, demanding the Makololo lower their flags. When sensationalist Lakes Company reports filtered back to London, the press were seized with patriotic praise for the Africans refusing to lower Queen Victoria's standard.[285] It seemed as if a war with Portugal might be

FIGURE 16. Sir Harry Johnston's depiction of the devastation after a slave raid in Central Africa. *Graphic*, 29 Sep. 1888, 340–41. By permission of Mary Evans Picture Library, ref. 10012234.

imminent. Waller quickly released a pamphlet that explained the strength of Britain's "title-deeds to Nyassaland" and the Company's moral purpose "of introducing legitimate commerce, which is the surest and safest cure for the slave trade."[286] In Glasgow, journalist supporters crowed that "it will become a national necessity to support our missionaries and traders" and "that which Lord Salisbury was reluctant to do a year ago will now be forced upon him."[287] Other commentators counseled caution, warning that commercial agents of the Lakes Company had a vested interest in government action, so it was best to wait for Johnston's impartial consular assessment.[288] In fact, the consul was as keen as the missionaries and the traders were to exploit the opportunity.

The Lakes Company, its missionary cheerleaders such as Waller, supportive officials such as Johnston, and even the shadowy support of Rhodes, formed a successful alliance to win greater state support. There was no war with Portugal, and some Britons, not just the Peace Society, thought it would have been a gross mistake. Although critics were well aware of the Lakes Company's self-interest in propagandizing against Portugal, considerable sympathy for British influence against the slave trade remained.[289] There is evidence that Salisbury actively solicited an outcry from the African Lakes Company's supporters in the Church of Scotland to strengthen his bargaining position with the Portuguese over East Africa.[290] What lay at issue, as in other political conflicts, were questions of method (the use of imperial power) and assessment of opportunity (whether the lakes region represented poor value for the moral or financial capital required).

The expulsion of the Portuguese came with the declaration of a British protectorate over the Shire Highlands. In 1891, Johnston was appointed as the British resident. In the post, he continued to write popular accounts of the benefits of British imperialism, mining Dr. Livingstone's legacy.[291] By the end of 1892, he had used this power to free slaves taken by local rivals and impose treaties suppressing the slave trade, welcoming commerce, and acknowledging the British protectorate's right of taxation. Johnston argued that government money would be spent more efficiently on his efforts than on perpetual naval suppression at sea, and throughout his work he emphasized that security from slave raids was the purpose of Britain's presence in the area.[292] Complex political and economic struggles with African leaders could be easily reduced in reports home to stories of British officers fighting villains addicted to slave trading.[293] Whereas Elton had imagined that his elephants would undermine the slave trade in the region, Johnston used a combination of steamers, diplomacy, and brute force to pursue the same objective.

A similar combination of large-scale and small-scale anti-slavery calculation can be seen in Britain's advance into Nigeria. The city of Lagos had been, in 1861, one of the earliest anti-slavery annexations. Successive governments were content to protect British trade on the Niger River from European rivals and African resistance. From 1886, the Royal Niger Company, organized by merchant George Goldie, developed a British protectorate over the "Oil Rivers."[294] Serving as Britain's consular representative there before his exploits in Central Africa, Johnston infamously deposed and abducted JaJa, a Bonny ruler, for his perfectly legal defiance.[295] Incidents such as this—and the 1894 attack on Nana, the Benin River governor—had no immediate connection to slave-trade suppression, but reflected the local obsession and metropolitan acquiescence in measures developing "legitimate commerce" in place of slavery. Moreover, the bridgeheads of imperial expansion had been laid by initiatives earlier in the century, such as the missionary dominance at Abeokuta.[296]

With hostility toward chartered companies from politicians such as Chamberlain, the Company tried to use anti-slavery issues to win popular support. Paul Lovejoy and Jan Hogendorn have unearthed Goldie's calculated publicity for the Company's anti-slavery work, which extended well beyond the hundreds of treaties he signed with Nigerian rulers for slave-trade suppression and the promotion of commerce. Goldie pressed for expansion to the north, against the Sokoto Caliphate, which was blamed for widespread slave trading in the Company's protectorate.[297] He insisted that his actions were those of a gentleman defending a woman or child from an abusive "ruffian." Although we may doubt his philanthropy in this matter, the economic motives he harbored were predicated on the presumption that prosperity must follow suppression of the slave trade and its resultant disruptions.[298]

Although the Company lost its charter and Nigeria was split into two official protectorates, anti-slavery priorities remained similar under Lugard, who was appointed high commissioner of the northern half of Nigeria. His military forces advanced on the caliphate by the end of 1900 with the stated aim of suppressing slave raiding.[299] Similarly, Sir Ralph Moor attacked the Aro people in 1901.[300] These military expansions fulfilled Chamberlain's prediction that force was needed to "destroy the practices of barbarism, of slavery, of superstition" just as "you cannot have omelettes without breaking eggs."[301] Men like Goldie, Johnston, and Lugard played up these motives to secure government and public support, but they may have held the views sincerely too. Sincere if bigoted, British colonizers did assume that the suppression of slave raids was necessary for both morality and their own enrichment.[302] As Sir Gilbert Carter, a former governor of Lagos, insisted in an 1897 lecture, "the slave question is at the root of all trade difficulties in West Africa."[303]

British expansion was not determined by some objective test of economic interest but by a contingent political struggle. If the result was uncertain, the question of slavery remained at the forefront of political calculations and public interest in Africa. Hence, state involvement in Africa was vitally shaped by public enthusiasm for slave-trade suppression. Frederic Holmwood, the assistant political agent at Zanzibar, contributed an essay to Elton's published memoirs in 1879 in which he diplomatically argued that "the period of cheap journalism" helped cabinet ministers survey and secure "the unmistakable expression of the nation's wishes" for "the purely philanthropic action of slave-trade suppression." Put more bluntly, popular pressure framed the possibilities for government action.[304] Holmwood's statement was prophetic for the following two decades as well as the period he surveyed in the 1870s. Anti-slavery offered an easy message for popularizing the exertion of British imperial power abroad—from the Zanzibar mission to Livingstone's funeral, from the fugitive slave circulars to the Uganda annexation. Governments knew that anti-slavery was the popular aspect of imperial expansion.

## IMPERIAL MOTIVES

Political support for imperial intervention and eventual imperial rule depended on public perceptions of what interests were at stake. A chaotic, pluralist range of interests and objections aligned for or against action in particular circumstances; officials and statesmen judged whether they could be counted as a national interest and this subjective judgement depended largely on the disposition of the public and—particularly—the press.[305] Anti-slavery ideologies were one of the principal ways that commercial, strategic, spiritual, and moral objectives could be combined. Anti-slavery helped create commercial interests; anti-slavery translated commercial interests into national interests; anti-slavery was a principle public expression of imperial enthusiasm.

Only the last of these can be judged a "decoy." A keen enthusiast for imperial power in Uganda and Central Africa, Horace Waller had a nuanced view of morality and material interest. He denied that British commercial penetration of Africa "must surely have let in light." Rather, he mourned "if it be so, it is the blaze of the burning village" all too often.[306] Yet, for all his cynicism about commercial exploitation, Waller himself supported imperial power in order to blaze a path for anti-slavery progress. Not all commerce was good, but his tolerance for burning villages was greater when it let in the light of anti-slavery and he believed that would promote the right sort of legitimate trade. Similarly, statesmen knowingly balanced public enthusiasm for anti-slavery against other pressures, but they could use commercial interests, such as those of the IBEAC or the Royal Niger

Company, for anti-slavery ends as easily as they used anti-slavery means for commercial purposes.

Therefore, anti-slavery was not the decoy elephant of Frederic Elton's imagination, tricking Britons into following a route they would have otherwise ignored. Rather, the relationship between anti-slavery and imperial expansion was akin to the organic wild elephant trains of East Africa, marching in step under mutual protection and encouragement. A contingent process of negotiation between officials, activists, and the British public decided which paths were taken.[307] Far from being undermined by the rise of new imperial and racist thought, anti-slavery was intimately involved in its development. It is not so much that "the anti-slavery movement and the imperialist one finally met" at the end of the century but that British imperial thought had been critically shaped by strains of anti-slavery.[308] The suppression of the slave trade provided much early interest in Africa where otherwise there would have been little or none. The rise of the "new imperialism" undoubtedly complicated the nature of British attitudes toward Africa and concepts of empire more generally; still, anti-slavery continued to be woven into European imperialist perspectives on Africa.[309] Where there were commercial objectives, anti-slavery assumptions provided faith in future wealth, and where commercial gain was denied, anti-slavery provided a moral and spiritual reward for action regardless. There were four ways that anti-slavery contributed to British imperial expansion to Africa. Far from disguising motivations, anti-slavery fueled and directed them. First, in practical terms, the British cruisers that patrolled the west coast of Africa, and by then the east coast too, were there because of the slave-trade policy. This provided military protection not only for traders but also for missionaries who, in certain situations, from Abeokuta to Uganda, established "bridgeheads" for expansion. Anti-slavery assumptions and the slave-trade squadrons acted as bridge-builders for imperial bridgeheads. This was often consciously rooted in attaching anti-slavery to "legitimate" commerce as an alternative to the slave trade. Seeing this relationship as a decoy for economic ambitions is missing the point. The promotion of a free-labor world was seen as both a moral duty and a boon for all nations of the earth—a second reason anti-slavery aided imperial power. Although the terms of free-labor superiority had evolved over time and continued to be debated, there seemed little doubt from any quarter that slavery was incompatible with progress. Securing access to African territory for British interests was desirable only because of anti-slavery assumptions that fertile and extensive lands would be cultivated by African hands just as soon as the slave trade was suppressed. Moreover, private commercial concerns, which the British government did not always support, could be converted into national interests by the question of slave-trade suppression. This was a proper area for state power, not private enterprise.[310] Third, and partly because of this fact, public anti-slavery sentiment proved a powerful force in favor of those who could capture its support, for or against particular state policies. Anti-slavery was one of the few genuinely popular questions relating to the Empire beyond the white settler colonies.[311] There was still a great deal of division over the practical details of anti-slavery policy on any given issue. However, convincing public arguments could unleash terrifying outcries against negligent statesmen. But, fourth, and finally, so far as anti-slavery had any implications for understandings of race, for many Britons it favored increased contempt toward and intolerance of Africans. The complicity of African chieftains in slave trading, the failure of West Indian laborers to conform to free-labor expectations, and the pervasive presence of slavery among African societies all reinforced racist attitudes. This apparent incongruity is the subject of the next chapter.

It is remarkable, given how closely we today associate slave trading with the worst excesses of British imperialism, to note the peculiar connection between ideas about anti-slavery and empire. A last example may illustrate this. At the 1843 Anti-Slavery Convention, the Seminole Indian prince Econchatti was displayed to abolitionist delegates, who passed a motion condemning the American government's war against his people.[312] British delegates, however, were less keen to see parallels when American abolitionists complained of Britain's attacks "on the poor Affghans, on the Caffres, on the Chinese," considering these remarks obtusely political and irrelevant to their exclusive focus on anti-slavery.[313] The foregoing survey of British colonial practices, even when accompanied by detailed research into anti-slavery politics within Britain, can only begin to uncover the strange contradictions of philanthropy and colonialism in Victorian empire. Like the baffled Britons at the 1843 Convention, it has been hard for generations since to see the immediate link between anti-slavery beliefs and the practice of colonial expansion.[314]

# 7

## The Anti-Slavery Empire

"QUEEN VICTORIA EYE, see too far" was the verdict of some Africans living near the River Gambia when they encountered the electric searchlight of HMS *Racer* in January 1887. According to Edwin Parker, who recorded his service aboard the ship in a private journal, the new light was useful for the sailors' regular attempts to intimidate African societies along the west coast of Africa. On this occasion, the Royal Navy was intervening to enforce peace between local African communities at Swarra Cunda Creek because "commerce is prevented by civil wars, as native farmers and others will not cultivate the ground." It was two decades since the end of the transatlantic slave trade, but British forces still sought to promote civilizing commerce using intimidation at the best and brutality at the worst. Just a month earlier, Parker had recorded in his diary the exploits of his colleagues who had revenged two white traders alleged to have been murdered on the River Niger: "Expedition returned, after having burned, torn down, blown up, shelled, and otherwise destroyed several villages & canoes, and killed a few hundred niggers."[1]

With British power directed toward stability and commercial freedom in these kinds of ways, it is unsurprising that African peoples felt as if Queen Victoria's eye peered too far into African societies. Why, twenty years after the end of the intercontinental slave trade from West Africa, was the Royal Navy still directing violence against and pursuing control of local communities?[2] We have already seen the surprising ways in which anti-slavery supported Victorian territorial expansion in Africa, and now examine why coerced labor in the British Empire—from the West Indies and India to African protectorates—troubled British anti-slavery consciences so rarely.

The use of violence and British force in the pursuit of stability and order complemented British accommodation with forced labor.

Far from careless hypocrisy or willful negligence, most Victorians tolerated indentured labor, social repression, and "indigenous slavery" as proper engines of an anti-slavery world. This chapter looks at coerced labor in the West Indies and in emigration from India, how local African slaveries were tolerated and harnessed within an anti-slavery empire, and the development of racial attitudes during this period.

## FROM BOMBAY TO MORANT BAY

In the final two decades of the nineteenth century, India assumed an important place in British anti-slavery thinking as a precedent for balancing desires for stability with a rejection of human bondage. The subcontinent had been somewhat overlooked earlier in the century, since the Emancipation Act of 1833 applied to Britain's West Indian colonies but not to the "East Indies," as Britain's Indian territories and satellites were dubbed. Emancipation arrived there slowly, quietly, and without the fanfare of freedom in the western sugar islands. Because India was not a colony ruled from London, the colony's slave-holding had been addressed during the East India Company's rechartering in 1833. This produced a demand for abolition, but without any urgency or stringency. Initial plans for a radical, uncompensated emancipation of Indians' slaves were quashed by politicians including the Tory Duke of Wellington and the Whig historian Thomas Babington Macaulay; the latter argued that Britain should attempt cultural reforms slowly and sensitively. Any abolitionist concerns about India were eclipsed by the debates over the West Indian Emancipation Act, which passed Parliament at the same time.[3]

However, campaigners slowly turned their attention to the inaction of the East India Company's court of directors. In 1841 the India Law Commission headed by Macaulay reported to Parliament on the nature of slavery in the subcontinent. Because concern centered on Indian exploitation of other Indians, cultural anxiety was muted. Lord Auckland, the governor general of India, accepted that British sympathies would demand action, but insisted that "we ought not, through a misuse of names, to form an erroneous idea of things, or seek violently to disturb relations" that were "a service of mutual advantage, or even an honour and distinction."[4] Responding to the report, the BFASS announced their "feelings of disgust and detestation" at the forms of slavery they had heard of in India: "Domestic slavery though less revolting in the case of some of its victims...cannot be contemplated, even in its mildest form" and required termination, so "that henceforth, the whole of the British empire shall be, not only theoretically but practically, as sacred to freedom as Great Britain itself."[5] A new Conservative government under Sir Robert Peel acceded to their demands, though Auckland's successor, Lord Ellenborough, found a cautious way to comply. India's Act V of 1843 made slaves equal to free subjects before the law in property rights, civil liberties, and protection from punishment. Rather than actively emancipating slaves, breaking customary relationships, the Act removed any legal protection for such ownership. Masters had no rights under the law, but slaves were left to assert their freedom for themselves, if they chose to. This was "delegalization," not emancipation.[6]

Having agitated for the emancipation of slaves in India and in the eastern colonies of Ceylon (modern Sri Lanka), Penang and Malaca (both in Malaysia), and Singapore, the BFASS was remarkably content with the limited law it secured from the East India Company.[7] Thomas Clarkson wrote to Queen Victoria in 1843, advising her that, despite abolition being "not openly declared," the BFASS accepted the Act as "identical with the abolition of slavery."[8] It seems strange that not only British officials but the BFASS had accepted the qualitatively different nature of forced labor in India from interracial slavery elsewhere.

India could be treated differently because there seemed to be no interracial slavery. That conclusion was founded on a piece of legal redefinition. British residents in India had treated their own enslaved household servants, in many cases, as extensions of their family, often leaving specific instructions in their wills for adoption or manumission of "slaves." However, government inquiries had erased use of the word "slave" from local vocabularies; official reports denounced household slavery as un-British and re-christened slaves as "servants." After disappearing from British households, cases where Indians were holding other Indians as slaves could be reinterpreted as a familial bond closer to domestic service, best regulated through British master-and-servant law. Historian Margot Finn rightly observes that these two pieces of legal trickery left Britons "to coerce labour through contracts and legal processes, generating 'unfree' labour from 'free' servants hired outside systems of slavery."[9]

By suspending the legal status of slavery in 1843, British rulers were able to imagine adjusted Indian traditions as compatible with Western free-labor practices even if the realities on the ground had not changed for the better. The dean of the "Subaltern Studies" school of Indian history, Gyan Prakash, convincingly argues that "a bourgeois political economy was installed as the hegemonic discourse" of freedom, where "slavery, serfdom, and debt-bondage emerged as progressive steps in the direction towards free labor."[10] Coercion, then, was legitimized by a wholly dominating concept of freedom that British officials applied to India to justify an exploitative system.

The easy redefinition of domestic slavery as service would have consequences far beyond the borders of British India because it opened the possibility of legitimizing British access to Indian labor by deeming it indenture,
debt bondage, and other forms of contract under master-and-servant law.
Overseas debt and contract labor were attractive for employers when
the cost of transportation was significantly higher than the capital a free
emigrant could hope to accumulate. For this reason, indentured labor
proved more significant to non-European than white migrations within the
nineteenth-century British Empire.[11] Indian indentured labor had first been
used to supplement the work of freed black Britons in the Indian Ocean
island of Mauritius and the Caribbean colony of Demerara. In the latter
place, the driving force for migration was John Gladstone, father of the MP
and future prime minister William Gladstone, and from 1836 he sought to
bring Indian indentured laborers to work on his sugar estates.

Concerns about exploitative conditions in the destination colonies very
soon led to a humanitarian outcry in Britain. The Demerara Governor-
General's Council enforced a ban on the importation of indentured servants
in 1838, which was followed by similar legislation in India by 1839.[12] In
1840 Lord John Russell opposed any fresh emigration, fearing that indenture risked becoming "a new system of slavery." After beating his party the
next year, the Conservatives permitted indentured labor migration to Mauritius in 1843 and to other British colonies in the following year, accepting assurances of greater efforts to prevent deception or physical coercion
when signing up laborers. As we have seen, Russell and his Whig colleagues
turned to emigration after 1846 as a form of compensation to West Indian
planters for the loss of sugar protection. When Russell returned to power
as prime minister, he too became an enthusiast for greater indentured immigration from India to the faltering sugar colonies.[13]

Racial prejudice hampered any state protection of indentured Indian
laborers during their voyages. Anxious about the stinking and deadly ships
used to transport European migrants to the United States and to the white
dominions, Parliament passed a series of Passenger Acts. Although these
protections were extended to subjects traveling to the West Indies in 1840,
gross differences remained between the regulation of voyages.[14] For example, the emigration commissioners in London gave smaller incentives for
surgeons to repeat their service on voyages of Indian emigration than they
gave doctors aboard ships of white Britons bound for Australia. This meant
that experience and competence was only properly valued when it would
save white emigrants' lives.[15] The law protected subjects equally, but some
more equally than others.

Historians studying systems of indenture and contract-labor migration in the British Empire have disagreed fiercely over the degree to which

coercion was involved. Evidence suggests that force and lies were often used, though many indentured laborers did enjoy a longer life expectancy in the new colonies than in India. Whereas historian Hugh Tinker endorsed Russell's (initial) judgment that it was "a new system of slavery," optimists such as Pieter Emmer have suggested that Indian migrants were canny self-improvers.[16] Economic coercion makes this "free" emigration highly suspect, but it was treated similarly under law to employment in Britain itself.[17]

On arriving at their destination, laborers might encounter disease, strict labor conditions, or abuse. Close empirical studies of different regions suggest that the experiences of passage and labor for Indian emigrants were incredibly varied.[18] However, in a broad evaluation of the system of indenture, scholar Madhavi Kale understandably characterizes the claim that slave and free systems of migration and labor were categorically different as "post-abolition fiction."[19] British satisfaction with apparently "free" bonded labor failed to recognize the messy reality of human interactions and the abusive nature of much imperial labor. Britons imagined a clear binary when, in reality, indentured labor schemes relied on a toxic cocktail of local poverty and colonial opportunity. Still, they remained distinct from the Atlantic slave trade, even if they shared an abusive and exploitative character.[20]

When viewing the immense scale of intercontinental migrations within the British Empire, it is hardly surprising that imperial practices and individual experiences must have varied widely. More than 1.5 million Indians left their homeland in the 1838–1922 period on contracts of indenture. Some served in other European nations' colonies, but the vast majority remained on British soil in such far-flung colonies as British Guiana in South America (from 1838), Natal in South Africa (from 1860), and Fiji in the Pacific (from 1878).[21] Alongside this army of Indians, nineteenth-century British planters also sought indentured and contract labor from Africa, China, and the islands of Melanesia to the east of Fiji, though never in such great numbers (fig. 17). Painstaking research has considered the circumstances and adaptations of particular communities of laborers in different contexts.[22]

For the present study, the fundamental question is how British officials reconciled what they knew of this great migration with purported anti-slavery principles. Given Britain's opposition to the Atlantic slave trade, the migration of laborers from West Africa was always likely to cause particular unease and outrage. The British government promoted the recruitment of labor from African communities, though contemporary critics feared that premiums paid to find volunteers would simply encourage new slave wars to capture fake recruits.[23] On the other hand, it looked equally suspicious when newly liberated slaves, rescued from foreign slave

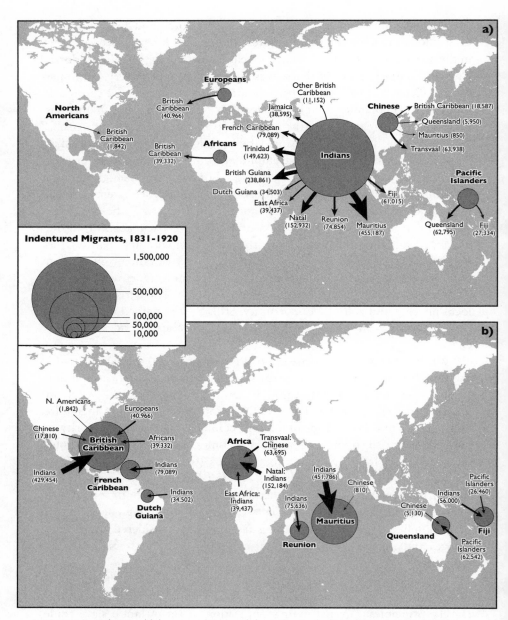

**FIGURE 17.** Indentured laborers arriving and departing in the British Empire, 1831–1920. Figures in the two maps may differ based on actual or estimated deaths en route. *Source:* David Northrup, *Indentured Labor in the Age of Imperialism, 1834–1922* (Cambridge, 1995), 155–61. Produced by Cartography Unit, Plymouth University.

ships, were then strong-armed into "free" labor for Britain.[24] As poor as conditions for liberated Africans were in Sierra Leone and at other points of disembarkation, officials resented the cost of supporting them. The British offered few meaningful opportunities for these escapees to create independent lives and so promoted migration to the Caribbean.[25] This resettlement of freed Africans made one historian suspicious that Britain's slave-trade-suppression system was entirely intended to supply de facto slaves to her West Indian colonies.[26] However, the move to supply British colonies with laborers freed from slave ships was opportunistic, resulting from the demands of the sugar colonies and the challenge of rehousing liberated Africans. There was no conscious plan to reintroduce a secret form of slavery, but successive British governments of both parties were happy to make indenture attractive to many freed people because the alternative was destitution.[27]

West Indian planters' efforts to restore productivity after emancipation provided the impetus for the recruitment of indentured labor from India and Africa, since freed black workers understandably refused to return to slave plantations as poorly paid wage laborers. There were plenty of reasons why freed West Indian slaves might prefer to work for themselves, but none of these were rational in the eyes of the dominant British officials, politicians, and commentators. Enterprise and self-reliance were condemned as ignorance and sloth.[28] James Stephen, under-secretary for the Colonial Office, author of the Emancipation Act, and son of a leading abolitionist, argued that freed people "must be stimulated to Industry by positive Laws which shall enhance the difficulty of obtaining a mere subsistence." He hoped that the "dread of starving is thus substituted for the dread of being flogged."[29]

The Colonial Office hoped that new indentured Indian and African labor would force down wages and force up productivity, keeping local blacks in their place. In the cases of both indentured immigrants and freed people, officials sought ostensibly free means of coercing subjects of color to behave according to British expectations of rationality. When race was involved, government policy toward labor resorted to new coercive practices without compromising mainstream understandings of anti-slavery. The huge social and economic differences among the West Indian islands depended on the precise circumstances of postemancipation work regimes.[30] In the varied islands of the British Caribbean, government officials or local assemblies passed strict rules against "vagrancy," punishing blacks who did not have jobs with criminal sanctions and forcing them into the employed workforce as plantation workers.[31] Ironically, in Mauritius, many Indian indentured laborers, brought to the island to drive down wages, followed black West Indians in preferring independence to plantation labor; they too found colonial ordinances directed against their "vagrancy."[32] The Colonial Office in London had consistently opposed former slaves' flight from low wages on the plantations to independent subsistence in free villages. Unable to adapt to the consequent social and demographic tendencies, all West Indian colonies had struggled to address poverty and squalor in these communities or to provide hospitals to replace plantation facilities.[33]

These social tensions provided the backdrop for the 1865 "Morant Bay rebellion" in Jamaica. The revolt had its roots in Governor Edward Eyre's relationship with the Jamaican representative assembly. This had soured over his removal of Jewish and black officials from their positions, but also reflected broader tensions over the Assembly's relationship with successive governors and the colony's Executive Council.[34] However, this political alienation merely exacerbated black laborers' frustrations at their economic suffering. Supported by Baptist missionaries, a series of meetings had been convened to petition Queen Victoria and her government to relieve material distress. The Colonial Office ignorantly replied to one such address from the people of St. Anne's in Jamaica. The missive from London, circulated throughout the island with fifty thousand copies, insisted that "working for Wages, not unsteadily and capriciously, but steadily and continuously" would be their salvation and that "it is from their own industry and prudence, in availing themselves of the means of prospering that are before them"—not government help—"that they must look for an improvement to their condition."[35] Apparently, "positive laws" might support the welfare of planters but not black workers.

George Gordon, a mixed race Baptist member of the Jamaican Assembly, emerged as the leading advocate for amelioration of Jamaican suffering, criticizing Indian immigration, corporal punishment of workers, heavy taxation of the poor, and the corruption of parish officials. Although not present at Morant Bay during the uprising, Gordon's previous activity there was blamed by Eyre, his long-standing nemesis, for inflaming the local population to violent revolt against the local magistrates.[36] As well as declaring martial law in the region and brutally killing more than eight hundred rebels, Eyre speedily tried and executed Gordon in a manner many judged to be a political assassination outside of English traditions of justice. Rival British newspapers declared sympathy with either the soldiers and their commander or the "eight miles of dead bodies" left in the wake of Eyre's repression. The BFASS played a leading role in agitating against the governor, with 250 of its members calling at the Colonial Office. Humanitarians helped convince Edward Cardwell, the colonial secretary, to recall Eyre, which unleashed a three-year-long public-relations struggle between his detractors and supporters with Mill and Carlyle heading up the opposing sides' ranks of celebrity lobbyists.[37]

Although BFASS objections to the conditions of emancipated slaves and indentured laborers in the West Indies after 1840 had little impact in Whitehall or in the press, the crisis in Jamaica following Morant Bay drew metropolitan opinion—and political controversy—firmly back to the Caribbean.[38] Some historians have seen Eyre's defenders as a "pro-slavery lobby" and his opponents as humanitarians influenced by the same forces that had promoted abolition. However, we should exercise some caution in assuming the Governor Eyre incident reflected "the movement away from an anti-slavery ideology and towards a more overt form of racism."[39] Eyre's defenders charged that critics were mindlessly bleating on behalf of "their pet black lambs" who had simply been "chastened for misconduct." Such abuse was unsurprising; more interesting was the criticism that the BFASS had stumbled onto "a subject apparently altogether foreign to the object for which it was established."[40] In many quarters, abolitionist concern for black British subjects was dismissed as irrelevant to anti-slavery. Antiracism logically bred anti-slavery, but anti-slavery did not logically require antiracism. They were independent, if often intertwined, ideas.

These attitudes stemmed from prejudices against the poor and black workers that had survived after slavery had been extinguished. The author Anthony Trollope, rather like Thomas Carlyle, condemned black West Indians as a "servile race" who required mastery even in freedom.[41] Planters such as Neville Lubbock insisted that "the position of the employers and employed was completely reversed" after emancipation in the sugar colonies, and as late as 1883 made this case to win further favorable concessions. Lubbock concluded as a general rule that "absolute freedom, unaccompanied by any kind of restraint, is not good for man," especially "races upon whom civilization has only recently dawned."[42] For many British observers, not just West Indian planters, free labor would be acceptable only when accompanied by sufficient state intervention to maintain existing racial and economic hierarchies. Sir John Pope-Hennessy, governor of Barbados, won censure from the Colonial Office after the island's unrest in 1876 because of his public attacks on white planters for demanding the old conditions of "slavery." His belief that anti-slavery required a less exploitative model of imperial rule in West Indian race relations was a maverick position.[43]

The abolition of the Assembly and the imposition of crown colony rule by the governor in the wake of the uprising reflected a wider Colonial Office disenchantment with black Britons in the West Indies. Although racist violence against the Jamaican protests of 1865 won significant censure, far fewer liberals criticized the balance of power that the state promoted between West Indian employers and laborers. Just as indentured Indian and African labor could be accepted as a logical consequence of emancipation, so the economic legislation against former slaves seemed necessary.

In this sense, contests—such as the clash between Eyre's supporters and enemies—raged over very narrow terms of disagreement. To many Britons, indentured labor and West Indian coercion secured rather than scuppered their country's anti-slavery goals.

## THE ROAD TO HELL

The goals of stability and prosperity dominated the application of anti-slavery principles to India and the West Indies, and these values informed British approaches to subjects and protected peoples in later-nineteenth-century Africa. Although officials consistently attacked interracial export slave trades, policy remained cautious regarding "traditional" forms of slavery within African societies. This was consistent with a long-standing foreign-policy focus on slave trading rather than domestic institutions. Whereas intraracial slave-holding was accepted as a natural frailty common to the early stages of civilization, foreign slaveries were cast as a malign block on the economic and racial development of Africans.[44] Precedents from British anti-slavery policy were therefore developed and adapted when new imperial expansion presented moral problems concerning the legal status of African slavery, the treatment of runaway slaves, and the use of coerced labor by imperial officials.

The Indian precedent of "delegalization" informed British attitudes toward indigenous societies in Africa, alongside experiences in the Gold Coast, one of Britain's few colonies on the continent before the last third of the century. The Gold Coast's forts offered a model of cheap, informal influence against slavery and raiding for slaves in the neighboring interior.[45] By 1840, Governor George Maclean exercised an improvised judicial authority beyond the borders of British territory in a "protectorate" painted yellow rather than red on maps of the area, because it was not formal British territory.[46] However, his implicit recognition of slavery, when arbitrating in cases of ill-treatment, sacrifice, or runaways from the protectorate, struck observers back in London as distasteful and legally dubious.[47] In March 1841, a proclamation affirmed that British and European residents of the Gold Coast could not hold slaves and that there would be no recognition of pawning (a form of debt bondage) within the colony. However, African slavery in the informal protectorate could be left alone, since it was not British territory.[48] Future governors would decline to adjudicate in cases in the protectorate that required any acknowledgement of slavery, even if they still enjoyed authority over the protectorate.[49] The 1865 Select Committee on Africa reasserted this principle that customs such as pawning could be gradually ameliorated in non-British territories by the good influence of judicial power.[50]

Although British policymakers considered the rights and wrongs of acknowledging "traditional" slavery in law, proactive attacks on intraracial slave systems were barely considered. An assumption that domestic slavery among "uncivilized" people was not morally equivalent to black slavery in Western economies survived for more than sixty years in a variety of African contexts. In 1842, many witnesses for the Select Committee on West Africa questioned whether slavery could reasonably share a name with New World forms of bondage, given its character.[51] Speaking in 1865 of what he had seen in Central Africa, Livingstone was sure that domestic slaves "are called the children of the man who has purchased them, and if he is not kind to them they may change to any one in the kingdom."[52] He attributed this benign slavery to "uncivilized" masters' "laziness" and feared it would become a threat only when Africans became "civilized", ambitious, and commercial.[53] Frederic Elton, in an 1877 letter from East Africa, declared that "the feudal form of slavery I do not so much object to." It "might continue, being an institution of the country, which the piratical slave trade of later years is not."[54] During his 1894–95 stay near Lake Malawi, the missionary Arthur Sim reflected that "until Christianity introduces the system we are accustomed to" this was probably the only way to maintain order in society.[55] Sim feared that immediate freedom for the local slaves would lead to their starvation, as "these poor fellows are not ready for freedom yet."[56]

Across these four examples, apologies for intraracial slavery reflected European weakness as much as ideological choice; Sim's predecessors in the 1860s and 1870s had offered asylum to fugitive slaves and openly undermined slave-holding, only to be attacked and punished by indignant neighbors.[57] Both principle and pragmatism led Britons to doubt that ending intraracial slavery would lead to anything besides disruption, poverty, and suffering, which could only encourage the real evil of Africa: the external slave trade.[58] As Colonel Henry Ord suggested in 1865, British efforts could be focused on the industrial-scale trafficking of Africans for export. Only in his lesser goals did he include the "civilization" of native peoples—in which category he included the eradication of domestic slavery. Passive attitudes toward slavery within African societies did not, however, give governments license to become actively complicit in upholding it by law in British territory. The suppression of slave raiding and slave trading could require intervention, whereas "uncivilized" slavery within African communities did not.[59] Among witnesses to the 1865 committee on West Africa, it seemed as if avoiding the difficult question of domestic slavery was one of the primary arguments for formal colonies in West Africa.[60] Local slaveries were embarrassing problems to be managed acceptably while attacking the export slave trade and promoting free-labor commerce.[61] In shaping British imperial policy, "missionaries and imperialists seeking territories to conquer" had little success using "domestic slavery as a justification for intervention" rather than the suppression of the slave trade.[62]

The favored method of tackling "domestic slavery" was "delegalization," that old conceit from India.[63] William Wylde, still at the Slave Trade Department in 1865, suggested that by abolishing the legal recognition of slavery, any unhappy "servant" in Lagos and Sierra Leone could transfer his work to another master or seek the protection of the British authorities. He was "neither *de facto* or *de jure* a slave."[64] Under the formula of delegalization, British and "native" courts in the expanded Gold Coast Colony, formed in 1874 following the Ashanti War, were forbidden to recognize slavery. British officials did not seek to violently disturb African relationships and did not actively encourage slaves to assert their freedom, even if the 1874 proclamation of delegalization was periodically repromulgated.[65] The reorganization of the colony had required a new legal formula because of a combination of hostility in the House of Commons, press criticism, and suspicion from civil servants. Seeing public anger at the idea of slavery in a colony, the delegalization formula was deployed over the wishes of commercial interests.[66] An anti-slavery activist such as Horace Waller could crow, in 1891, that "British rule has been a Providence in this respect to India" by managing to "throttle slavery" through the power of law.[67] It was this model officials adopted beyond the Gold Coast, in the scramble for African dominion, as a way of honoring anti-slavery law without risking "general emancipation."[68] This conceit allowed Britons to reject "a principle which is repugnant to English ideas" without attempting to "entirely subvert the principles on which African society rests."[69]

Later nineteenth-century episodes of expansion also relied on the legal concept of a protectorate developed in the 1840s Gold Coast to accommodate African slave-holding and British morality.[70] When the African "protectorate," distinct from a colony, emerged as a legal concept in the course of the 1884 Berlin conference, British officials ultimately accepted the device as a useful distinction between full colonies where anti-slavery laws were applied actively and these nominally independent areas.[71] The protectorate permitted "hegemony on a shoestring" and clean hands for British rulers.[72]

Indeed, the concept of protectorates even allowed the British to introduce delegalization slowly without breaking the letter of their own law. This was the case in Zanzibar and Pemba during their 1890 adoption as a protectorate. In the years before the kingdom became a protectorate, slavery had gradually come under attack as a side effect of British slave-trade-suppression efforts. From the late 1850s consul Christopher Rigby cracked down on slave-holding by merchants from British India.[73] An active new policy of policing the activities of British Indians in East

Africa saw official tours of the Zanzibari mainland territories, giving cer-
tificates of freedom to their slaves and actively spreading word that the
queen's subjects could not participate in slavery. The advance against Arab
ownership of African slaves was much slower.[74] It was not until 1897, seven
years after establishing a protectorate, that so much as the legal status of
slavery was abolished.[75] As Lugard observed in 1893, it was "a scandal" to
find that "our policy regarding slavery should be an active & pushing one
so long as the whole difficulty of the matter fell on the shoulders of a native
ruler...but should be a distinctly retrogressive one from the day it devolved
upon us to carry out measures ourselves."[76] Another critic of the seven-year
delay insisted that "England could do better with the loss of her cloves and
her cocoanuts than she could with the loss of her honour, her traditional
philanthropy." Such a radical view was not shared by Foreign Office men,
who assumed that a sustainable form of free labor required stability of
production.[77] As weak an anti-slavery measure as "delegalization" was, the
legal device of a "protectorate" could delay even this move against settled
systems of slavery.

In 1895, Sir Arthur Hardinge, consul in Zanzibar, explained to Liberal
foreign secretary Lord Kimberley that if "the maintenance of slavery, even
if only for a few years longer[,] entailed real suffering," then no economic
argument could justify it. He denied, however, that it caused any suffering.
This apology for slave-holding, reminiscent of Confederate Southerners
thirty years earlier, was only sustainable so long as officials and the bulk of
public opinion back in Britain accepted that a stable transition to free labor
was the best moral calculation. Missionaries in Zanzibar were wheeled out
to dutifully testify that slaves would be massacred in a rebellion or left des-
titute if immediate emancipation were forced upon the Arab masters, hor-
rifying the London-based mission societies.[78] Kimberley's under-secretary
of state for foreign affairs, Sir Edward Grey, explained the policy toward
slavery in protectorates during an 1895 debate on Zanzibar: "Against the
slave trade the British Government had made, and would continue to make,
constant warfare; but the institution of domestic slavery was common to all
Mohammedan countries, and certainly it had not been our general practice, upon assuming a Protectorate, to force a complete change in the institutions" of the native state.[79]

Although a sense of caution was common to all Britons considering
African slavery, this state of affairs seemed unacceptable to critics. Lugard
and Waller played leading roles in a public and private campaign for delegalization in the Zanzibar Protectorate, despite Foreign Office reticence.
For them, nonrecognition in law was the bare minimum, not a gradual
goal, of anti-slavery policy in a protected territory.[80] In parallel with his
campaign to retain Uganda, Lugard lobbied MPs, seeking support from

beyond the traditional critics in the BFASS. Lugard's argument that delegalization should be required in a protectorate appealed to his politician
allies since it was a compromise between humanitarian utopianism and
official pragmatism. Although there would be little effect on the ground,
British moral standards could be upheld. As Sir Charles Dilke told him,
the fact that "the impartial and well-informed" like Lugard shared "the
view expressed by the fanatics" made statesmen take notice and listen.[81]
This alliance emerged after the BFASS committee members with the stron-
gest links to imperial governance, Waller and Wylde, had drawn up the
Society's position on slavery in East Africa.[82] It is striking, however, that
political controversy over African slavery was confined to such a narrow,
legalistic set of differences as delegalization immediately and delegalization
gradually. In the House of Commons in 1892, MP Joseph Pease argued
passionately "that the abolition of the legal status was to be preferred to
emancipation, because the latter would mean the sudden withdrawal of
all labor," resistance from slaveholders, and possible suffering for slaves,
"whereas the abolition of the legal status would not involve any distur-
bance."[83] Even such a critic of Foreign Office gradualism as Pease wished
to disavow any practical steps to emancipation. Lugard adopted exactly
the same position in making his case about Zanzibar to Chamberlain and
Arthur Balfour when Salisbury's Conservative government took office in
1895. Explaining how he differed from the Liberals and the Foreign Office, he maintained in a confidential memo for them that "I do *not* advocate 'emancipation' viz. forcible abolition, and making it criminal to hold
a slave, *but* 'non-recognition by law', viz. permissive freedom to those who
desire to claim it."[84] Such criticism demanded few differences in reality, but
put great store in a difference of principles on paper. Although there were
two visions of Britain's moral and legal responsibility for slavery in protectorates (as opposed to colonies), the outrage masked an ongoing consensus
against "active" emancipation in "uncivilized" societies.

Although the stakes were low, passions still ran high, and it is not obvious why. In Lugard's case it is hard to find any mercenary or political
motive for his enthusiastic support for immediate removal of the legal status. His later policy toward slavery in Nigeria has been scrutinized and,
understandably, condemned by historians as legalistic trickery. However,
the Zanzibar campaign reveals a sincere personal investment in the importance of "legal status." As pedantic a cause as this was, Lugard had no
self-interest in challenging the Foreign Office's Sir Percy Anderson, chief of
the Africa Department, who he feared was "really England's Foreign minister." Sir George Goldie argued that Lugard's entire future career would
be thrown away by pursuing the issue, when he should be "what the French
politicians called 'opportuniste'."[85] Lugard was probably grandstanding

when he declared to his brother, in private, that delegalization would be "the greatest triumph I've ever scored."[86] However, his attachment to the paper emancipation, "which affects the welfare of thousands of 'British protected persons',," was real enough.[87] He may have sought the personal glory of claiming Wilberforce's mantle, but it is hard to find baser motives in his protest given that it clearly undermined rather than advanced his imperial career.[88] Rather, it seems that Lugard and Waller successfully revived the traditional BFASS criticism of Foreign Office policy and repackaged delegalization as the honorable, pragmatic, traditional, and patriotic approach rather than an anxiety restricted to Quaker radicals.

The principle of abolishing slavery's legal status in protectorates was repeated, with modifications and delays, throughout the British Empire. However, fear of public controversy and pressure for reforms officials deemed unworkable encouraged them to turn to secrecy. Following the outcry over the Zanzibar protectorate, in 1897 the Colonial Office advised Governor McCallum of Lagos "to avoid committing himself in writing to any general statement of policy on slavery," in case it made it back to Britain and caused controversy there.[89] After the British reconquest of the Sudan in 1898, the Anglo-Egyptian administration removed legal sanction to any form of forced labor. However, both Lord Kitchener, governor of the province, and Lord Cromer, Britain's consul general in the puppet state of Egypt, sought to leave slave-holding alone. In future years, the Sudan's chief official for slavery matters warned subordinates he would "cut off the right hand finger of any" who used the term "slave" rather than "servant" in official correspondence.[90] With deliberate deception, the colonizers sought to hide their active support for traditional institutions from the prying eyes of Westminster.

Even then, the distinction between the abolition of slavery and the abolition of the "legal status" could create opportunities for politicking. Joseph Chamberlain, speaking for the Conservatives, was happy to give partisan criticism of Grey's Zanzibar policy in 1895, as advised by his confidant Lugard. However, four years later, as secretary of state for the colonies, Chamberlain himself came under attack over Britain's policies in Nigeria. The Liberals suggested that he would repeat the sins for which he had castigated them in Zanzibar, by tolerating slavery once a chartered company's protectorate had become an imperial protectorate. As Chamberlain explained, the Royal Niger Company had "abolished the legal status of slavery" and that would remain true when their territories transferred to British protectorates, even if it was "a pious opinion" that could not be enforced in areas that "had not been trodden by white men." Still, his admission that delegalization would not change much in Nigeria looked bad after his insistence on the importance of immediate delegalization in Zanzibar.[91]

Although there was only a technical difference between the Liberals' legal recognition of slavery in Zanzibar before 1897 and the Conservatives' impotent delegalization in Nigeria after 1899, his opponents mercilessly accused Chamberlain of hypocrisy.[92] Ironically, the colonial secretary's adviser had foreseen this. A year earlier, Lugard had confided to his diary his doubts about Chamberlain's ambitions of cultivating the "great estates" of Nigeria through state, not Company, administration. Given the Conservatives' stand against the Liberals over Zanzibar, Lugard thought Chamberlain was creating a liability in accepting government responsibility for problems such as African slavery.[93]

Those who wanted immediate or gradual abolition of the legal status could agree on one thing: slavery itself could be left to decline without a formal act of emancipation, guaranteeing orderly, stable transitions to free labor.[94] The greatest danger to economic and political order seemed to be self-sufficiency and independence by freed people.[95] Stability was a requirement of the legitimate commerce needed to supplant slave trading and slave raiding. Therefore, immediate steps for meaningful African emancipations were deferred as threats to the political order and the economic development required for anti-slavery policies' long-term triumph.[96] Emancipation in the West Indies and hopes for a peaceful end to American slave-holding had seen most Britons seeking no disruption to the global export of commodities hitherto produced with slave labor. Similarly, the Foreign Office advised the prime minister, Lord Salisbury, in 1891 that "the disappearance of the status of slavery should be carried through with as little alteration as possible in the existing relations between master and slaves." Even BFASS activists accepted that liberated slaves in Africa would be compelled to work for wages, using feudal tithes or vagrancy laws in order to maintain productivity.[97]

Lugard had a chance to pursue his anti-slavery ideas when he was appointed high commissioner for Northern Nigeria in 1900. While British law in Nigeria ignored slavery, the Islamic courts continued to recognize it.[98] Children could not be born into slavery after 1901 and, reinterpreting religious law, Lugard promoted a version of self-manumission by slaves.[99] In 1933, while helping create the League of Nations' anti-slavery policy, Lugard would maintain that the abolition of legal status was a pragmatic and humane triumph of British policy.[100] However, far from affecting the lives of slaves, the policy was directly intended to allow the practical functions of African slavery to continue under newly evolved legal, moral, and political sanction.[101] This would avoid the fears of British officials, as expressed in 1900, that "if the existing labour system is broken down *before* the new one to replace it nothing but ruin and famine can result."[102] It was on this basis, following his experience in Uganda and Zanzibar alongside a national tradition of delegalization, that Lugard could promote noninter-ference with African slavery as an anti-slavery policy.

As perverse as an anti-slavery policy of noninterference may be, the logic that led to British complicity in actively supporting African systems of slavery is even stranger. The clearest case of this comes when colonial regimes acted against runaway slaves. In 1897, in the new East Africa Pro-tectorate, administered by Sir Arthur Hardinge from Zanzibar, missionar-ies refused to honor the earlier practice of surrendering fugitive slaves to masters. This prompted an outcry in the House of Commons, with the Liberal opposition exploiting the government's humiliation. Although the legal abolition of slavery was not extended to this protectorate for another decade, Salisbury's government insisted, with embarrassment, that it was illegal for any British subjects to assist in the capture of slaves and officials should not encourage the missionaries to do so.[103]

In the Lagos colony's southern Nigerian protectorate, runaway slaves had long been seen as a threat to good order. H. E. McCallum argued in 1897 "that questions relative to domestic slaves are to be dealt with by the Native Authorities only" and so fugitives lacking evidence of maltreatment could be sent back to their owners.[104] After complaints the following year about McCallum's officials assisting in the return of fugitives, Chamberlain ordered that they must not do so, even when the slaves had escaped from neighboring areas where there was no ban on the legal status of slavery.[105] In Northern Nigeria, the government similarly restrained British officials' connivance in the institution of slavery. Responding to resistance and al-leged slave trading, the British led African allies in a raid on the Nigerian nation of Obohia in 1896. Despite the anti-slave-trade purpose of the mis-sion, Consul-General Ralph Moor permitted his supporting troops to re-turn home with captured slaves from Obohia. His logic was that they were better off in British-controlled territory, but the Foreign Office was unim-pressed and intervened to restore them to their former home.[106]

After Lugard assumed rule in Northern Nigeria in 1900, he success-fully resisted attempts by some subordinates to legally recognize—so as to regulate—slavery. Instead, he adopted an obtuse policy toward fugitive slaves. Although his officials were banned from assisting in recaptures, they were encouraged to make it difficult for slaves to run away from masters.[107] In this distinction, Lugard once again drew on his experience in other parts of Africa. Missionaries in the Central African lakes had quickly discov-ered that the liberation of fugitive slaves could make their presence unten-able with former owners. In his years there, Lugard developed a scheme to permit fugitive slaves to be rewarded with wages for self-redemption, to provide an alternative.[108] It was this dubious balance between stability and noncomplicity that he sought to replicate in Nigeria. A man who put such great store in delegalization was all the more enthusiastic to "manage" the dismantling of slavery on the ground.

Accommodation with slavery and the deterrence of dislocation were not simply hypocritical; they flowed naturally from anti-slavery plans to create new wealth in Africa. Britain's whole anti-slave-trade policy rested on creating value in African labor rather than letting it be exported to the New World; that implicitly required tolerance for alternative forms of co-erced labor in Africa.[109] The suppression of the slave trade was presented as an enabling gift, benefiting Britain, Africans, and the rest of the world be-cause it would lead to new wealth from settled labor within Africa.[110] Anti-slavery policy therefore prized a stable system of production that would mirror African slaveries in all respects except the legal ownership of other humans. A glacial attitude toward dismantling intraracial slaveries was a requirement for, not in contradiction with, the dominant expectations for a postemancipation society. This led to a peculiar system of logic, whereby de facto tolerance for intraracial slavery guaranteed stability, the suppres-sion of interracial slave trading, and the safe dismantling of African slavery in the future.

The fact that greater African wealth could come only from African free labor offered imperially minded authors comfort, ironically, that empire building would produce benevolent results. As Waller argued in 1891, "Af-rica's real safety lies in the fact, that the man born of her soil is the one who must inevitably develop her riches," guaranteeing, among European colo-nists, a "wholesome rivalry begotten of a demand for native free labour."[111] Similarly, Sir Harry Johnston suggested in 1896 that Britain's presence in Central Africa was benevolent because it "has resulted in no confiscation of the black man's land, but in his being taught to develop its resources in the most profitable manner, since it has been followed by the steady suppres-sion of the slave trade and diffusion of real and reasonable liberty."[112] Yet far from cultivating respect for Africans, a hunger for cheap labor led to even more innovative means of making African laborers fit the demands of colonial economies. This was what Conservative foreign secretary George Curzon meant when he declared that "free labour, paid labour, is not in-digenous...it would have to be carefully tended and watered to enable it to grow."[113]

This growth was anything but tender. Following the example of the West Indies, colonial authorities sought new ways to maintain racial and economic inequalities. "Free labor" required an end to slavery, but it did not mean freedom of choice for the laborers. After his proclamation of 1874, the governor of the Gold Coast colony, George Strahan, was shocked when large numbers of slaves and pawns—who made up perhaps a quarter of the African population—began to leave their servitude in the interior portions of the territory. The massive disruption to the existing labor economy would entail, in the next twenty years, a policy of recruiting indentured laborers from elsewhere in Africa.[114] As in other parts of the empire, indentured labor provided a palatable way to coerce nonwhites without the structures of slavery.[115] An 1888 article in the *Graphic* suggested moving Africans to areas lacking workers, proposing that "the most effectual way to kill the slave-trade is to encourage voluntary emigration under careful supervision. If the Chinese emigrate why should not the African negroes?"[116] Although such schemes were attempted on a smaller scale than intercontinental indentured migration, colonial authorities were happy to support this way of driving down the cost of African labor.[117]

South Africa demonstrated a similar pattern of racial order and new coercion alongside anti-slavery piety. In the Cape Colony, African slaves were freed from white masters in 1838, but colonists soon looked for laws controlling labor mobility and preserving old hierarchies as far as seemed possible.[118] Laws controlling employee-employer relations provided a de facto form of racism.[119] This discrimination did not stop the BFASS or the Conservative Party from presenting the Dutch settlers as villains plotting the expansion of slavery during the first and second Boer wars.[120] However, the language of anti-slavery would haunt the warmongers afterward. The British labor movement attacked the "Chinese slavery" subsequently promoted by the Conservatives in South Africa, and the Liberal Party was delighted to take up this attack in the 1905 election. But this did not represent a damascene conversion against indentured labor arrangements. Rather, popular mobilization supported the rights of white British emigrants to jobs that might have been "stolen" by Chinese rivals. Immediately after taking office, the Liberals permitted indentured Chinese labor to continue with minor regulations. Although the particular conditions of indentured labor were criticized, there was only marginal criticism of the concept of coercing non-European labor.[121] When it came to these new forms of coercion, the grounds of political criticism were very narrowly defined.

Still, the threat of public scandal frightened politicians, who feared, for example, that railway building in Uganda would see the employment of slave labor. Given the railway's touted benefits in suppressing the slave trade, they were keen to avoid this.[122] Chamberlain, for the Conservative opposition, made political capital of taunting Sir William Harcourt for his inability to guarantee that the initial construction of the railway would avoid slave labor. For the Liberals, Harcourt argued weakly that it was impossible to build an anti-slavery railroad without doing so.[123] Having previously supported a railway, the BFASS hesitated in 1894 when it seemed likely that slave porters would be used to transport materials for its construction.[124] The Uganda railway would be largely built by indentured

Indians, avoiding this problem with a different form of coerced labor.[125] Typically, it was the condition of slavery that scared politicians or outraged the public, not the conditions under which non-Europeans would work.

A semantic distinction between slave trading and European labor regimes hampered British criticism of reported abuses in the empires of other powers. In an 1878 letter, R. B. D. Morier confessed that the Portuguese in Mozambique were legally permitted to buy slaves and free them, even though this method of obtaining labor would stimulate new slave catching. This seemed regrettable, but it was not easy to make them stop.[126] The Foreign Office was slow to stir even in cases in which British business interests might be complicit in foreign practices akin to slavery. In 1894, the Quaker abolitionist Joseph Pease drew officials' attention to Portuguese practices on the island of São Tomé, off the coast of their colony of Angola. Lord Kimberley, the foreign secretary, agreed to the civil service recommendation that "we had better leave it alone."[127] George Cadbury, who bought chocolate from São Tomé, insisted in 1901 that missionaries' "quiet work is perhaps the best means" of redressing any abuses resembling slavery. It was only later that the controversy exploded onto the public stage.[128]

The infamous abuses exposed in King Leopold's Congo Free State in the early twentieth century were only the most horrific of a spectrum of practices in European empires. Missionary groups in Britain would successfully mobilize popular outrage against the atrocities of the Belgian Congo, "the New African Slavery," as E. D. Morel labeled it. However, there was no similar introspection about British accommodations and adaptations to forced labor within African societies; in this sense, the Congo agitation is an exception that proves the rule of British myopia about labor regimes. In the case of Britain, anti-slavery principles prohibited the ownership of people but permitted—in fact, encouraged—many other forms of coerced labor.[129] In an era when the rights of organized labor were being won within Britain and "free labor" was adopted as a description of non-unionized labor, it is perhaps unsurprising that coercive forms of "free labor" were developed for nonwhite peoples in British colonies and protectorates.[130] In many circumstances, colonial officials deliberately erased the word "slavery" from their vocabulary, since "judicious silence" was safer than rousing anger back home.[131]

With complex African economies and societies responding to the material effects of global trade and imperial labor schemes, local working practices perpetually adapted, catching British politicians and their agents off guard. As one historian of slavery in Africa has argued, "if there was a passive agent in the history of slavery during the nineteenth century, it was Europe, not Africa."[132] Though British anti-slavery ideologies would be adapted or refitted to accommodate imperial reality and commercial greed, there was no fundamental break with the spirit of the 1833 Emancipation Act. Then, many campaigners, most politicians, and the general public embraced an end to the legal institution of slavery, but fully expected black people to retain a submissive role. While the Victorian empire confronted slavery in very different parts of the world using a variety of methods, this original tension remained. In 1869, embarking on an expedition to conquer Sudan for the khedive of Egypt, Samuel Baker wrote Samuel Wilberforce, the bishop of Oxford, promising to attack slavery with "a firm but delicate hand," suppressing the slave trade by means of the coercion of African workers. Baker's "practical philanthropy" would use "despotic power" to develop "people who in their ignorance must be regarded in the light of children." Therefore, he promised a system of coerced labor to raise *"the value of the human being upon his own soil to a rate that will render him too valuable for exportation."*[133] The letter is remarkable not only as an early example of how imperialists would adapt anti-slavery ideas in the following twenty-five years but because it was addressed to Wilberforce's son. There was but a short generational gap between the "heroic" age of British abolitionism and the imperial age of anti-slavery, just as there was but a short intellectual gap between the anti-slavery ideologies of the two eras.

Baker expressed his goal more starkly than others, but the assumptions he made reflected Victorian political realities. Although there were real arguments over the means of mitigating African slavery or regulating indentured and coerced labor, those differences were slight.[134] It is interesting, though, that the same men who aligned anti-slavery piety with imperial expansion could make selfless stands against Africans' mistreatment when their own standards were breached. From his role in the expansions documented in the previous chapter, Waller might seem to be a simple propagandist for the invasions of Zanzibar, Central Africa, and Uganda. However, he led ferocious public attacks on Henry Morton Stanley for his treatment of indigenous Africans in the 1870s and 1890s. In the latter period, following the "relief" of Emin Pasha, the explorer's reputation was destroyed by the APS and the BFASS, even though the latter had initially supported the expedition.[135] Stanley had used hired slaves on his nominally anti-slavery Emin Pasha Relief Expedition, while his ally, Leopold, relied on slaves to build his Congo railway.[136] Explorers such as Richard Burton justified this, when challenged, as the only way to secure porters, insisting that he paid the slaves wages individually and treated them as free laborers.[137]

Beyond the questionable pieties and moral certainties, there was still some meaning to British pretensions. Writing a book for public consumption in 1897, Sir Harry Johnston took great pride in a policy of nonrecognition of slavery in the Central African Protectorate, even though many slaves remained in traditional relationships to their masters.[138] On the ground, many of his junior officials acknowledged that their policies were glossed for domestic audiences and Johnston's knighthood roused the cynicism of one subordinate. Wordsworth Poole, a young doctor in the protectorate, confided to his mother that "it is a considerable farce this slave freeing business" but "freed slaves pay well at home" and earned knighthoods.[139] "It is," he told her, "with many digs in the ribs and chuckles that we read the effusions of the Rev. Horace Waller and others in the papers from home." He was amused at the likelihood that the official utterances of Johnston and his colleagues would delude "a stupid old historian taking infinite pains to get to the original Foreign Office despatches and thinking that at last he had hit on the truth." Poole's casual contempt reflected the fact that Johnston's gift of freedom meant little in practice.[140] Although progress against local slavery was clearly slow and exaggerated for the gratification of metropolitan audiences, such cynicism toward philanthropists did not undercut such Britons' own assumptions about how imperial prosperity required the suppression of slave trading and would help dismantle slave systems. Even when the sources are thick with self-promotion and self-justification, a "stupid old historian" can recognize that a greedy accommodation with indentured labor, African slavery, and coerced labor developed through, and not in contradiction with, dominant anti-slavery expectations.

## RACE, FREE LABOR, AND SEEING TOO FAR

It is time to return to the Africans who encountered the HMS *Racer*'s electric searchlight at Swarra Cunda Creek. They suggested that "Queen Victoria eye, see too far," but British officials' obsession with stability, prosperity, and authority meant they saw little hypocrisy in "freeing" Africa through new adaptations of slavery. Far from masking baser interests, anti-slavery shaped assumptions about the transition to free-labor societies and economies. At the heart of such beliefs, though, were ideas about "uncivilized" black societies, shaped by ideas blending slavery with race. Holmwood, vice-consul at Zanzibar, suggested that "there is a trait in the character of Africans generally which has done much to keep them in a state of barbarism—it is a disinclination to any settled employment, no matter what the incentive to labor." Abstaining from a view on the cause of this "disinclination," he summed up the range of theories he had heard: "This may be a consequence of generations of slavery or the defect may be inherent in the race; it is fostered by the warm equable climate and by the immense fertility of the soil.…It is none the less a tendency to be combated in every possible way, and should on no account be lost sight of."[141] This account of black racial inferiority blurred climate, biology, and culture together, but emphasized the need to *force* free-labor production as a substitute for slavery. Victorians' complex ideas about race and slavery can be better understood by tracing their connection throughout this period and across the American and African continents.

Historian Douglas Lorimer is correct to argue that anti-slavery "quickened English sympathies, but at the cost of intensifying the race consciousness of the Victorians."[142] In many cases, anti-slavery arguments about the dehumanizing effect of slave labor destroyed faith in the potential of newly emancipated peoples. Even after slavery, people of African origin could be dismissed as a people of toil.[143] Racialized myths about black laziness became more common throughout the nineteenth century, not the least because of debates since the 1840s concerning Caribbean decline. The sugar-duties crisis helped make a clear break between anti-slavery principle and pro-black sentiment. In 1853, the conservative *Fraser's Magazine* observed that Great Britain had hitherto assumed that every black man was a slave entitled to the nation's protection and affection; now they were learning to discriminate between sympathy for slaves and contempt for black people. This distinction signaled a growing frustration that free African peoples did not act out the roles scripted for them by British political enthusiasms.[144] In this respect, the "Morant Bay Rebellion" of 1865 confirmed a division between anti-slaveries rather than a challenge to a declining anti-slavery consensus. There was never a consensus over race relations, labor discipline, and imperial governance after slavery.

This is not to suggest uniformity or continuity in British racial attitudes.[145] Frederick Douglass was surely correct to detect a shift in racial prejudice between his 1846 and 1859 visits.[146] New racisms imagined that certain groups were slower to realize the advantages of advancement, civilization, and self-improvement than respectable classes of Britons.[147] This did not mean a neat transition from more traditional views of cultural or environmental differences to scientific racism, since science followed popular racial attitudes more than it led them.[148] Far from narrowing, ideas about race expanded fluidly in the period, as prejudice found more and more forms of investigation and explanation.[149] Polygenesis, a theory of separate origins for races, gained ground in Victorian Britain despite its troubling implications for the accuracy of the book of Genesis, but monogenesis, the idea of a common human origin, survived in mainstream theology and also in Charles Darwin's theory of evolution.[150] What united this melting pot of biological, cultural, and geographical racisms was growing pessimism for the "development" of nonwhite races—and that was strongly influenced by anti-slavery.

What these diverse forms of racial thinking shared, be they scientific or civilizational, was a tendency to elongate the time expected for nonwhite peoples to "develop." In traditional cultural or climatic racism, individuals could be improved within their lifetimes, and a baby transferred at birth to Britain would have the chance of becoming the equal of a Briton. By the mid-nineteenth century, the timescale was expanding, as both civilizational and biological theories of human difference became pessimistic about racial development.[151] The cases of Indian indentured labor and West Indian labor oppression demonstrate how British anti-slavery aspirations could unleash new forms of coercion toward nonwhite peoples; in both cases, by 1865 desires to maintain pre-emancipation prosperity and social order provided new methods of controlling imperial subjects. But beyond India or Jamaica—indeed, beyond the borders of Britain's empire at that time— there were more methods to come. Just as coercive forms of "free" labor flowed, perversely, from anti-slavery victories in India and the Caribbean, anti-slavery endeavors in Africa begot new forms of domination.

Anti-slavery and racial stereotyping, which had evolved together after West Indian emancipation, made this perverse logic possible. The racial theorist Benjamin Kidd applied Darwinian evolution to races, imagining competition between them that would inevitably lead to the annihilation of weaker peoples through extermination or, in modern times, through assimilation. He traced the strength of Anglo-Saxon peoples to the end of slavery in Europe. Because European societies had used free labor since the fourteenth century, the market competition within them had driven them to better things, giving them dominance. This strange view of inherited culture—"social evolution"—did not view slavery as the proper station for nonwhites. Rather, Kidd's innovative theory suggested that black people would continue their role as servants in a free-labor economy by virtue of their uncivilized social inheritance.[152] These ideas of race and "social evolution" were new and controversial in 1894, but the place of slavery and free labor was quite orthodox. Emancipation was not a benevolent gift of freedom; emancipation freed slaves for the real competition of the labor market, self-reliance, and self-improvement.

Presumably influenced by his family experience of the Caribbean, Samuel Baker insisted that Africans "must be compelled to work, by some stringent law against vagrancy" as "the negro does not appreciate the blessings of freedom."[153] The intimate connection that British thinkers drew between the promotion of legitimate trade and the suppression of the slave trade meant that strong anti-slavery feeling could exist alongside the most virulent racial hatred. Officials expressed contempt for Africans in the same letters where they eagerly discussed strategy against the slave trade. As Governor Freeman of Lagos declared to Wylde in 1864, "blessed are ye who have no personal communication with niggers." He admired Richard Burton's recent book for avoiding "the snivelling missionary tone about the 'poor oppressed black man'," which was adopted by others "in order to curry favor with the higher powers who are usually rather afraid of if not attached to Exeter Hall [where BFASS meetings were held] & its parasites."[154] In 1865, Commodore Wilmot, commanding the West Africa squadron, also endorsed Burton's racial pessimism "about the African race," stating that "they never will become a great people."[155] This was, however, a purer, less diluted version of the pessimism that crept even into the corridors of "Exeter Hall."

If emancipation in the West Indies or slave-trade suppression in Africa did not instantly create happy, contented wage laborers, then race seemed to be to blame. Sir Harry Johnston, in an 1889 paper, argued that "we cannot expect the negroes of West Africa to become all at once and in one or even three generations normally intelligent, self-governing people," even if there were excellent individuals.[156] If these elongated expectations of racial progress still held out hope of improvement, it was often imagined to come under imperial stewardship. This mix of pessimism and optimism was summed up in 1893 by Lugard's argument that "if you freed three slaves to-day, two of them (given the opportunity) would sell the third to-morrow" and so civilized superintendence was required.[157]

In 1858, the *London Cotton Plant*, a journal linked to American planters, insisted that "avowing utter detestation of Slavery in any form whatever, we hold that negro servitude to the white man is not human slavery, but the normal condition of the inferior race." The *Anti-Slavery Reporter* mocked this attempt to rebrand Southern slave-holding as "negro servitude" and questioned the sanity of investors who thought pro-slavery apology would sell well in an anti-slavery nation.[158] However, while any defense of slave ownership got short shrift, assumptions about the "normal condition" of black people had wider currency in Victorian Britain than the *Reporter* liked to think. In this sense, Thomas Carlyle's infamous *Discourse on the Nigger Question* of the 1850s was closer to mainstream British views of labor relations with nonwhites than it might seem. The cynicism and racial venom of Carlyle's work drew public censure and his views on race were hugely controversial, but his faith in the coercion of black labor was less radical. A focus on the slave trade and enslavement as the principal sufferings of "the African race" easily led to censure when freed people failed to act as they were intended.[159]

Expectations of cheap, pliant, "free" labor shaped racial beliefs. Parallel European and American developments in racial thought suggest that Britain's peculiar anti-slavery tradition was not the only source of racial prejudice. However, particular features of popular anti-slavery ideas permitted them to be combined with developing racial pessimism.[160] In many cases, anti-slavery ideology incubated a variety of racial prejudices, rather than egalitarian respect. A few mourned that the more radical implications of being an anti-slavery nation were ignored. Thomas Hodgkin, founder of the Aborigines' Protection Society (APS), despaired of the directions taken by anti-slavery in the hands of missionaries and anti-slavery societies.[161] To a handful of contemporaries, it seemed clear that the principles of anti-slavery were violated by imperial expansion and contract labor coercion. However, this represented a narrow sliver on the spectrum of public opinion.

While "Queen Victoria eye" looked far and wide across non-European societies, a relentless focus on the slave trade and anti-slavery obscured most Britons' views of humanitarian imperialism. So long as this eye focused narrowly on the legal ownership of human beings rather than Hodgkin's grander project of opposing racial prejudice, coerced labor, and the theft of land, this was not hypocrisy so much as fidelity. As noted at the start of this book, "parallax" is an optical effect, suggesting something has moved position when, in fact, it is the viewer that has done so. As "Queen Victoria eye" examined nonwhite peoples in different circumstances, contexts, and times, racial pessimism loomed larger in the foreground, but this did not mean that the rejection of Hodgkin's view heralded a dramatic departure from anti-slavery ideas.

# 8

## Ideologies of Freedom

THIS BOOK began with the burning of a village on the Gallinas River. The Royal Navy's self-righteous arson epitomizes the dilemma of Victorian anti-slavery in the question of whether freedom burned bright. Having looked at various theaters of politics and culture, high and low, touched by this same problem, it is appropriate to return to the metaphor. Comparisons between fire and freedom are not just a fanciful conceit. Buxton hoped that Africa would, in the future, follow Britain's development away from the afflictions of similar superstition, rude intellect, and slavery to become "a blaze of light, liberty, religion, and happiness."[1] The American poet John Greenleaf Whittier had complained that "freedom's fire is dim with us" when compared to Britain's burning commitment to anti-slavery.[2] Harriet Beecher Stowe suggested that ambivalence toward the Union cause in the American Civil War meant the "decline of the noble anti-slavery fire" in Britain.[3] Frederick Douglass had hoped to see his home country and others around the world emulate Britain in kindling an "anti-slavery fire."[4] In all these examples, British freedoms would ignite the spread of liberty around the globe. Yet, more than a century later, it is easier to conclude that the hopes and possibilities of abolition and emancipation were consumed by the raging ambition of Victorian imperialists.

Dispute, discontent, and discord have been recurring themes in the previous chapters. British politicians and the public they governed and represented could not agree on the implications of emancipation. The transformation of Britain into an anti-slavery nation—meaning the nationalization of anti-slavery sentiment—was a messy, bloody, and confused process. Rather than shelter behind this complexity, it seems more satisfying to venture some broad conclusions about three things: first, how public anti-slavery sentiment interacted with elite or official policymaking; second, how anti-slavery operated as an ideology; and, third, how far the outcomes of struggles over anti-slavery policy were contingent and not inevitable.

## ELITE AND POPULAR ANTI-SLAVERIES

The prominence of diverse anti-slavery impulses in Victorian Britain was well hidden by rivalries over method that opposing factions presented as questions of principle. Disputes over free trade, the use of force, the treatment of fugitive slaves, and public subsidy for imperial enterprise stood or fell on questions of principle, but not on a principle of enmity or apathy toward slavery. Samuel Ringgold Ward, the African American abolitionist, said that he was sometimes asked why Britons should discuss slavery "as there are no slaves in the British empire now, there is nothing for the British people to do on the subject" and "that as the discussion of slavery is necessarily, now, the discussion of a subject affecting other nations and governments than our own, such discussion will be regarded by them as an interference in their affairs."[5] Such hostility reflected uncertainty over what being an anti-slavery nation meant in practice and perhaps some apathy on the part of the public as to what they could do. Yet, when Ward turned to name pro-slavery Britons, his list was thin and necessarily subjective; convinced that *"the elevation of the British negro"* was intrinsic to anti-slavery, he concluded that racists were intrinsically pro-slavery.[6] However, if we accept his definition of anti-slavery as racial egalitarianism, very few people in Britain had ever supported anti-slavery. There was no golden age of mass support for egalitarian, radical abolitionism, even if the earlier crusade against national slave-holding had successfully hidden divisions within popular anti-slavery politics and culture.[7]

Ward was right to be disquieted by some British elite attitudes, but he was perhaps too optimistic when he celebrated that among the public "I found, in every part of England, Ireland, Scotland and Wales, that abolitionism is not a mere abstract idea, but a practical question of great importance. It is not because, to a certain extent, anti-slavery sentiments are fashionable and natural, that these persons approve them, but because of their intrinsic character."[8] It is impossible to gauge with any quantitative certainty whether Ward exaggerated the extent of his welcome, or perhaps sought to flatter his audience. In his London-published autobiography, Ward admitted that anti-slavery sentiment might be a meaningless variety of cultural chauvinism. He noted that some Britons, on immigrating to the United States, quickly became pro-slavery because for them "abolitionism is mere sentimentality at home, and therefore good for nothing abroad.

They only *drifted* with the current."[9] Frequent and recurring references to global slavery or the slave trade in Victorian print journalism might have reflected a public appetite for such material, but it is hard to provide any empirical proof that this was more than "drifting with the current." Editors and authors deployed this material in publications that may have been purchased for quite different reasons. The audiences for liberated African Americans' lectures or the widespread readers of books by Stowe and Livingstone suggest, though, a genuine fascination with the continuing suppression of slavery and the slave trade. How such sentiment and sympathy would translate into politics and action is as tricky for us to assess in the twenty-first century as it was for politicians in the nineteenth.

A real fear of public wrath over slavery issues, however, meant that politicians had to tread carefully if they were to avoid the censure of opponents. This was a negative impulse for their actions, as they were motivated by wanting to avoid the perception of being weak on anti-slavery principles rather than having any positive agenda for policy. In the opening stages of the Civil War, Russell and Palmerston had considered armed mediation, fearing that reunion would mean Northern capitulation to pro-slavery demands. However, the Emancipation Proclamation made intervention impossible, since, as Palmerston put it, anti-slavery public opinion created "the Shackles of Principle and of Right & Wrong" on any policy.[10] As the previous chapters have shown, officials or politicians could find that their interpretation of anti-slavery was too pragmatic or subtle for the passions of the press, while the BFASS often found its brand of anti-slavery, especially in the earlier period, sidelined as quixotic and unworldly. However, the triumph of certain anti-slavery views within government leaves unanswered whether anti-slavery commitment was organic or merely a vein of sentiment that wily imperialists or politicians could tap for their own ends.

Popular politics were forged by both the entrepreneurship of leaders and the preexisting sympathies of the populace. The Liberal caucuses in the fugitive-slave circular crisis, Bartle Frere in the Zanzibar controversy, Livingstone in his life and death, and Tories in the Uganda debate could publicize their political preferences as test cases of the nation's anti-slavery duty. However, these strategies were only successful because of a widespread popular affection for such a duty.[11] Waller, an actor in those episodes, argued near the end of the century that "if our Foreign Office is to take up what is called philanthropic work, it can only be brought by pressure from without." This was not meant as criticism of his friends and allies in the imperial establishment as indifferent to anti-slavery. Rather, he argued that, "in no case does the fault lie with the Ministry of the day; the initiative must be with the public."[12] Even if he sought support for his favored societies when he said this, Waller was right to emphasize the role of popular support. Public notions of anti-slavery politics were not fixed, but there was no room in political discourse for pro-slavery views, only for competing debates about anti-slavery methods.

## ANTI-SLAVERY AS IDEOLOGY

Historians of slavery and abolition have long been attracted to "ideology" as a way of understanding the Western world's conversion from an active promoter of human bondage to its pious enemy. In his work on the ideology of slavery in African societies, Paul Lovejoy suggests that "ideology" means "a system of ideas pertaining to social and political subjects which justify and legitimate culture," acting like a mirror on the material interests of society's rulers.[13] Such theories assume that "ideology" culturally normalizes and rationalizes the economic interests of a ruling class among all parts of a society.[14] In the Victorian period, it makes more sense to understand anti-slavery as an ideology in itself rather than focusing on anti-slavery as a reflection or aspect of some other ideology. It is more satisfying to see ideologies as belief systems through which economic realities or interests are created, imagined, and pursued, rather than as a product of them.[15] This does not mean that ideologies are altruistic, but rather that political economy rarely presents simple, unambiguous calculations of self-interest. Complex, speculative choices are made through the filter of political ideology; economic rationality is itself an act of political belief, not a neutral assessment of predicted costs and benefits, limited only by the quality of information available.[16]

Neither discourse nor material circumstances drive human history; rather, individuals and societies clash over how to assimilate new ideas or circumstances into their understanding of the world.[17] As historian Frederick Cooper defines it, a study of ideology "means looking beyond the artificial dichotomy of idealist and materialist explanations." This permits "an understanding of which aspects of humanity were and were not objects of concern and what the context and uses of those ideals were"—how ideology "obscured and illuminated" material reality.[18] Paradoxically, human experience is understood through ideology, yet ideology is made by human experience. Ideologies both help people to interpret events or arguments and translate them into familiar and understandable terms. They can be remade, as orbiting elements of the ideology drift away to found new separate cores, new ideologies. It is semantic to argue when this process occurred for anti-slavery and it would be stretching the atomic or orbital metaphors to the breaking point to pursue them any further. Suffice to say, charting and understanding the mainstream and aberrant currents within anti-slavery ideology is vital to understanding Victorian politics and policy, even if it is a messy business. Governments and nations, not to mention individuals, do not have the consistent, thought-through belief systems of political philosophers, but it is still possible to piece their broad ideology together and come closer to understanding what essentially happened in Victorian Britain.[19]

Even if the British Empire is best understood as part of an interconnected world system with diverse and competing interests and values in each historical situation, certain ideologies still shaped the metropolitan response to events, opportunities, and threats. As imperial power was projected, mediated, and balanced in a British world system, statesmen, officials, and public opinion chaotically forged an anti-slavery world system.[20] There was little consensus on how and where to pursue anti-slavery goals most effectively, but anti-slavery ideology loosely bound together providential prosperity and the suppression of the transnational slave trade. Developing anti-slavery ideologies changed the ways in which officials and the wider public interpreted, understood, and responded to events. The Victorians and their historians could happily ignore, most of the time, the connections between the different spheres of diplomatic action, trade policy, colonial occupation, domestic culture, religious fervor, and electoral politics, but they still remained connected, if disparate. There was such a thing as British anti-slavery ideology, however divided. The content and consequences of this ideology played a central role in the politics of empire.

It was not true, as one official in Africa argued, that Britain "put her shoulder steadily to the wheel, by interfering for the suppression of the unnatural traffic, without for a moment counting the cost or regarding the danger."[21] Even if the cost was counted and even if some imperialists manipulated anti-slavery to support their material greed, the standards of modern economic rationality cannot explain the popular and official appeal of anti-slavery politics. Britons continued to agree that moral ends, such as anti-slavery, drove national and global prosperity, even when they could not agree on the mechanisms through which virtue did so.[22] This superiority could be as vague as God's providential support for the continued supremacy of the British Empire or as specific as the positive expectations of cotton production in an African colony. The flows of capital and trade within the white-settler empire were assisted by cultural networks of Anglo-Saxon kinship, and in a similar manner material interests in nonwhite peoples were shaped by cultural concerns such as anti-slavery.[23] Other European empires, without the same traditions of popular support, still adopted many assumptions from Britain's commitment to slave-trade suppression and the coercive promotion of free labor, certain that it must be materially beneficial if perfidious Albion was so keen on it.[24]

As we have seen, remarkably few voices in Britain took a neutral or friendly position towards slavery. In that sense, opposition to human slavery was moving from the ideology of a section of the public to a social fact; anti-slavery had become a hegemonic ideology. However, differences over particular anti-slavery issues and methods disguised a narrow consensus behind rancorous contentions.[25] Instead of experiencing a decline in anti-slavery sentiment, Victorian Britons created the fragmentation of anti-slavery ideology into competing ideologies of freedom. Modern democracies still struggle with the burning question of what "freedom" means and how particular freedoms should be judged against one another. In thinking about the differences within anti-slavery ideology, it is useful to consider the intended impact on those saved from slavery. Doing so may provide a useful corrective to this book's necessary focus on metropolitan passions and policies.

The capabilities approach for human development developed by philosophers Amartya Sen and Martha Nussbaum can help us examine Victorian Britons' expectations for the social and political conditions of postemancipation societies and what "freedoms" they prized. British penetration and colonialism has been described as a "first development plan for Africa," so it is not so odd to use the capabilities approach, which was created to analyze modern development economics.[26] The capabilities approach has cast off crude measures of development such as economic growth, considering life expectancy, educational opportunity, political liberty, legal equality, and individual self-expression as meaningful freedoms. Far from imposing a modern theory on nineteenth-century society, the framework offers a means of understanding the historically specific content of Victorian anti-slavery.[27] Applying the capabilities approach, it becomes clear that very few Britons ever expected to promote the social opportunities or political agency of enslaved peoples.[28] The experiences of countries besides Britain demonstrate that emancipation did not automatically unleash a wider set of progressive, tolerant forces, and indeed could happily coexist alongside racism.[29] Sen uses freed African Americans' resistance to plantation employment, despite its alleged advantages, as an example of rational individuals choosing the security and dignity of self-sufficiency over impersonal economic logic. His attention to such choices is highly pertinent for Victorian Britain, given the similar experiences of Africans and black Britons. In neither the United States nor Britain did emancipation usher in wholesale opportunities for black people to fully participate in free labor, a free society, or a free market.[30] British policy defined free labor primarily as the development of civilizing prosperity, not as the development of independent agency after slavery.

This meant that many white Britons condemned black people for failing to behave according to the dictates of anti-slavery ideology. Such a shift reinforced a gradual evolution in racial thinking, as perceived "inferiorities" were cast as long-term, communal failings rather than individual, transient inadequacies. Perversely, the terms of British emancipation strengthened Victorian pessimism about the improvement and freedom of individual Africans. A dominant ideology of freedom saw economic development as the best way to develop West Indian or African societies. Livingstone popularized such an approach and focused not on the conversion of individuals but on the transformation of whole African communities. By contrast, a missionary such as Bishop William Tozer was in a minority for respecting indigenous customs and defining civilization as something besides technology and economy.[31] Most Britons continued to think of former slaves as corporate objects rather than as individuals.

Criticism of the consensus more usually came from reactionaries, not antiracist radicals. James Froude, in 1888, worried that "it has been the absence of restraint which has prevented them [Africans] becoming civilised" and thought the nation's moral duty in the West Indies had been betrayed fifty years earlier by setting black Britons "free to follow their own devices."[32] He argued that "Acts of Parliament cannot make us equal. Some must lead and some must follow, and the question is only of degree and kind." He concluded, "Slavery is gone, with all that belonged to it; but it will be an ill day for mankind if no one is to be compelled any more to obey those who are wiser than himself, and each of us is to do only what is right in our own eyes." He maintained that there "may be authority, yet not slavery: a soldier is not a slave, a sailor is not a slave, a wife is not a slave; yet they may not live by their own wills or emancipate themselves at their own pleasure from positions in which nature has placed them."[33] By such a prescription, Britain had done too little to maintain the social and economic order of slavery, not too much. Compared to Froude's virulent racism, the colonial administrator Sir Harry Johnston was positively charitable when he warned, in his history text, that "the Negro has been given back his freedom that he may use it with a man's sense of responsibility." Menacingly, he predicted that Africans would likely be enslaved again, by "the pressure of eager, hungry, impatient outside humanity," if they did not choose to embrace free labor.[34]

The triumph of anti-slavery ideas, ironically, gave a new life to British racial prejudice. Racism had been tainted by association with pro-slavery in the years before 1838. With British slavery and the slave trade placed beyond mainstream political debate, Britons were freer to villainize and mock Africans, African Americans, and British blacks without condoning human bondage. Anti-slavery had never challenged the fundamental notion that black people, poor men, and all women were incapable of being full agents.[35] Fixed anti-slavery views about the rational interests of black Britons or Africans fermented racist venom and contempt.

In the British Empire, as we have seen, Africans were partly blamed for the slave trade and condemned to regimes of forced labor and imperial occupation in order to establish regimented "free" labor economies.[36] Indentured labor from Africa and India was used to pressure the freed people of colonies such as Jamaica into conformity with economic expectations. Because almost all Britons intended and expected emancipation to maintain existing racial and economic hierarchies, the full social and economic implications of a free-labor society were muted by state intervention whenever the free market seemed to be to the advantage of black over white interests. As Frederick Cooper puts it, "anti-slavery ideology separated slavery from its economic context."[37] Moreover, while the theory of indirect rule in British protectorates allowed for devolution and self-determination for African communities, in practice it devolved traditional rule to despots and supported existing labor practices, when possible, as slavery dissolved into wage labor.[38] Paid labor, accompanied by state protection of colonial employers, was a combination almost as likely as slavery to leave the talents and energies of black people unrealized.[39]

Similar differences in approach are clear when domestic reformers tried to extend the ideology of anti-slavery to other marginalized and oppressed Britons. Radicals saw women or workers as enslaved by legal disabilities, while, for more conservative politicians, such people were permitted freedom commensurate to their abilities. In this sense, radical, egalitarian ideologies of freedom struggled, in different contexts, against more discriminatory and limited ideologies of freedom. Anti-slavery opened up wider questions of positive and negative freedoms, or, more precisely, freedom as the development of self-determining capabilities versus freedom as self-ownership and pliant wage labor.

## ANTI-SLAVERY ENDS AND MEANS

After emancipation, the ideology of anti-slavery fractured as different perspectives were thrust in diverse and conflicting directions by the new political pressures. It is entirely unsurprising that Victorian anti-slavery failed to have the radical implications for racial equality and self-determination that modern observers might hope for; it is more surprising that anti-slavery ideology played such a crucial part not merely in justifying but in creating these new impulses for expansion and domination.[40] The road to hell was paved with anti-slavery intentions. Britain bullied rival countries and scrambled into Africa with an anti-slavery compass. But could anti-slavery have developed into a popular force for racial equality rather than racial difference, or a political campaign for commercial partnership rather than economic domination?

Alternative anti-slavery ideologies were available. The development of anti-slavery policy was the aggregate of individual decisions, not the sad inevitability of conspiracy or material circumstance. African agency challenged the preset notions of imperial power, while canny mobilization of public opinion could destroy the best-laid plans of politicians and officials.[41] The deep diversity of opinion over every issue or dilemma concerning slavery was, in itself, evidence that Victorian Britons could conceptualize alternative choices. In 1841, the governor of Sierra Leone, Sir John Jeremie, had argued that anti-slavery treaties should treat Africans as they treated European nations. His views were dismissed by Palmerston, the foreign secretary, and James Stephen, the under-secretary of the Colonial Office, who did not wish "to indulge these petty Chiefs."[42] The issue of African sovereignty rarely reappeared. What it lacked was a champion, speaker, or campaigner who could convince Britons of the more radial implications of being an anti-slavery nation. An anti-imperial, antiracist brand of anti-slavery would have required an exceptional group of individuals campaigning to change public attitudes since it would have required a greater leap from preconceived notions, but that was not impossible.

The early Victorian BFASS offered one potential source for such leadership, but it was hampered in doing so. On the level of policy, the support of pacifism rather than naval suppression of the transatlantic slave trade and of protectionism in colonial sugar hampered any wider campaign against vagrancy laws and indenture in the emancipated West Indies. Before 1870, the BFASS seemed too radical and unworldly to lead a new national campaign; after roughly 1874, the principles and commitments of its committee members, not least Wylde and Waller, converged more closely with those of the Foreign Office. The Niger expedition can be seen as a prelude to the scramble for Africa, but if Buxton, its architect, had not lost reelection to the House of Commons then he could have emerged as leader for some alternative brand of anti-slavery. Rather than founding a society to promote the doomed expedition, he could have chosen to champion a broader range of questions. Buxton's impeccable Whig establishment credentials would have mirrored William Wilberforce's friendship with Pitt and other Tories; he might have led a challenging but credible abolitionist movement, given his passionate defense of the African Xhosa people's territory from British colonization. He could have made a movement for universal human capabilities more publicly and politically palatable than did his friend Thomas Hodgkin, the Aborigines' Protection Society (APS) founder.[43] Given the terms on which the crusade for emancipation had triumphed it would have been immensely difficult to develop the antiexploitative themes of anti-slavery politics, but the possibility existed. In fact, the APS itself could be liable to imperial impulses, such as the annexation of Fiji, on the basis that Britain could then more effectively protect the inhabitants from the deprivations of Australian labor recruiters.[44] APS secretary Frederick Chesson successfully coordinated a campaign in 1875 to retain Gambia for Britain, rather than trading it with France. Even the APS thought about "responsible empire" as much as the self-determination or individual dignity of people of color.[45]

When considering the suppression of the transatlantic slave trade, historian David Eltis poses a chilling question: Would it have been desirable for the slave trade to have been suppressed earlier if, as seems likely, that would have required further British colonization in Africa and the more violent exercise of British imperial power?[46] A similar question presents itself when looking at anti-slavery politics in the British Empire. A more radical movement for abolition and emancipation would have taken much longer to succeed; the essential nonradicalism of mainstream anti-slavery ideology before 1833 is what secured emancipation. How can one wish that West Indian emancipation be delayed in the hopes of a more perfect, less abusive, anti-slavery imperialism? Such questions of perfectionism versus compromise can only be answered with perfect knowledge of the counterfactuals—the "what ifs"—that damningly elude any historian.

On the one hand, this interpretation might be mistaken as an excuse for British colonial, racial, and labor abuses. Although prejudice should not be rescued from the condescension of posterity, understanding is quite different from excusing. There is no vindication for colonialism or racism in the truth that Victorian politics and culture were not fundamentally mercenary, conspiratorial, or amoral. Rather, an exploration of sincere bigotry and genuine righteousness helps explain how these events happened. It also renders them more disturbing. As a historian of Nazi Germany has observed, it is far more unsettling to understand the worldview of those who perpetrated past abuses—to see how their actions were rationalized— rather than dismiss them as aberrant, unthinking monsters.[47] We do not have to choose simply between anti-slavery as a "perfectly virtuous" crusade and anti-slavery as perfidious, bigoted insincerity.[48] The historical truth, being the result of human endeavor, is far more delicately shaded and complex. In this sense, I explain without forgiving. On the other hand, these conclusions could be seen to unremittingly condemn and deprecate all anti-slavery ideology. Although anti-slavery politics were intimately connected with British imperialism, there was an alternative. The editor and publisher James Knowles advised Lugard, during one of his campaigns over anti-slavery policy, that public opinion could be impressed "with the desired view while yet plastic & before it becomes hardened & settled."[49] He was right. At different points, anti-slavery sentiment could have unleashed a wider program of reform, rejecting racial prejudice rather than encouraging it, and we will mourn that this did not happen and was rather unlikely to happen. Still, it is not the task of historians to censure or praise the past, even if it is common to look to them for the laws of history.

Perhaps the only applicable guidance from studying nineteenth-century anti-slavery is that simple moral beliefs quickly generate complex practical dilemmas. To modern eyes, it is clear that many Victorian conceptions of freedom had deeply oppressive and tragic consequences, intended and unintended. Writing about Russian revolutionary thinkers, the philosopher Slavoj Žižek declares that "there is nothing ethically more disgusting than revolutionary Beautiful Souls who refuse to recognise, in the Cross of the postrevolutionary present, the truth of their own flowering dreams about freedom."[50] Many of the Victorians studied in this book pursued anti-slavery sentiments sincerely, but they did not allow the coercive, racist, or imperialist consequences of British policy to dent their faith in anti-slavery assumptions—not least in the ultimate coexistence of perfect morality and maximum profit. Today, legal definitions of slavery are still problematic and contested, while humanitarian sentiment drags individuals, publics, and governments into complex, practical challenges with competing ethical, economic, and political priorities.[51] Although we will not like all the actions or attitudes fostered by anti-slavery ideology, it is chastening to recall that twenty-first-century citizens still struggle to know what ends justify which means. It is not always easy to recognize the difference between proud commitments to freedom burning bright and such devotions burning up.

# Abbreviations

## ARCHIVES

| | |
|---|---|
| BL | British Library, London |
| Bod. | Bodleian Library, Oxford |
| GLC | Gilder Lehrman Collection, New-York Historical Society, New York |
| HBSC | Harriet Beecher Stowe Center, Hartford, Connecticut |
| JJC | John Johnson Collection, Bodleian Library |
| NA | National Archives, Kew |
| RH | Rhodes House Library, Oxford |

## PUBLICATIONS

| | |
|---|---|
| DCB/DBS | *Dictionary of Canadian Biography* |
| EHR | *English Historical Review* |
| HJ | *Historical Journal* |
| ILN | *Illustrated London News* |
| JICH | *Journal of Imperial and Commonwealth History* |
| ODNB | *Oxford Dictionary of National Biography* |
| PH | *Parliamentary History* |
| PP | *Parliamentary Papers* |

## ORGANIZATIONS

| | |
|---|---|
| APS | Aborigines' Protection Society |
| BFASS | British and Foreign Anti-Slavery Society |
| CO | Colonial Office |
| FO | Foreign Office |
| IBEAC | Imperial British East Africa Company |

# Notes

___

## PROLOGUE

1. *PP* 1846, l, "Class A Correspondence with the British Commissioners relating to the Slave Trade," 38–39: Commodore Jones to the Lieut.-Governor of Sierra Leone, 7 Feb. 1845; ibid., 39–40: Commodore Jones to the Chiefs of the Gallinas, 24 Jan. 1845.

2. *PP* 1846, l, 42: Commander C. H. M. Buckle to Commodore Jones, 3 Feb. 1845; ibid., 38–39: Commodore Jones to the Lieut.-Governor of Sierra Leone, 7 Feb. 1845. The communications rarely agree on the spelling of the towns' names, presumably because the British were anglicizing Mende names.

3. PP 1846, l, 38–39: Commodore Jones to the Lieut.-Governor of Sierra Leone, 7 Feb. 1845; ibid., 53–54: Commodore Jones to Hon. Sidney Herbert, 1 Mar. 1845.

4. PP 1846, l, 53–54: Commodore Jones to Hon. Sidney Herbert, 1 Mar. 1845; ibid., 57–58: Commodore Jones to Lieut.-Governor of Sierra Leone, 24 Feb. 1845; ibid., 53–54: Commodore Jones to Hon. Sidney Herbert, 1 Mar. 1845.

5. William Kingston, *Blue Jackets or, Chips of the Old Block: A Narrative of the Gallant Exploits* (London, 2006 [1854]), 261. For this and other naval sources, the author is indebted to independent historian Peter Davis, "William Loney RN," http://home.wxs.nl/~pdavis/Loney.htm.

## 1. AN ANTI-SLAVERY NATION

1. Conder's poem "The Last Night of Slavery" was written in 1834 and published in 1837: Josiah Conder, *The Choir and the Oratory* (London, 1837), 285–87; Marcus Wood, ed., *The Poetry of Slavery: An Anglo-American Anthology* (Oxford, 2003), 320–22.

2. For a sample of the vast literature on these subjects, readers might begin with these suggestions. On abolitionism: Christopher Leslie Brown, *Moral Capital: Foundations of British Abolitionism* (Chapel Hill, N.C., 2006); David Brion Davis, *Inhuman Bondage: The Rise and Fall of Slavery in the New World* (Oxford, 2006); Seymour Drescher, *Abolition: A History of Slavery and Antislavery* (Cambridge, 2009). For the human stories of enslaved Africans in the middle passage: Marcus Rediker, *The Slave Ship: A Human History* (London, 2007); Stephanie Smallwood, *Saltwater Slavery: A Middle Passage from Africa to American Diaspora* (Cambridge, Mass., 2007). On the West Indies: Thomas C. Holt, *The Problem of Freedom: Race, Labor and Politics in Jamaica and Britain, 1832–1938* (Baltimore, 1992); Gad Heuman and David V. Trotman, *Contesting Freedom: Control and Resistance in the Post-Emancipation Caribbean* (Warwick, 2005). For histories of African experience: John

Thornton, *Africa and Africans in the Making of the Atlantic World, 1400–1800,* 2nd ed. (Cambridge, 1998); Robin Law, *The Oyo Empire, c.1600–c.1836: A West African Imperialism in the Era of the Atlantic Slave Trade* (Oxford, 1977).

3. Linda Colley, *Britons: Forging the Nation 1707–1837,* rev. ed. (New Haven, Conn., 2009 [1992]), 367.

4. Seymour Drescher, *The Mighty Experiment: Free Labour versus Slavery in British Emancipation* (Oxford, 2002), 166; Howard Temperley, *British Anti-Slavery 1833–1870* (London, 1972), 167; Drescher, *Abolition,* 277; Christopher Lloyd, *The Navy and the Slave Trade: The Suppression of the African Slave Trade in the Nineteenth-Century* (London, 1949), 101–3; Catherine Hall, *Civilising Subjects: Metropole and Colony in the English Imagination 1830–67* (Oxford, 2002), 338–39. Marika Sherwood has completely dismissed anti-slavery pieties after 1807: Marika Sherwood, *After Abolition: Britain and the Slave Trade since 1807* (London, 2007), 175–77.

5. For aspects of this perspective, see David Turley, *The Culture of English Anti-Slavery, 1780–1860* (London, 1991), 4–5, 227–28; Brown, *Moral Capital,* esp. 459.

6. Andrew S. Thompson, *Imperial Britain: The Empire in British Politics, c. 1880–1932* (Harlow, Essex, 2000), 11–12, similarly focuses on public debates, in his case outside of parties as much as outside of particular anti-slavery societies.

7. Thomas Clarkson, *The History of the Rise, Progress, and Accomplishment of the Abolition of the African Slave-Trade by the British Parliament* (London, 1839 [1808]), map insert facing 164; Temperley, *British Anti-Slavery,* ix, xvii. Whereas Temperley considers the "abolitionist" currents after 1833, this book explores and expands on his suggestion that anti-slavery survived outside the societies. For a recent discussion of this problem, see William Mulligan, "The Fugitive Slave Circulars, 1875–76," *JICH* 37 (2009): 183–205, at 184. Regarding Clarkson's impact on later historians, see Brown, *Moral Capital,* 5–8.

8. Michael Freeden, "Ideology and Political Theory," *Journal of Political Ideologies* 11 (2006): 3–22; Michael Freeden, *Ideologies and Political Theory: A Conceptual Approach* (Oxford, 1996), 82.

9. Freeden, "Ideology," 20; for a more recent use of the concept, see Duncan Bell, *The Idea of Greater Britain: Empire and the Future of World Order, 1860–1900* (Princeton, 2007), 21. For a similar application by a historian, see William H. Sewell, "Ideologies and Social Revolutions: Reflections on the French Case," *Journal of Modern History* 57 (1985): 57–85.

10. See, on national identity, H. Alan Cairns, *Prelude to Imperialism: British Reactions to Central African Society 1840–1890* (London, 1965), 171.

11. *Anti-Slavery Reporter,* 1 July 1872, as quoted in R. J. Gavin, "The Bartle Frere Mission to Zanzibar, 1873," *HJ* 5 (1962): 122–148, at 139.

12. *Times,* 24 July 1834, 7.

13. On the politics and finance of compensation, see Nicholas Draper, *The Price of Emancipation: Slave-Ownership, Compensation and British Society at the End of Slavery* (Cambridge, 2010).

14. Temperley, *British Anti-Slavery,* 12–13.

15. Sir George Stephen, *Antislavery Recollections: In a Series of Letters addressed to Mrs. Beecher Stowe, at Her Request* (London, 1854), 167.

16. Temperley, *British Anti-Slavery,* 25–26.

17. *Hansard,* 3rd ser., 1833, xviii, 357.

18. Ibid., 34–35; Izhak Gross, "Parliament and the Abolition of Negro Apprenticeship, 1835–1838," *EHR* 96 (1981): 560–76, at 560–65.

19. Joseph Sturge and Thomas Harvey, *The West Indies in 1837: Being a Visit to Antigua, Montserrat, Dominica, St. Lucia, Barbados and Jamaica* (London, 1838), v–vi; Elwood H. Jones, "John Scoble," *DCB/DBS.*

20. Gross, "Parliament," 565.

21. Hall, *Civilising Subjects,* 320–23; James Williams, *A Narrative of Events, Since the First of August, 1834, by James Williams, An Apprenticed Labourer in Jamaica,* ed. Diana Paton (Durham, N.C., 2001 [London, 1837]).

22. Alex Tyrrell, "The 'Moral Radical Party' and the Anglo-Jamaican Campaign for the Abolition of the Negro Apprenticeship System," *EHR* 99 (1984): 481–502, quote at 490 and assessment of Glenelg's actions at 498–99.

23. Gross, "Parliament," 560–76, and Tyrrell, "'Moral Radical Party'," 481–502, provide the fullest account of parliamentary maneuvers; see also Temperley, *British Anti-Slavery*, 37–41. On the nature of apprenticeship and the colonial legislatures' voluntary termination, see William A. Green, *British Slave Emancipation: The Sugar Colonies and the Great Experiment 1830–1865* (Oxford, 1976), 129–62.

24. *British Emancipator*, 25 Apr. 1838, 73–74, contains an analysis of the vote.

25. Howard Temperley, "The O'Connell Stevenson Contretemps: A Reflection of the Anglo-American Slavery Issue," *Journal of Negro History* 47 (1962): 217–33, at 218–19. See Christine Kinealy, *Daniel O'Connell and the Anti-Slavery Movement: "The Saddest People the Sun Sees"* (London, 2010), on his abolitionism.

26. On apprenticeship campaigning and the formation of the BFASS, see Temperley, *British Anti-Slavery*, 38–41, 62–66.

27. On its broader history, see "One of the Protestant party," *Random Recollections of Exeter Hall* (London, 1838), for some accounts of its meetings and speakers.

28. *Times*, 17 May 1841, 4. The newspaper had actually criticized the Civilization Society's methods too, and similarly evoked Quaker influence on that occasion. Similar religious controversy dogged the launch of the Garrisonian Anti-Slavery League a decade later: *Mirror of Literature, Amusement and Instruction*, 1 Oct. 1846, 252–33. On the breadth of support for the expedition, see Richard R. Follett, "After Emancipation: Thomas Fowell Buxton and Evangelical Politics in the 1830s," *PH* 27 (2008): 119–29, at 127–28.

29. As quoted by Hall, *Civilising Subjects*, 339.

30. *Chambers's Edinburgh Journal*, 30 Apr. 1842, 116.

31. *Spectator*, 13 Mar. 1852, 249.

32. *Chambers's Journal*, 18 Apr. 1857, 244.

33. *Times*, 13 Sept. 1861, 6.

34. My distinction is similar, but not identical, to divisions drawn by American historians between supporters of immediate abolition and those who sought to stifle the spread of slaveholding. On the differences between these terms, see David Brion Davis, "Review: Antislavery or Abolition?" *Reviews in American History* 1 (1973): 95–99.

35. On these alignments, see Turley, *Culture*, 100–107; C. Duncan Rice, *The Scots Abolitionists* (Baton Rouge, La., 1981), 78–83; Temperley, *British Anti-Slavery*, 208–9; Clare Taylor, introduction to *British and American Abolitionists: An Episode in Transatlantic Understanding*, ed. Clare Taylor (Edinburgh, 1974), 2–3.

36. Indeed, there remains great scope for research on the local impact of anti-slavery societies in provincial towns and cities. On Armistead, see Alexis Bisset, "Wilson Armistead and the Leeds Anti-Slavery Association" (BA thesis, Leeds University, 2007). See also Temperley, *British Anti-Slavery*, 239; Clare Midgley, *Women against Slavery: The British Campaigns, 1780–1870* (London, 1992), 133–35.

37. BFASS, *Proceedings of the General Anti-Slavery Convention, called by the committee of the British and Foreign Anti-Slavery Society, and held in London, from Friday, June 12th, to Tuesday, June 23rd, 1840* (London, 1841), quote at 46; on Godwin, see Alan Sell, *Philosophy, Dissent and Nonconformity* (Cambridge, 2004), 170.

38. BFASS, *Proceedings ... 1840*, 134–38.

39. Ibid., 47–76.

40. Ibid., 465–72.

41. Ibid., 239–40; A. G. L. Shaw, "Charles Fitzgerald," *ODNB*.

42. BFASS, *Proceedings ... 1840*, 23–46, quote at 29; Schlesinger Library, Alma Lutz Collection, A-110, fo. 12, microfilm M59, Mary Grew Diary for 1840: 40; Kathryn Kish Sklar, "'Women Who Speak for an Entire Nation': American and British Women Compared at the World Anti-Slavery Convention, London, 1840," in *The Abolitionist Sisterhood: Women's Political Culture in Antebellum America*, ed. John Fagin Yellin and John C. Van Horne (Ithaca, N.Y., 1994), 301–34; Wendell Phillips Garrison and Francis Jackson Garrison, *William Lloyd Garrison: The Story of his life, told by his children* (4 vols., New York, 1885–89), 2:374.

43. Benjamin Robert Haydon, *The Diary of Benjamin Robert Haydon*, ed. Willard Bissell Pope (5 vols., Cambridge, Mass., 1963), 4:644: entry for 29 June 1840; Douglas A. Lorimer, *Colour, Class and the Victorians: English Attitudes to the Negro in the Mid-Nineteenth Century* (Leicester, 1978), 35. For a different example, see Hall, *Civilising Subjects*, 321–32.

44. BFASS, *Proceedings ...1840, 557*.

45. BFASS, *Proceedings of the General Anti-Slavery Convention called by the Committee of the British and Foreign Anti-Slavery Society and held in London from Tuesday, June 13th, to Tuesday, June 20th, 1843* (London, 1843).

46. Temperley, *British Anti-Slavery*, 244, 261: The next conference organized by the BFASS would be held in Paris in 1867.

47. Seymour Drescher, "Whose Abolition? Popular Pressure and the Ending of the British Slave Trade," *Past and Present* 143 (1994), 136–66, at 166.

48. *Chambers's Edinburgh Journal*, 30 Apr. 1842, 116. On such difficulties, see Temperley, *British Anti-Slavery*, 227–28.

49. The 1840 Convention saw Sturge and Bowring disagree on this question: BFASS, *Proceedings ...1840*, 203–6.

50. See Frederick Douglass, *The Frederick Douglass Papers: Series One*, ed. John W. Blassingame (5 vols., New Haven, 1979), 1:363; Benjamin Quarles, "Ministers without Portfolio," *Journal of Negro History* 39 (1954), 27–42, at 28.

51. David Judge, "Public Petitions and the House of Commons," *Parliamentary Affairs* 31 (1978): 391–405, at 393–94.

52. Temperley, *British Anti-Slavery*, xvi.

53. George Stephen, introduction to *American Slavery Discussed in Congress*, ed. George Stephen (London, 1853), viii.

54. "Hegemony," invoked here to describe anti-slavery rather than explain it, has been used in a very different way by earlier anti-slavery historians: David Brion Davis, *The Problem of Slavery in the Age of Revolution 1770–1823* (New York, 1999 [Ithaca, N.Y., 1975]), 349–50; the applicability of Gramscian hegemony to British abolitionism is debated in the essays comprising Thomas Bender, ed., *The Antislavery Debate: Capitalism and Abolitionism as a Problem in Historical Interpretation* (Berkeley, 1992).

55. *Uncle Tom's Cabin Almanack, or Abolitionist Momento* (London, 1853), 4.

56. Zoë Laidlaw, "Heathens, Slaves and Aborigines: Thomas Hodgkin's Critique of Missions and Anti-Slavery," *History Workshop Journal* 64 (2007), 133–161, at 133; James Heartfield, *The Aborigines' Protection Society: Humanitarian Imperialism in Australia, New Zealand, Fiji, Canada, South Africa, and the Congo, 1836–1909* (London, 2011), 36.

57. Niks Erik Enkvist, "The Octoroon and English Opinions of Slavery," *American Quarterly* 8 (1956): 166–70. Enkvist equates British ambivalence toward the Union in the American Civil War as further evidence of a decline of sympathy; his defense of the play on these grounds is unconvincing.

58. Douglass, *Frederick Douglass Papers*, 1:475.

59. Kenneth D. Nworah, "The Aborigines' Protection Society, 1889–1909: A Pressure-Group in Colonial Policy," *Canadian Journal of African Studies* 5 (1971): 79–91, at 88.

60. On black minstrelsy, see J. S. Bratton, "English Ethiopians: British Audiences and Black-Face Acts, 1835–65," *Yearbook of English Studies* 11 (1981): 127–42; Michael Pickering, "Mock Blacks and Racial Mockery: The 'Nigger' Minstrel and British Imperialism," in *Acts of Supremacy: The British Empire and the Stage, 1790–1930*, ed. J. S. Bratton, Richard Allen Cave, Brendan Gregory, Heidi J. Holder and Michael Pickering (Manchester, 1991), 179–236; Lorimer, *Colour*, 86; Sarah Meer, "Competing Representations: Douglass, the Ethiopian Serenaders, and Ethnic Exhibition in London," in *Liberating Sojourn: Frederick Douglass & Transatlantic Reform*, ed. Alan J. Rice and Martin Crawford (Athens, Ga., 1999), 146–51; Robert Nowatzki, *Representing African Americans in Transatlantic Abolitionism and Blackface Minstrelsy* (Baton Rouge, La., 2010). For Harriet Beecher Stowe's debt to minstrel traditions, see Sarah Meer, *Uncle Tom Mania: Slavery, Minstrelsy, and Transatlantic Culture in the 1850s* (Athens, Ga., 2005), 9–16.

61. Hazel Waters, *Racism on the Victorian Stage: Representations of Slavery and the Black Character* (Cambridge, 2007), 107–18, 127–29, 151–73; Nowatzki, *Representing*, 4, 78–81, 98. On anti-slavery and excitement, see Audrey Fisch, *American Slaves in Victorian Britain* (Cambridge, 2000), 54.

62. Richard Altick, *The Shows of London* (Cambridge, Mass., 1978), 396.

63. *Chambers's Journal*, 12 Feb. 1870, 110.

64. J. R. Oldfield, *Chords of Freedom: Commemoration, Ritual and British Transatlantic Slavery* (Manchester, 2007).

65. Anthony Trollope, *The West Indies and the Spanish Main* (London, 1859), 63.

66. The author thanks S. Heath Mitton for suggesting parallax as a useful way to describe the thesis of this book. For a different use of "parallax" as a metaphor, see Slavoj Žižek, *The Parallax View* (Boston, 2006). There, the parallax view highlights the unseen differences between two ideological positions viewing reality, rather than two chronological positions viewing the same idealistic positions.

67. Lydia Maria Child Papers, Library of Congress microfilm copies, letter 10/236: Ellis Gray Loring to Lydia Maria Child, 21 Jan. 1841.

68. William Hart Benton, *Thirty Years View* (2 vols., New York, 1856), 2:447; Robin W. Winks, *Blacks in Canada*, 2nd ed. (London, 1997), 173.

69. *Daily News*, 6 Oct. 1862, 4; *Leeds Mercury*, 21 Oct. 1862, 2. Both writers complained about Britain's lack of sympathy for the Union in the Civil War.

70. Don Fehrenbacher, *The Slaveholding Republic: An Account of the United States Government's Relationship with Slavery* (New York, 2001).

71. On patriotic language in British anti-slavery, see Turley, *Culture*, 178–81; Srividhya Swaminathan, *Debating the Slave Trade: Rhetoric of British National Identity, 1759–1815* (Farnham, Surrey, 2009). On the idea of imperial reform, see Brown, *Moral Capital*, 456–57.

## 2. UNCLE TOM'S BRITAIN

1. *Examiner*, 29 May 1852, 341

2. Richard Altick, *The English Common Reader: A Social History of the Mass Reading Public, 1800–1900*, 2nd ed. (Columbus, Ohio, 1998), 301, 384; Meer, *Uncle Tom Mania*, 4.

3. Stephen, "Introduction," viii; Marcus Wood, *Blind Memory: Visual Representations of Slavery in England and America, 1760–1865* (Manchester, U.K., 2000), 144. On the consumer aspects of earlier abolitionism, see J. R. Oldfield, *Popular Politics and British Anti-Slavery 1787–1807* (London, 1998 [Manchester, 1995]), 155–79.

4. For examples of theatrical productions, see New York Historical Society, GLC, GLC05508: "Slave Life!," broadside advertisement, 1852; *Examiner*, 4 Dec. 1852, 773. On local talks, see *North Wales Chronicle and Advertiser*, 28 Jan. 1853, 4; on figurines, Louise L. Stevenson, "Virtue Displayed: The Tie-Ins of Uncle Tom's Cabin" (http:///www.iath.virginia.edu/utc/interpret/exhibits/stevenson/steveson.html); toys, wallpaper and dolls: Meer, *Uncle Tom Mania*, 134; Lorimer, *Colour*, 85.

5. Wendy F. Hamand, "'No Voice from England': Mrs. Stowe, Mr. Lincoln, and the British in the Civil War," *New England Quarterly* 61 (1988): 3–24, at 4–5. All twenty-six volumes of the petition survive at the Harriet Beecher Stowe Center, Hartford, Conn.

6. *Leeds Mercury*, 16 Oct. 1852, 4.

7. *North Wales Chronicle*, 15 Apr. 1853, 5; Charles Beecher, *Harriet Beecher Stowe in Europe: The Journal of Charles Beecher*, ed. Joseph S. Van Why and Earl French (Hartford, Conn., 1986), 20–22. Examples of such crowds abound in Beecher's journal. In Stowe's second trip to England, the public zeal had not abated: HBSC, Katharine S. Day Collection: Mary Perkins to "my dear friends," 10–11 Sept. 1856.

8. Victoria herself first became aware of the book's popularity in late 1852, remarking on Carlisle's introduction to it in a letter: GLC, GLC01587: Victoria to Duchess of Sutherland, 29 Oct. 1852. She appears not to have encountered the copy sent by the author to her husband: GLC, GLC01585: Harriet Beecher Stowe to Prince Albert, 20 Mar. 1852.

9. Lords Russell, Palmerston, and Argyle, and the archbishop of Dublin (Richard Whateley) were among them: Beecher, *Harriet Beecher Stowe in Europe*, 84; *Reynold's Newspaper*, 15 May 1853.

10. Joseph Willard, *Letter to an English Friend on the Rebellion in the United States and British Policy* (Boston, 1863), 3; see Bright's criticism of "the infamous Times": John Bright, *The Struggle in America in Relation to the Working Men of Britain* (n.p., 1863), 8.

11. Harriet Beecher Stowe, *A Reply to "The Affectionate Address of the Women of Great Britain and Ireland"* (London, 1863), 62.

12. R. J. M. Blackett, *Divided Hearts: Britain and the American Civil War* (Baton Rouge, La., 2001), 9; Duncan Andrew Campbell, *English Public Opinion and the American Civil* War (Woodbridge, Suffolk, 2003); Douglas A. Lorimer, "The Role of Anti-Slavery Sentiment in English Reactions to the American Civil War," *HJ* 19 (1976): 405–20; Lawrence Goldman, "'A Total Misconception': Lincoln, the Civil War, and the British" in *The Global Lincoln*, ed. Richard Carwardine and Jay Sexton (New York, 2011), 107–22.

13. For example, A. J. B. Beresford Hope, *The American Disruption* (London, 1862), 37–38.

14. [Frances Power Cobbe], *Rejoinder to Mrs. Stowe's Reply to the Address of the Women of England* (London, 1863); Sally Mitchell, *Francis Power Cobbe: Victorian Feminist, Journalist, Reformer* (Charlottesville, Va., 2004), 132.

15. Lorimer, "Role," 420, 406. See also the editorial comment in Charles Adams, ed., *Slavery, Secession & Civil War: Views from the United Kingdom and Europe* (Lanham, Md., 2007), 53.

16. Stowe, *Reply*, 14.

17. Quarles, "Ministers," 30. This approach can be seen in James Spence, *The American Union* (London, 1861), as noted by Donald Bellows, "A Study of British Conservative Reaction to the American Civil War," *Journal of Southern History* 51 (1985): 505–26, at 516. On economic aspects, see Jay Sexton, *Debtor Diplomacy: Finance and American Foreign Relations in the Civil War Era 1837–1873* (Oxford, 2005), 134–89. For U.S. considerations on these matters, see Kinley J. Brauer, "The Slavery Problem in the Diplomacy of the American Civil War," *Pacific Historical Review* 46 (1977): 439–69.

18. E. L. Blackman, *Shall We Recognise the Confederate States?* (Ipswich, 1863), 14–15, 18. See also Beresford Hope, *American Disruption*, 67; Thomas Colley Grattan, *England and the Disrupted States of America* (London, 1861), 17.

19. *Household Words*, 18 Sept. 1852, 4; Mrs. [Favell Lee] Mortimer, *Far Off; or Africa and America Described* (2 vols., London, 1854), 2:154; Charles Lyell, *Travels in North America with Geological Observations on the United States, Canada and Nova Scotia* (2 vols., London, 1845), 1:212–14; Frederick Marryat, *A Diary in America* (3 vols., London, 1839), 1:295.

20. A point being made just twenty-five years later: Sydney Buxton, *Finance and Politics: An Historical Study 1763–1885* (2 vols., London, 1888), 1:272. Early in the war, supporters of the South taunted that Lincoln had not issued a proclamation against slavery: Grattan, *England*, 40.

21. As quoted in Royden Harrison, *Before the Socialists: Studies in Labour and Politics, 1861–1881* (London, 1965), 45.

22. On the long-standing fear of servile insurrection, see Seymour Drescher, "John Brown's Body in Europe," *Journal of American History* 80 (1993): 499–524, at 506–12.

23. Christopher Herbert, *War of No Pity: The Indian Mutiny and Victorian Trauma* (Princeton, 2008).

24. *Fraser's Magazine*, Feb. 1863, 203–4; *Law Magazine and Review*, Feb. 1862, 3; "Philo-Americanus," in *The American Struggle: An Appeal to the People of the North* (London, 1862), 13–14, 26–27.

25. *Fraser's Magazine*, Feb. 1862, 262.

26. Correspondents supporting the CSA very occasionally attempted an apology for slavery, such as the Todmorton working man quoted by Blackett, *Divided Hearts*, 10. Perhaps the only British publication that supported the Confederacy by defending slavery was the *Anthropological Review*, the house journal of British racism, with secret funding from the CSA government in Richmond: Lorimer, *Colour*, 149.

27. *Times*, 3 Sept. 1852, 5.

28. *Times*, 6 Jan. 1863, 8.

29. *Times*, 25 Dec. 1852, 4.

30. *Fraser's Magazine*, Aug. 1852, 242; "The author of 'Friends in Council'" [Arthur Helps], *A Letter on Uncle Tom's Cabin* (Cambridge, 1852), 22. Helps was fascinated with Western slavery, and dedicated himself to a four-volume history of its rise in the Americas: *The Spanish Conquest in America and its Relation to the History of Slavery and the Government of the Colonies* (4 vols., London, 1855–61), 1:7.

31. *Wesleyan-Methodist Magazine*, June 1853, 565. For alternative interpretations of the Haitian Revolution, see Edward Bartlett Rugemar, *The Problem of Freedom: The Caribbean Roots of the American Civil War* (Baton Rouge, La., 2008), 42–65.

32. Lyell, *Travels*, 1:185–90.

33. *Fraser's Magazine*, Nov. 1842, 620; ibid., Aug. 1852, 243. The latter article, which was full of praise for *Uncle Tom's Cabin*, solicited a reply from "a Carolinian" that rehearsed the difficulties Southerners faced and the usual arguments against abolitionists: ibid., Oct. 1852, 476–90. This pity for slaveholders trapped in slavery continued into the Civil War: ibid., Feb. 1863, 192. On the claimed martyrdom of slaveowners, see Marcus Wood, *Slavery, Empathy and Pornography* (Oxford, 2002), 3.

34. Lyell, *Travels*, 1:193. For his *Principles of Geology*, see Martin Rudwick, "Sir Charles Lyell," *ODNB*. Lyell's evolutionary views influenced and were influenced by Darwin: Adrian Desmond and James Moore, *Darwin's Sacred Cause: How a Hatred of Slavery Shaped Darwin's Views on Human Evolution* (Boston, 2009), 329–30.

35. *Household Words*, 23 Aug. 1856, 133; this is consistent with an earlier concern for method, ibid., 18 Sept. 1852, 1.

36. Beecher, *Harriet Beecher Stowe in Europe*, frontispiece; *Bristol Mercury, and Western Counties Advertiser*, 8 Jan. 1853, 6; Midgley, *Women*, 148–49.

37. On the wider idea of reform in this period, see Joanna Innes and Arthur Burns, introduction to Joanna Innes and Arthur Burns, eds., *Re-thinking the Age of Reform* (Cambridge, 2003), 1–70, esp. 10. David Turley, "British Antislavery Reassessed," in *Re-thinking the Age of Reform*, ed. Innes and Burns, 182–99, discusses the relationship between anti-slavery and ideas of reform.

38. *National Review*, Jan. 1857, 215.

39. Russell Lant Carpenter, *Observations on American Slavery, After a Year's Tour in the United States* (London, 1852), 1; on this point in general, see Max Berger, "American Slavery as Seen by British Visitors, 1836–1860," *Journal of Negro History* 30 (1945): 181–201, at 196.

40. G. P. R. James, *The Old Dominion* (London, 3 vols., 1856), 1:296. For his career as a British consul in Virginia, see Michelle Anders Kinney, "'Doubly Foreign': British Consuls in the Antebellum South, 1830–1860" (PhD diss., University of Texas at Arlington, 2010), 125–28.

41. *National Review*, Jan. 1857, 235.

42. *Household Words*, 18 Sept. 1852, 6. A point Dickens was eager to remind Mrs. Cropper, Lord Denman's daughter, when he wrote to defend himself from her late father's attacks on his anti-slavery credentials. See Harry Stone, "Dickens and Harriet Beecher Stowe," *Nineteenth-Century Fiction* 12 (1957): 188–202, at 195.

43. Lyell, *Travels*, 1:190.

44. *Quarterly Review*, June 1849, 209; *Daily News*, 2 July 1849, 2; *Fraser's Magazine*, May 1850, 573–74.

45. *Chambers's Journal*, Apr. 1857, 245. Interestingly, this writer fears it would be Massachusetts that seceded from the Union, ushering in civil war and servile insurrection. The same was true for Frances Trollope, *Domestic Manners of the Americans*, 5th ed. (London, 1839), ii.

46. *Fraser's Magazine*, Nov. 1856, 617; ibid., Aug. 1852, 243; ibid., Nov. 1842, 620. See also the *Times*' criticism of Charles Sumner: *Times*, 18 June 1860, 8.

47. *Morning Chronicle*, 16 Sept. 1852, 3.

48. *Leeds Mercury*, 16 Oct. 1852, 4. On his concerns about interfering directly in American politics, or of being seen as aligned with Garrison, see Betty Fladeland, *Men and Brothers: Anglo-American Antislavery Cooperation* (Chicago, 1972), 352.

49. *Household Words*, Aug. 1856, 133.

50. *Times*, 24 Aug. 1859, 8; on their retardation of progress, see also Lyell, *Travels in North America*, 1:187–88.

51. *Spectator*, 4 Dec. 1852, 1163.

52. *Chamber's Edinburgh Journal*, Apr. 1842, 116. See also Charles Dickens to Mrs. Cropper, 20 Dec. 1852, reprinted in Stone, "Charles Dickens," 194.

53. *Examiner*, 11 Aug. 1849, 499; *Supplement to the Leeds Mercury*, 18 Aug. 1849, 11.

54. *Examiner*, 4 Sept. 1852, 563.

55. Meer, *Uncle Tom Mania*, 13. Some productions made the abolitionist Van Tromp the central character of the narrative: *Weekly Review and Dramatic Critic*, Oct. 1852, 61.

56. Meer, *Uncle Tom Mania*, 225.

57. Forrest Wilson, *Crusader in Crinoline: The Life of Harriet Beecher Stowe* (Philadelphia, 1941), 424.

58. Anon., *Uncle Tom's Cabin Almanack, or Abolitionist Momento* (London, 1853).

59. *Chambers's Journal*, Apr. 1857, 244.

60. On the emergence of gradualist and immediatist anti-slavery on either side of the Atlantic—and the problems of such terminology—see David Brion Davis, "The Emergence of Immediatism in British and American Antislavery Thought," *Mississippi Valley Historical Review* 49 (1962): 209–30.

61. *Household Words*, Aug. 1856, 133; ibid., 18 Sept. 1852, 1.

62. Trollope, *Domestic*, 200.

63. *Times,* 18 June 1860, 8; see also Amelia Murray, *Letters from the United States, Cuba and Canada* (London, 1857), 39.

64. *National Review*, Jan. 1857, 214; see also *Chambers's Journal*, Apr. 1857, 243.

65. *Chambers's Journal*, Mar. 1857, 179.

66. *Fraser's Magazine*, July 1854, 79; *Mirror*, Oct. 1846, 252; D. P. Crook, "Portents of War: English Opinion on Secession," *Journal of American Studies* 4 (1971): 163–79, at 172.

67. *Economist*, 4 Oct. 1856, 1089–90; ibid., 3 Nov. 1860, 1204; ibid., 24 Nov. 1860, 1303–34. Jay Sexton directed the author to this surprising editorial choice.

68. *Fraser's Magazine,* Feb. 1862, 259; *Leeds Mercury*, 21 Oct. 1862, 2; *Fortnightly Review*, June 1869, 708–9.

69. Crook, "Portents," 174–79.

70. *Times*, 9 Sept. 1861, 8.

71. *Times*, 13 Apr. 1859, 7.

72. Crook, "Portents," 172; *Chambers's Journal*, Mar. 1857, 180; ibid., Apr. 1857, 243–45; *Times*, 12 Mar. 1861, 9. The tariff provoked the *Times*, albeit temporarily, to imply that the Confederacy's internal institutions were not so much the business of the world as the North's external tariff.

73. *Times*, 6 Jan. 1863, 9. For a Northern attempt to rebut these appeals, see Robert Trimble, *The Negro, North and South* (London, 1863), 2.

74. *Times,* 16 Aug. 1861, 8; for its antebellum promotion by British abolitionists, see J. B. Estlin, *A Brief Notice of American Slavery and the Abolition Movement* (London, 1853), 31.

75. *ILN*, 7 Feb. 1863, 154; *Chambers's Journal*, Mar. 1857, 181; R. J. M. Blackett, "Cracks in the Antislavery Wall: Frederick Douglass's Second Visit to England (1859–60) and the Coming of the Civil War," in *Liberating Sojourn: Frederick Douglass & Transatlantic Reform*, ed. Alan J. Rice & Martin Crawford (Athens, Ga., 1999), 191–93, 198; on British perceptions in these critical months, see Blackett, *Divided Hearts*, 21–22.

76. *ILN*, 18 Oct. 1862, 427; *All The Year Round*, Dec. 1862, 329.

77. *Daily News*, 8 Oct. 1862, 4; Rev. Alfred C. Thomas, *Prayer Sympathy Invoked for America: A sermon preached at Cross Street Chapel, Islington* (Philadelphia, 1863), 16.

78. Marquis of Lothian, *The Confederate Secession* (London, 1864), 81–83, 90; William Devereux Jones, "The British Conservatives and the American Civil War," *American Historical Review* 58 (1953): 527–543, at 528.

79. Lothian, *Confederate Secession*, 91–99.

80. When Mill wrote for *Westminster Review,* July 1862, 489–510, he accepted that a victorious Confederacy would emancipate her slaves. See Lorimer, "Role," 416–17.

81. "A Poor Peacemaker," *The Slavery Quarrel* (London, 1863).

82. Duke University, Francis Yates Aglionby papers: E. Aglionby[?] to "My dear cousin" [probably Charles Yates Aglionby], 17 Feb. 1861; Duke University, Francis Yates Aglionby papers: E. Aglionby[?] to Fanny Aglionby, 11 May 1863. For family genealogy and history, see H. R. T. Summerson, *"An Ancient Squires Family": The History of the Aglionbys, c. 1130–2002* (Carlisle, 2007).

83. D. W. Mitchell, *Ten Years Residence in the United States* (London, 1862), 245–46, 249; *Westminster Review*, 1 Apr. 1863, 571–72.

84. Seymour Drescher, "The Ending of the Slave Trade and the Evolution of European Scientific Racism," *Social Science History* 14 (1990): 415–50, at 441–42.

85. Carpenter, *Observations,* 4.

86. *Daily News,* 16 Dec. 1864, 3.

87. *Examiner,* 4 Dec. 1852, 778. It was praised by Lady Byron in a letter to Stowe: Schlesinger Library, Beecher-Stowe Family Papers, A-012, microfilm M-45, folder 245: Lady Byron to Harriet Beecher Stowe, 1 Sept. 1856.

88. *Daily News,* 9 May 1853, 4.

89. HBSC, Acquisitions collection: Harriet Beecher Stowe to Sir Arthur Helps, 22 Aug. 1852.

90. *Punch,* May 1851, 218; Marcus Cunliffe, "America at the Great Exhibition of 1851," *American Quarterly* 3 (1951): 115–26, at 20.

91. *Liberator,* 18 July 1851, 116; William Wells Brown, *Three Years in Europe; or, Places I Have Seen and People I Have Met* (London, 1852), 207–17; William Farrison, *William Wells Brown: Author & Reformer* (Chicago, 1969), 187–88; Richard Blackett, *Beating against the Barriers: The Lives of Six Nineteenth-Century Afro-Americans* (Ithaca, N.Y., 1989), 101–3.

92. Josiah Henson, *Father Henson's Story of His Own Life* (Boston, 1858), 187–93; John Lobb, *The Young People's Illustrated Edition of Uncle Tom's Story of His Life (from 1789 to 1877)* (London, 1877), 123. On concerns at the accuracy of some of the claims made regarding Henson's life, see Mary Ellen Doyle, "Joseph Henson's Narrative: Before and After," *Negro American Literature Forum* 8 (1974): 176–83; Winks, *Blacks,* 187–90; Sharon A. Roger Hepburn, "Henson, Josiah (1789–1883)," *ODNB.*

93. John Scoble, *Great Exhibition and American Slavery* (n.p., 1850).

94. Brown, *Three Years,* 248–49. See also Farrison, *William Wells Brown,* 216.

95. Trollope, *Domestic Manners,* ii.

96. BFASS, *Proceedings ... 1840* (London, 1841), 121; see also Bell, *Idea,* 64.

97. Douglass, *Frederick Douglass Papers,* 1:138, 295; see also Willi Coleman, "'Like Hot Lead to Pour on the Americans...': Sarah Redmond Parker—From Salem, Mass., to the British Isles," in *Women's Rights and Transatlantic Antislavery in the Era of Emancipation,* ed. Kathryn Kish Sklar and James Brewer Stewart (New Haven, Conn., 2007), 173.

98. Douglass, *Frederick Douglass Papers,* 1:354, 420.

99. The BFASS's *Anti-Slavery Reporter* helped spread such tales of abuse to other journals: Lorimer, *Colour,* 73.

100. *Times,* 13 Apr. 1859, 7; Martin Crawford, *The Anglo-American Crisis of the Mid-Nineteenth Century: The Times and America, 1850–62* (Athens, Ga., 1962), 57.

101. *Chambers's Journal,* Mar. 1856, 207; *Household Words,* July 1854, 539.

102. Fisch, *American Slaves,* 23.

103. *Times,* 25 Dec. 1852, 4.

104. On American slavery in earlier British literature, see Matthew Mason, "The Battle of the Slaveholding Liberators: Great Britain, the United States, and Slavery in the Early Nineteenth Century," *William and Mary Quarterly* 59 (2002):665–96, at 679–83.

105. Meer, *Uncle Tom Mania,* 180, 201, 205; Cunliffe, *Chattel Slavery and Wage Slavery: The Anglo-American Context, 1830–1860* (Athens, Ga., 1979), 40; C. Duncan Rice, "Literary Sources and British Attitudes to Slavery" in, *Anti-Slavery, Religion and Reform,* ed. Christine Bolt and Seymour Drescher (Folkestone, Kent, 1980), 329–32.

106. Oscar Maurer, "'Punch' on Slavery and the Civil War in America 1841–1865," *Victorian Studies* 1 (1957): 9.

107. Mortimer, *Far Off,* 2:144–53, and frontispiece.

108. Richard Blackett, *Building an Anti-Slavery Wall: Black Americans in the Atlantic Abolitionist Movement, 1830–1860* (Baton Rouge, La., 1983), xi, 46, 141. See also Quarles, "Ministers," 27–42; Fisch, *American Slaves.*

109. Fisch, *American Slaves,* 52; Julia Sun-Joo Lee, *The American Slave Narrative and the Victorian Novel* (Oxford, 2010).

110. Douglass, *Frederick Douglass Papers,* 1:291; Blackett, *Building,* 27.

111. C. Duncan Rice, *The Rise and Fall of Black Slavery* (London, 1975), 46; Blackett, *Building,* 27.

112. Jeffery A. Auerbach, *The Great Exhibition of 1851: A Nation on Display* (New Haven, Conn., 1999), 168; Rachel Teukolsky, *The Literate Eye: Victorian Art Writing and Modern Aesthetics* (Oxford, 2009), 264.

113. Henry Russell, *Henry Russell's New and Vocal Pictorial Entertainment entitled The Far West or the Emigrants' Progress from the Old World to the New and Negro Life!* (London, n.d.), 23–32; Andrew Lamb, *A Life on the Ocean Wave: The Story of Henry Russell* (Croydon, 2007), 259, 266. Some of Russell's songs for "Negro Life!" were composed long before Tom-mania; for example, the slave ship song was first advertised in 1845 (358–62).

114. C. Peter Ripley, ed., *The Black Abolitionist Papers* (5 vols., London, 1985), 1:191–223: "A description of William Wells Brown's Original Panoramic Views of the Scenes in the Life of an American Slave, from his birth in slavery to his death or his escape to his first home of freedom on British soil," 1849; Farrison, *William Wells Brown,* 173–76.

115. *Ballad Sheet of "Song composed by H.B. Brown on his escape from slavery," "The slave's sing," and "Freedom's Star"* (n.d., n.p.) [found in JJC, Slavery 2].

116. Fisch, *American Slaves,* 80; Lorimer, *Colour,* 53–54. Brown's oft-recounted libel victory over them shows that his performance, by far the most populist of the slaves' tours, did arouse fears and loathing.

117. Fisch, *American Slaves,* 54–55, 99; Audrey Fisch, "'Exhibiting Uncle Tom in Some Shape or Other': The Commodification and Reception of Uncle Tom's Cabin in England," *Nineteenth-Century Contexts* 17 (1993): 145–58.

118. *National Review,* Jan. 1857, 212.

119. *ILN,* 27 Sept. 1856, 316.

120. *National Review,* Jan. 1857, 230.

121. *ILN,* 29 Nov. 1856, 555.

122. *Uncle Tom's Cabin Almanack,* 8. Stowe herself suggested this in an Irish context: GLC, GLC08360 (Maria Lamb Scrapbook): Harriet Beecher Stowe to Dublin Ladies Anti-Slavery Society, 23 Sept. 1853; GLC, GLC08360 (Maria Lamb Scrapbook): R. R. Madden to Mrs. Maria Webb, 1 Jan. 1852.

123. *Wesleyan-Methodist Magazine,* June 1853, 565.

124. *Uncle Tom's Cabin Almanack,* 4, 63. See the identical object behind *Uncle Tom in England* (London, 1852), 166, 186–87.

125. Brown, *Narrative,* iv.

126. Douglass, *Frederick Douglass Papers,* 1:325.

127. *Fraser's Magazine,* July 1855, 43. On efficacy, see Gabor S. Boritt, "Punch Lincoln: Some Thoughts on Cartoons in the British Magazine," *Journal of the Abraham Lincoln Association* 15 (1994): 1–22, at 4.

128. *Fraser's Magazine,* Feb. 1862, 258.

129. John Elliot Cairnes, *The Slave Power,* 2nd ed. (London and Cambridge, 1863), 209–302.

130. Indeed, it seems American abolitionist societies were not particularly well financed. The Garrisonian American Anti-Slavery Society raised c. $30,000 per annum, while the American and Foreign Anti-Slavery Society took perhaps $5,000: Benjamin Quarles, "Sources of Abolitionist Income," *Mississippi Valley Historical Review* 32 (1945): 36–76, at 76.

131. Ibid., 65.

132. The Garrisonians in Boston had pioneered an anti-slavery bazaar in 1834. Quarles, "Sources," 71–73, 75; Ripley, *Black Abolitionist Papers,* 1:216–23; Blackett, *Building,* 114–15.

133. Douglass, *Frederick Douglass Papers,* 1:370–71, 381–82; ibid., 2:7.

134. F. K. Prochaska, "Charity Bazaars in Nineteenth-Century England," *Journal of British Studies* 16 (1977): 62–84, at 70.

135. On his ability to do this, see Blackett, "Cracks," 190; Blackett, *Building,* 114–15.

136. Quarles, "Ministers without Portfolio," 27, 33.

137. *Preston Chronicle and Lancashire Advertiser,* 30 Oct. 1852, 2; *Bristol Mercury and Western Counties Advertiser,* 18 Jan. 1853, 6.

138. *Leeds Mercury,* 5 Mar. 1853, 5; HBSC, Acquisitions collection: Shaftesbury et al. to Harriet Beecher Stowe, 18 July 1853; Beecher, *Harriet Beecher Stowe in Europe,* 31, 45; Wilson, *Crusader in Crinoline,* 372.

139. Douglass, *Frederick Douglass Papers,* 1:269–70.

140. Brown, *Three Years,* 249–50.

141. Douglass, *Frederick Douglass Papers,* 1:352.

142. Ripley, *Black Abolitionist Papers*, 1:336: Speech by Samuel Ringgold Ward, Poultry Chapel, London, 9 May 1853.

143. Rugemar, *Problem*.

144. For example, Douglass, *Frederick Douglass Papers*, 1:261, 324, 369, 477; Brown, *Three Years*, 250; Anon., *Uncle Tom in England*, 190–91.

145. Ripley, *Black Abolitionist Papers*, 1:66: James McCune Smith, Speech to Glasgow Emancipation Society, 15 Mar. 1837.

146. Wood, *Slavery*, 9.


## 3. THE ANTI-SLAVERY STATE

1. This pithy summary of the argument—"from imperial morality to moral imperialism"—was generously proposed to the author by Jan-George Deutsch.

2. Draper, *Price*.

3. Temperley, *British Anti-Slavery*, ix

4. For case studies in particular regions, see, for example, Joseph C. Dorsey, *Slave Traffic in the Age of Abolition: Puerto Rico, West Africa and the Non-Hispanic Caribbean, 1815–59* (Gainesville, Fla., 2003); J. L. Wright, "Nothing Else But Slaves: Britain and the Central Saharan Slave Trade in the Nineteenth Century" (unpublished PhD thesis, School of Oriental and African Studies, University of London, 1998).

5. John Gallagher and Ronald Robinson, "The Imperialism of Free Trade," *Economic History Review*, 2nd ser., 6 (1953): 1–15, at 1.

6. Ibid., 6–12.

7. John Darwin, *The Empire Project: The Rise and Fall of the British World-System* (Cambridge, 2009), 16, 3.

8. Leslie Bethell, "The Mixed Commissions for Suppression of the Slave Trade in the Nineteenth Century," *Journal of African History* 7 (1966): 79–93, at 80; Richard W. Van Alstyne, "The British Right of Search and the African Slave Trade," *Journal of Modern History* 2 (1930): 37–47. As David Eltis notes, no slave-trade treaty was ever signed without Great Britain being one of the parties to it. The French, from 1856, were unique in providing their own slave-trade patrols, meaning Britain did not require the right to search ships under the Tricolour: David Eltis, *Economic Growth and the Ending of the Transatlantic Slave Trade* (Oxford, 1987), 90.

9. Ibid., 96.

10. Due to an accounting change in 1854, the figures before this date are for years ending 5 January, while those in this year and after are for years ending 31 March. I have excluded expenditures in the first three months of 1854, when this change happened, to avoid double counting it and artificially inflating figures. Source for price indices and state expenditure: Brian R. Mitchell, *British Historical Statistics*, 2nd ed. (Cambridge, 1988), 721–74, 587–95. Many thanks to David Eltis for his advice in constructing my data for this graph.

11. Bethell, "Mixed Commissions," 87.

12. Eltis, *Economic Growth*, 92.

13. NA, Russell Papers, PRO 30/22/31: Copy of Russell to Duke of Newcastle, 7 Sept. 1862.

14. NA, Russell Papers, PRO 30/22/26: Somerset to Russell, 9 Jan. 1865. Colin White was preparing a paper at the time of his death arguing that the charges against the Admiralty were unjust, which he was sadly unable to publish in Keith Hamilton and Patrick Salmon, eds., *Slavery, Diplomacy and Empire: Britain and the Suppression of the Slave Trade, 1807–1975* (Eastbourne, Sussex, 2009).

15. Aberdeen as quoted by Andrew Porter, "Trusteeship, Anti-Slavery and Humanitarianism," in *The Oxford History of the British Empire*, ed. Andrew Porter (5 vols., Oxford, 1999), 3:211; Keith Hamilton, "Zealots and Helots: The Slave Trade Department of the Nineteenth-Century Foreign Office," in, *Slavery, Diplomacy and Empire*, ed. Hamilton and Salmon, 20. Hamilton's advice on the difficulty of dating the Department's birth is gratefully acknowledged.

16. This rearrangement coincided with the dismissal of two clerks for misuse of departmental funds: Ray Jones, *The Nineteenth Century Foreign Office* (London, 1971), 27–32; J. M. Collinge, *Office-Holders in Modern Britain: Volume 8: Foreign Office Officials 1782–1870* (London, 1979), 34. The regular establishment of the Slave Trade Department reflected a belief that employing a larger number of poorly paid clerks was less economical than one with fewer high-skilled clerks. It represented a victory for Palmerston's long-running campaign to improve the pay of senior clerks in the Department: see Draft Report of 1850 Treasury Committee of Enquiry into the Foreign Office, as reproduced in Jones, *Nineteenth Century Foreign Office*, 153–54.

17. The draft report of the 1850 "Treasury Committee of Enquiry into the Foreign Office" is reproduced in Jones, *Nineteenth Century Foreign Office*, 150.

18. Jones, *Nineteenth Century Foreign Office*, 19; T. G. Otte, "The Foreign Office, 1856–1914," in *Imperial Defence: The Old World Order 1856–1956*, ed. Greg Kennedy (Abingdon, Oxfordshire, 2008), 9–29.

19. Hamilton, "Zealots and Helots," 33.

20. Duke University Library, Bandinel Papers, Box 2: Memorandum from James Stephen to Lord John Russell, n.d., regarding letter of John Bandinel to James Stephen, 10 Apr. 1840.

21. Duke University Library, Backhouse Papers, Box 12: John Backhouse (snr.) to George Canning Backhouse, 27 July 1841; Hamilton, "Zealots and Helots," 25–26; Duke University Library, Bandinel Papers, Box 2: Aberdeen to John Bandinel, 12 Oct. 1843.

22. Hamilton, "Zealots and Helots," 21, 30–34.

23. Ibid., 32–33.

24. Ibid., 34.

25. Durham University, Wylde papers, WYL 27/8–9: Commodore A. P. E. Wilmot to W. H. Wylde, 20 Mar. 1864.

26. Durham University, Wylde papers, WYL 29/12: Edmund Sturge to W. H. Wylde, 22 Apr. 1892.

27. On the use of secret service funds for anti-slavery espionage in Brazil and Cuba, see Eltis, *Economic Growth*, 115–17.

28. Durham University, Wylde papers, WYL 27/38–40: Alexander Graham Dunlop to Wylde, 20 Sept. 1864.

29. T. G. Otte, "'A Course of Unceasing Remonstrance': British Diplomacy and the Suppression of the Slave Trade in the East," in *Slavery, Diplomacy and Empire*, ed. Hamilton and Salmon, 100–101.

30. NA, FO 84/373, fo. 291: Palmerston to Sir John McNeil, 9 July 1841; FO 83/486, NA, fo. 5: Aberdeen to Captain Hamerton, 30 May 1843.

31. NA, FO 84/333, fos. 78–80: Sir Thomas Reade to John Backhouse, 29 June 1840. Note the difficulty of achieving a tangible outcome, even if the Foreign Office network shared information efficiently.

32. NA, FO 84/373, fo. 8: Palmerston to Sir Edmund Lyons, 20 Apr. 1841.

33. NA, Russell papers, PRO 30–22/21, fo. 355: Palmerston to Russell, 9 Dec. 1860.

34. Eltis, *Economic Growth*, 98–99.

35. Ibid., 97–98.

36. Bethell, "Mixed Commissions," 80, 85–87. We cannot recover the full cost of compensation claims against the squadron: Eltis, *Economic Growth*, 96; Farida Shaikh, "Judicial Diplomacy: British Officials and the Mixed Commission Courts," in *Slavery, Diplomacy and Empire*, ed. Hamilton and Salmon (Eastbourne, 2009), 47–49, 51.

37. Ibid., 42.

38. NA, FO 315/8, fo. 38: Copy of Commissioners at Havana to Aberdeen, 9 June 1846.

39. NA, FO 315/8, fo. 349: Copy of Commissary Judge at Havana to Palmerston, 25 Apr. 1848.

40. NA, FO 315/8, fo. 89: Copy of Commissioners at Havana to Aberdeen, 6 Nov. 1846.

41. NA, FO 315/8, fo. 515: Copy of Commissioners at Havana to Palmerston, 25 Jan. 1849.

42. Duke University Library, Backhouse Papers, Box 27: George Canning Backhouse 1851 diary, entries for 22 Sept. 1851, 23 Sept. 1851, 2 Sept. 1851; Duke University Library, Backhouse Papers, Box 27: George Canning Backhouse 1852–53 diary, entry for 31 Dec. 1852.

43. Duke University Library, Backhouse Papers, Box 27: George Canning Backhouse 1852–53 diary, entry for 10 Feb. 1853.

44. Duke University Library, Backhouse Papers, Box 27: George Canning Backhouse 1852–53 diary, entry for 10 May 1853.

45. Duke University Library, Backhouse Papers, Box 27: George Canning Backhouse 1852–53 diary, entry for 31 May 1853.

46. Duke University Library, Backhouse Papers, Box 27: George Canning Backhouse 1852–53 diary, entry for 21 Oct. 1853.

47. Duke University Library, Backhouse papers, Box 17: Consul General Crawford to "My Lord" [Clarendon], 1 Sept. 1855; Duke University Library, Backhouse Papers, Box 17: copy of Thomas Callaghan to Thomas Staveley, 8 Sep 1855. There seems to be no documentary evidence that this was an assassination connected with his diligence in suppressing the slave trade: Luis Martinez-Fernandez, *Fighting Slavery in the Caribbean: The Life and Times of a British Family in Nineteenth-Century Havana* (Armonk, N.Y., 1998), 146–50.

48. Dorsey, *Slave Traffic,* 174

49. NA, FO 84/1034, fo. 54: Foreign Office to Rear Admiral Fanshawe, 27 June 1857.

50. For the idea of a "man on the spot," see John S. Galbraith, *Crown and Charter: The Early Years of the British South Africa Company* (Berkeley, Calif., 1974), 8; John S. Galbraith, *Reluctant Empire: British Policy on the South African Frontier, 1834–1854* (Berkeley, Calif., 1963), 23.

51. NA, FO 84/333: fo. 6: Sir Edmund Lyons to Palmerston, 7 Oct. 1840.

52. *ASR,* 11 Jan. 1843, 3.

53. NA, FO 84/373, fos. 486–90: Sir Thomas Reade to Palmerston, 30 Apr. 1841; NA, FO 84/373, fos. 441–42: Draft to Sir Thomas Reade, 22 June 1841.

54. NA, FO 84/373, fo. 532: Sir Thomas Reade to Palmerston, 7 Sept. 1841; NA, FO 84/648, fo. 66: Sir Thomas Reade to Aberdeen, 24 Jan. 1846.

55. NA, FO 84/598, fo. 77: Sir Thomas Reade to Aberdeen, 10 Jan. 1845.

56. NA, FO 84/333, fo. 66: Col. Warrington to John Bidwell Esq., 10 Aug. 1840. On the intellectual descent of his plans for the improvement of the interior, via Bentham and D'Ghies, see Wright, "Nothing," 124. See 133–38 below for its parallels with Buxton's plans for civilization of the Niger.

57. NA, FO 84/333, fos. 66–67: Col. Warrington to John Bidwell Esq., 10 Aug. 1840

58. NA, FO 84/648, fo. 122: Drummond Hay to Lord Aberdeen, 12 June 1846.

59. Dorsey, *Slave Traffic,* 173

60. The "gravitational field" metaphor is borrowed from Darwin, *Empire Project,* 23.

61. Ronald Robinson, John Gallagher, and Alison Denny, *Africa and the Victorians: The Official Mind of Imperialism,* 2nd ed. (London, 1981), 19–23. The "official mind" remains useful in discussing anti-slavery policy within the Foreign Office, notwithstanding the caution offered by John Darwin, "Imperialism and the Victorians: The Dynamics of Territorial Expansion," *EHR* 112 (1997): 614–42.

62. Roger T. Anstey, "Capitalism and Slavery—A Critique," *Economic History Review,* 2nd ser., 21 (1968): 307–20; Rice, *Rise and Fall,* 231.

63. Bernard Semmel, *Liberalism and Naval Strategy: Ideology, Interest, and Sea Power during the Pax Britannica* (Boston, 1986), 44–45; Paul Michael Kielstra, *The Politics of Slave Trade Suppression in Britain and France* (Basingstoke, Hampshire, 2000), 207–38.

64. NA, FO 97/430, fo. 4: Memorandum on the State of Questions in the Slave Trade Department of the Foreign Office, 3 Jan. 1852.

65. University of Southampton, Palmerston papers, Broadlands Manuscripts, SLT 12: Anonymous memorandum on Brougham's proposals, 18 Feb. 1838; Kielstra, *Politics,* 190; Eltis, *Economic Growth,* 85.

66. Ibid., 86–87.

67. Edward Keene, "A Case Study of the Construction of International Hierarchy: British Treaty-Making against the Slave Trade in the Early Nineteenth Century," *International Organization* 61 (2007): 313, 320.

68. Ephraim D. Adams, *British Interests and Activities in Texas, 1838–1846* (Baltimore, 1910), 16–18; David Turley, "Anti-Slavery Activists and Officials: 'Influence,' Lobbying and the Slave Trade, 1807–1850," in *Slavery, Diplomacy and Empire,* ed. Hamilton and Salmon, 88–90.

69. William E. Channing, *Thoughts on the Evils of a Spirit of Conquest, and on Slavery* (London, 1837), 6; John Scoble, *Texas: Its Claims to be Recognised as an Independent Power by Great Britain examined in a Series of Letters* (London, 1839), 4–5. See also RH, Anti-Slavery Society papers, MSS. Brit. Emp. s.20 E2/6, fo.98: min. 65, 28 Sept. 1840; RH, Anti-Slavery Society papers, MSS. Brit. Emp. s.20 E2/20, fos.197–99; RH, Anti-Slavery Society papers, MSS. Brit.Emp.s.19 E2/19, BFASS memorials and petitions book, 222–31: Thomas Clarkson to Sam Houston, 6 Oct. 1843.

70. Adams, *British Interests,* 54–60; Leila M. Roeckell, "Bonds over Bondage: British Opposition to the Annexation of Texas," *Journal of the Early Republic* 19 (1999): 257–78, at 268, 270.

71. See Steven Heath Mitton, "The Free World Confronted: The Problem of Slavery and Progress in American Foreign Relations, 1833–1844" (PhD diss., Louisiana State University, 2005), esp. 7.

72. Duff Green papers, Microfilm reel 2: Duff Green to President Tyler, 18 May 1843.

73. Duff Green papers, Microfilm reel 2: Duff Green to John C. Calhoun, 29 Sept. 1843.

74. Lewis Tappan Papers, Microfilm reel 1: Journal entries for 19 June and 12 July 1843.

75. Duff Green papers, Microfilm reel 2: Duff Green to Lucretia Green, 16 Aug. 1842. Peel seems to have dealt with Green politely. For their later discussions, see Duff Green papers, Microfilm reel 2: Duff Green to President Tyler, 31 May 1843.

76. Duff Green papers, Microfilm reel 2: Duff Green to unknown recipient, 1 Aug. 1843. On his suspicions of Palmerston: Duff Green papers, Microfilm reel 2: Duff Green to Abel Upshur, 16 Nov. 1843.

77. This is why consuls did not act against domestic slave-holding or the internal slave trade in the U.S. South, as Kinney, "'Doubly Foreign,'" 78, 143–62, 337–38, finds.

78. David Turley, "'Free Air' and Fugitive Slaves: British Abolitionists versus Government over American Fugitives 1834–61," in *Anti-Slavery, Religion and Reform,* ed. Caroline Bolt and Seymour Drescher (Folkestone, Kent, 1980), 163–82.

79. University of Southampton, Palmerston papers, Broadlands manuscript, SLT 20: Palmerston's note to Stephens, 7 Jan. 1837 & 2 May 1839.

80. Edward D. Jervey and C. Harold Huber, "The Creole Affair," *Journal of Negro History* 65 (1980): 196–211.

81. As quoted by ibid., 205–6.

82. Daniel Webster, *The Works of Daniel Webster,* ed. Edward Everett, 6th ed. (6 vols., Boston, 1853), 6:316–17: Lord Ashburton to Daniel Webster, 2 Aug. 1842; Jervey and Heuber, "Creole Affair," 205–6.

83. Henry E. Landry, "Slavery and the Slave Trade in Atlantic Diplomacy, 1850–1861," *Journal of Southern History* 27 (1961): 184–207, at 192.

84. RH, Anti-slavery papers, MSS Brit. Emp. S.19 E2/19: Petitions and Memorials book, 159: Ashburton to John Scoble, 4 Nov. 1842.

85. For full details of the treaty, see Ephraim D. Adams, "Lord Ashburton and the Treaty of Washington," *American Historical Review* 17 (1912): 764–82, at 765–66.

86. Winks, *Blacks,* 170–71, 704. Winks notes that one of the law officers who argued this line, adopted by Glenelg, was John Campbell, the biographer of Lord Mansfield who probably invented the quote attributed to him regarding British air being "free."

87. Lewis Tappan papers, Microfilm reel 1: 1843 journal, entry for 12 July 1843. Aberdeen was responding to Tappan's suggestion that John Quincy Adams and other American anti-slavers thought him "not so friendly" to their cause, on account of the treaty's extradition clause.

88. RH, Anti-slavery papers, MSS Brit. Emp. S20: BFASS Petitions and Addresses book, 44–7: Thomas Clarkson to Lewis Tappan, 10 Jan. 1844; RH, Anti-Slavery Papers, MSS Brit. Emp. S20: BFASS Petitions and Addresses book, 40: Thomas Clarkson to Sir Charles Metcalfe, 7 Dec. 1843; Duke University: Wilder scrapbook, 107: Thomas Clarkson to [Benjamin Hawes?], 10 July 1845.

89. Alexander L. Murray, "The Extradition of Fugitive Slaves: A Re-evaluation," *Canadian Historical Review* 43 (1962): 298–314, at 298.

90. Winks, *Blacks,* 170–71, 704.

91. Turley, "'Free Air'," 171, 174–75, 177–78; Murray, "Extradition," 298; Winks, *Blacks,* 173–76.

92. Webster, *Works of Daniel Webster,* 6:367: General Cass to Daniel Webster, 29 Aug. 1842; Landry, "Slavery," 186–87. For a different interpretation, see Mitton, "Free World," 90–107.

93. Donald L. Canney, *Africa Squadron: The U.S. Navy and the Slave Trade, 1842–1861* (Washington D.C., 2006), 222–23.

94. NA, Russell papers, PRO 30/22/24, fo. 54: Somerset to Russell, 29 Aug. 1860.

95. Richard D. Fulton, "The London *Times* and the Anglo-American Boarding Dispute of 1858," *Nineteenth-Century Contexts* 17 (1993): 133–44. The *Times* was incensed at suggestions it was "a partisan of slavery," rather than an opponent of unjust and ineffectual methods (139).

96. *Hansard, Parliamentary Debates,* 3rd ser., 1851, cli, 2087; Semmel, *Liberalism,* 47.

97. Russell Papers, NA, PRO 30/22/24, fo. 70: Somerset to Russell, 7 Feb. 1861.

98. Manisha Sinha, *The Counter-revolution of Slavery: Politics and Ideology in Antebellum South Carolina* (Chapel Hill, N.C., 2000), 183–84; Matthew Mason, "Keeping Up Appearances: The International Politics of Slave Trade Abolition in the Nineteenth-Century Atlantic World," *Williams and Mary Quarterly,* 3rd ser., 66 (2009): 809–32, at 829–30.

99. Russell Papers, NA, PRO 30/22/21, fos. 563–65: Palmerston to Russell, 24 Sept. 1861; Howard Jones, *Blue & Grey Diplomacy: A History of Union and Confederate Foreign Relations* (Chapel Hill, N.C., 2010), 39, 122; on Palmerston's attitude to the conflict, see Duncan Andrew Campbell, "Palmerston and the American Civil War," in *Palmerston Studies II,* ed. David Brown and Miles Taylor (Southampton, 2007), 144–67.

100. Duke University Library, Great Britain Savannah Consulate Papers: E. M. Archibald to Lord Lyons, 13 Mar. 1860.

101. Duke University Library, Great Britain Savannah Consulate papers: Copy of Lyons to Molyneux, 25 July 1860.

102. Duke University Library, Great Britain Savannah Consulate papers: Lyons to Molyneux, 28 Apr. 1860. Kinney, "'Doubly Foreign,'" 177–95, also considers the Brodie case and draws different conclusions.

103. Darwin, *Empire Project,* 18–19.

104. A brief exception came during Henry Ellis's mission to Rio de Janiero in 1842, when Aberdeen initially instructed him to offer reform of the sugar duties, benefitting Brazilian planters, in exchange for a commitment to gradual emancipation: Leslie Bethell, *The Abolition of the Brazilian Slave Trade: Britain, Brazil and the Slave Trade Question 1807–1869* (Cambridge, 1970), 231–33.

105. Leslie Bethell, "The Independence of Brazil and the Abolition of the Brazilian Slave Trade: Anglo-Brazilian Relations, 1822–1826," *Journal of Latin American Studies* 1 (1969): 115–147, at 143–46; Bethell, *Abolition,* 242.

106. As quoted in Leslie Bethell, "Britain, Portugal and the Suppression of the Brazilian Slave Trade: The Origins of Lord Palmerston's Act of 1839," *EHR* 80 (1965): 761–84, 781.

107. As quoted in Bethell, *Abolition,* 243. See also his insightful contrast of the Aberdeen and Palmerston acts: 259.

108. Quoted in Bethell, *Abolition,* 255.

109. *Hansard,* 3rd ser., 1850, cix, 1136; Russell papers, NA, PRO 30/22/48, fos. 32–34: Christie to Russell, 21 Sept. 1860.

110. Eltis, *Economic Growth,* 90.

111. *PP 1847–48,* xxii (1), 9, 15, 19–20; *Hansard,* 3rd ser., 1851, cli, 1338. On the actual causes of Brazilian abolition, see Jeffrey Needell, "The Abolition of the Brazilian Slave Trade in 1850: Historiography, Slave Agency and Statesmanship," *Journal of Latin American Studies* 33 (2001): 681–711.

112. Bethell, "Mixed Commissions," 89.

113. As quoted by Bethell, *Abolition,* 266.

114. Robert Conrad, "Neither Slave nor Free: The Emancipados of Brazil, 1818–1868," *Hispanic American Review* 53 (1973): 50–70, at 65–66.

115. BFASS, Proceedings ... *1840,* 207, 265, 415.

116. *Uncle Tom's Almanack,* 21.

117. See Keene, "Case Study," 320.

118. Otte, "'A Course'," 103.

119. NA, FO 84/1324, fos. 62–64: Barron to Clarendon, 18 Jan. 1870.

120. NA, FO 84/1324, fos. 94–97: Elliot to Granville, 14 Aug. 1870.

121. NA, FO 84/1324, fo. 82: Elliot to Granville, 17 July 1870.

122. NA, FO 84/1354, fo. 201: Foreign Office to Cumberbatch, 27 Sept. 1872.

123. NA, FO 84/1305, fo. 28: Clarendon to Elliot, 22 Sept. 1869. Presumably it had been an "exceptional" case when, in 1853, Clarendon approved the purchase of Croat slaves by one consul: NA, FO 84/919, fos. 16–22: Sidney Smith Saunders to Clarendon, 5 Aug. 1853.

124. On Egypt, see Gabriel Baer, "Slavery in Nineteenth Century Egypt," *Journal of African History* 8 (1967): 417–41, at 431.

125. Yusuf Erdem, "Slavery in the Ottoman Empire and Its Demise" (DPhil thesis, Oxford University, 1993), 160; Otte, "'A Course'," 104.

126. NA, FO 84/1305, fo. 103: Henry Elliot to Clarendon, 27 Oct. 1869.

127. NA, FO 84/1324, fos. 109–110: Elliot to Granville, 16 Aug. 1870.

128. Erdem, "Slavery," 154, 160.

129. Erdem suggests that Palmerston never intended to act against the domestic institutions of the Ottoman Empire. Far from being an early ambition from which Britain backed away, the demands of 1840 were a false start: ibid., 140–41.

130. Durham University, Wylde papers, WYL 54/39–40: A. H. Layard to W. H. Wylde, 31 Mar. 1880; Durham University, Wylde papers, WYL 54/53: A. H. Layard to W. H. Wylde, 23 Apr. 1880; Otte, "'A Course'," 112–13.

131. It is not possible to do this topic justice, but see Matthew S. Hopper, "Globalization and the Economics of African Slavery in Arabia in the Age of Empire," *Journal of African Development* 12 (2010): 125–46; Matthew S. Hopper, "Imperialism and the Dilemma of Slavery in Eastern Arabia and the Gulf, 1873–1939," *Itinerario* 30 (2006): 76–94.

132. NA, FO 84/1324, fos. 66–67: Enclosed copy of Barron to Hay, 11 Jan. 1870.

133. Ehud R. Toledano, *As if Silent and Absent: Bonds of Enslavement in the Islamic Middle East* (New Haven, 2007), 62–66.

134. For example: NA, FO 84/1305, fo. 9: Clarendon to Henry Elliot, 15 July 1869; NA, FO 84/1305, fo. 117: Sir Philip Francis to Clarendon, 28 Sept. 1869; NA, FO 84/1305, fos. 125–26: Sir Philip Francis to Clarendon, 1 Dec. 1869.

135. NA, FO 84/1324, fos. 200–4: R. A. O Dalyell to H. P. J. Barron, 4 Feb. 1870. For a similar case, see NA, FO 84/1341, fo. 3: Granville to Elliot, 18 Apr. 1871.

136. Erdem's observations of British official attitudes toward the Ottoman Empire may be generalized across the Foreign Office more broadly: Erdem, "Slavery in the Ottoman Empire," 154, 160. So may Oldfield's conclusions regarding Palmerston: John Oldfield, "Palmerston and Anti-Slavery," in *Palmerston Studies II,* ed. David Brown and Miles Taylor (Southampton, 2007), 35.

137. Bethell, *Abolition*, 54.

138. Ibid., 344–45.

139. NA, FO 84/1305, fos. 11, 14–17: Memorandum, 31 Aug. 1869.

140. NA, FO 84/373, fos. 441–442: Draft of FO to Sir Thomas Reade, 22 June 1841; see also: NA, FO 84/648, fo. 58: Aberdeen to Sir Thomas Reade, 24 June 1846.

141. Kielstra, *Politics*, 1, 215.

142. Anstey, "Capitalism," 318.

143. The topic has received the recent and worthy attention of essayists in Hamilton and Salmon, eds., *Slavery*.

144. On "legal imperialism," in the context of the extension of extraterritorial courts, see Turan Kayaoğlu, *Legal Imperialism: Sovereignty and Extraterritoriality in Japan, the Ottoman Empire, and China* (Cambridge, 2010).

145. Helps, *Spanish Conquest*, 1:3.

146. Henry Maine, *Ancient Law: Its Connection with the Early History of Society and its Relation to Modern Ideas*, 3rd American ed. (New York, 1873 [London, 1861]), 163–64; Karuna Mantena, *Alibis of Empire: Henry Maine and the Ends of Liberal Imperialism* (Princeton, 2010).

147. On the idea of civilization as an alternative to "national character," never wholly eclipsed, see Peter Mandler, *The English National Character: The History of an Idea from Edmund Burke to Tony Blair* (New Haven, Conn., 2006), 77, 40–41, 58.

148. Joseph Denman, *West India Interests, African Emigration, and Slave Trade* (Worcester, 1848), 4. He agreed with the government, though disagreeing on free trade.

149. *Times*, 15 Feb. 1876, 9.

150. As quoted by Otte, "'A Course'," 113.

151. *Fraser's Magazine*, Aug. 1852, 240.

152. Darwin, *Empire Project*, 15.

153. Durham University, Wylde papers, WYL 27/10–11: Frederick William Gray to Commodore A. P. E. Wilmot, 23 Mar. 1864; Durham University, Wylde papers, WYL 27/8–9: Wilmot to Wylde, 20 Mar. 1864.

154. Durham University, Wylde papers, WYL 46/46–47: Copy of William Houghton A. Burzacott, 13 Dec. 1876; Durham University, Wylde papers, WYL 47/1: Note from Wylde to Lord Tenterden, 8 Jan. 1877; Durham University, Wylde papers, WYL 47/2: Foreign Office memorandum annotated by Tenterden and Wylde, 9 Jan. 1877.

155. Duke University Library, Backhouse Papers, Box 27: George Canning Backhouse 1852–53 diary, entry for 15 Sept. 1853; Martinez-Fernandez, *Fighting Slavery*, 141, 55.

156. Shaikh, "Judicial Diplomacy," 55–57.

157. Martinez-Fernandez, *Fighting Slavery*, 46–48.

158. For similar conclusions regarding Mixed Commission judges, see Shaikh, "Judicial Diplomacy," 59. For alleged corruption by British officials, see ibid., 53–54.

159. Rice, *Rise*, 231–32.

160. BFASS, *Proceedings ...1840*, 203.

161. NA, FO 84/373, fo. 291: Palmerston to Sir John McNeil, 9 July 1841.

162. BFASS, *Proceedings ...1840*, iii.

163. Ibid., 243.

164. See Turley, "Anti-Slavery Activists," 86–87, and, on humanitarian lobbying of the Colonial Office, Zoë Laidlaw, *Colonial Connections, 1815–45: Patronage, the Information Revolution and Colonial Government* (Manchester, 2005), 27–29.

165. Tyrrell, "The 'Moral Radical Party'," 499.

166. University of Southampton, Palmerston Papers, Broadlands manuscripts, SLT 8: Thomas Fowell Buxton to Palmerston, 29 May 1837.

167. A. F. Madden, "The Attitude of the Evangelicals to the Empire & Imperial Problems, 1820–50" (DPhil thesis, Oxford University, 1950), 42.

168. NA, FO 84/373, fo. 11: Draft to Sir Edmund Lyons, 11 May 1841. For the pressure, see BFASS, *Proceedings ...1840*, 264, 461. For the original minutes, see RH, Anti-Slavery Society Papers, MSS British Emp. S20 E/218.

169. NA, FO 84/373, fo. 438: Draft to Sir Thomas Reade, 18 Mar. 1841.

170. Eltis, *Economic Growth*, 83.

171. Duke University Library, Backhouse Papers, Box 9: William Hamilton to John Backhouse Snr., 25 Feb. 1837.

172. Duke University Library, Backhouse Papers, Box 12: William Hamilton to John Backhouse Snr., 6 Sept. 1841; for American examples, see Kinney, "'Doubly Foreign'," 131–33.

173. Ibid., 242–56, 335–36, 163.

174. Duke University Library, Backhouse Papers, Box 27: George Canning Backhouse 1852–53 diary, entry for 12 Apr. 1853.

175. Hugh Tinker, *A New System of Slavery: The Export of Indian Labour Overseas 1830–1920*, 2nd ed. London, 1993([Oxford, 1974]), 69, 74; Green, *British Slave Emancipation*, 267.

176. NA, FO 84/846, fo. 79: Aberdeen to Lt. Col. Barnett, 23 Dec. 1843.

177. RH, Anti-Slavery Papers, MSS Brit. Emp. S20, Memorials and petitions book, 27: [Copy of] Addington to J. H. Hinton, 16 Dec. 1843.

178. As so often happened in these cases, sufficient evidence could not be found. RH, Anti-Slavery Papers, MSS. Brit.Emp.s.19 E2/19, Memorials and petitions book, 161–66: John Scoble to John Cropper, 9 Nov. 1842; RH, Anti-Slavery Papers, MSS. Brit.Emp.s.19 E2/19, Memorials and petitions book: John Scoble to John Cropper, 11 Nov. 1842; RH, Anti-Slavery Papers, MSS. Brit.Emp.s.19 E2/19, Memorials and petitions book: George Hope to John Scoble, Colonial Office, 10 Nov. 1842; RH, Anti-Slavery Papers, MSS. Brit. Emp.s.19 E2/19, Memorials and petitions book: John Cropper to John Scoble, 11 Nov. 1842.

179. University of Southampton, Palmerston papers, Broadland manuscripts, SLT 20: Palmerston's draft reply to the committee of the Anti-Slavery Society, 18 Oct. 1842. The final version is recorded in RH, Anti-Slavery papers, MSS. Brit.Emp.s.20 E2/19, Memorials and petitions book, 156–59: Palmerston's reply to BFASS Delegation, 17 Oct. 1842.

180. Kielstra, "Politics," 236; Peter Jones, "Palmerston and the Slave Trade" (unpublished article, draft supplied by the author, 2007), 10. Many thanks to Jones for sharing his forthcoming article.

181. Dorsey, *Slave Trade*, 72–73, 76; Manuel Llorca-Jaña, "David Turnbull," *ODNB*.

182. University of Southampton, Palmerston papers, Broadlands Manuscripts, SLT/26: Undated memo c.1845, as cited in Jones, "Palmerston and the Slave Trade"; Eltis, *Economic Growth*, 121.

183. Kielstra, *Politics*, 1, 215.

184. Ibid., 209–11.

185. Ibid., 237.

186. Eltis, *Economic Growth*, 89; Bethell, *Abolition*, 275.

187. See Roeckell, "Bonds," 273.

188. For example: Duke University Library, Lord John Russell Papers: Palmerston to Russell, 6 Feb. 1844. He had been criticized in 1840: University of Southampton, Palmerston papers, Broadlands manuscripts, SLT 16: William Hawksworth to Palmerston, 14 Jan. 1860.

189. *Times*, 15 Aug. 1876, 6; Mulligan, "Fugitive Slave Circulars," 183–205, Wylde's opinion as quoted at 188.

190. Yale Divinity School, Horace Waller Papers, Record Group 72, Box 1, Folder 2, 1876 Diary: Entries for 14 Feb., 10 Jan., 1 Feb., 12 Feb., 23 Feb., 4 Mar 1876.

191. *Punch*, 2 Oct. 1875, 331. See also ibid., 19 Feb. 1876, 59; ibid., 4 Mar. 1876, 79.

192. As quoted by Mulligan, "Fugitive Slave Circulars," 187–89, 195.

193. As quoted by ibid., 193.

194. Durham University, Wylde papers, WYL 24/26–29: Clement Hill to W. H. Wylde, 29 Sept. 1876.

195. Mulligan, "Fugitive Slave Circulars," 198.

196. R. J. Gavin, "Bartle Frere Mission," 138–41.

197. On the relationship between domestic politics and foreign policy, see comments by T. G. Otte, "'Avenge England's Dishonour': By-elections, Parliament and the Politics of Foreign Policy in 1898," *EHR* 121 (2006): 385–428.

198. NA, FO 84/333, fos. 48–49: Draft dispatch to Lord Ponsomby, 9 Nov. 1840.

199. For examples: NA, FO 84/373, fo. 293: Palmerston to Sir John McNeil, 9 July 1841; NA, FO 84/486, fo. 8: Aberdeen to the Imam of Muscat, 2 Aug. 1843; NA, FO 84/373, fos. 487–88: Sir Thomas Reade to Palmerston, 30 Apr. 1841.

200. Kielstra, *Politics*, 233.

201. Charles Livingstone and David Livingstone, *Narrative of an Expedition to the Zambesi and its Tributaries* (London, 1865), 595.

## 4. BRITONS' UNREAL FREEDOM

1. The "guzzling slave" belongs to William Lovett, *Social and Political Morality* (London, 1853), 43; "the slavery of ignorance" is from *Fraser's Magazine*, Sept. 1835, 270. The danger of reading abolitionism into any contemporary mention of "slavery" is noted by Turley, *Culture*, 184, and Kelly J. Mays, "Slaves in Heaven, Laborers in Hell: Chartist Poets' Ambivalent Identification with the (Black) Slave," *Victorian Poetry* 39 (2001): 137–63, at 144. I am grateful to David Turley for his advice on this methodological problem.

2. As observed by D. W. Bebbington in his review of "G.I.T. Machin, *Politics and the Churches in Great Britain* (Oxford, 1977) and Robert Currie, Alan Gilbert, and Lee Horsley, *Churches and Churchgoers: Patterns of Church Growth in the British Isles Since 1700* (Oxford, 1977)," *HJ* 21 (1978): 1013–16, at 1014.

3. Timothy Larsen, *Friends of Religious Equality: Nonconformist Politics in Mid-Victorian England* (Woodbridge, Suffolk, 1999), 143.

4. Huzzey, "L.A. Chamerovzow," *ODNB*; Turley, *Culture*, 104–5.

5. Alexander Tyrrell, "Making the Millennium: The Mid-Nineteenth Century Peace Movement," *HJ* 21 (1978): 75–95, see 83–85.

6. Alexander Tyrrell, *Joseph Sturge and the Moral Radical Party in Early Victorian Britain* (London, 1987).

7. Larsen, *Friends,* 220.

8. Turley, *Culture,* 187–95.

9. Ibid., 108.

10. Douglass, *Frederick Douglass Papers,* 1:295, 339.

11. *Free Church Alliance with Manstealers: Send Back the Money* (Glasgow, 1846), 27. For the complexities of Anglo-Irish relations, see Kinealy, *Daniel O'Connell;* Angela Murphy, *American Slavery, Irish Freedom: Abolition, Immigrant Citizenship, and the Transatlantic Movement for Irish Repeal* (Baton Rouge, La., 2010), and forthcoming work by David Sim.

12. Samuel Ringgold Ward, *Autobiography of a Fugitive Negro: His Anti-Slavery Labours in the United States, Canada and England* (London, 1855), 253.

13. Wilson, *Crusader,* 374; see also Blackett, *Building,* 14–15.

14. Beecher, *Harriet Beecher Stowe in Europe,* 34.

15. Quarles, "Ministers," 40.

16. For a later example, see Brown, *Three Years,* 249–50.

17. *The Free Church and Her Accusers: The Question at Issue* (Glasgow, 1846); George Thompson and Henry C. Wright, *The Free Church of Scotland and American Slavery* (Edinburgh, 1846); Alasdair Petty, "Send Back the Money: Douglass and the Free Church of Scotland," in *Liberating Sojourn: Frederick Douglass & Transatlantic Reform,* ed. Alan J. Rice and Martin Crawford (Athens, Ga., 1999), 31–41; Blackett, *Building,* 80–81.

18. *Free Church Alliance,* 28; *Free Church and Her Accusers,* 6.

19. Blackett, *Building,* 99–103; see also Thomas F. Harwood, "British Evangelical Abolitionism and American Churches in the 1830s," *Journal of Southern History* 28 (1962): 287–306; BFASS, *Proceedings…1840,* 62–63, 115, 137.

20. Antoninette Burton, "New Narratives of Imperial Politics in the Nineteenth Century," in *At Home with the Empire: Metropolitan Culture and the Imperial World,* ed. Catherine Hall and Sonya O. Rose (Cambridge, 2006), 212–13.

21. Clare Midgley, "Bringing the Empire Home: Women Activists in Imperial Britain, 1790s–1930s," in *At Home with the Empire,* ed. Hall and Rose, 233.

22. *Hansard,* 3rd ser., 1852, cxx, 1207.

23. Colley, *Britons,* 366–68, quotation at 368; see also David Brion Davis, *Slavery and Human Progress* (New York and Oxford, 1984), 210.

24. Seymour Drescher, *Capitalism and Antislavery: British Popular Mobilization in Comparative Perspective* (New York, 1987), 151.

25. For an excellent recent account of the Chartists, see Malcolm Chase, *Chartism: A New History* (Manchester, 2007).

26. William Lovett, *The Life and Struggles of William Lovett,* ed. R. H. Tawney (2 vols., New York, 1920 [London, 1876]), 1:201.

27. *Morning Chronicle,* 7 Jan. 1837, 3.

28. As quoted by Temperley, *British Anti-Slavery,* 16.

29. *Fraser's Magazine,* Nov. 1859, 638.

30. *Uncle Tom in England,* 205; Fisch, *American Slaves,* 48.

31. On the broader context of American democracy, African American emancipation, and British ideas of representation, see Richard Huzzey, "British Liberties, American Emancipation and the Democracy of Race," in *The American Experiment and the Idea of Democracy in British Culture, 1776–1914,* ed. Ella Dzelzainis and Ruth Livesey (forthcoming).

32. Lovett, *Life and Struggles,* 1:132–37.

33. *Times,* 25 Dec. 1852, 4.

34. Frances Trollope, *Domestic Manners of the Americans,* 5th ed. (London, 1839), 195; Harriet Martineau, *Society in America* (3 vols., London, 1837; repr., New York, 1966), 2:313; see also Charles Dickens, *American Notes for General Circulation,* ed. Patricia Ingham (London, 2000 [1842]), 265.

35. Douglass, *Frederick Douglass Papers*, 1:367.

36. As quoted by *Proceedings...1840*, 122; presumably due to Stanton's faulty memory or the secretaries' error, the punctuation and word choices vary from the version printed in John Greenleaf Whittier, *Poems Written During the Progress of the Abolition Question in the United States, Between 1830 and 1838* (Boston, 1837), 38. On Stanton and his unusual choice of honeymoon, see Ann D. Gordon, ed., *The Selected Papers of Elizabeth Cady Stanton and Susan B. Anthony* (New Brunswick, N.J., 1997), xiix.

37. Mortimer, *Far Off*, 2:182; Meer, *Uncle Tom Mania*, 142; Ripley, *Black Abolitionist Papers*, 1:213: "A description of William Wells Brown's Original Panoramic Views of the Scenes in the Life of an American Slave...," 1849.

38. Douglass, *Frederick Douglass Papers*, 1:362; Brown, *Three Years*, 9.

39. *Economist*, 3 Nov. 1860, 4. I thank my student Lesley Kiger for drawing my attention to this reference in her Yale undergraduate senior essay.

40. Lothian, *Confederate Secession*, 100–101.

41. R. W. Russell, *America Compared with England: The Respective Social Effects of the American and English Systems of Government and Legislation* (London, 1849).

42. As quoted by Kathryn Gleadle, *The Early Feminists: Radical Unitarians and the Emergence of the Women's Rights Movement* (Basingstoke, Hampshire, 1995), 119.

43. Ibid., 84.

44. Ibid., 62–70.

45. Midgley, "Bringing the Empire Home," 232–33.

46. Midgley, *Women*, 72–73.

47. Ibid., 155–56.

48. Ibid., 84.

49. David Brion Davis, "Declaring Equality: Sisterhood and Slavery," in *Women's Rights and Transatlantic Antislavery in the Era of Emancipation*, ed. Kathryn Kish Sklar and James Brewer Stewart (New Haven, 2007), 15; Karen Offen, "How (and Why) the Analogy of Marriage with Slavery Provided the Springboard for Women's Rights Demands in France, 1640–1848," in *Women's Rights and Transatlantic Antislavery*, ed. Sklar and Stewart, 57–81; Seymour Drescher, "Women's Mobilization in the Era of Slave Emancipation: Some Anglo-French Comparisons," in *Women's Rights and Transatlantic Antislavery*, ed. Sklar and Stewart, 98–120.

50. Midgley, "Bringing the Empire Home," 232; Midgley, *Women*, 81.

51. *Spectator*, 4 Dec. 1852, 1163. See also *Lloyd's Weekly Newspaper*, 27 Mar. 1853, 1; *Daily News*, 9 May 1853, 4.

52. Midgley, *Women*, 149.

53. Meer, *Uncle Tom Mania*, 176.

54. As quoted in Sklar, "'Women'," 315.

55. As quoted in Midgley, *Women*, 162.

56. As quoted in Gleadle, *Early Feminists*, 84.

57. Midgley, *Women*, 173–74; Clare Midgley, "British Abolition and Feminism in Transatlantic Perspective," in *Women's Rights and Transatlantic Antislavery*, ed. Sklar and Stewart, 122; Judith Walkowitz, *Prostitution and Victorian Society: Women, Class and the State* (Cambridge, 1980), 123–24.

58. Midgley, *Women*, 172, 200–204.

59. Sklar, "'Women'," 321; Midgley, "British Abolition," 125–29.

60. Drescher, "Women's Mobilization," 114–15.

61. But see Midgley's brilliant objections to discounting white female campaigners' concern for black women as bearing only instrumental rather than intrinsic value to "feminism" in her "British Abolition," 125–29.

62. Turley, *Culture*, 194–95; Drescher, *Capitalism*, 144–45; see Innes and Burnes, introduction to *Rethinking the Age of Reform*, ed. Innes and Burnes, 68, n190, for reservations.

63. Gleadle, *Early Feminists*, 63.

64. Turley, *Culture*, 182.

65. The relevant sections of Davis, *Problem of Slavery in the Age of Revolution*, are reprinted with the ensuing *AHR* debate in Bender, ed., *Antislavery Debate*. Davis's recent reflections on the topic can be found in David Brion Davis, *In the Image of God: Religion, Moral Values, and Our Heritage of Slavery* (New Haven, Conn., 2001), 217–34.

66. See, for example, Robert Cruikshank, *The Condition of the West India Slave contrasted with that of the Infant Slave in our English Factories* (London, n.d.), discussed by Wood, *Blind Memory*, 273-74. In the earlier period, see "A Plain Man," *The True State of the Question* (London, 1792).

67. John C. Cobden, *The White Slaves of England: Compiled from Official Documents* (New York, 1860); see also Cunliffe, *Chattel Slavery*.

68. James Henry Hammond, *Letter of His Excellency Governor Hammond to the Free Church of Glasgow on the Subject of Slavery* (Columbia, S.C., 1844), 5-6.

69. *Leeds Mercury*, 16 Oct. 1852, 4

70. *Fraser's Magazine*, Aug. 1852, 238-39; HBSC, Acquisitions collection: Harriet Beecher Stowe to Sir Arthur Helps, 22 Aug. 1852. In this letter, Stowe proposed that both American slavery and the problems of industrial labor could be tackled only through "gradual amelioration."

71. *Examiner*, 26 Mar. 1853, 196.

72. For example: Brown, *Three Years in Europe*, 91-92; Judie Newman, "Stowe's Sunny Memories of Highland Slavery," in *Special Relationships: Anglo-American Affinities and Antagonisms 1854-1936*, ed. Janet Beer and Bridget Bennett (Manchester, 2002), 28-31.

73. Ibid., 28-42; George Shepperson, "Harriet Beecher Stowe and Scotland, 1852-53," *Scottish Historical Review* 32 (1953): 40-46; K. D. Reynolds, *Aristocratic Women and Political Society in Victorian Britain* (Oxford, 1998), 123-28.

74. *People's Paper*, 12 Mar. 1853, reprinted in Karl Marx and Frederick Engels, *The Collected Works of Karl Marx and Frederick Engels* (47 vols. to date, London, 1978-present), 11:495.

75. *Reynold's Newspaper*, 16 Jan. 1853, 7.

76. *All The Year Round*, 15 June 1867, 585.

77. *Punch*, 22 Jan. 1853, 37. See also *Punch*, 29 Jan. 1853, 52; *Punch*, 26 Feb. 1853, 89; Richard D. Altick, *Punch: The Lively Youth of a British Institution 1841-51* (Columbus, Ohio, 1997), 369-70; Altick, *Shows of London*, 283.

78. Thompson and Wright, *Free Church*, 35.

79. For Isaiah Berlin's famous complaint that liberty should be defined in only a negative, not a positive, sense, see Isaiah Berlin, *Two Concepts of Liberty* (Oxford, 1958).

80. Cunliffe, *Chattel Slavery*, 10.

81. Tom L. Franzmann, "Antislavery and Political Economy in the Early Victorian House of Commons: A Research Note on 'Capitalist Hegemony'," *Journal of Social History* 27 (1994): 579-93; the quotation is from Eltis, *Economic Growth*, 122, which Franzmann critiques on the first page of his article.

82. Robert J. Steinfeld, *Coercion, Contract, and Free Labor in the Nineteenth Century* (Cambridge, 2001), 39, 47, 82-84.

83. *Times*, 8 Mar. 1788, as cited in Brown, *Moral Capital*, 371.

84. Douglass, *Frederick Douglass Papers*, 1:343; Richard Bradbury, "Frederick Douglass and the Chartists," in *Liberating Sojourn: Frederick Douglass & Transatlantic Reform*, ed. Alan J. Rice and Martin Crawford (Athens, Ga., 1999), 169-87.

85. Ward, *Autobiography*, 237-40.

86. Douglas B. A. Ansdell, "William Lloyd Garrison's Ambivalent Approach to Labour Reform," *Journal of American Studies* 24 (1990): 402-7, at 403-4.

87. Chase, *Chartism*, 54-55.

88. Karl Marx, "The Poverty of Philosophy," in Marx and Engels, *Collected Works*, 4:169.

89. Steinfeld, *Coercion*, 13.

90. Wilfried Nippel, "Marx, Weber, and Classical Slavery," *Classics Ireland* 12 (2005): 31-49, at 40; Gerald Runkle, "Karl Marx and the American Civil War," *Comparative Studies in Society and History* 6 (1964): 117-41.

91. *Hansard*, 3rd ser., 1848, xcvi, 85.

92. J. S. Mill, *Principles of Political Economy* (2 vols., London, 1848), 1:293-98. Mill departed from many other political economists in defending trade unionism as a necessary guard against free labor becoming a new slavery: ibid., 2:498.

93. On Mill, see Steinfeld, *Coercion*, 236-37.

94. Ibid.

95. Joseph Persky, "Wage Slavery," *History of Political Economy* 30 (1998): 627–51, at 641–49.

96. G. D. H. Cole, *Chartist Portraits* (London, 1941), 84–86; Cecil Driver, *Tory Radical: The Life of Richard Oastler* (New York, 1946), 40–41.

97. *Leeds Mercury,* 16 Oct. 1830, reprinted in Patricia Hollis, ed., *Class and Class Conflict in Nineteenth-Century England, 1815–1850* (London, 1976), 194. See also Persky, "Wage Slavery," 640.

98. Seymour Drescher, "Cart Whip and Billy Roller: Antislavery and Reform Symbolism in Industrializing Britain," *Journal of Social History* 15 (1981): 3–24, at 13.

99. *Examiner,* 19 Aug. 1848, quoted in John Butt, "'Bleak House' in the Context of 1851," *Nineteenth-Century Fiction* 10 (1955): 1–21, at 14–15.

100. *Wesleyan-Methodist Magazine,* Mar. 1854, 224; see, earlier, Sir Charles Lyell, *A Second Visit to the United States of North America* (2 vols., London, 1849), 1:367.

101. *Times,* 6 Aug. 1834, 6; *Times,* 1 Aug. 1834, 5.

102. Thomas Carlyle, "Occasional Discourse on the Negro Question," in *Fraser's Magazine,* Dec. 1849, 670–79; Thomas Carlyle, *Occasional Discourse on the Nigger Question* (London, 1853), see 26 for "tom-foolery." On the differences between the two editions, see Wood, *Slavery,* 376.

103. Rice, *Rise,* 365; Wood, *Slavery,* 364.

104. John Morrow, *Thomas Carlyle* (London, 2006), 126–33.

105. *Punch,* 12 Jan. 1850, 19.

106. Brown, *Three Years,* 217.

107. Carlyle, *Occasional Discourse,* 17.

108. Ibid., 26. He referred to the "Exeter Hall" meeting place for many humanitarian groups, including anti-slavery organizations.

109. One of the only positive responses was a pro-slavery pamphlet dedicated to Carlyle during the American Civil War: "A Poor Peacemaker," *Slavery Quarrel.*

110. For his private remarks on American slavery, which seem to endorse gradual emancipation, see Thomas Carlyle to Beverley Tucker, 21 Oct. 1850, reprinted in *Harper's Magazine,* Oct. 1885, 797–800.

111. Morrow, *Thomas Carlyle,* 126.

112. See also Chris R. Vanden Bosschep, *Carlyle and the Search for Authority* (Columbus, Ohio, 1991), 202, n67.

113. Chase, *Chartism,* 307.

114. Norbert J. Gossman, "William Cuffay: London's Black Chartist," *Phylon* 44 (1983): 56–65.

115. Chase, *Chartism,* 54.

116. As quoted in Harrison, *Before the Socialists,* 59; Turley, *Culture,* 183.

117. Mays, "Slaves," 153.

118. Blackett, *Building,* 24; Fladeland, "'Our Cause'," 69–99.

119. Patricia Hollis, "Anti-Slavery and British Working-Class Radicalism in the Years of Reform," in *Anti-slavery, Religion and Reform,* ed. Christine Bolt and Seymour Drescher (Folkestone, Kent, 1988), 310–11.

120. Neville Kirk, "In Defence of Class: A Critique of Recent Revisionist Writing upon the Nineteenth-Century English Working Class," *International Review of Social History* 32 (1987): 2–47, at 23; Turley, *Culture,* 183.

121. Lovett, *Life,* 1:143.

122. As quoted in Jonathan Rose, *The Intellectual Life of the British Working Classes* (New Haven, Conn., 2002), 383. For the wider debate on the attitudes of working people during the war, see Blackett, *Divided Hearts;* Mary Ellison, *Support for Secession: Lancashire and the Civil War* (Chicago, 1972); Philip Foner, *British Labor and the American Civil War* (New York, 1981).

123. Robert Harborough Sherard, *The White Slaves of England* (London, 1895); Robert Harborough Sherard, *The Child Slaves of Britain* (London, 1905).

124. Sherard, *White Slaves,* 22, 208.

125. Joseph Arch, *Joseph Arch: The Story of his Life,* ed. Countess of Warwick (London, 1898), 29; Rose, *Intellectual Life,* 382.

126. Paula Bartley, *Prostitution: Prevention and Reform in England, 1860–1914* (London, 2000), 170–73.

127. *Times,* 18 Jan. 1904, 12; *Broad Views,* Feb. 1904, 190.

128. Blackett, *Building,* xi, 19.

129. Brown, *Three Years,* 114. The involvement of children would be consistent with other benevolent causes, in which they were often donors and key sympathizers: Prochaska, "Charity Bazaars," 75.

130. All quoted in Rose, *Intellectual Life,* 383–84.

131. Beecher, *Stowe in Europe,* ed. Van Why and French, 28–29.

132. Ibid., 23, 27.

133. Ward, *Autobiography,* 330–37.

134. Drescher, "Cart Whip," 3–24.

135. Richard Huzzey, "Free Trade, Free Labour and Slave Sugar in Victorian Britain," *HJ* 53 (2010): 359–79.

136. *Hansard,* 3rd ser., 1840, lv, 76–77; the effect of the duties in directly increasing the cost to the consumer had been noted by the Report of the 1840 Select Committee on Import Duties: *PP 1840,* v (601), v.

137. *Hansard,* 3rd ser., 1846, lxxxviii, 537. See also *Hansard,* 3rd ser., 1846, lxxxviii, 651; *Hansard,* 3rd ser., 1840, lv, 80; *Hansard,* 3rd ser., 1846, lxxxviii, 141.

138. *Hansard,* 3rd ser., 1848, xcix, 1242.

139. Huzzey, "Free Trade," 364.

140. *Hansard,* 3rd ser., 1846, lviii, 129.

141. *Hansard,* 3rd ser., 1846, lviii, 103; *Hansard,* 3rd ser., 1840, lv, 80–81; *PP 1840,* v (601), 209–14.

142. *Hansard,* 3rd ser., 1840, lv, 90–91.

143. *Hansard,* 3rd ser., 1841, lviii, 102, 129.

144. *Hansard,* 3rd ser., 1846, lxxxviii, 523

145. *Hansard,* 3rd ser., 1841, lviii, 134; *Hansard,* 3rd ser., 1846, lxxxviii, 509.

146. *Hansard,* 3rd ser., 1846, lxxxviii, 44.

147. *Hansard,* 3rd ser., 1848, c, 347–48.

148. *Hansard,* 3rd ser., 1841, lviii, 31–34. There are echoes of this speech in Carlyle, *Occasional Discourse,* even though Russell is one of this work's targets.

149. *Hansard,* 3rd ser., 1840, lviii, 131. Similar sentiments are expressed in *Hampshire Telegraph and Sussex Chronicle,* 25 July 1846, 8.

150. *Hansard,* 3rd ser., 1848, xcvi, 17; see also *Hansard,* 3rd ser., 1841, lviii, 128–29.

151. *Hansard,* 3rd ser., 1848, xcix, 876; James Ewing Ritchie, *Thoughts on Slavery and Cheap Sugar. A Letter to the members and friends of the British and Foreign Anti-Slavery Society* (London, 1844), 26; *PP 1842,* xiii (479), 272; *Hansard,* 3rd ser., 1848, xcix, 1374; *PP 1842,* xiii (479), 440.

152. Ritchie, *Thoughts,* 37

153. *Hansard,* 3rd ser., 1846, lxxxviii, 472.

154. For example, see the resolutions of the 1842 Select Committee on the West India Colonies: *PP 1842,* xiii (479), iv. Drescher identifies the role of the sugar duties in fostering racist attitudes toward West Indian blacks by 1848: Drescher, *Mighty Experiment,* 218–19.

155. K. N. Bell and W. P. Morrell, eds., *Select Documents on British Colonial Policy 1830–60* (Oxford, 1928), 412: Russell to Light (British Guiana), 15 Feb. 1840; see also W. P. Morrell, *British Colonial Policy in the Age of Peel and Russell* (Oxford, 1930), 151. In the same letter he opposes any new immigration to the West Indies.

156. Also see Labouchere, when speaking in defense of the duties in 1840: *Hansard,* 3rd ser., 1840, lv, 87–88; note Gladstone's schadenfreude: *Hansard,* 3rd ser., 1840, lv, 101.

157. G. R. Porter, *The Progress of the Nation, in its Various Social and Economical Relations* (London, 1843 [1836]), 40, 430.

158. Ibid., 436

159. Green, *British Slave Emancipation,* 165, 187–88.

160. *Hansard,* 3rd ser., 1840, lv, 97.

161. Herman Merivale, *Lectures on Colonization and Colonies* (2 vols., London, 1840–41), 1:313, 326. Merivale was haunted by the possibility that anti-slavery would be

undermined if emancipation resulted in a repetition of Haitian-style barbarity and economic decline in the West Indies.

162. Hall, *Civilising Subjects,* 379.

163. As quoted by David Eltis, "Abolitionist Perceptions of Society after Slavery," in *Slavery and British Society, 1776–1846,* ed. James Walvin (Baton Rouge, La., 1982), 209.

164. Holt, *Problem,* xxiii–iv.

## 5. POWER, PROSPERITY, AND LIBERTY

1. *Hansard,* 3rd ser., 1846, lxxxviii, 482.

2. The quotation is from MP William Ewart. *Hansard,* 3rd ser., 1841, lviii, 101.

3. Benjamin Disraeli, *Lord George Bentinck* (London, 1852), 529. This section is adapted from Huzzey, "Free Trade," 359–79.

4. G. Kitson Clark, "The Repeal of the Corn Laws and the Politics of the Forties," *Economic History Review,* n.s., 4 (1951): 1–13, at 4.

5. Robert Livingston Schulyer, "The Abolition of British Imperial Preference, 1846–1860," *Political Science Quarterly* 33 (1918): 77–92, at 84.

6. Statistical analysis of voting rolls from 1833 to 1840 has suggested that MPs who voted for emancipation were highly likely to support free trade in corn (an English term at the time for any cereal grain), but far less enthusiastic about free trade in sugar: Franzmann, "Antislavery," 584–86.

7. Hume gave his evidence shortly after retiring from the Board of Trade. Drescher, *Mighty Experiment,* 162–63. For his exclusion of sugar from a general enthusiasm for free trade, see *PP 1840,* v (601), 119. He was mentioned often: *Hansard,* 3rd ser., 1840, lviii, 122; *Hansard,* 3rd ser., 1848, xcvi, 102; H. V. Huntley, *Observations upon the Free Trade Policy of England in Connexion with the Sugar Act of 1846* (London, 1849), 39.

8. The 1833 bill had merely attempted to remove the privilege from West Indian planters by equalizing their duties with those of East Indian producers of sugar; *Hansard,* 3rd ser., 1833, xx, 256. For his shift toward complete free trade in sugar, see *Hansard,* 3rd ser., 1839, xlviii, 1023; *Hansard,* 3rd ser., 1840, lv, 78.

9. *Hansard,* 3rd ser., 1840, lv, 106.

10. *Hansard,* 3rd ser., 1841, lviii, 667, 1241.

11. When amendments to Peel's 1844 budget tested the two ideas, equalization lost by only 197 to 128, whereas complete free trade lost by 259 to 56: *Hansard,* 3rd ser., 1844, lxxv, 219, 468.

12. *Hansard,* 3rd ser., 1846, lxxxviii, 115, 182.

13. *Hansard,* 3rd ser., 1848, xcix, 1362–63.

14. *Hansard,* 3rd ser., 1840, lv, 95. See also *Hansard,* 3rd ser., 1846, lxxxviii, 514; *Hansard,* 3rd ser., 1848, xcix, 1467.

15. *Hansard,* 3rd ser., 1841, lviii, 121. Another blood metaphor was used in Samuel Wilberforce, *Cheap Sugar Means Cheap Slaves* (London, 1848), 13

16. *Hansard,* 3rd ser., 1846, lxxxviii, 533–34.

17. *Hansard,* 3rd ser., 1846, lxxxviii, 501–2. See also: *Hansard,* 3rd ser., 1846, lxxxviii, 510–12.

18. *Hansard,* 3rd ser., 1846, lxxxviii, 652–54.

19. Discriminating between produce on the basis of how it was produced fell foul of "most favoured nation" trading treaties. If the 1846 Act had not been passed, three thousand tons of slave-grown sugar still would have been admissible under this loophole in the 1844 Act: *Hansard,* 3rd ser., 1848, xcvi, 50–53.

20. See *Hansard,* 3rd ser., 1840, lv, 81; *Hansard,* 3rd ser., 1848, xcvi, 85; *Hansard,* 3rd ser., 1846, lxxxviii, 482–83; *Hansard,* 3rd ser., 1841, lviii, 98; *Liverpool Mercury,* 24 July 1846, 10.

21. *Hansard,* 3rd ser., 1841, lviii, 37–38.

22. *Hansard,* 3rd ser., 1846, lxxxviii, 517.

23. BL, Joseph Sturge papers, Add. Ms. 43845, fos. 13–14: Bright to Sturge, 1 Jan. 1843.

24. *Hansard,* 3rd ser., 1846, lxxxvii, 1335–36. See also *Hansard,* 3rd ser., 1841, lviii, 86; *Hansard,* 3rd ser., 1846, lxxxviii, 505. For the Whigs' earlier view in 1840, see *Hansard,* 3rd ser., 1840, lv, 86.

25. Herman Merivale, for example, conceded that the consumption of slave-grown goods involved Britons in the guilt of slavery, but he could not see how it was possible to abstain completely "while our system of manufacture exists." The "great social evil" must therefore be addressed, he reasoned, through other national activity than abstention: Merivale, *Lectures,* 1:296–97.

26. *Hansard,* 3rd ser., 1841, lviii, 43.

27. For criticism, see *Economist,* 1 Aug. 1846, 987.

28. *Hansard,* 3rd ser., 1846, lxxxviii, 23.

29. *Economist,* 25 July 1846, 956–57; *Economist,* 1 Aug. 1846, 987. See also *Hansard,* 3rd ser., 1846, lxxxviii, 515–16; *Hansard,* 3rd ser., 1848, xcvi, 50–52.

30. *Hansard,* 3rd ser., 1841, lviii, 40–41.

31. *Hansard,* 3rd ser., 1846, lxxxvii, 1311–12. See also *Hansard,* 3rd ser., 1841, lviii, 101.

32. *Morning Chronicle,* 11 May 1841, 7.

33. For example: *Manchester Examiner,* 11 July 1846, 4; *Hansard,* 3rd ser., 1848, xcvi, 85–86; *Hansard,* 3rd ser., 1848, c, 59; *Hansard,* 3rd ser., 1846, lxxxviii, 24; *Hansard,* 3rd ser., 1848, xcix, 1466.

34. Ritchie, *Thoughts,* 26–27.

35. RH, Anti-Slavery papers, MSS Brit. Emp. s. 19, Petitions and memorials book, 9: minute of meeting of 2 Dec. 1840; RH, Anti-Slavery papers, MSS Brit. Emp. s. 19, Petitions and memorials book, 10: Leveson to Tredgold, 14 Dec. 1840.

36. *Hansard,* 3rd ser., 1846, lxxxviii, 122; see also *Hansard,* 3rd ser., 1841, lviii, 115.

37. On the rights of free commerce, see *Hansard,* 3rd ser., 1846, lxxxviii, 24. On receiving stolen goods, see Russell, *Hansard,* 3rd ser., 1846, lxxxvii, 1314. For a reply, see Wilberforce, *Cheap Sugar,* 8.

38. *Hansard,* 3rd ser., 1846, lxxxviii, 481–82, 487–88. See also *Leeds Mercury,* 25 July 1846, 4; *Hansard,* 3rd ser., 1848, xcvi, 53.

39. *Hansard,* 3rd ser., 1846, lxxxviii, 486, 508, 516–17.

40. For an eccentric exception, see *Hansard,* 3rd ser., 1848, xcix, 1324–25.

41. For example, *Slave Sugar In A Nutshell* (London, 1850).

42. Drescher, *Mighty Experiment,* 162.

43. *Hansard,* 3rd ser., 1840, lv, 79; *Hansard,* 1848, c, 57.

44. *Hansard,* 3rd ser., 1846, lxxxviii, 479–80.

45. *Hansard,* 3rd ser., 1840, lv, 79–80.

46. *Economist,* 25 July 1846, 956; *Economist,* 15 Aug. 1846, 1051; *Economist,* 19 Sept. 1846, 1221; see also *Hansard,* 3rd ser., 1846, lxxxviii, 478–79.

47. Ritchie, *Thoughts,* 10, 6.

48. *Hansard,* 3rd ser., 1848, xcvi, 62–64, 71.

49. *Hansard,* 3rd ser., 1846, lxxxviii, 115.

50. For examples from Conservatives, see *Hansard,* 3rd ser., 1848, xcix, 757, 782. By contrast, John Bright likened the planters to Oliver Twist, as they continually begged for more: *Hansard,* 3rd ser., 1848, xcix, 1428.

51. *Hansard,* 3rd ser., 1846, lxxxviii, 127.

52. "A resident in the West Indies for thirteen years," *The British West India Colonies* (London, 1853), 4.

53. *Hansard,* 3rd ser., 1846, lxxxviii, 141–43.

54. *Hansard,* 3rd ser., 1846, lxxxviii, 38; *Hansard,* 3rd ser., 1848, xcvi, 15–16, 31.

55. *Hansard,* 3rd ser., 1840, lv, 102. Emancipation was never attacked as a point of principle during the sugar duty debates, but MPs were happy to criticize the way in which it had been implemented: *Hansard,* 3rd ser., 1848, xcix, 754–55.

56. *Hansard,* 3rd ser., 1840, lv, 93–94.

57. Wilberforce's revisionism is noted by Drescher, *Mighty Experiment,* 180.

58. *Hansard,* 3rd ser., 1846, lxxxviii, 661. He repeated the arguments in an 1848 speech reprinted as Wilberforce, *Cheap Sugar,* 3–4. See also *Hansard,* 3rd ser., 1840, lviii, 84.

59. Huzzey, "Free Trade," 359–79; Drescher, *Mighty Experiment.*

60. Joseph Beldam, *A Review of the Late Proposed Measure for the Reduction of the Duties on Sugar* (London, 1841), 17; *Hansard,* 3rd ser., 1848, c, 12.

61. *Hansard,* 3rd ser., 1840, lv, 97; *Hansard,* 3rd ser., 1846, lxxxviii, 539.

62. *Hansard*, 3rd ser., 1848, xcvi, 103, 160.

63. Frank Trentmann, "Political Culture and Political Economy: Interest, Ideology and Free Trade," *Review of International Political Economy* 5 (1998): 217–51, at 239; Frank Trentmann, "Before 'Fair Trade': Empire, Free Trade, and the Moral Economies of Food in the Modern World," *Environment and Planning D: Society and Space* 25 (2007): 1079–1102. See E. P. Thompson, *Customs in Common: Studies in Traditional Popular Culture* (New York, 1993), 259–351, esp. 271, 351, on why Thompson did not deny moral thinking about market economics.

64. See Gladstone's audacity in this regard: *Hansard*, 3rd ser., 1840, lv, 99–106.

65. *Hansard*, 3rd ser., 1846, lxxxviii, 542–43.

66. *Hansard*, 3rd ser., 1846, lxxxviii, 650.

67. *Hansard*, 3rd ser., 1846, lxxxviii, 139. On his interests, see Holt, *Problem*, 243–44.

68. *Hansard*, 3rd ser., 1840, lv, 94–95.

69. Wilberforce, *Cheap Sugar*, 13; *Hansard*, 3rd ser., 1846, lxxxviii, 666.

70. C. Duncan Rice, "'Humanity Sold for Sugar!' The British Abolitionist Response to Free Trade in Slave-Grown Sugar," *HJ* 13 (1970): 402–18, at 406–7.

71. *Hansard*, 3rd ser., 1848, xcix, 751–52.

72. Sturge papers, BL, Add. Ms. 43845, fos. 13–14: Bright to Sturge, 1 Jan. 1843.

73. *Economist*, 25 July 1846, 953.

74. Temperley, *British Anti-Slavery*, 155.

75. *Hansard*, 3rd ser., 1848, xcix, 748; for other examples of such "moral economics" behind the free traders' case, see *Hansard*, 3rd ser., 1848, xcix, 1341–42; *Economist*, 25 July 1846, 956.

76. Morrell, *British Colonial Policy*, 233. For similar assessments, see Schulyer, "Abolition," 78–79; Elsie Pilgrim, "Anti-Slavery Sentiment in Great Britain 1841–1854: Its Nature and Its Decline, with Special Reference to Its Influence upon British Policy towards the Former Slave Colonies" (PhD thesis, Cambridge University, 1952), 95–96; Lloyd, *The Navy*, 101–3; Bethell, *Abolition*, 273; Hall, *Civilising Subjects*, 338–39. On the negative treatment of the sugar duties equalization as opposed to the corn laws, see Philip D. Curtin, "The British Sugar Duties and West Indian Prosperity," *Journal of Economic History* 14 (1954): 157–64.

77. Eric Williams, "Laissez Faire, Sugar and Slavery," *Political Science Quarterly* 58 (1943): 67–85, at 67.

78. Rice, "'Humanity'," 406–7.

79. Drescher, *Mighty Experiment*, 166, though see 174. For exceptions to pessimistic interpretations, see Eltis, "Abolitionist," 208; G. R. Searle, *Morality and the Market in Victorian Britain* (Oxford, 1998), 57–59, 62; Turley, *Culture*, 126–29.

80. Huntley, *Observations*, 29; see also *Hansard*, 3rd ser., 1848, xcvi, 137.

81. *Economist*, 25 July 1846, 961.

82. John Brown, *Slave Life in Georgia: A Narrative of the Life, Sufferings, and Escape of John Brown, a Fugitive Slave, Now in England*, ed. L. A. Chamerovzow (London, 1855), 209.

83. On the earlier period, see Midgley, *Women*, 35–40.

84. Elihu Burritt, *Twenty Reasons for the Total Abstinence from Slave Produce* (London, n.d. [1853?]), 3. The pamphlet is undated, but a copy in the Bodleian Library, JJC, Slavery 2, is annotated "August 1853," which fits with internal and external evidence for its date.

85. BFASS, *Proceedings ...1840*, esp. 415, 420, 428–29, 433–47.

86. On the efforts of Sturge and other Quakers to establish a free produce movement after 1846, see also Ruth Ketring Nuermberger, *The Free Produce Movement: A Quaker Protest against Slavery* (New York, 1942), 57; Temperley, *British Antislavery*, 165; Ripley, *Black Abolitionist Papers*, 1:232–33: Henry Highland Garnet to Samuel Rhoads, 5 Dec. 1850; Blackett, *Building*, 174–75.

87. Clare Midgley, *Feminism and Empire: Women Activists in Imperial Britain, 1790–1865* (Abingdon, Oxfordshire, 2007), 63.

88. Beecher, *Harriet Beecher Stowe in Europe*, 60, 64, 115.

89. *Times*, 18 May 1853, 4.

90. *Hansard*, 3rd ser., 1841, lviii, 101.

91. Beecher, *Harriet Beecher Stowe in Europe*, 118–19.

92. Duke University Library, Charles Gilpin Papers: Richard Cobden to Charles Gilpin, 6 Oct. 1850.

93. BFASS, *Proceedings … 1843*, 144.

94. "T.H," *Are the West India Colonies to be Preserved* (London, 1840), 7.

95. Ritchie, *Thoughts*, 26. See also Merivale, *Lectures*, 1:310; *Hansard*, 3rd ser., 1846, lxxxviii, 133–34.

96. Jacob Omnium, *Is Cheap Sugar The Triumph of Free Trade?* (London, 1847), 5.

97. *Hansard*, 3rd ser., 1846, lxxxviii, 138–40.

98. Green, *British Slave Emancipation*, 271, 275.

99. Merivale, *Lectures*, 1:326; Leslie Stephen and Donovan Williams, "Herman Merivale," *ODNB*.

100. For example, some West Indians attacked protection for distillers in the British Isles, and sought free importation for colonial rum. This highlighted the temporary nature of their alliance with the Tory protectionists. Bentinck criticized those planters who would undermine the mainland's rum protection while claiming sugar protection for themselves: *Hansard*, 3rd ser., 1848, xcvi, 10.

101. John Innes, *Thoughts on the Present State of the West India Colonies* (London, 1840), 14, 28.

102. Merivale, *Lectures*, 1:297.

103. Innes, *Thoughts*, 39.

104. *Hansard*, 3rd ser., 1846, lxxxvii, 1315.

105. *Economist*, 6 June 1846, 730; *Economist*, 1 July 1846, 889; *Economist*, 15 Aug. 1846, 1051.

106. *Hansard*, 3rd ser., 1848, xcix, 1383–84.

107. Trollope, *West Indies*, 64–67, 74, 87–88, 102.

108. Ibid., 106.

109. Drescher, *Great Experiment*, 227.

110. *Free Trade in Negroes*, (London, 1849); "A Barrister" [Sir George Stephen], *Analysis of the Evidence Given Before The Select Committee on the Slave Trade* (London, 1850), 10. On the Jamaican Chamber's response, see Holt, *Problem of Freedom*, 202.

111. Morrow, *Thomas Carlyle*, 126–27.

112. *Hansard*, 3rd ser., 1848, xcix, 1217–19; *Hansard*, 3rd ser., 1848, xcix, 1427.

113. *Hansard*, 3rd ser., 1846, lxxxvii, 1336–37.

114. *Hansard*, 3rd ser., 1848, xcvi, 1103, 1131.

115. For example, *PP 1847–48*, xxii (1), 194.

116. *PP 1847–48*, xxii (1), 65; *PP 1847–48*, xxii (283), 22–24, 29, 81; *PP 1847–48*, xxii (1), 194, 196, 202; *PP 1847–48*, xxii (283), 84.

117. *PP 1847–48*, xxii (1), 261; *PP 1847–48*, xxii (467), 17, 81, 96.

118. Sensitivity to their desire for free labor emigration from West Africa led Hutt to expand the remit of his committee to include considerations of where it could come from: *PP 1847–48*, xxii (705), 9.

119. Denman, *West India Interests*, 5.

120. *Hansard*, 3rd ser., 1848, xcvi, 1107. "Anti-coercionists" is a historians' label, usefully coined by W. L. Mathieson, *Great Britain and the Slave Trade* (London, 1929), 48, maintained by Bethell, *Abolition*, 304, and most other authors.

121. Buxton was quoted by Hutt, *Hansard*, 3rd ser., 1848, xcvi, 1096, and also by Gladstone, *Hansard*, 3rd ser., 1850, cix, 1164.

122. *PP 1847–48*, xxii (1), 194

123. *Hansard*, 3rd ser., 1845, lxxxi, 1156–82.

124. For example, *Hansard*, 3rd ser., 1846, lxxxviii, 502–3.

125. *Hansard*, 3rd ser., 1848, xcvi, 1091–92.

126. On the resolutions, see *PP 1847–48*, xxii (705), 25; *PP 1849*, ixx (1), xix.

127. *Hansard*, 3rd ser., 1850, cix, 1094. The committee's division on the key issue of withdrawal was decided only by Hutt's casting his vote as chairman.

128. Sir George Stephen, *The Niger Trade Considered in Connection with the African Blockade* (London, 1849), 53.

129. *PP 1847–48*, xxii (1), 225

130. Report of the commissioners, Messrs. Macaulay and Doherty, 31 Dec. 1838, reprinted in *PP 1847–48*, xxii (1), 202. See also Joseph Denman's robust argument for improving the squadron, before calls for its withdrawal had gathered any momentum: Joseph Denman, *Practical Remarks on The Slave Trade of the West Coast of Africa* (London, 1839), 15.

131. *PP 1847–48*, xxii (1), 155; *PP 1847–48*, xxii (283), 14; *PP 1847–48*, xxii (1), 91. Concerns about the quality of ships continued into the next decade: NA, Russell papers, PRO 30/22/24, fos. 115–16: Somerset to Russell, 16 Nov. 1861; NA, Russell papers, PRO 30/22/26, fo. 440: Somerset to Russell, 9 Jan. 1865.

132. David Turnbull, *Travels in the West* (New York, 1969 [London, 1840]), 393.

133. *PP 1847–48*, xxii (1), 6–7, 23. Ideas for a migratory mixed commission court were also floated, but got little support. *PP 1847–48*, xxii (1), 121

134. *PP 1847–48*, xxii (1), 9; *PP 1847–48*, xxii (1), 75, 254.

135. *PP 1847–48*, xxii (1), 101; *PP 1847–48*, xxii (283), 14.

136. Denman, *Practical Remarks*, 20–21.

137. He ascribed the tactic to the inexperience of the squadron commander, Sir Charles Hotham: *PP 1847–48*, xxii (1), 42.

138. *PP 1847–48*, xxii (1), 32. See also Lloyd, *Navy*, 81.

139. *PP 1847–48*, xxii (1), 22; the memorandum is reprinted in ibid., 27–29. For support, see ibid., 123.

140. *PP 1847–48*, xxii (1), 24, 62–67; Amanda Perreau-Saussine, "British Acts of State in English Courts," *British Yearbook of International Law* 78 (2008): 220–21.

141. Perreau-Saussine, "British Acts," 222–23.

142. As quoted in ibid., 223.

143. Ibid., 228. On Palmerston's opposition to Denman's proposed redeployment of cruisers from Brazil, see Kielstra, *Politics*, 236.

144. Eltis, *Economic Growth*, 121. The Foreign Office had initially misinterpreted the queen's advocate's advice: Lloyd, *Navy and the Slave Trade*, 97–99; *PP 1847–48*, xxii (1), 30.

145. *PP 1847–48*, xxii (1), 121.

146. *PP 1847–48*, xxii (1), 30.

147. *PP 1847–48*, xxii (1), 236, 256. On his memorandum, see Kielstra, *Politics*, 191.

148. For example, *PP 1847–48*, xxii (1), 200, 227, 232.

149. *Hansard*, 3rd ser., 1845, lxxxi, 1166.

150. *Hansard*, 3rd ser., 1849, civ, 784–87.

151. *PP 1847–48*, xxii (283), 71; *Hansard*, 3rd ser., 1848, xcvi, 1111–12.

152. *PP 1847–48*, xxii (283), 37, 144.

153. *Hansard*, 3rd ser., 1845, lxxxi, 1171–2; *PP 1847–48*, xxii (1), 193, 258.

154. *Hansard*, 3rd ser., 1848, xcvi, 1101.

155. See *PP 1847–48*, xxii (283), 127.

156. *Chambers's Edinburgh Journal*, Aug. 1848, 120.

157. For example, *PP 1847–48*, xxii (1), 195.

158. *Hansard*, 3rd ser., 1848, xcvi, 1098.

159. *PP 1847–48*, xxii (1), 196, 201; *PP 1847–48*, xxii (283), 69, 85; *PP 1847–48*, xxii (467).

160. For example, the anti-coercionist *Lloyd's Weekly London Paper*, 24 Mar. 1850, 7. On a "rhetoric of sensibility," see Brycchan Carey, *British Abolitionism and the Rhetoric of Sensibility: Writing, Sentiment, and Slavery, 1760–1807* (Basingstoke, Hampshire, 2005).

161. *Hansard*, 3rd ser., 1848, xcvi, 1092; *PP 1847–48*, xxii (1), 38.

162. *Hansard*, 3rd ser., 1845, lxxxi, 1168–69.

163. *PP 1847–48*, xxii (1), 2.

164. Denman argued that the greater cramming was compensated for by the shorter length of the middle passage in faster ships, *PP 1847–48*, xxii (1), 23, 37.

165. Lord Denman, *A Letter from Lord Denman to Lord Brougham on the Final Extinction of the Slave Trade* (London, 1848), ix.

166. *Hansard*, 3rd ser., 1846, lxxxvii, 1267–68.

167. *PP 1847–48*, xxii (1), 4, 18; Sir George Stephen ["A Barrister"], *Analysis*, 12–13.

168. *Hansard*, 3rd ser., 1848, xcvi, 1092.

169. NA, Russell papers, PRO 30/22/8D, fo. 91: Lord John Russell's speech in Downing Street, 19 Mar. 1850; *Hansard*, 3rd ser., 1850, cix, 1121; Sir George Stephen ["A Barrister"], *Analysis*, 6.

170. For example, *PP 1847–48*, xxii (1), 142, 158, 173.

171. *Daily News*, 18 Aug. 1849, 4.

172. Duke University, Charles Gilpin papers: Richard Cobden to Charles Gilpin, 6 Oct. 1850.

173. *Hansard*, 3rd ser., 1845, lxxxi, 1169.

174. *Punch*, 20 Mar. 1850, 125.

175. *PP 1847–48*, xxii (1), 18.

176. *PP 1847–48*, xxii (1), 140.

177. Palmerston was at least consistent in emphasizing the early interception of slaves, rather than ending slaveholding abroad. During the American Civil War, he still believed the Royal Navy should refocus its efforts on catching ships before they had embarked slaves, or else the dealers on the shore would have made their profit. NA, Russell papers, PRO 30/22/22, fos. 92–4: Sir Charles Wood to Russell, 13 Aug. 1862.

178. *PP 1847–48*, xxii (283), 15, 84, 103, 119; *Household Words*, 9 Jan. 1858, 84.

179. *PP 1847–48*, xxii (283), 29, 35, 137.

180. *PP 1847–48*, xxii (283), 17–20.

181. *PP 1847–48*, xxii (1), 26.

182. Extracts from two West Africa commissioners reprinted in *PP 1847–48*, xxii (1), 262. Support assertion at 216.

183. *PP 1847–48*, xxii (1), 17–18; see also *Hansard*, 3rd ser., 1850, cix, 1149.

184. *PP 1847–48*, xxii (1), 25, 107, 202, 233. *PP 1847–48*, xxii (283), 13, 88, 115. Missionaries were keen on retaining the cruisers: *PP 1847–48*, xxii (467), 152–53, 156. Note also the publication of Townsend's correspondence on the issue as Samuel Crowther and Henry Townsend, *Slave Trade – African Squadron, Letters from the Rev. Samuel Crowther, A Native of the Yoruba Country, and a Clergyman of the Church of England at Abbeokuta and the Rev. Henry Townsend of the Church Missionary Society at Abbeokuta* (London, 1850). For actual reduction of presence after withdrawal, see Paul Mmegha Mbaeyi, *British Military and Naval Forces in West African History, 1807–1874* (New York, 1978), 172–73.

185. *PP 1847–48*, xxii (467), 119.

186. *PP 1847–48*, xxii (1), 236–37.

187. *PP 1847–48*, xxii (1), 178. See also ibid., 34–55; *Morning Chronicle*, 19 Mar. 1850, 4.

188. *PP 1847–48*, xxii (467), 23.

189. A rebuttal motion prepared and reedited by Palmerston and Russell certainly emphasized this: NA, Russell papers, PRO 30/22/8D, fos.10–15: "Draft motion on suppression of the slave trade," n.d. It seems likely that this is the draft designed to "go down more easily" with "wavering friends," as referred to in NA, Russell papers, PRO 30/22/8D, fo.75: Palmerston to Russell, 17 Mar. 1850; NA, Russell papers, PRO 30/22/8D, fo.77: Sir Charles Wood to Russell, 17 Mar. 1850.

190. NA, Russell papers, PRO 30/22/8D, fo. 75: Palmerston to Russell, 17 Mar. 1850.

191. Sir George Stephen ["A Barrister"], *Analysis*, 5.

192. It seems likely that a sizeable number of Whigs voted with Russell and Palmerston, but would have been inclined to support the motion if it had been a free vote. The vote split: 176 Liberal Whigs, 23 Peelites, and 33 Protectionists for the cruisers, with 48 Liberal Whigs, 17 Peelites, and 89 Protectionists in favor of the motion: microfilm of BL, Hobhouse papers, Add. 61829, Hobhouse diary: entry for 19 Mar. 1850; Bethell, *Abolition*, 323–24.

193. *Hansard*, 3rd ser., 1850, cix, 1110–16, 1126.

194. Microfilm of BL, Hobhouse papers, Add. 61829, Hobhouse diary: 19 Mar. 1850; Bethell, *Abolition*, 324.

195. *Hansard*, 3rd ser., 1850, cix, 1130.

196. Temperley, *British Anti-Slavery*, 178. For earlier predictions, see *Economist*, 19 Sept. 1846, 1221.

197. *PP 1847–48*, xxii (1), 55, 104, 153, 201.

198. This analysis is based on a comparison of divisions on the sugar duties and slave trade bills of 19 Mar. 1850 (*Hansard,* 3rd ser., 1850, cix, 1184–86) and 31 May 1850 (*Hansard,* 3rd ser., 1850, cxi, 593–96). There were 331 MPs who voted in both divisions. Forty-five MPs voted for protection and coercion, 155 for free trade and coercion (the ministry position), 87 MPs for protection and pacifism, and just 44 MPs voted for free trade and pacifism. The comparison excludes both Robert Palmer and Sir Roundell Palmer, as it is not possible to correlate their votes on division lists where they both featured as "R. Palmer."

199. Reprinted at *PP 1847–48,* xxii (283), 174. This petition was cited by Hutt in the 1845 debate: *Hansard,* 3rd ser., 1845, lxxxi, 1161.

200. Joseph Denman, *The Slave Trade, The African Squadron and Mr. Hutt's Committee* (n.p, n.d [1848?]), 9.

201. Duke University, Charles Gilpin Papers: Richard Cobden to Charles Gilpin, 6 Oct. 1850.

202. David Turnbull, *The Jamaica Movement* (London, 1849), 126.

203. Ibid., 16, 363, 367.

204. *Jamaica Despatch,* 13 June 1849, as quoted in Turnbull, *Jamaica Movement,* 408–10.

205. *Hansard,* 3rd ser., 1850, cix, 1140–41.

206. *Hansard,* 3rd ser., 1850, cix, 1111–16.

207. Carpenter, *Observations,* 18.

208. *Punch,* 20 Mar. 1850, 130.

209. NA, Russell papers, PRO 30/22/8D, fos. 124A-125: Minto to Russell, 17 Mar. 1850.

210. NA, Russell papers, PRO 30/22/8D, fos. 124A-125: Minto to Russell, 17 Mar. 1850.

211. Bethell, *Abolition,* 325–27.

212. Ibid., 340–41.

213. Lord Denman, *Uncle Tom's Cabin, Bleak House, Slavery and the Slave Trade* (London, 1853), 7; *Daily News,* 31 Dec. 1852, 4; *The Destruction of Lagos* (London, 1852), 2; Bethell, *Abolition,* 344, 360. See Needell, "Abolition," on debates in Brazilian history over the real causes.

214. "Slave Voyages Database," ed. David Eltis (Atlanta, Ga., 2008–present), http://www.slavevoyages.org.

215. Sir George Stephen ["A Barrister"], *Analysis,* 95; David Murray, *Odious Commerce: Britain, Spain and the Abolition of the Cuban Slave Trade* (Cambridge, 1980), 211–12.

216. *Liverpool Mercury,* 18 July 1851, 6; for later anti-coercionism, see *Manchester Examiner and Times,* 19 Mar. 1851, 6.

217. Landry, "Slavery and the Slave Trade in Atlantic Diplomacy, 1850–1861," 188.

218. Lloyd, *Navy,* 104–6; Mathieson, *Great Britain,* 88–90.

219. *Manchester Examiner,* 29 Feb. 1848, 4. See also *Morning Chronicle,* 19 Mar. 1850, 4.

220. *Leeds Mercury,* 23 Mar. 1850, 4.

221. *PP 1849,* xix (410), xxiv–xxvi.

222. *Caledonian Mercury,* 22 July 1850, 2.

223. Denman, *Slave Trade,* 7; *PP 1847–48,* xxii (1), 288, 256, 247–49; *PP 1847–48,* xxii (283), 31, 73.

224. Interestingly, Hutt had been one of the radicals supporting O'Connell's 1833 plan to pay apprentices: *Hansard,* 3rd ser., 1833, xviii, 547.

225. *Hansard,* 3rd ser., 1845, lxxxi, 1157–58.

226. Eltis, *Economic Growth,* 213.

227. Seymour Drescher, "Brazilian Abolition in Comparative Perspective," in *The Abolition of Slavery and the Aftermath of Emancipation in Brazil,* ed. Rebecca J. Scott (Durham, N.C., 1995), 28.

228. Curtin, "British Sugar Duties," 160–62.

229. Trollope, *West Indies,* 62, 90.

230. Ibid., 101, 100, 105–6.

231. Drescher, *Mighty Experiment,* 227, 210–11.

232. *Hansard,* 3rd ser., 1846, lxxxvii, 1315–16; *Hansard,* 3rd ser., 1846, lxxxviii, 116, 133–34; *Hansard,* 3rd ser., 1848, xcix, 1384; Innes, *Thoughts,* 14, 28, 39; Ritchie, *Thoughts,* 26; Drescher, *Mighty Experiment,* 165.

233. James Stirling, *Letters from the Slave States* (London, 1857), 120–21. Stirling is inconsistent, talking of moral benefits in some chapters but emphasizing economic superiority in others, for example, 222, 229–31, 239.

234. J. S. Mill, *Principles*, 1:297–98, 303–9; 2:243; for a nuanced account of his views on free labor and a comparison with American thought, see James L. Huston, "Abolitionists, Political Economists, and Capitalism," *Journal of the Early Republic* 20 (2000): 496.

235. Cairnes, *The Slave Power*, 65–72, 341–45; see Davis, *Slavery*, 254–55.

236. George B. Wheeler, ed., *The Southern Confederacy and the African Slave Trade: The Correspondence between Professor Cairnes, A.M., and George McHenry Esq.* (Dublin, 1863), 23; Robert W. Fogel, "The Origin and History of Economic Issues in the American Slavery Debate," in *Without Consent or Contract: The Rise and Fall of American Slavery: Evidence and Methods*, ed. Robert W. Fogel, Ralph A. Galantine, and Richard L. Manning (New York, 1992): 161–63; Adam Rothman, "Review of Seymour Drescher, The Mighty Experiment (Oxford, 2002)," *Journal of Interdisciplinary History* 24 (2004): 634–36.

237. Thomas Ellison, *Slavery and Secession in America, Historical and Economical; Together with a Practical Scheme of Emancipation*, 2nd ed. (London, 1862 [1861]); D. A. Farnie, "Thomas Ellison," *ODNB*.

238. *Hansard*, 3rd ser., 1850, cix, 1183.

239. *Hansard*, 3rd ser., 1848, xcvi, 85.

240. A possible exception is Carlyle, whose ideal of "servantship for life" was idiosyncratic and iconoclastic. However, his goal was new forms of paternal authority, and he defended this as a future model rather than defending the abuses under chattel slavery: Thomas Carlyle, *Shooting Niagara – and after?* (London, 1867), 5–8, 26–28.

241. Sven Beckert, "Emancipation and Empire: Reconstructing the Worldwide Web of Cotton Production in the Age of the American Civil War," *American Historical Review* 109 (2004): 1405–38, at 1429, 1432–33; *Economist*, 12 Feb. 1859, 166–68.

242. *Chambers's Edinburgh Journal*, 8 Feb. 1851, 90. See also *Journal of the Society of Arts*, 12 Mar. 1858, 261.

243. Duke University, Marquis of Ripon papers: William Henry Hulbert to Lord Godrich, 12 Dec. 1857. For Hulbert's idiosyncratic views on slavery and secession, see Daniel W. Crofts, *A Secession Crisis Enigma: William Henry Hulbert and "The Diary of a Public Man"* (Baton Rouge, La., 2010), 52–53.

244. J. S. Mill, *Dissertations and Discussions: Political, Philosophical, and Historical* (3 vols., Boston, 1865 [4 vols., London, 1859–79]), 3:240–41; Semmel, *Liberalism*, 62.

245. Mill, *Dissertations*, 3:238–40.

246. Although Mill clearly believed that the dissemination of free labor was not an anticompetitive weapon, there was justice in foreigners' broader fears about the expansion of British power through the slave trade treaties' right of search: Perreau-Saussine, "British Acts," 220.

247. *Hansard*, 3rd ser., 1848, xcvi, 206.

248. Beckert, "Emancipation," 1413–15, 1420, 1424.

249. For one of the occasional half-hearted attempts, see *The London Cotton-plant*, as discussed in *ASR*, 1 July 1858, 161.

250. *Hansard*, 3rd ser., cli, 1334–38.

251. *Hansard*, 3rd ser., cli, 1340–41; Semmel, *Liberalism*, 49.

252. For a superb account of Palmerston's faith and religious policy in general, see John Wolffe, "Lord Palmerston and Religion: A Reappraisal," *EHR* 120 (2005): 907–36, at 916–17, for his view of providence in particular.

253. As quoted by Kielstra, *Politics*, 237.

254. See also Davis, *Slavery*, 303.

255. *Quarterly Review*, Oct. 1872, 538–40.

## 6. AFRICA BURNING

1. Jane Burbank and Frederick Cooper, *Empires in World History: Power and the Politics of Difference* (Princeton, N.J., 2010), 293; Suzanne Miers, *Britain and the Ending of the Slave Trade* (London, 1975), 37.

2. Jan-Georg Deutsch's thoughts on how to conceptualize this transformation were invaluable. On the "cultural imperialism" of earlier abolitionists, see Howard Temperley, "Anti-Slavery as Cultural Imperialism," in *Anti-Slavery, Religion and Reform,* ed. Christine Bolt and Seymour Drescher (Folkestone, Kent, 1980), 335–50.

3. Compare with Drescher, *Abolition,* 377, 390.

4. Robinson, Gallagher, and Denny, *Africa and the Victorians,* 14–15.

5. Darwin, "Imperialism," 640–41.

6. The quotations are from ibid., 627, and Cairns, *Prelude,* 140.

7. K. Onwuka Dike, *Trade and Politics in the Niger Delta* (Oxford, 1966 [1956]), 152–58; a debate on the "crisis of adaptation" forms the focus of the essays in *From Slave Trade to 'Legitimate' Commerce,* ed. Robin Law (Cambridge, 1995); David Richardson, "Background to Annexation: Anglo-African Credit Relations in the Bight of Biafra, 1700–1891," in *From Slave Trade to Empire: Europe and the Colonisation of Black Africa, 1780s–1880s,* ed. Olivier Pétré-Grenouilleau (Abingdon, Oxfordshire, 2004), 62; David M. Gordon, "The Abolition of the Slave Trade and the Transformation of the South-Central African Interior during the Nineteenth Century," *William and Mary Quarterly,* 3rd ser., 66 (2009): 915–38.

8. Bernard Porter, *The Absent-Minded Imperialists: Empire, Society and Culture in Britain* (Oxford, 2004), 112.

9. Lord Melbourne, *Lord Melbourne's Papers,* ed. L. C. Sanders (London, 1880), 376–77: Melbourne to Lord John Russell, 3 Sept. 1838.

10. See parallels with the "imperialism of human rights" in Abigail Green, "The British Empire and the Jews," *Past and Present* 199 (2008): 175–205.

11. Miers, as quoted by Kevin Grant, *A Civilised Savagery: Britain and the New Slaveries in Africa, 1884–1926* (New York, 2005), 26; see also Frederick Cooper, "From Free Labor to Family Allowances: Labor and African Society in Colonial Discourse," *American Ethnologist* 16 (1989): 748.

12. This conceptualization owes a great debt to Andrew Porter's analysis of missionary diversity in "Church History, History of Christianity, Religious History: Some Reflections on British Missionary Enterprise since the Late Eighteenth Century," *Church History* 71 (2002): 581–82. The "agent, scribe and moral alibi" quote is a subversion of Jean Comaroff and John Comaroff, *Of Revelation and Revolution* (2 vols., Chicago, 1991–97), 1:88.

13. Mortimer, *Far Off,* 2:1, 52.

14. Philip Curtin, *The Image of Africa* (London, 1965), 293.

15. Sir George Stephen ["A Barrister"], *Analysis,* 4.

16. In particular, see Deidre Coleman, *Romantic Colonization and British Anti-slavery* (Cambridge, 2005), 198–99.

17. Brown, *Moral Capital,* chap. 5; Michael Turner, "The Limits of Abolition: Government, Saints and the 'African Question', c.1780–1820," *EHR* 112 (1997): 319–57; Dike, *Trade,* 13; Suzanne Schwartz, "Commerce, Civilization and Christianity: The Development of the Sierra Leone Company," in *Liverpool and Transatlantic Slavery,* ed. David Richardson, Suzanne Schwarz and Anthony J. Tibbles (Liverpool, 2007), 252–76; William A. Green, "The West Indies and British West African Policy in the Nineteenth Century—A Corrective Comment," *Journal of African History* 15 (1974): 247–59; Christa Dierksheide, "'Capable of Improvement': Commerce, Christianity, and the Idea of an Independent Africa, c. 1740–1810," (unpublished paper, International Seminar on the History of the Atlantic World, Harvard University, 2006); Cairns, *Prelude,* 198; Thomas Fowell Buxton, *The African Slave Trade and Its Remedy,* 2nd ed. (London, 1840), 362.

18. Buxton, *African Slave Trade and Its Remedy,* 400–436. Buxton found supporters from such diverse sources as administrators (Charles McCarthy and Colonel Edward Nichols, for example), explorers (Mungo Park, Macgregor Laird, and Richard Lander), seamen (Capt. William Allen, R.N.), and even Mohammad Ali, the pasha of Egypt (362–65).

19. Thomas Fowell Buxton, *Letter on the Slave Trade to the Lord Viscount Melbourne* (London, 1838); Thomas Fowell Buxton, *The African Slave Trade* (London, 1839); Thomas Fowell Buxton, *The Remedy* (London, 1840); Society for the Extinction of the Slave Trade and for the Civilization of Africa, *Prospectus of the Society for the Extinction of the Slave Trade, and for the Civilization of Africa* (London, 1840).

20. Buxton, *Remedy*, 302, 437, 279; Brodie Cruikshank, *Eighteen Years on the Gold Coast* (2 vols., London, 1853), 2:277.

21. Buxton, *Remedy*, 343.

22. Buxton, *Letter*, ix.

23. Macgregor Laird and R. A. K. Oldfield, *Narrative of an Expedition into the Interior of Africa* (2 vols., London, 1837), 2:354, 399–400; *PP 1865*, v (1), 227.

24. Laird and Oldfield, *Narrative*, 1:3; ibid., 2:360, 390; Buxton, *Remedy*, 230; Buxton, *Letter*, 33–36; *PP 1842*, xi (1), 131; John Beecham, *Ashantee and the Gold Coast* (London, 1841), 119–21.

25. BL, Aberdeen papers, Add. MS 43238, fos. 279–80: T. F. Buxton to Aberdeen, 22 Dec. 1841. Curtin suggests that Buxton deliberately played up the role of Christianity when marketing his expedition idea in order to enlist the support of missionaries and their supporters: Curtin, *Image*, 302.

26. Laird and Oldfield, *Narrative*, 2:390.

27. Andrew Porter; "'Commerce and Christianity': Providence Theory, the Missionary Movement, and the Imperialism of Free Trade, 1842–1860," *HJ* 26 (1983): 71–94; Andrew Porter, "'Commerce and Christianity': The Rise and Fall of a Nineteenth-Century Missionary Slogan," *HJ* 28 (1985): 597–621. For the argument Porter resists, see Brian Stanley, *The Bible and the Flag: Protestant Missions and British Imperialism in the Nineteenth and Twentieth Centuries* (Leicester, 1990), 56–61, 70–74. On links between anti-slavery and missionaries, see also C. Duncan Rice, "The Missionary Context of the British Anti-Slavery Movement," in *Slavery and British Society 1776–1846*, ed. James Walvin (London, 1982), 150–63.

28. Beecham, *Ashantee*, 338–39; *PP 1842*, xi (1), 191: evidence of John Beecham.

29. William Tait, *Slave-Trade Overruled for the Salvation of Africa* (London, 1851), 9.

30. Yale Divinity School, Horace Waller Papers, Record Group 72, Box 2, Folder 19, 1875 Diary: entry for 21 May 1875.

31. See, for example, Elizabeth Dimock, "Women, Missions and Modernity: From Anti-Slavery to Missionary Zeal, 1780s to 1840s," *Itinerario* 34 (2010): 53–66.

32. Esther Copley, *A History of Slavery and its Abolition*, 2nd ed. (London, 1844), 581.

33. A. E. M. Anderson-Morshead, *The History of the Universities' Mission to Central Africa, 1859–1896* (London, 1897), xx.

34. For examples, *Central Africa*, 1 Jan. 1883, 10; *Central Africa*, Apr. 1896, 66.

35. Buxton, *African Slave Trade and Its Remedy*, 13, 271, 289; for "great family," see Laird and Oldfield, *Narrative*, 1:vi.

36. Laird and Oldfield, *Narrative*, 2:376–79; Thomas Hutchinson, *Impressions of Western Africa* (London, 1858), 263; Francis Thornhill Baring, *Journals and Correspondence of Francis Thornhill Baring*, ed. T. G. Baring (2 vols., London, 1902), 1:168.

37. Laird and Oldfield, *Narrative*, 2:380, 388–89.

38. *PP 1842*, xi (1), xxi.

39. Buxton, *African Slave Trade and Its Remedy*, 273, 308; Buxton, *Letter*, xiii; Laird and Oldfield, *Narrative*, 1:vi.

40. Ibid., 2:354, 363–64, 379. The idea of this peculiarly British burden is also evident in Cruikshank, *Eighteen Years*, 1:6–7.

41. A. G. Hopkins, "The 'New International Economic Order' in the Nineteenth Century: Britain's First Development Plan for Africa," in *From Slave Trade to Legitimate Commerce*, ed. Robin Law (Cambridge, 1995), 247–48. On potential gains, see John S. Galbraith, *Mackinnon and East Africa 1878–1895: A Study in the 'New Imperialism'* (Cambridge, 1972), 3–4.

42. Burke is also quoted directly by Hutchinson, *Impressions*, 264.

43. Buxton, *Letter*, ix–x; Buxton, *African Slave Trade and Its Remedy*, 278–79, 302, 342–43, 439.

44. Laird and Oldfield, *Narrative*, 2:361.

45. For example: *Popular Science Review*, Jan. 1862, 109; Frederick L. Barnard, *A Three Years' Cruize in the Mozambique Channel for the Suppression of the Slave Trade* (London, 1848), 105; Baring, *Journals and Correspondence*, 1:167: Sir Francis Baring to Thomas Baring, 17 Oct. 1859; Hutchinson, *Impressions*, vi; *PP 1865*, v (1), 17–18, 310;

*PP 1842*, xi (1), 64, 91, 153, 252, 327, 403, 409. On consistency, see Ralph A. Austen and Woodruff D. Smith, "Images of Africa and British Slave-Trade Abolition: The Transition to an Imperialist Ideology, 1787–1807," *African Historical Studies* 2 (1969): 69–83, at 81–83.

46. *Hansard*, 3rd ser., 1845, lxxxi, 1171.

47. *Times*, 20 Sept. 1864, 6; *Times*, 14 Nov. 1864, 3; Andrew Porter, *Religion versus Empire? British Protestant Missionaries and Overseas Expansion, 1700–1914* (Manchester, 2004), 187; Jones, "Palmerston and the Slave Trade." On Palmerston's early skepticism toward the Niger expedition, which make this later interpretation most ironic, see John Gallagher, "Fowell Buxton and the New African Policy, 1838–1842," *Cambridge Historical Journal* 10 (1950): 10, 36–58, at 44.

48. *Times*, 2 Dec. 1857, 6.

49. *Times*, 30 Jan. 1857, 6.

50. Bouda Etemad, "Economic Relations between Europe and Black Africa, c.1780–1936: A Quantitative Analysis," in *From Slave Trade to Empire: Europe and the Colonisation of Black Africa, 1780s–1880s*, ed. Olivier Pétré-Grenouilleau (Abingdon, Oxfordshire, 2004), 69–81; Imanuel Geiss, "Free Trade, Internationalization of the Congo Basin, and the Principle of Effective Occupation," in *Bismarck, Europe, and Africa: The Berlin Africa Conference 1884–1885 and the Onset of Partition*, ed. Stig Förster, Wolfgang J. Mommsen, and Ronald Robinson (Oxford, 1988), 266.

51. *Hansard*, 3rd ser., vol. 151, 1335–38.

52. Harold Temperley, "Lord Granville's Unpublished Memorandum on Foreign Policy, 1852," *Cambridge Historical Journal* 2 (1928): 298–302, at 299–300; D. C. M. Platt, *Finance, Trade, and Politics in British Foreign Policy 1815–1914* (Oxford, 1968), xiv–xvi.

53. *Chambers's Journal*, May 1854, 278–80.

54. *PP 1865*, v (1), 113.

55. *The Massacres at Dahomey* (n.p., 1862?), 1–2; *William Craft's Mission to Dahomey* (n.p., 1863?); copies of these consulted in JJC, Slavery 2. See also Blackett, *Building*, 175–86; Blackett, *Beating*, 108–22.

56. *Morning Chronicle*, 25 Jan. 1861, 3.

57. Miers, *Britain*, 37; Davis, *Slavery*, 299.

58. Barrie M. Ratcliffe, "Cotton Imperialism: Manchester Merchants and Cotton Cultivation in West Africa in the Mid-Nineteenth Century," *African Economic History* 11 (1982): 87–113.

59. Dike, *Trade*, 66; on the anti-slavery operations there, see Robert T. Brown, "Fernando Po and the Anti-Sierra Leonean Campaign: 1826–1834," *International Journal of African Studies* 6 (1973): 249–264.

60. Cruikshank, *Eighteen Years*, 2:277; Hutchinson, *Impressions*, 78; Baring, *Journals and Correspondence*, 1:167: Sir Francis Baring to Thomas Baring, 17 Oct. 1859; Dike, *Trade*, 96; Colin W. Newbury, *The Western Slave Coast and Its Rulers* (Oxford, 1961), 58; *Times*, 11 Feb. 1857, p. 5; NA, FO 84/1034, fo. 60: Shelburne to Chamerovzow, 11 Aug. 1857; NA, FO 84/1034, fo. 105: Thomas Clegg, "Notice of sale," 23 Aug. 1853; NA, FO 84/1034, fo. 87: Foreign Office to Cotton Supply Association of Manchester, 14 Nov. 1857; NA, FO 84/1034, fo. 94: Foreign Office to Cotton Supply Association of Manchester, 18 Nov. 1857.

61. Richard Whately, *Life and Correspondence of Richard Whately*, ed. E. J. Whately (London, 1866, 2 vols.), 2:285: Whateley to Mrs. Hill, 12 Feb. 1853.

62. For details of the "trust" system of credit and contemporary criticism, see Dike, *Trade*, 102–13, 122–25. The 1860s saw Palmerston subsidizing Macgregor Laird's commercial trading posts farther up the Niger, in a bid to break the monopoly of existing traders using this system (179).

63. NA, CO 267/170, fos. 9–10: Russell to Madden, 26 Nov. 1840. See also Stephen, *Niger Trade*, 25; *PP 1842*, xi (1), 316, 177–79, 215.

64. *PP 1842*, xi (1), xvii–xviii.

65. Cruikshank, *Eighteen Years*, 2:ii–iv.

66. Their conclusions on this point are stated in *PP 1842*, xi (1), xix–xx. For objections to any restriction on legitimate trade: *PP 1842*, xi (1), 17–19, 36–37, 43–46, 72, 78, 117, 124, 129, 157, 375–78.

67. *PP 1842,* xi (1), 2, 129, 228, 312–13, 344–45.

68. In the event, it saw more significant criticism leveled by traders at those occasions when the Royal Navy had become overzealous in its duties and disrupted their business. For example, *PP 1842,* xi (1), 140, 375–76. For William Forster's complaints, see NA, CO 267/170, fos. 216–17: William Forster to Russell, 16 Aug. 1841.

69. *PP 1842,* xi (1), 43–46, 75, 103, 173–74, 212–13. For a particularly farcical example of a trader evading suggestions of his association with slave dealing, see the evidence of William Mackintosh Hutton, ibid., 210–12. See also Akosa Admoa Perbi, *A History of Indigenous Slavery in Ghana* (Accra, Ghana, 2004), 159.

70. NA, CO 267/170, fo. 226: William Foster to R.R. Madden, 19 July 1841.

71. Curtin, *Image,* 448; Temperley, *White Dreams,* 58–59.

72. Dike, *Trade,* 114–15.

73. Curtin, *Image,* 292.

74. Buxton, *Letter,* xiv–xv; Temperley, *White Dreams,* 16–23. Compare with Gallagher, "Fowell Buxton," 42. See also Richard Brent, *Liberal Anglican Politics: Whiggery, Religion and Reform 1830–1841* (Oxford, 1987), 275–76.

75. Temperley, *White Dreams,* xiii, 23–29. The cost, Temperley observes, was incredible, given that a small increase in the budget for West African forts, to £4,000 total, had been recently refused (43). The cabinet was initially skeptical; see the memorandum inserted in the Earl of Minto's copy, held by the Bodleian Library: Buxton, *Letter,* at Bod., Bod. 2475 d.67. See also NA, Russell papers, PRO 30/22/3B, fo. 157: Tavistock to Russell, June 1838; Temperley, *White Dreams,* 5.

76. Temperley, *White Dreams,* 40.

77. Martin Lynn, "'The Imperialism of Free Trade' and the Case of West Africa, c.1830–1870," *JICH* 15 (1986): 22–40, at 24; Curtin, *Image,* 290, 304–5.

78. *PP 1842,* xi (1), xxi; and again in *PP 1865,* v (1), 8.

79. Curtin, *Image,* 343; Butt, "'Bleak House'," 14–15.

80. Temperley, *White Dreams; Times,* 3 May 1841, 4; *Times,* 24 Jan. 1842, 4; *Times,* 28 Jan. 1842, 4.

81. Curtin, *Image,* 372–77, 384.

82. For his rebuttal of Africans' imperviousness to improvements, see *PP 1865,* v (1), 232; on the *Times:* Gavin, "Bartle Frere Mission," 143.

83. NA, CO 96/2, fo. 111: James Stephen, "Memorandum on West African Select Committee," 23 Dec. 1842.

84. *PP 1842,* xi (1), 345, 348.

85. *Spectator,* 3 Apr. 1853, 322–23.

86. But see Drescher, "Ending," 443–44.

87. Eltis, *Economic Growth,* 240.

88. Keene, "Case Study," 327.

89. Durham University, Wylde Papers, WYL 28/6–7: Printed report to Russell by the commission revising naval instructions for slave-trade suppression, 18 Jan. 1865.

90. Eltis, *Economic Growth,* 121; Robin Law, "Abolition and Imperialism: International Law and the British Suppression of the Atlantic Slave Trade," in *Abolitionism and Imperialism in Britain, Africa and the Atlantic,* ed. Derek R. Peterson (Athens, Ohio, 2010), 150–74; Jennifer Pitts, "Boundaries of International Law," in *Victorian Visions of Global Order: Empire and International Relations in Nineteenth-Century Political Thought,* ed. Duncan Bell (Cambridge, 2007), 67–88.

91. *ILN,* 14 Apr. 1849, 237; ibid., 18 Jan. 1851, 44. The British also attacked African settlements which existed alongside barracoons: Kingston, *Blue Jackets,* 355.

92. Buxton, *African Slave Trade and its Remedy,* 302–4; Buxton, *Letter,* xiii; Cruikshank, *Eighteen Years,* 2:6–7; Curtin, *Image,* 457–58, 467. On the antecedents, see Richardson, "Background," 47.

93. Gallagher and Robinson, "Imperialism of Free Trade," 1–15; Robinson, Gallagher, and Denny, *Africa and the Victorians,* 2–3, 28–33. For earlier formulations, see John Flint, "African Historians and African History," *Past and Present* 10 (1956): 96–101; Dike, *Trade,* 159.

94. *PP 1865,* v (i), xiv: "Report from the Select Committee appointed to consider the State of the British Establishments on the Western Coast of Africa"; Colin Newbury, "Great

Britain and the Partition of Africa, 1870–1914," in *Oxford History of the British Empire*, ed. Andrew Porter (Oxford, 5 vols., 1999), 4:624–50, at 624.

95. Henry Landor, *The Best Way to Stop the Slave Trade* (London, 1850), 5; *PP 1842*, xi (1), 37, 46, 406; for opposition: ibid., 136.

96. Temperley, *White Dreams*, 28; Palmerston could see the advantage of state involvement on Fernando Po, but not Mombass, which could be used for civilizing trade by private initiative. See NA, FO 54/2, fo. 109: Glenelg to Palmerston, 10 Sept. 1838; NA, FO 54/2, fo. 140: Captain Colgan to Palmerston, 15 Sept. 1838; NA, FO 54/2, fo. 181: Palmerston to Glenelg, 14 Oct 1838.

97. *PP 1842*, xi (1), iv.

98. *Caledonian Mercury*, 22 July 1850, 2.

99. Dike, *Trade*, 65.

100. Laird and Oldfield, *Narrative*, 2:354, 357–58; Cruikshank, *Eighteen Years*, 2:334.

101. *PP 1865*, v (1), iii, 84. See Charles Adderley's lengthy draft report for exegesis on the short resolutions adopted by the committee: *PP 1865*, v (1), iii, xiii–xiv. Adderley took his lead from Colonel Ord's "Report of the Commissioner appointed to inquire into the condition of the British settlements on the West Coast of Africa," in ibid., 362–65.

102. *PP 1865*, v (1), 50. Adderley, among all the members of the select committee, seems to have been alone in welcoming the imperial domination of some African tribes over others as the best means of civilized native government emerging in Africa (135, 163). Sir Francis Baring was happily surprised at the nonexpansionist result: Baring, *Journals and Correspondence*, 1:175. For Livingstone's skepticism, see *PP 1865*, v (1), 228.

103. For those supporting the protection of trade only, see NA, CO 267/170, fo. 226: William Foster to R. R. Madden, 19 July 1841; NA, CO 267/170, fos. 216–17: William Forster to Russell, 16 Aug. 1841.

104. Dike, *Trade*, 87–92.

105. Ibid., 131–45.

106. Newbury, *Western Slave Coast*, 48.

107. Robert Smith, "The Lagos Consulate, 1851–1861: An Outline," *Journal of African History* 15 (1974): 396–97, 415; Anthony G. Hopkins, "Property Rights and Empire Building: Britain's Annexation of Lagos, 1861," *Journal of Economic History* 40 (1980): 781; Cairns, *Prelude*, 140.

108. Buxton, *Letter*, xi; see also Hutchinson, *Impressions*, 76.

109. Austen and Smith, "Images of Africa," 82–83.

110. *PP 1865*, v (1), 320.

111. Dike, *Trade*, 66, 83; NA, FO 84/2, fo. 113: Denis Le Marchant to John Backhouse, 7 Dec. 1839. Britain frequently failed to meet financial obligations under these treaties due to bureaucratic incompetence: Dike, *Trade*, 83–86; Eltis, *Economic Growth*, 88.

112. NA, CO 96/24, fo. 126: Straith to Palmerston, 20 Aug. 1851.

113. *PP 1865*, v (1), 363; *Uncle Tom's Almanack*, 54–56; Robin Law, "The White Slaver and the African Prince: European and American Depictions of Pre-Colonial Dahomey," in *Images of Africa*, ed. Martin Gray and Robin Law (Stirling, 1990), 22–41; Smith, "Lagos Consulate," 414.

114. NA, CO 96/24, fo. 163: Palmerston to Lords Commissioners of the Admiralty, 27 Sept. 1851. It was later suggested that Akitoye's legitimacy was by no means clear: *PP 1865*, v (1), 66. See also Newbury, *Western Slave Coast*, 47

115. NA, CO 96/24, fo. 126: Straith to Palmerston, 20 Aug. 1851.

116. NA, CO 96/24, fo.159: Palmerston to Lords Commissioners of the Admiralty, 27 Sept. 1851; NA, FO 97/430: "Memorandum of the State of Questions in the Slave Trade Department of the Foreign Office," 3 Jan. 1852. Lagos may well have ended up being targeted for reprisal because Whydah and the rest of Dahomey territory presented too many military complications: NA, Russell papers, PRO 30/22/24, fo. 89: Somerset to Russell, 24 June 1861.

117. Southampton University, Palmerston papers, Broadlands manuscripts, GC/RU/424: Russell to Palmerston, 24 Sept. 1851, as cited by Law, "International Law," 163, and Jones, "Palmerston and the Slave Trade."

118. NA, CO 96/24, fo. 164: Palmerston to Lords Commissioners of the Admiralty, 27 Sept. 1851.

119. Robert S. Smith, *The Lagos Consulate 1851–1861* (London, 1978), 26.

120. Newbury, *Western Slave Coast*, 54.

121. *Spectator,* 10 Jan. 1852, 27; *Destruction,* 19; Hutchinson, *Impressions,* 76.

122. *PP 1865,* v (1), 59, 117.

123. NA, FO 84/1141, fos. 52–53: Russell to Foote, 22 June 1861. A memorandum from Wylde noted that the threat of a new attack on Abeokuta by Dahomey would be an excellent opportunity to take possession of Lagos, suggesting it was the occasion for a long-awaited formal occupation. NA, FO 84/1141, fo. 8: William Wylde, "Memorandum," 22 June 1861.

124. *PP 1865,* v (1), 449–50: Newcastle to Freeman, 1 Dec. 1862.

125. Kristin Mann, *Slavery and the Birth of an African City, Lagos, 1700–1900* (Bloomington, Ind., 2007), 84–85, 91. For different interpretations, see also Hopkins, "Property Rights," 795; Smith, *Lagos Consulate,* 31–33, 120–24. Newbury emphasizes Brand's concern with stable government: Newbury, *Western Slave Coast,* 65.

126. Baring, *Journals and Correspondence,* 1:168–71. Baring used the 1865 select committee to promote this agenda: *PP 1865,* v (1), 86.

127. Dike, *Trade,* 129, 147.

128. Michael Craton, *Sinews of Empire* (London, 1974), 292.

129. Durham University, Wylde Papers, WYL 27/16–20: Governor Freeman to W. H. Wylde, 9 June 1864.

130. *ILN,* 13 Mar. 1852, 224. See also Kingston, *Blue Jackets,* 256–60.

131. Durham University, Wylde Papers, WYL 48/12–18: Frederic Elton to W. H. Wylde, 23 Aug. 1877.

132. John Tillotson, *Tales About Animals* (London, 1858), 4–5.

133. Durham University, Wylde Papers, WYL 48/12–18: Frederic Elton to W.H. Wylde, 23 Aug, 1877.

134. Galbraith, *Mackinnon,* 76–77, 82.

135. Wood, *Slavery,* 9. See also, for example, Patrick Manning, "Slavery and Slave Trade in West Africa," in *Themes in West Africa's History,* ed. Emmanuel Kwaku Akyeampong (Athens, Ohio, 2006), 114.

136. On earlier Indian Ocean slave-trade suppression, see Richard B. Allen, "Suppressing a Nefarious Traffic: Britain and the Abolition of Slave Trading in India and the Western Indian Ocean, 1770–1830," *William and Mary Quarterly,* 3rd ser., 66 (2009): 873–94.

137. For a similar argument about networks of Africanists, see Dorothy O. Helly, "'Informed' Opinion on Tropical Africa in Great Britain, 1860–1890," *African Affairs* 68 (1969): 195–217, at 204, 208, 215–17. On networks and empire, see Frederick Cooper, "Networks, Moral Discourse, and History," in *Intervention and Transnationalism in Africa: Global-Local Networks of Power,* ed. Thomas Callaghy, Ronald Kassimir, and Robert Latham (Cambridge, 2001), 23–46; Gary B. Magee and Andrew S. Thompson, *Empire and Globalisation: Networks of People, Goods and Capital in the British World, c. 1850–1914* (Cambridge, 2010), 16–19, 26–29.

138. Charles and David Livingstone, *Narrative,* 3:596.

139. Church Missionary Society, *The Slave Trade of East Africa* (London, 1868), 32; see also *London Quarterly Review,* Oct. 1872, 249–50.

140. Charles and David Livingstone, *Narrative,* v–vi; Dorothy O. Helly, *Livingstone's Legacy: Horace Waller and Victorian Mythmaking* (Athens, Ohio, 1987), 237–39; Reginald Coupland, *The Exploitation of East Africa, 1856–1890: The Slave Trade and the Scramble* (London, 1939), 148.

141. R. W. Beachey, *The Slave Trade of Eastern Africa* (London, 1976), 99–103; *PP 1871,* xii (420), iii–x.

142. For the background, see Moses Nwulia, *Britain and Slavery in East Africa* (Washington, D.C., 1975), 53, 59, 67.

143. Ibid., 43.

144. Durham University, Wylde Papers, WYL 34/13–16: *Answer to a Confidential Memorandum on the East Africa Slave Trade* (London, 1872).

145. Gavin, "Bartle Frere Mission," 132–36.

146. Ibid., 136.

147. *Aberdeen Journal*, 31 Jan. 1872, 2; *Birmingham Daily Post*, 7 Feb. 1872, 5.

148. *Royal Cornwall Gazette*, 14 Oct. 1871, 7.

149. *Birmingham Daily Post*, 9 Feb. 1872, 4; *Birmingham Daily Post*, 27 July 1872, 5.

150. *Morning Post*, 26 July 1872, 7; *Sheffield and Rotherham Independent*, 8 Aug. 1872, 2.

151. *Leeds Mercury*, 29 July 1872, 3; *Glasgow Herald*, 29 July 1872, 5.

152. On his skepticism, see Richard Huzzey, "Gladstone and the Suppression of the Slave Trade," in *William Gladstone: New Studies and Perspectives*, ed. Ruth Clayton Windscheffel, Roland Quinault, and Roger Swift (forthcoming).

153. Gavin, "Bartle Frere Mission," 135–41; see also William Mulligan, "British Anti-Slave Trade and Anti-Slavery Policy in East Africa, Arabia, and Turkey in the Late Nineteenth Century," in *Humanitarian Intervention: A History*, ed. Brendan Simms and D. J. B. Trim (Cambridge, 2011), 257–80.

154. John Benyon, "Bartle Frere," *ODNB*; F. V. Emery, "Geography and Imperialism: The Role of Sir Bartle Frere," *Geographical Journal* 150 (1984): 342–50.

155. *Daily News*, 13 Feb. 1872, 6.

156. Gavin, "The Bartle Frere Expedition," 138–43.

157. Helly, *Livingstone's Legacy*, viii–xiv, 13–15, 42–43, 53, 175, 247–48; David Livingstone, *Livingstone's Last Journals*, ed. Horace Waller (2 vols., London, 1874).

158. *ILN*, 25 Apr. 1874, 2–3.

159. *ILN*, 17 Dec. 1881, 586.

160. Roy Bridges, "Prelude to the Partition of East Africa," in *Imperialism, Decolonisation and Africa*, ed. Roy Bridges (Basingstoke, Hampshire, 2000), 74–75, 90–95.

161. As quoted by Norman Etherington, "Frederic Elton and the South African Factor in the Making of Britain's East African Empire," *JICH* 2 (1981): 255–74, 260.

162. Wylde Papers, Durham University, WYL 46/26–29: Clement Hill to W. H. Wylde, 29 Sept. 1876.

163. Dike, *Trade*, 168; Hamilton, "Zealots and Helots," 33–34.

164. Gavin, "Bartle Frere," 145–47.

165. D. K. Fieldhouse, *Economics and Empire 1830–1914* (London, 1973), 363–64, 370–71.

166. Michael D. McMullen, "Sir John Kirk," *ODNB*; Nwulia, *Britain and Slavery*, 43, 137.

167. FO 84/1391, NA, Memorandum on Zanzibar, 17 Apr. 1873, as quoted by Etherington, "Frederic Elton," 257.

168. Galbraith, *Mackinnon*, 49.

169. As quoted by Etherington, "Frederic Elton," 269.

170. Galbraith, *Mackinnon*, 42–43, 56, 62; Yale Divinity School, Horace Waller Papers, Record Group 72, box 2, folder 19, 1876 Diary: entry for 5 Apr. 1876; Etherington, "Frederic Elton," 269: Etherington shows that Elton had long viewed East Africa through the prism of South African interests; his career had begun as an agent for the Natal colony when it sought to recruit African free labor from Portuguese Mozambique.

171. Ibid., esp. 262–65.

172. Durham University, Wylde Papers, WYL 51/6–7: R. B. D. Morier to W. H. Wylde, 27 Jan. 1879. On Morier, see Richard Davenport-Hines, "Robert Morier," ODNB.

173. J. Frederic Elton, *Travels and Researches Among the Lakes and Mountains and Central Africa: From the Journals of the Late J. Frederic Elton, FRGS*, ed. H. B. Cotterill (London, 1879), xii.

174. Miers, *Ending*, 117.

175. Ibid., 169–74, quotation at 173.

176. Ibid., 173.

177. But see Wm. Roger Louis, *Ends of British Imperialism: The Scramble for Empire, Suez, and Decolonization* (London, 2006), 116–17.

178. Galbraith, *Mackinnon*, 89; Darwin, *Empire Project*, 128; Miers, *Ending*, 190–92.

179. Galbraith, *Mackinnon*, 85–86, 127, 129–33.

180. D. A. Low, *Fabrication of Empire: The British and the Uganda Kingdoms* (Cambridge, 2009), 92–95; Galbraith, *Mackinnon*, 111–15.

181. Galbraith, Mackinnon, 139–40.

182. Ibid., 130, 139.

183. Ibid., 127, 141, 145, 147.

184. Ibid., 147, 159.

185. Etherington, "Frederic Elton," 268.

186. For an interesting Marxist account along these lines, see R. M. A. Zwanenberg, "Anti-Slavery, The Ideology of 19th Century Imperialism in East Africa," typescript conference paper, Historical Association of Kenya Annual Conference 1972 (Sterling Memorial Library, Yale University, call number SML DT32.5.V35 1972).

187. Galbraith, Mackinnon, 111, 138, 143; for a convincing interpretation that Mackinnon's commercial interests resulted from his shipping empire, see J. Forbes Munro, "Shipping Subsidies and Railway Guarantees: William Mackinnon, Eastern Africa and the Indian Ocean, 1860–93," Journal of African History 28 (1987): 209–30.

188. Harry Johnston, "British West Africa and the Trade of the Interior," Proceedings of the Royal Colonial Institute 20 (1889): 90–111, at 91.

189. Galbraith, Mackinnon, 156.

190. Contrast with H. D. Perraton, "British Attitudes towards East and West Africa, 1880–1914," Race and Class 8 (1967): 223–46, at 224–25.

191. Suzanne Miers, "Slavery and the Slave Trade as International Issues, 1890–1939," Slavery & Abolition 19 (1998): 16–37, at 21. See, as a statement of ambitions, Sir Harry Johnston's anonymous article in the Times, 22 Aug. 1888, 8; Roland Oliver, Sir Harry Johnston and the Scramble for Africa (London, 1964), 140–41.

192. Nwulia, Slavery, vii.

193. Etherington, "Frederic Elton," 256–57.

194. Barrie M. Ratcliffe, "Commerce and Empire: Manchester Merchants and West Africa, 1873–1895," JICH 7 (1979): 293–320.

195. Elton, Travels and Researches, ed. Cotterill, 13–14.

196. Charles New, Life, Wanderings, and Labours in Eastern Africa (London, 1874), 508.

197. Miers, Britain, 116–17.

198. Elton, Travels and Researches, ed. Cotterill, 22–23. Helly, "'Informed Opinion'," 206, 209–10; Edward Hutchinson, The Slave Trade of East Africa (London, 1874).

199. Hamilton, "Zealots and Helots," 34.

200. M. E. Chamberlain, "Clement Hill's Memorandum and the British Interest in East Africa," EHR 87 (1972): 533–47, at 533.

201. Ibid., 535–37.

202. Ibid., 546.

203. Durham University, Wylde Papers, WYL 46/26–29: Clement Hill to W. H. Wylde, 29 Sept. 1876.

204. Coupland, Exploitation, 386.

205. Abbas Ibrahim Muhammad Ali, The British, the Slave Trade and Slavery in the Sudan, 1820–1881 (Khartoum, Sudan, 1972), 45–54.

206. Richard Davenport-Hines, "Charles George Gordon," ODNB; Ali, Slavery in the Sudan, 82–87.

207. RH, Horace Waller Papers, MSS.Afr.s.16, fos. 86–90: Charles Gordon to Horace Waller, 11 Sept. 1877; on their relationship, see Yale Divinity School, Horace Waller Papers, box 2, folder 2: diary entry for 26 Jan. 1877; Ali, Slavery in the Sudan, 103.

208. Ibid., 105–11, 116, 124–29.

209. Darwin, Empire Project, 71–74, quotation at 74.

210. Miers, Britain, 80–81; Ali, Slavery in the Sudan, 114.

211. Pollock, Gordon, 288; Ahmad Alawad Sikainga, Slaves into Workers: Emancipation and Labor in Colonial Sudan (Austin, Tex., 1996), 13–14.

212. Graphic, 8 Mar. 1884, 226.

213. Penny Illustrated Paper, 9 Aug. 1884, 85.

214. John Pollock, Gordon: The Man behind the Legend (London, 1993), 1–7; Richard Davenport-Hines, "Charles George Gordon," ODNB.

215. Bernard M. Allen, "Livingstone and Gordon," Journal of the Royal African Society 40 (1941): 121–27, at 123–24.

216. *Hansard,* 3rd ser., 1889, cccxxxiv, 902–3.
217. Pollock, *Gordon,* 268.
218. *Graphic,* 18 July 1885, 63.
219. *Penny Illustrated Paper,* 16 May 1885, 308
220. Durham Library, Wylde Papers, WYL 65/5–6: Printed memorandum by Charles Allen for the committee of the Anti-Slavery Society, 21 Dec. 1888; B. A. Riffenburgh, "Verney Lovett Cameron," *ODNB.*
221. *Graphic,* 29 Jan. 1887, 113.
222. Miers, *Britain,* 204.
223. *Graphic,* 4 Aug. 1888, 110.
224. Miers, *Britain,* 207; Hamilton, "Zealots," 35–36.
225. *Hansard,* 3rd ser., 1889, cccxxxiv, 916–18.
226. *Penny Illustrated Paper,* 6 Apr. 1889, 214; Miers, *Britain,* 211; quotation from *Graphic,* 30 Mar. 1889, 310.
227. Miers, *Britain,* 233–34, 242–44.
228. Ibid., 218–19, 246–47, 284–85; see also Daniel Laqua, "The Tensions of International-ism: Transnational Anti-Slavery in the 1880s and 1890s," *International History Review* 33 (2011): 705–26, at 711–13.
229. Miers, *Britain,* 253–56.
230. Ibid., 290.
231. Ibid., 258–61.
232. Galbraith, *Mackinnon,* 167, 170–72.
233. *Hansard,* 4th ser., 1894, xxv, 242–44.
234. RH, Lugard Papers, MS Brit Emp.s.45, fo. 1: Ernest Bentley to Frederick Lugard, 29 Jan. 1892.
235. D. A. Low, *Buganda in Modern History* (London, 1971), 56; M. Louise Pirouet, "Alfred Tucker," *ODNB;* Tudor Griffiths, "Bishop Alfred Tucker and the Establishment of a British Protectorate in Uganda 1890–94," *Journal of Religion in Africa* 31 (2001): 92–114, at 105.
236. A. H. M. Kirk-Greene, "Frederick Lugard," *ODNB;* Galbraith, *Mackinnon,* 198; Low, *Buganda,* 56.
237. *Pall Mall Gazette,* 3 Mar. 1892, 2.
238. *Pall Mall Gazette,* 3 Mar. 1892, 1–2.
239. *Essex County Standard,* 10 Sept. 1892, 4.
240. Galbraith, *Mackinnon,* 201–2, 205–9; RH, Lugard Papers, MS Brit Emp.s.45, fos. 12–15: George Mackenzie to Lugard, 12 Aug. 1892.
241. *Morning Post,* 4 Oct. 1892, 4; Miers, *Ending,* 294.
242. *Huddersfield Chronicle and West Yorkshire Advertiser,* 20 Feb. 1982, 5; *Aberdeen Weekly Journal,* 16 Feb. 1892, 7; *Birmingham Daily Post,* 3 Mar. 1892, 4; *Glasgow Herald,* 13 Feb. 1892, 9; *Derby Mercury,* 18 May 1892, 5; William G. Hynes, *The Economics of Empire: Britain, Africa and the New Imperialism, 1870–95* (London, 1979), 129.
243. Low, *Buganda,* 61–62, 70, 73–74.
244. Durham University, Wylde Papers, WYL 69/15: BFASS memorial to Rosebery, Oct. 1892.
245. *Birmingham Daily Post,* 13 Oct. 1892, 4.
246. *Leeds Mercury,* 24 Sept. 1892, 10.
247. *Leeds Mercury,* 24 Sept. 1892, 10.
248. *Pall Mall Gazette,* 21 Oct. 1892, 1.
249. Lady Grogan, *Reginald Bosworth Smith: A Memoir* (London, 1909), 244–45; *Morning Post,* 21 Oct. 1892, 2.
250. *Dundee Courier and Argus,* 21 Oct. 1892, 5.
251. *Morning Post,* 30 Sept. 1892, 8.
252. RH, Lugard Papers, MS Brit Emp. s.53, fos. 7–8: "Speech to Kensington Town Hall," 10 Nov. 1892; RH, Lugard Papers, MS Brit Emp. s.53, fo. 11: "Speech to Birmingham Town Hall," 2 Dec. 1892; see also Stanley: *Leeds Mercury,* 4 Oct. 1892, 8.
253. *Morning Post,* 4 Oct. 1892, 4.
254. *Punch,* 22 Oct. 1892, 1872; see also *Punch,* 21 Apr. 1894, 187.

255. Low, *Buganda*, 76–77.

256. RH, Lugard Papers, MS Brit. Emp. s.53, fo. 12: "Speech to Birmingham Town Hall," 2 Dec. 1892.

257. RH, Lugard Papers, MS Brit. Emp. s.45, fos. 12–15: George Mackenzie to Lugard, 12 Aug. 1892.

258. *Central Africa*, Apr. 1896, 58.

259. RH, Lugard Papers, MS. Brit. Emp. s.57, fos. 106–8: Transcript of Frederick Lugard to Edward Lugard, 3 June 1894.

260. RH, Lugard Papers, MS. Brit. Emp. s.71, fos. 20–23: Horace Waller to Frederick Lugard, 27 Dec. 1895.

261. Compare with the cleaner distinction perceived by Helly, *Livingstone's Lost Legacy*, 355.

262. *Penny Illustrated Paper*, 8 Oct. 1892, 238; H. C. G. Matthew, *The Liberal Imperialists: The Ideas and Politics of a Post-Gladstonian Élite* (Oxford, 1973), 16.

263. Leo McKinstry, *Rosebery: Statesman in Turmoil* (London, 2005), 240–49, quotations at 248 and 246; John Davis, "Archbibald Primrose, Fifth Earl of Rosebery," *ODNB*; Low, *Buganda*, 59.

264. RH, Lugard Papers, MS Brit. Emp.s.57, fos. 102–3: Transcript of Frederick Lugard to Edward Lugard, 27 Mar. 1894.

265. RH, Lugard Papers, MS Brit. Emp.s.57, fos. 106–8: Transcript of Frederick Lugard to Edward Lugard, 3 June 1894.

266. *Hansard*, 4th ser., 1894, xxv, 240.

267. *Hansard*, 4th ser., 1894, xxv, 240–43.

268. *Graphic*, 14 Apr. 1894, 414

269. *Hansard*, 4th ser., xxv, 243–44.

270. *Hansard*, 4th ser., 1895, xxxiv, 1112.

271. Low, *Fabrication*, 340–41.

272. See Richard J. Hammond, "Economic Imperialism: Sidelights on a Stereotype," *Journal of Economic History*, 21 (1961): 582–98, at 588.

273. Oliver, *Sir Harry Johnston*, 145; James Stevenson, *The Water Highways of the Interior of Africa, with notes on Slave Hunting and the means of its Suppression* (Glasgow, 1883).

274. Porter, *Religion*, 268–74.

275. Owen J. M. Kalinga, "The Karonga War: Commercial Rivalry and Politics of Survival," *Journal of African History* 21 (1980): 209–18.

276. *Glasgow Herald*, 25 Feb. 1888, 8.

277. RH, Lugard Papers, MS. Brit. Emp. s.35, fos. 42–4: "Nyassa Anti-Slavery and Defence Fund" (n.d.).

278. *Dundee Courier & Argus*, 25 Apr. 1888, 2; *Birmingham Daily Post*, 28 Dec. 1888, 3.

279. *Manchester Times*, 18 May 1888, 5.

280. *Birmingham Daily Post*, 19 Apr. 1889, 5.

281. *Graphic*, 29 Sept. 1888, 340–41, 343.

282. Alex Johnston, *The Life and Letters of Sir Harry Johnston* (London, 1929), 91–95; Oliver, *Sir Harry Johnston*, 144.

283. Roland Oliver, "Sir Harry Johnston," *ODNB*; Hammond, "Economic Imperialism," 586–87.

284. *Aberdeen Journal*, 6 Jan. 1890, 4.

285. *Huddersfield Daily Chronicle*, 6 Jan. 1890, 3.

286. *Pall Mall Gazette*, 8 Jan. 1890, 7; Horace Waller, *Nyassaland: Great Britain's Case against Portugal* (London, 1890).

287. *Glasgow Herald*, 7 Jan. 1890, 4. See also *Lancaster Gazette*, 11 Jan. 1890, 3.

288. *Liverpool Mercury*, 7 Jan. 1890, 5.

289. *Northern Echo*, 9 Jan. 1890, 2.

290. Oliver, *Sir Harry Johnston*, 15.

291. Johnston, *Life and Letters*, 120.

292. Oliver, *Sir Harry Johnston*, 200–201, 206–8; Colin Baker, "Tax Collection in Malawi: An Administrative History, 1891–1972," *International Journal of African Historical Studies* 8 (1975): 40–62.

293. Harry Johnston, "The British Central Africa Protectorate," *Geographical Journal* 5 (1895): 193-214.

294. Michael Crowder, *West Africa under Colonial Rule* (London, 1969), 116-17.

295. Ibid., 119-21.

296. Ibid., 122, 126-29; Nworah, "Aborigines' Protection Society," 83; for commercial motives, see Philip A. Igbafe, "The Fall of Benin: A Reassessment," *Journal of African History* 11 (1970): 385-400.

297. Paul E. Lovejoy and Jan S. Hogendorn, *Slow Death for Slavery: The Course of Abolition in Northern Nigeria, 1897–1936* (Cambridge, 1993), 1, 16; Crowder, *West Africa,* 130-31. See also John D. Hargreaves, *West Africa Partitioned* (2 vols., Basingstoke, Hampshire, 1985), 2:117-18.

298. Lovejoy and Hogendorn, *Slow Death,* 17.

299. Ibid., 20-22.

300. C. W. Newbury, ed., *British Policy towards West Africa: Select Documents 1875–1914* (Oxford, 1971), 242-43: Sir Ralph Moor to Joseph Chamberlain, 24 Nov. 1901.

301. As quoted by Crowder, *West Africa,* 128.

302. Lovejoy and Hogendorn, *Slow Death,* 29.

303. Sir Gilbert Carter, "The Colony of Lagos," *Proceedings of the Royal Colonial Institute* 28 (1896–97): 275-305, at 278.

304. Elton, *Travels and Researches,* ed. Cotterill, 12.

305. Darwin, *Empire Project,* 90-93, 96.

306. Horace Waller, *Ivory, Apes, Peacocks: An African Contemplation* (London, 1891), 88; Felix Driver, "Henry Morton Stanley and His Critics: Geography, Exploration and Empire," *Past & Present* 133 (1991): 134-66, at 164.

307. Thompson, *Imperial Britain,* 11-12.

308. Rice, *Rise,* 369. See Lovejoy and Hogendorn, *Slow Death,* 27, 29, for uncertainty about colonizers' synthesis of genuine abhorrence with clear self-interest.

309. Miers, *Britain,* xi, 317; A. E. Afigbo, *The Abolition of the Slave Trade in Southeastern Nigeria, 1885–1950* (Rochester, N.Y., 2006), 31; Geiss, "Free Trade," 271.

310. For a parallel state intervention, see R. E. Dumett, "Joseph Chamberlain, Imperial Finance and Railway Policy in British West Africa in the Late Nineteenth Century," *EHR* 90 (1975): 287-321, at 302.

311. For the focus on settler colonies or defense and its widespread appeal, see Thompson, *Imperial Britain,* 37-39.

312. BFASS, *Proceedings …1843,* 62-64.

313. Ibid., 68.

314. Frederick Cooper, *From Slaves to Squatters: Plantation Labour and Agriculture in Zanzibar and Coastal Kenya, 1890–1925* (New Haven, Conn., 1980), 32.

## 7. THE ANTI-SLAVERY EMPIRE

1. Plymouth and West Devon Record Office, 335/4, Edwin Parker's journal aboard HMS *Racer:* entries for 24 Nov. 1886 and 10 Dec. 1886.

2. See also Roger Anstey, *Britain and the Congo in the Nineteenth Century* (Oxford, 1962), 26-27.

3. Howard Temperley, "The Delegalization of Slavery in British India," *Slavery and Abolition* 21 (2000): 169-71.

4. Ibid., 174-76, quote at 175-76.

5. RH, Anti-Slavery Papers, MSS. Brit.Emp.s.19 E2/19, BFASS Memorials and petitions book, 65-71: Memorial of the Committee of the BFASS to Sir Robert Peel, First Lord of the Treasury, on Slavery in British India, 10 Sept. 1841.

6. Temperley, "Delegalization," 181-83.

7. RH, Anti-Slavery Papers, MSS. Brit.Emp.s.19 E2/19, BFASS Memorials and petitions book, 174-82: John Scoble to Lord Fitzgerald, 11 Feb 1843; RH, Anti-Slavery Papers, MSS. Brit.Emp.s.19 E2/19, BFASS Memorials and petitions book, 183-87: Scoble to Lord Stanley, 10 Feb 1843.

8. RH, Anti-Slavery Papers, MSS. Brit.Emp.s.19 E2/19, BFASS Memorials and petitions book, 232–33: Thomas Clarkson to Queen Victoria, 11 Oct. 1843.

9. Margot Finn, "Slaves out of Context: Domestic Slavery and the Anglo-Indian Family, c. 1780–1830," *Transactions of the Royal Historical Society* 19 (2009): 181–203, quotation at 201; Michael Anderson, "India, 1858–1930: The Illusion of Free Labor," in *Masters, Servants, and Magistrates in Britain and the Empire, 1562–1955,* ed. Douglas Hay and Paul Craven (Chapel Hill, N.C., 2004), 422–54.

10. Gyan Prakash, *Bonded Histories: Genealogies of Labor Servitude in Colonial India* (Cambridge, 2002 [1992]), 9–11.

11. David W. Galeson, "The Rise and Fall of Indentured Servitude in the Americas: An Economic Analysis," *Journal of Economic History* 44 (1984): 1–26.

12. Tinker, *New System,* 63–69; David Northrup, *Indentured Labour in the Age of Imperialism, 1834–1922* (Cambridge, 1995), 24.

13. Tinker, *New System,* 71–81; Grant, *Civilised Savagery,* 23. For BFASS opposition to Russell's proposals to reopen the trade to Mauritius in 1840, see RH, Anti-slavery papers, MSS. Brit. Emp. s.19 E2/19, Memorials and petitions book, 12–17: BFASS deputation to Lord John Russell, 4 June 1840.

14. Tinker, *New System,* 70–71.

15. Ibid., 147–48.

16. Pieter Emmer, "'A Spirit of Independence' or Lack of Education for the Market? Freedmen and Asian Indentured Labourers in the Post-Emancipation Caribbean, 1834–1917," *Slavery and Abolition* 21 (2000): 150–68, at 151–52, 164–65.

17. Gad Heuman, "The British West Indies," in *The Oxford History of the British Empire,* ed. Andrew Porter (5 vols., Oxford, 1999), 3:483–84; Prabhu P. Mohapatra, "Assam and the West Indies, 1860–1920: Immobilizing Plantation Labor," in *Masters, Servants, and Magistrates in Britain and the Empire, 1562–1955,* ed. Douglas Hay and Paul Craven (Chapel Hill, N.C., 2004), 455–80.

18. Northrup, *Indentured Labour,* 108.

19. Madhavi Kale, *Fragments of Empire: Capital, Slavery, and Indian Indentured Labor in the British Caribbean* (Philadelphia: University of Pennsylvania Press, 1998), 174–75.

20. On this debate, see Northrup, *Indentured Labour,* 6.

21. Stanley Engerman, "Servants to Slaves: Contract Labour and European Expansion," in *Colonialism and Migration: Indentured Labour before and after Slavery,* ed. Pieter Emmer (Dordrecht, Netherlands, 1986), 272.

22. See for example, Northrup, *Indentured Labour;* Doug Munro, "The Labor Trade in Melanesians to Queensland: An Historiographic Essay," *Journal of Social History* 28 (1995): 609–25; Ralph Shlomowitz, "Markets for Indentured and Time-Expired Melanesian Labour in Queensland, 1863–1906: An Economic Analysis," *Journal of Pacific History* 16 (1981): 70–91.

23. *PP 1847–48,* xxii (467), 131.

24. *PP 1847–48,* xxii (467), 44, 56–57.

25. On African emigration, see Rosanne Marion Adderley, *"New Negroes from Africa": Slave Trade Abolition and Free African Settlement in the Nineteenth-Century Caribbean* (Bloomington, Ind., 2006), 72–76; Monica Schuler, *"Alas, Alas, Kongo": A Social History of Indentured African Immigration into Jamaica, 1841–1865* (Baltimore, Md., 1980); K. O. Laurence, *Immigration into the West Indies in the 19th Century* (St. Lawrence, Barbados, 1971). For moral arguments, see *PP 1842,* xi (1), xi–xv, 143–45, 149, 197, 247, 253–56, 318, 327, 399–401.

26. Johnson U. J. Asiegbu, *Slavery and the Politics of Liberation: A Study of Liberated African Emigration and British Anti-Slavery Policy* (London, 1969); Johnson U. J. Asiegbu, "The Dynamics of Freedom: A Study of Liberated African Emigration and British Antislavery Policy," *Journal of Black Studies* 7 (1976): 95–106.

27. For cautionary notes on Asiegbu's overall argument and evidence, see Humphrey J. Fisher, "Review of Johnson U. J. Asiegbu, *Slavery and the Politics of Liberation* (London, 1969)," *Bulletin of the School of Oriental and African Studies* 34 (1971): 188–90.

28. Davis, *Slavery,* 221.

29. As quoted by Davis, *Slavery*, 215–16, also 308.

30. Thanks to Stanley Engerman for suggesting this theme.

31. Holt, *Problem*, 126–28, 173–76, 184–87; Green, *British Slave Emancipation*, 395–97, 403.

32. Laurence Brown, "Inter-colonial Migration and the Refashioning of Indentured Labour: Arthur Gordon in Trinidad, Mauritius and Fiji (1866–1880)," in *Colonial Lives across the British Empire: Imperial Careering in the Long Nineteenth Century*, ed. David Lambert and Alan Lester (Cambridge, 2006), 216–17.

33. Green, *British Slave Emancipation*, 300–315.

34. Ibid., 373–79.

35. As quoted in ibid., 384–85.

36. Ibid., 386–89.

37. Bernard Semmel, *Jamaican Blood and Victorian Conscience: The Governor Eyre Controversy*, 2nd ed. (Westport, Conn., 1972), 22–23; Gad Heuman, *The Killing Time: The Morant Bay Rebellion in Jamaica* (London, 1994), 164–65.

38. For effects on racial attitudes, see James Patterson Smith, "The Liberals, Race, and Political Reform in the British West Indies, 1866–74," *Journal of Negro History* 79 (1994): 131–64.

39. Rice, *Rise*, 365; Heuman, *Killing Time*, 172; Catherine Hall, "The Economy of Intellectual Prestige: Thomas Carlyle, John Stuart Mill, and the Case of Governor Eyre," *Cultural Critique* 12 (1989): 167–96, at 185.

40. *Anti-Teapot Review*, Feb. 1867, 5–7.

41. Trollope, *West Indies*, 7.

42. *Nineteenth Century*, Dec. 1883, 1062–1074; Thomas C. Holt, "The Essence of the Contract: The Articulation of Race, Gender, and Political Economy in British Emancipation Policy, 1838–1866," in *Beyond Slavery: Explorations of Race, Labor, and Citizenship in Postemancipation Societies*, ed. Frederick Cooper, Thomas C. Holt, and Rebecca J. Scott (Chapel Hill, N.C., 2000), 54–57.

43. Philip Howell and David Lambert, "Sir John Pope Hennessy and Colonial Government," in *Colonial Lives across the British Empire: Imperial Careering in the Long Nineteenth Century*, ed. David Lambert and Alan Lester (Cambridge, 2006), 242–43.

44. Cruikshank, *Eighteen Years*, 1:305–11, 327–33; PP 1865, v (1), 229.

45. Buxton, *Remedy*, 392; Cruikshank, *Eighteen Years*, 1:190; Perbi, *History*, 153.

46. *PP 1865*, v (1), 82, 127.

47. Cruikshank, *Eighteen Years*, 1:188–89; ibid., 2:50; PP 1842, xi (1), 196, 204; Raymond Dumett and Marion Johnson, "Britain and the Suppression of Slavery in the Gold Coast Colony, Ashanti and the Northern Territories," in *The End of Slavery in Africa*, ed. Suzanne Miers and Richard Roberts (London, 1988), 75; Curtin, *Image*, 307; Temperley, *White Dreams*, 85.

48. NA, CO 96/2, fo. 49: George Maclean to Stanley, 13 Sept. 1843; NA, CO 96/2, fo. 54: Stanley to Maclean, 7 Dec. 1843; NA, CO 267/170, fos. 233–34: William Foster to R. R. Madden, 19 July 1841; Cruikshank, *Eighteen Years*, 1:195; PP 1842, xi (1), v, 25, 42, 50, 151, 193, 262; Perbi, *History*, 159, 160–65.

49. *PP 1865,* v (1), 131–32.

50. Lyons McLeod made a strong claim in 1865 that toleration of pawning in British possessions such as the Gold Coast had gone on long enough, and that Britain now had enough muscle to abolish the institution. However, the committee's report did not make this a priority, whereas the case of Lagos was specifically highlighted. See *PP 1865*, v (1), 168–69. For the reality of "pawning" in African societies, see Miers, *Britain*, 140–43.

51. For examples of this opinion, see PP 1842, xi (1), 32, 60, 164, 259, 276; PP 1865, v (1), 79–81, 84, 112, 200.

52. *PP 1865*, v (1), 229.

53. Cairns, *Prelude*, 139.

54. Durham University, Wylde Papers, WYL/47/60–61: Elton to Wylde, 15 July 1877. The views mirrored Waller's, expressed more than a decade earlier; Yale Divinity School, Horace Waller Papers, Record Group 72, box 1, folder 2: Waller to parents, 20 Oct.–12 Nov. 1861, fo. 4.

55. Arthur Sim, *The Life and Letters of Arthur Fraser Sim: Priest in the Universities' Mission to Central Africa* (London, 1896), 110.

56. Sim, *Life,* 173.

57. Paul Lovejoy, *Transformations in Slavery: A History of Slavery in Africa,* 2nd ed. (Cambridge, 2000 [1983]), 264–65.

58. Cruikshank, *Eighteen Years,* 1:300. It was feared that unleashing such trauma on a society would only cause its collapse, rather than reform: *PP 1865,* v (1), 85, 143.

59. Sir Harry H. Johnston, *A History of the Colonization of Africa by Alien Races* (Cambridge, 1899), 91.

60. *PP 1865,* v (1), 94, 112; for the contrary view, see ibid., 310. See also Perbi, *History,* 164.

61. Compare with Patrick Brantlinger, *Rule of Darkness: British Literature and Imperialism, 1830–1914* (Ithaca, N.Y., 1988), 194–95.

62. Toyin Falola, *Colonialism and Violence in Nigeria* (Bloomington, Ind., 2009), 5.

63. Miers, *Britain,* 157; Suzanne Miers and Richard Roberts, introduction to *The End of Slavery in Africa,* ed. Miers and Roberts (London, 1988), 12–13. As Miers and Roberts note, the comparison between this model and the Gold Coast was problematic, as the Indian Act did not apply to Indian client states.

64. *PP 1865,* v (1), 116.

65. Kwabena Opare-Akurang, "The Administration of the Abolition Laws, African Responses, and Post-Proclamation Slavery in the Gold Coast, 1874–1940," *Slavery and Abolition* 19 (1998): 149–66, at 149–51, 154–56.

66. Raymond E. Dumett, "Pressure Groups, Bureaucracy, and the Decision-making Process: The Case of Slavery Abolition and Colonial Expansion in the Gold Coast, 1874," *JICH* 9 (1981): 193–215, at 203–8.

67. Waller, *Ivory,* 82.

68. As quoted by Cooper, *Slaves to Squatters,* 42; see also Nwulia, *Slavery,* 189.

69. *PP 1865,* v (1), 131; Mann, *Slavery,* 167–79.

70. Bernard Porter, "Review Article: Imperialism and the Scramble," *JICH* 9 (1980): 80.

71. Louis, *Ends,* 116–17; Heartfield, *Aborigines' Protection Society,* 49–54.

72. Sara Berry, "Hegemony on a Shoestring: Indirect Rule and Access to Agricultural Land," *Africa* 62 (1992): 327–55.

73. Nwulia, *Slavery,* 53, 59, 67.

74. Elton, *Travels and Researches,* ed. Cotterill, 72–73, 103, 109–10; Nwulia, *Slavery,* 89, 136–39, 147–48.

75. The coastal strip of Zanzibari territory incorporated into the East Africa Protectorate would wait until 1907 for the legal abolition of slavery: Nwulia, *Slavery,* 196–97.

76. RH, Lugard Papers, Brit. Emp. s.71, fos. 74–78: Frederick Lugard to Sir Charles Dilke, 1 Dec. 1893.

77. Cooper, *Slaves to Squatters,* 47; Nwulia, *Slavery,* 175, 184. Quotation from ibid., 184. See also RH, Lugard Papers, Brit. Emp. s.71: Horace Waller to Frederick Lugard, 18 Oct. 1895.

78. As quoted by Nwulia, *Slavery,* 185, see also 186–87.

79. *Hansard,* 4th ser., 8 Mar. 1895, xxxi, c. 667.

80. RH, Lugard Papers, MS Brit. Emp.s.57, fos. 121–22: Transcript of Frederick Lugard to Edward Lugard, 1 May 1895; RH, Lugard Papers, MS. Brit. Emp. s.71, fos. 14–15: Horace Waller to Frederick Lugard, 22 Jan. 1894; RH, Lugard Papers, MS. Brit. Emp. s.71, fos. 16–17: Horace Waller to Frederick Lugard, 18 Oct. 1895; Horace Waller, *The Case of Our Zanzibar Slaves: Why Not Liberate Them?* (London, 1896).

81. RH, Lugard Papers, MS. Brit. Emp. s.71, fo. 79: Sir Charles Dilke to Frederick Lugard, 2 Dec. 1893.

82. Durham University, Wylde Papers, WYL 67/8: Charles Allen to W. H. Wylde, 13 Mar. 1890; Durham University, Wylde Papers, WYL 67/31: Charles Allen to W. H. Wylde, 25 Mar. 1890.

83. *Hansard,* 4th ser., 1894, xxv, 237.

84. RH, Lugard Papers, MS. Brit. Emp.s.71, fo. 112: "Summary of memorandum re: non-recognition," 22 Aug. 1895.

85. RH, Lugard Papers, MS. Brit. Emp. s.57, fos. 126–27: Transcript of Frederick Lugard to Edward Lugard, 28 Sept. 1895; RH, Lugard Papers MS. Brit. Emp. s.71, fos. 88–89: George Goldie to Frederick Lugard, 21 Aug. 1895.

86. RH, Lugard Papers, MS Brit. Emp. s.57, fos. 106–8: Transcript of Frederick Lugard to Edward Lugard, 3 June 1894.

87. RH, Lugard Papers, Brit. Emp. s.71, fos. 74–78: Frederick Lugard to Sir Charles Dilke, 1 Dec. 1893.

88. On the sincere pursuit of anti-slavery for personal or national glory, see Brown, *Moral Capital.*

89. As quoted by Anne Phillips, *The Enigma of Colonialism: British Policy in West Africa* (London, 1989), 31.

90. Taj Hargey, "Festina Lente: Slavery Policy and Practice in the Anglo-Egyptian Sudan," *Slavery and Abolition* 19 (1998): 250–72, at 251–53, quotation at 252.

91. *Hansard,* 4th ser., 1899, lxxv, 949.

92. For examples of confusion over the legal technicalities, see ibid. and *Hansard,* 4th ser., 1899, lxxv, 672.

93. Frederick Lugard, *The Diaries of Lord Lugard,* ed. Margery Perham, (4 vols., Evanston, Ill., 1959), 4:343–44: entry for 13 Mar. 1898.

94. Lovejoy, *Transformations,* 252–54.

95. Cooper, *Slaves to Squatters,* quotations at 24, 42, but see also 33–41; and Frederick Cooper, *Plantation Slavery on the East Coast of Africa* (Portsmouth, N.H., 1997), 253.

96. Toyin Falola and Matthew M. Heaton, *A History of Nigeria* (Cambridge, 2008), 84.

97. Cooper, *Slaves to Squatters,* 38; Cooper, "From Free Labor," 748.

98. Lovejoy and Hogendorn, *Slow Death,* 5.

99. Paul Lovejoy and J. S. Hogendorn, "The Reform of Slavery in Early Colonial Northern Nigeria," in *The End of Slavery in Africa,* ed. Suzanne Miers and Richard Roberts (Madison, Wis., 1988), 394–95.

100. Lord Frederick Lugard, "Slavery in All its Forms," *Africa* 6 (1933): 1–14.

101. Jan Hogendorn and Paul E. Lovejoy, "Keeping Slaves in Place: The Secret Debate on the Slavery Question in Northern Nigeria, 1900–1904," in *The Atlantic Slave Trade: Effects on Economies, Societies, and Peoples in Africa, the Americas, and Europe,* ed. Joseph E. Inikori and Stanley L. Engerman (Durham, N.C., 1992), 49–76.

102. As quoted by Phillips, *Enigma,* 29.

103. Nwulia, *Slavery,* 199–200.

104. Toyin Falola, "The End of Slavery among the Yoruba," *Slavery and Abolition* 19 (1998): 232–49, at 236–41. For earlier complicity at Lagos, see *PP 1865,* v (1), 69.

105. *Hansard,* 4th ser., 1898, liii, 1355; on Lugard's policy after 1900, see Lovejoy and Hogendorn, *Slow Death,* 32, 38, 81–88.

106. Afigbo, *Abolition,* 30.

107. Hogendorn and Lovejoy, "Keeping Slaves in Place," 49–76.

108. Margery Perham, *Lugard: The Years of Adventure, 1858–1898* (London, 1956), 191–92; on later policy, see C. N. Uba, "Suppression of the Slave Trade in the Nigerian Emirates," *Journal of African History* 32 (1991): 447–70.

109. Hutchinson, *Impressions,* vi; *PP 1842,* xi (1), 36, 153, 169; Miers, *Britain,* 147; Eltis, *Economic Growth,* 28; Curtin, *Image,* 452–53; *Times,* 26 Nov. 1842, 4; Temperley, *White Dreams,* 161.

110. Wm. Roger Louis, "The Berlin Congo Conference and the (Non-) Partition of Africa," in *Ends of British Imperialism: The Scramble for Empire, Suez, and Decolonization* (London, 2006), 84–85.

111. Waller, *Ivory,* 26.

112. Sir Harry Johnston, "England's Work in Central Africa," *Proceedings of the Royal Colonial Institute* 28 (1896–97): 50–75, at 62.

113. As quoted by Cooper, *Slaves to Squatters,* 41.

114. Gerald McSheffrey, "Slavery, Indenture, Legitimate Trade and the Impact of Abolition in the Gold Coast, 1874–1901: A Reappraisal," *Journal of African History* 24 (1983): 349–63, at 353–58.

115. Lovejoy and Hogendorn, *Slow Death,* 12.

116. *Graphic,* 4 Aug. 1888, 110.

117. Eltis, *Economic Growth,* 213–14. He notes that personal taxation was not used to create an artificial need for labor in the colonial period very often.

118. John Edwin Mason, *Social Death and Resurrection: Slavery and Emancipation in South Africa* (Charlottesville, Va., 2008), 10; Wayne Dooling, *Slavery, Emancipation and Colonial Rule in South Africa* (Athens, Ohio, 2007), 149; Elizabeth Elbourne, *Blood Ground: Colonialism, Missions, and the Contest for Christianity in the Cape Colony and Britain, 1799–1853* (Montreal, 2002).

119. Mason, *Social Death,* 252.

120. Davis, *Slavery,* 307; see also Antoinette Burton, "States of Injury: Josephine Butler on Slavery, Citizenship, and the Boer War," *Social Politics* 5 (1998): 338–61; British and Foreign Anti-Slavery Society, *The Boers and Slavery in South Africa: Statement of the British and Foreign Anti-Slavery Society* (London, 1881).

121. Grant, *Civilised Savagery,* 80–92, 104–6; Andrew S. Thompson, *The Empire Strikes Back? The Impact of Imperialism on Britain from the Mid-Nineteenth Century* (Harlow, Essex, 2005), 69–74.

122. *Hansard,* 4th ser., 1894, xxv, 243.

123. *Hansard,* 4th ser., 1895, xxxiv, 1094, 1113, 1116–17.

124. Durham University, Wylde Papers, WYL 69/1920: BFASS Memorial to Lord Kimberley regarding the Mombassa-Victoria railroad, 21 July 1894.

125. Thomas R. Metcalf, *Imperial Connections: India in the Indian Ocean Arena, 1860–1920* (Berkeley, 1998), 188.

126. Durham University, Wylde Papers, WYL 49/10–14: R. B. D. Morier to W. H. Wylde, 27 Feb. 1878.

127. As quoted by Grant, *Civilised Savagery,* 118.

128. As quoted by ibid., 119.

129. Ibid., 29, 40–42; Frederick Cooper, "Conditions Analogous to Slavery: Imperialism and Free Labor Ideology in Africa," in *Beyond Slavery: Explorations of Race, Labor, and Citizenship in Postemancipation Societies,* ed. Frederick Cooper, Thomas C. Holt, and Rebecca J. Scott (Chapel Hill, N.C., 2000), 129–30.

130. Lovejoy, *Transformations,* 267; Lorimer, *Colour,* 100; on British labor and "free labor," see Mark Curthoys, *Governments, Labour, and the Law in Mid-Victorian Britain: The Trade Union Legislation of the 1870s* (Oxford, 2004).

131. As quoted by Phillips, *Enigma,* 28.

132. Lovejoy, *Transformations,* 252; see also the excellent case study by G. Ugo Nwokegi, "The Slave Emancipation Problematic: Igbo Society and the Colonial Equation," *Comparative Studies in Society and History* 40 (1998): 318–55.

133. Duke University, Samuel Wilberforce papers: Samuel Baker to Samuel Wilberforce, 24 Oct. 1869; emphasis in original.

134. Note the situation in Fiji: Heartfield, *Aborigines' Protection Society,* 189.

135. Driver, "Henry Morton Stanley," 159, 162.

136. Waller, *Ivory,* 45–50.

137. Nwulia, *Slavery,* 105.

138. Sir Harry H. Johnston, *British Central Africa: An Attempt to Give Some Account of the Territories Under British Influence North of the Zambezi* (London, 1897), 156–57.

139. Cairns, *Prelude,* 237, 299 n21.

140. Ibid., 237.

141. Elton, *Travels and Researches,* ed. Cotterill, 19–20.

142. Lorimer, *Colour,* 69.

143. Ibid., 92–93, 210–11.

144. The significance of this remark is highlighted in Bratton, "English Ethiopians," 128.

145. Though, for caution over evidence of tolerance for African Americans in the 1850s, see Rice, *Rise,* 47–48; Blackett, *Building,* 159–61.

146. Blackett, "Cracks," 201.

147. Lorimer, *Colour,* 202.

148. Ibid., 160–61.

149. Drescher, "Ending," 419–20, 430; Sadiah Querishi, "Robert Gordon Latham, Displayed Peoples, and the Natural History of Race, 1854–1866," *HJ* 54 (2011): 143–66, at 163–66.

150. Colin Kidd, *The Forging of Races: Race and Scripture in the Protestant Atlantic World, 1600–2000* (Cambridge, 2006), 152–63.

151. Nancy Stepan, *The Idea of Race in Science: Great Britain, 1800–1960* (London, 1982), 40–82; Cairns, *Prelude*, 91.

152. Benjamin Kidd, *Social Evolution* (London, 1894), 49, 140–42, 160.

153. As cited in Ali, *Slavery in the Sudan*, 35.

154. Durham University, Wylde Papers, WYL 27/13–15: Governor Freeman to W. H. Wylde, 9 Apr. 1864; Durham University, Wylde Papers, WYL 27/16–20: Governor Freeman to W. H. Wylde, 9 June 1864.

155. Durham University, Wylde Papers, WYL 28/21–26: Commodore Wilmot to W. H. Wylde, 14 May 1865.

156. Johnston, "British West Africa," 97–98; Oliver, *Sir Harry Johnston*, 271; Cairns, *Prelude*, 90.

157. Frederick Lugard, *The Rise of Our East African Empire: Early Efforts in Nyasaland and Uganda* (London, 1893), 28.

158. *ASR*, 1 July 1858, 161; Deborah A. Logan, *Harriet Martineau, Victorian Imperialism, and the Civilizing Mission* (Farnham, Surrey, 2010), 235.

159. Holt, *Problem*, 283–85; Hall, *Civilising Subjects*, 348–51.

160. Lorimer, *Colour*, 209–10; Cooper, "Conditions," 115. See also Darwin's late accommodation with gradual "improvement" and racial inferiority: Desmond and Moore, *Darwin's Scared Cause*, 88–93, 100–116, 129–30, 330, 356, 365–68.

161. Laidlaw, "Heathens," 133, 137.

## 8. IDEOLOGIES OF FREEDOM

1. Buxton, *Remedy*, 13. He directly quoted the younger Pitt.

2. The poem is from BFASS, *Proceedings…1840* (London, 1841), 122; presumably due to Stanton's memory or the secretaries' error, the punctuation and word choices vary from the version printed in Whittier, *Poems*, 38.

3. Harriet Beecher Stowe, *A Reply to 'The Affectionate Address of the Women of Great Britain and Ireland'* (London, 1863), 62.

4. Douglass, *Frederick Douglass Papers*, ed. Blassingame, 1:420.

5. Ward, *Autobiography*, 290.

6. Ibid., 299.

7. Davis, *Slavery*, 213–14.

8. Ward, *Autobiography*, 206.

9. Ibid., 325.

10. As quoted by Brauer, "Slavery," 460, 466.

11. This point develops one made by Dumett, "Pressure Groups," 210–11; Mulligan, "British Anti-Slave Trade and Anti-Slavery Policy", 262–63.

12. Waller, *Ivory*, 79.

13. Paul Lovejoy, "Slavery in the Context of Ideology," in *The Ideology of Slavery in Africa*, ed. Paul Lovejoy (Beverly Hills, Calif., 1981), 16, 19.

14. In his early work on British anti-slavery, David Brion Davis suggests that anti-slavery succeeded because it did not challenge the free-labor ideology on which industrial exploitation was based. Davis does not maintain this as an explanation for the emergence and popularity of anti-slavery politics, merely for their acceptability to elites: David Brion Davis, *In the Image of God: Religion, Moral Values, and Our Heritage of Slavery* (New Haven, Conn., 2001), 218.

15. Bo Stråth, "Ideology and History," *Journal of Political Ideologies* 11 (2006): 23–42, at 39.

16. See Adam Tooze, *The Wages of Destruction: The Making and Breaking of the Nazi Economy* (London, 2006), xx–xxv; Trentmann, "Political Culture," 217–51. For similar

problems with "interest," see Thomas Haskell, "Capitalism and the Origins of Humanitarian Sensibility, I," in *The Antislavery Debate: Capitalism and Abolitionism as a Problem in Historical Explanation,* ed. Thomas Bender (Berkeley, 1992), 123; Porter, "Review Article," 77.

17. On the debate in the social sciences, see Joachim Zweynert, "Interests versus Culture in the Theory of Institutional Change?" *Journal of Institutional Economics* 5 (2009): 339–60.

18. Cooper, *Slaves to Squatters,* 24, 33.

19. This answers a challenge Cooper laid down thirty years ago in ibid.

20. Darwin, *Empire Project,* 3–4.

21. Frederick Holmwood, introduction to Elton, *Travels and Researches,* ed. Cotterill, 3.

22. On material interests and ideology, see Cooper, *Slaves to Squatters,* 24.

23. Magee and Thompson, *Empire,* 13, 38.

24. Cooper, "Conditions," 116, 129.

25. On ideology and knowledge, see Teun A. Van Dijk, "Ideology and Discourse Analysis," *Journal of Political Ideologies* 11 (2006): 115–40, at 130–31.

26. See Stanley L. Engerman, "Slavery, Freedom, and Sen," *Feminist Economics* 9 (2003): 185–211, for a consideration of slavery and gender using Sen's work; Hopkins, "'New International Economic Order'" for the "development plan"; Hopkins, "Property Rights," 777–78.

27. For a classic statement of his wide publications on the subject, see Amartya Sen, *Development as Freedom* (Oxford, 1999). The capabilities approach has also been developed by Martha Nussbaum in works such as *Creating Capabilities: The Human Development Approach* (Cambridge, Mass., 2011).

28. For a similar observation, see Cooper, "Conditions," 115.

29. For the spectrum of free-labor ideologies within American anti-slavery, see Eric Foner, *Free Soil, Free Labor, Free Men: The Ideology of the Republican Party before the Civil War* (Oxford, 1970).

30. Sen, *Development,* 28–30; Mason, *Social Death,* 252.

31. Cairns, *Prelude,* 197, 218.

32. James Froude, *The English in the West Indies, Or the Bow of Ulysses* (2 vols., London, 1888), 1:98–99.

33. Ibid., 1:235; Eric Williams, *British Historians and the West Indies* (London, 1966), 177.

34. Johnston, *History,* 101–2.

35. See, for example, Cooper, "Essence," 53–59; George Boulukos, *The Grateful Slave: The Emergence of Race in Eighteenth-Century British and American Culture* (Cambridge, 2008).

36. Framed in a very different way, Holt considers development economics in Holt, *Problem,* 401.

37. Cooper, *Squatters,* 27.

38. Mantena, *Alibis,* 173–75.

39. Lovejoy, "Slavery," 12–14.

40. On this dilemma, see Davis, *Slavery,* 306.

41. Cooper, "Networks," 46.

42. As quoted by Keene, "Case Study," 329.

43. Follett, "After Emancipation," 123–24; Andrew F. Walls, "The Legacy of Thomas Fowell Buxton," *International Bulletin of Missionary Research* 15 (1991): 74–77; Laidlaw, "Heathens," 152; Laidlaw, *Colonial Connections,* 145–53; Alan Lester, *Imperial Networks: Creating Identities in Nineteenth-Century South Africa and Britain* (London, 2001), 105–30; Elbourne, *Blood Ground,* 287–91.

44. On the origins of anti-imperialism, see Gregory Claeys, "The 'Left' and the Critique of Empire, c. 1865–1900: Three Roots of Humanitarian Foreign Policy," in *Victorian Visions of Global Order: Empire and International Relations in Nineteenth-Century Political Thought,* ed. Duncan Bell (Cambridge, 2007), 239–66; on Fiji, see O. W. Parnaby, *Britain and the Labor Trade in the Southwest Pacific* (Durham, N.C., 1964), 43; Heartfield, *Aborigines' Protection Society,* 164–203.

45. Andrew Porter, "Trusteeship," 215; H. C. Swaisland, "Frederick Chesson," *ODNB;* Douglas Lorimer, "From Victorian Values to White Virtues: Assimilation and Exclusion in British Racial Discourse, c. 1870–1914," in *Rediscovering the British World,* ed. Phillip Buckner and R. Douglas Francis (Calgary, Alberta, 2005), 109–134, at 127; Heartfield, *Aborigines' Protection Society,* 43, 306.

46. Eltis, *Economic Growth,* 122.

47. Tooze, *Wages,* xx.

48. On perfect virtue, see W. E. H. Lecky, *The Natural History of European Morals* (2 vols., London, 1869), 1:161. For a subtle consideration of Lecky's view, see Davis, *Inhuman Bondage,* 234. For a view of anti-slavery policy as conspiracy, see Sherwood, *After Abolition,* 175–77.

49. RH, Lugard papers, MS. Brit. Emp. s.71, fo. 94: James Knowles to Frederick Lugard, 17 Oct. 1895.

50. Žižek, *Parallax View,* 5.

51. Jean Allain, "The Definition of Slavery in International Law," *Howard Law Journal* 52 (2009): 239–75.

# Bibliography

———

PRIMARY SOURCES

*Private Papers and Manuscripts*

Aberdeen Papers, British Library, U.K.

Acquisitions Collection, Harriet Beecher Stowe Center, Hartford, Conn.

Anti-Slavery Papers, Rhodes House Library, Oxford, U.K.

Backhouse Papers, David M. Rubenstein Rare Books and Manuscript Library, Duke University, Durham, N.C.

Bandinel Papers, David M. Rubenstein Rare Books and Manuscript Library, Duke University, Durham, N.C.

Beecher-Stowe Family Papers, Schlesinger Library, Cambridge, Mass.

Lydia Maria Child Papers, Microfilms from Library of Congress, Washington, D.C.

Katharine S. Day Collection, Harriet Beecher Stowe Center, Hartford, Conn.

The Gilder-Lehrman Collection, New-York Historical Society, N.Y.

Great Britain Savannah Consulate Papers, David M. Rubenstein Rare Books and Manuscript Library, Duke University, Durham, N.C.

Duff Green Papers, Microfilms from Southern Historical Collection, University of North Carolina at Chapel Hill

Hobhouse Papers, Microfilms from British Library, London, U.K.

Lugard Papers, Rhodes House Library, Oxford, U.K.

Alma Lutz Collection, Schlesinger Library, Cambridge, Mass.

Palmerston Papers, Broadlands Manuscripts, University of Southampton, U.K.

Edwin Parker Journal, Plymouth and West Devon Record Office, U.K.

Marquis of Ripon Papers, David M. Rubenstein Rare Books and Manuscript Library, Duke University, Durham, N.C.

Russell Papers, National Archives, U.K.

Joseph Sturge Papers, British Library, London, U.K.

Lewis Tappan Papers, Microfilms from Library of Congress, Washington, D.C.

Horace Waller Papers, Rhodes House Library, Oxford, U.K.

Horace Waller Papers, Yale Divinity School, New Haven, Conn.

Samuel Wilberforce Papers, David M. Rubenstein Rare Books and Manuscript Library, Duke University, Durham, N.C.

Wilder Scrapbook, David M. Rubenstein Rare Books and Manuscript Library, Duke University, Durham, N.C.

Wylde Papers, Durham University, U.K.

Francis Yates Aglionby Papers, David M. Rubenstein Rare Books and Manuscript Library, Duke University, Durham, N.C.

*Official Papers*

Colonial Office Papers, National Archives
   CO 96/2
   CO 96/24
   CO 267/170
Foreign Office Papers, National Archives
   FO 54/2
   FO 84/2, 333, 373, 486, 598, 648, 919, 1034, 1141, 1305
   FO 97/430
Hansard, *Parliamentary Debates,* 3rd and 4th series
*Parliamentary Papers*

*Periodicals and Newspapers*

*Aberdeen Journal, Aberdeen Weekly Journal, All The Year Round, Anti-Slavery Reporter, Anti-Teapot Review, Birmingham Daily Post, Bristol Mercury and Western Counties Advertiser, British Emancipator, Broad Views, Caledonian Mercury, Central Africa, Chambers's Edinburgh Journal, Chambers's Journal, Daily News, Derby Mercury, Dundee Courier and Argus, Economist, Essex County Standard, Examiner, Fortnightly Review, Fraser's Magazine, Glasgow Herald, Graphic, Hampshire Telegraph and Sussex Chronicle, Household Words, Huddersfield Chronicle and West Yorkshire Advertiser, Illustrated London News, Journal of the Society of Arts, Lancaster Gazette, Law Magazine and Review, Leeds Mercury, Liberator, Liverpool Mercury, Lloyd's Weekly London Paper, Lloyd's Weekly Newspaper, Manchester Examiner and Times, Mirror of Literature, Amusement and Instruction, Morning Chronicle, Morning Post, Morning Star, National Review, Nineteenth Century, Northern Echo, North Wales Chronicle, Pall Mall Gazette, Penny Illustrated Paper, People's Paper, Popular Science Review, Preston Chronicle and Lancashire Advertiser, Proceedings of the Royal Colonial Institute, Punch, Quarterly Review, Reynolds's Newspaper, Royal Cornwall Gazette, Sheffield and Rotherham Independent, Spectator, Times, Weekly Review and Dramatic Critic, Wesleyan-Methodist Magazine, Westminster Review*

*Printed Publications*

Adams, Charles, ed. *Slavery, Secession & Civil War: Views from the United Kingdom and Europe* (Lanham, Md., 2007).
Anderson-Morshead, A. E. M. *The History of the Universities' Mission to Central Africa, 1859–1896* (London, 1897).
Arch, Joseph. *Joseph Arch: The Story of his Life,* ed. Countess of Warwick (London, 1898).
Ballad Sheet of *"Song composed by H.B. Brown on his escape from slavery," "The slave's song," and "Freedom's* Star" (n.d., n.p.) [JJC, Slavery 2].
Baring, Francis Thornhill. *Journals and Correspondence of Francis Thornhill Baring,* ed. T. G. Baring, 2 vols. (London, 1902).
Barnard, Frederick L. *A Three Years' Cruize in the Mozambique Channel for the Suppression of the Slave Trade* (London, 1848).
Beecham, John. *Ashantee and the Gold Coast* (London, 1841).
Beecher, Charles. *Harriet Beecher Stowe in Europe: The Journal of Charles Beecher,* ed. Joseph S. Van Why and Earl French (Hartford, Conn., 1986).
Beecher Stowe, Harriet. *A Reply to "The Affectionate Address of the Women of Great Britain and Ireland"* (London, 1863).
Beldam, Joseph. *A Review of the Late Proposed Measure for the Reduction of the Duties on Sugar* (London, 1841).
Bell, Kenneth N., and W. P. Morell, eds. *Select Documents on British Colonial Policy, 1830–1860* (Oxford, 1928).
Benton, William Hart. *Thirty Years View,* 2 vols. (New York, 1856).
Beresford Hope, A. J. B. *The American Disruption,* 6th ed. (London, 1862).
Blackman, E. L. *Shall We Recognise the Confederate States?* (Ipswich, 1863).

Bright, John. *The Struggle in America in Relation to the Working Men of Britain* (n.p., 1863).

British and Foreign Anti-Slavery Society. *The Boers and Slavery in South Africa: Statement of the British and Foreign Anti-Slavery Society* (London, 1881)

——. *Proceedings of the General Anti-Slavery Convention, called by the committee of the British and Foreign Anti-Slavery Society, and held in London, from Friday, June 12th, to Tuesday, June 23rd, 1840* (London, 1841).

——. *Proceedings of the General Anti-Slavery Convention, called by the Committee of the British and Foreign Anti-Slavery Society and held in London from Tuesday, June 13th, to Tuesday, June 20th, 1843* (London, 1843).

Brown, John. *Slave Life in Georgia: A Narrative of the Life, Sufferings, and Escape of John Brown, a Fugitive Slave, Now in England*, ed. L. A. Chamerovzow (London, 1855).

Brown, William Wells. *Three Years in Europe; or Places I have seen and People I Have Met* (London, 1852).

Burritt, Elihu. *Twenty Reasons for the Total Abstinence from Slave Produce* (London, n.d. [1853?]).

Buxton, Thomas Fowell. *The African Slave Trade* (London, 1839).

——. *The African Slave Trade and Its Remedy*, 2nd ed. (London, 1840).

——. *Letter on the Slave Trade to the Lord Viscount Melbourne* (London, 1838).

——. *The Remedy* (London, 1840).

Cairnes, John Elliot. *The Slave Power*, 2nd ed. (London, 1863).

Carlyle, Thomas. *Occasional Discourse on the Nigger Question* (London, 1853).

——. *Shooting Niagara–and after?* (London, 1867).

——. "Thomas Carlyle to Beverley Tucker, 21 Oct. 1850," reprinted in *Harper's Magazine*, Oct. 1885, 797–800.

Carpenter, Russell Lant. *Observations on American Slavery, After a Year's Tour in the United States* (London, 1852).

Carter, Sir Gilbert. "The Colony of Lagos." *Proceedings of the Royal Colonial Institute* 28 (1896–97), 275–305.

Channing, William E. *Thoughts on the Evils of a Spirit of Conquest, and on Slavery* (London, 1837).

Church Missionary Society. *The Slave Trade of East Africa* (London, 1868).

Clarkson, Thomas. *The History of the Rise, Progress, and Accomplishment of the Abolition of the African Slave-Trade by the British Parliament* (London, 1839 [1808]).

[Cobbe, Frances Power]. *Rejoinder to Mrs. Stowe's Reply to the Address of the Women of England* (London, 1863).

Cobden, John C. *The White Slaves of England: Compiled from Official Documents* (New York, 1860).

Conder, Josiah. *The Choir and the Oratory* (London, 1837).

Copley, Esther. *A History of Slavery and its Abolition*, 2nd ed. (London, 1844)

Crowther, Samuel, and Henry Townsend. *Slave Trade–African Squadron, Letters from the Rev. Samuel Crowther, A Native of the Yoruba Country, and a Clergyman of the Church of England at Abbeokuta and the Rev. Henry Townsend of the Church Missionary Society at Abbeokuta* (London, 1850).

Cruikshank, Brodie. *Eighteen Years on the Gold Coast*, 2 vols. (London, 1853).

Cruikshank, Robert. *The Condition of the West India Slave Contrasted with that of the Infant Slave in our English Factories* (London, n.d.).

Denman, Joseph. *Practical Remarks on the Slave Trade of the West Coast of Africa* (London, 1839).

——. *The Slave Trade, The African Squadron and Mr. Hutt's Committee* (N.p, n.d [1849?]).

——. *West India Interests, African Emigration, and Slave Trade* (Worcester, 1848).

Denman, Lord Thomas. *The Destruction of Lagos* (London, 1852).

——. *Uncle Tom's Cabin, Bleak House, Slavery and the Slave Trade* (London, 1853).

Dickens, Charles. *American Notes for General Circulation*, ed. Patricia Ingham (London, 2000 [1842]).

Disraeli, Benjamin. *Lord George Bentinck* (London, 1852).

Douglass, Frederick. *The Frederick Douglass Papers: Series One*, ed. John W. Blassingame, 5 vols. (New Haven, Conn., 1979).

Ellison, Thomas. *Slavery and Secession in America, Historical and Economical; Together with a Practical Scheme of Emancipation*, 2nd ed. (London, 1862 [1861]).

Elton, J. Frederic. *Travels and Researches Among the Lakes and Mountains and Central Africa: From the Journals of the Late J. Frederic Elton, FRGS*, ed. H. B. Cotterill (London, 1879).

Estlin, J. B. *A Brief Notice of American Slavery and the Abolition Movement* (London, 1853).

*Free Church Alliance with Manstealers: Send Back the Money* (Glasgow, 1846).

*The Free Church and Her Accusers: The Question at Issue* (Glasgow, 1846).

*Free Trade in Negroes* (London, 1849).

Froude, James. *The English in the West Indies, Or the Bow of Ulysses*, 2 vols. (London, 1888).

Garrison, Wendell Phillips, and Francis Jackson Garrison. *William Lloyd Garrison: The Story of his life, told by his children*, 4 vols. (New York, 1885–89).

Gordon, Ann D., ed. *The Selected Papers of Elizabeth Cady Stanton and Susan B. Anthony* (New Brunswick, N.J., 1997).

Grattan, Thomas Colley. *England and the Disrupted States of America* (London, 1861).

Hammond, James Henry. *Letter of his Excellency Governor Hammond to the Free Church of Glasgow on the Subject of Slavery* (Columbia, S.C., 1844).

Haydon, Benjamin Robert. *The Diary of Benjamin Robert Haydon*, ed. Willard Bissell Pope, 5 vols. (Cambridge, Mass., 1963).

Helps, Sir Arthur. *The Spanish Conquest in America and its Relation to the History of Slavery and the Government of the Colonies*, 4 vols. (London, 1855–61).

[Helps, Arthur]. "The author of 'Friends in Council.'" *A Letter on Uncle Tom's Cabin* (Cambridge, 1852).

Henson, Josiah. *Father Henson's Story of His Own Life* (Boston, Mass., 1858).

Hollis, Patricia, ed. *Class and Class Conflict in Nineteenth-Century England, 1815–1850* (London, 1976).

Huntley, H. V. *Observations upon the Free Trade Policy of England in Connexion with the Sugar Act of 1846* (London, 1849).

Hutchinson, Edward. *The Slave Trade of East Africa* (London, 1874).

Hutchinson, Thomas. *Impressions of Western Africa* (London, 1858).

Innes, John. *Thoughts on the Present State of the West India Colonies* (London, 1840).

James, G. P. R. *The Old Dominion*, 3 vols. (London, 1856).

Johnston, Sir Harry H. *British Central Africa: An Attempt to Give Some Account of the Territories Under British Influence North of the Zambezi* (London, 1897).

——. "The British Central Africa Protectorate." *Geographical Journal* 5 (1895): 193–214.

——. "British West Africa and the Trade of the Interior." *Proceedings of the Royal Colonial Institute* 20 (1889): 90–111.

——. "England's Work in Central Africa." *Proceedings of the Royal Colonial Institute* 28 (1896–97): 50–75.

——.*A History of the Colonization of Africa by Alien Races* (Cambridge, 1899).

Kidd, Benjamin. *Social Evolution* (London, 1894).

Kingston, William. *Blue Jackets or, Chips of the Old Block: A Narrative of the Gallant Exploits* (London, 2006 [1854]).

Laird, Macgregor, and R. A. K. Oldfield. *Narrative of an Expedition into the Interior of Africa*, 2 vols. (London, 1837).

Landor, Henry. *The Best Way to Stop the Slave Trade* (London, 1850).

Lecky, W. E. H. *The Natural History of European Morals*, 2 vols. (London, 1869).

Livingstone, Charles, and David Livingstone. *Narrative of an Expedition to the Zambesi and its Tributaries* (London, 1865).

Livingstone, David. *Livingstone's Last Journals*, ed. Horace Waller, 2 vols. (London, 1874).

——. *Missionary Travels and Researches in South Africa* (London, 1857).

Lobb, John. *The Young People's Illustrated Edition of Uncle Tom's Story of his Life (from 1789 to 1877)* (London, 1877).

Lothian, Marquis of. *The Confederate Secession* (London, 1864).

Lovett, William. *The Life and Struggles of William Lovett*, ed. R. H. Tawney, 2 vols. (New York, 1920 [London, 1876]).

——. *Social and Political Morality* (London, 1853)

Lugard, Frederick. *The Diaries of Lord Lugard*, ed. Margery Perham, 4 vols. (Evanston, Ill., 1959).

——. *The Rise of Our East African Empire: Early Efforts in Nyasaland and Uganda* (London, 1893).

——. "Slavery in All its Forms." *Africa* 6 (1933): 1–14.

Lyell, Charles. *A Second Visit to the United States of North America*, 2 vols. (London, 1849).

——. *Travels in North America with Geological Observations on the United States, Canada and Nova Scotia*, 2 vols. (London, 1845).

Maine, Henry. *Ancient Law: Its Connection with the Early History of Society and its Relation to Modern Ideas*, 3rd American ed. (New York, 1873 [London, 1861]).

Marryat, Frederick. *A Diary in America*, 3 vols. (London, 1839).

Martineau, Harriet. *Society in America*, 3 vols. (New York, 1966 [London, 1837]).

Marx, Karl, and Frederick Engels. *The Collected Works of Karl Marx and Frederick Engels* (47 vols. to date, London, 1978–).

*The Massacres at Dahomey* (n.p., n.d. [1862?]) [JJC, Slavery 2].

Melbourne, Lord. *Lord Melbourne's Papers*, ed. L. C. Sanders (London, 1880).

Memorandum by the Earl of Minto. Inserted in Bodleian Library's copy of T. F. Buxton, *A Letter on the Slave Trade* (London, 1838), Bod., shelfmark: Bod. 2475 d.67.

Merivale, Herman. *Lectures on Colonization and Colonies*, 2 vols. (London, 1840–41).

Mill, J. S. *Dissertations and Discussions: Political, Philosophical, and Historical*, 3 vols. (Boston, 1865 [4 vols., London, 1859–79]).

——. *Principles of Political Economy*, 2 vols. (London, 1848).

Mitchell, D. W. *Ten Years Residence in the United States* (London, 1862).

Mortimer, Mrs. Favell Lee. *Far Off; or Africa and America Described*, 2 vols. (London, 1854).

Murray, Amelia. *Letters from the United States, Cuba and Canada* (London, 1857).

New, Charles. *Life, Wanderings, and Labours in Eastern Africa* (London, 1874).

Newbury, C. W., ed. *British Policy towards West Africa: Select Documents 1875–1914* (Oxford, 1971).

Omnium, Jacob. *Is Cheap Sugar The Triumph of Free Trade?* (London, 1847).

"One of the Protestant party." *Random Recollections of Exeter Hall* (London, 1838).

"Philo-Americanus." *The American Struggle: An Appeal to the People of the North* (London, 1862).

"A Plain Man." *The True State of the Question* (London, 1792).

"A Poor Peacemaker." *The Slavery Quarrel* (London, 1863).

Porter, G. R. *The Progress of the Nation, in its Various Social and Economical Relations* (London, 1843 [1836]).

"A resident in the West Indies for thirteen years." *The British West India Colonies* (London, 1853).

Ritchie, James Ewing. *Thoughts on Slavery and Cheap Sugar* (London, 1844).

Ripley, C. Peter, ed. *The Black Abolitionist Papers*, 5 vols. (London, 1985).

Russell, Henry. *Henry Russell's New and Vocal Pictorial Entertainment entitled The Far West or the Emigrants' Progress from the Old World to the New and Negro Life!* (London, n.d.).

Russell, R. W. *America Compared with England: The Respective Social Effects of the American and English Systems of Government and Legislation* (London, 1849).

Scoble, John. *Great Exhibition and American Slavery* (n.p., 1850).

——. *Texas: Its Claims to be Recognised as an Independent Power by Great Britain Examined in a Series of Letters* (London, 1839).

Sherard, Robert Harborough. *The Child Slaves of Britain* (London, 1905).

——. *The White Slaves of England* (London, 1895).

Sim, Arthur. *The Life and Letters of Arthur Fraser Sim: Priest in the Universities' Mission to Central Africa* (London, 1896).

"Slave Life!" 1852 broadside advertisement [GLC, GLC05508].

*Slave Sugar In A Nutshell* (London, 1850).

Society for the Extinction of the Slave Trade and for the Civilization of Africa. *Prospectus of the Society for the Extinction of the Slave Trade, and for the Civilization of Africa* (London, 1840).

Spence, James. *The American Union* (London, 1861).

Stephen, Sir George ["A Barrister"]. *Analysis of the Evidence Given Before the Select Committee on the Slave Trade* (London, 1850).

——. *Antislavery Recollections: In a Series of Letters addressed to Mrs. Beecher Stowe, at Her Request* (London, 1854).

——. Introduction to *American Slavery Discussed in Congress*, ed. George Stephen (London, 1853), i–xxxvi.

——. *The Niger Trade Considered in Connection with the African Blockade* (London, 1849).

Stevenson, James. *The Water Highways of the Interior of Africa, with notes on Slave Hunting and the means of its Suppression* (Glasgow, 1883).

Stirling, James. *Letters from the Slave States* (London, 1857).

Sturge, Joseph, and Thomas Harvey. *The West Indies in 1837: Being a Visit to Antigua, Montserrat, Dominica, St. Lucia, Barbados and Jamaica* (London, 1838).

Tait, William. *Slave-Trade Overruled for the Salvation of Africa* (London, 1851).

Taylor, Clare, ed. *British and American Abolitionists: An Episode in Transatlantic Understanding* (Edinburgh, 1974).

"T. H." *Are the West India Colonies to be Preserved?* (London, 1840).

Thomas, Rev. Alfred C. *Prayer Sympathy Invoked for America: A Sermon Preached at Cross Street Chapel, Islington* (Philadelphia, 1863).

Thompson, George, and Henry C. Wright. *The Free Church of Scotland and American Slavery* (Edinburgh, 1846).

Tillotson, John. *Tales About Animals* (London, 1858).

Trimble, Robert. *The Negro, North and South* (London, 1863).

Trollope, Anthony. *The West Indies and the Spanish Main* (London, 1859).

Trollope, Frances. *Domestic Manners of the Americans*, 5th ed. (London, 1839 [1832]).

Turnbull, David. *The Jamaica Movement* (London, 1849).

——. *Travels in the West* (London, 1840; facsimile New York, 1969).

*Uncle Tom in England* (London, 1852).

*Uncle Tom's Cabin Almanack, or Abolitionist Momento* (London, 1853).

Waller, Horace. *The Case of Our Zanzibar Slaves; Why Not Liberate Them?* (London, 1896).

——. *Ivory, Apes, Peacocks: An African Contemplation* (London, 1891).

——. *Nyassaland: Great Britain's Case against Portugal* (London, 1890).

Ward, Samuel Ringgold. *Autobiography of a Fugitive Negro: His Anti-Slavery Labours in the United States, Canada and England* (London, 1855).

Webster, Daniel. *The Works of Daniel Webster*, ed. Edward Everett, 6th ed., 6 vols. (Boston, 1853 [1851]).

Whately, Richard. *Life and Correspondence of Richard Whately*, ed. E. J. Whately, 2 vols. (London, 1866).

Wheeler, George B., ed. *The Southern Confederacy and the African Slave Trade: The Correspondence between Professor Cairnes, A.M., and George McHenry Esq.* (Dublin, 1863).

Whittier, John Greenleaf. *Poems Written During the Progress of the Abolition Question in the United States, Between 1830 and 1838* (Boston, 1837).

Wilberforce, Samuel. *Cheap Sugar Means Cheap Slaves* (London, 1848).

Willard, Joseph. *Letter to an English Friend on the Rebellion in the United States and British Policy* (Boston, 1863).

*William Craft's Mission to Dahomey* (n.p., n.d. [1863?]) [JJC, Slavery 2].

Williams, James. *A Narrative of Events, Since the First of August, 1834, by James Williams, An Apprenticed Labourer in Jamaica*, ed. Diana Paton (Durham, N.C., 2001 [London, 1837]).

Wood, Marcus, ed. *The Poetry of Slavery: An Anglo-American Anthology* (Oxford, 2003).

## SECONDARY SOURCES

Adams, Ephraim Douglass. *British Interests and Activities in Texas, 1838–1846* (Baltimore, Md., 1910).

——. "Lord Ashburton and the Treaty of Washington." *American Historical Review* 17 (1912): 764–82.

Adderley, Rosanne Marion. *"New Negroes from Africa": Slave Trade Abolition and Free African Settlement in the Nineteenth-Century Caribbean* (Bloomington, Ind., 2006).

Afigbo, A. E. *The Abolition of the Slave Trade in Southeastern Nigeria, 1885–1950* (Rochester, N.Y., 2006).

Ali, Abbas Ibrahim Muhammad. *The British, the Slave Trade and Slavery in the Sudan, 1820–1881* (Khartoum, Sudan, 1972).

Allain, Jean. "The Definition of Slavery in International Law." *Howard Law Journal* 52 (2009): 239–75.

Allen, Bernard M. "Livingstone and Gordon." *Journal of the Royal African Society* 40 (1941): 121–27.

Allen, Richard B. "Suppressing a Nefarious Traffic: Britain and the Abolition of Slave Trading in India and the Western Indian Ocean, 1770–1830." *William and Mary Quarterly,* 3rd ser., 66 (2009): 873–94.

Altick, Richard. *The English Common Reader: A Social History of the Mass Reading Public, 1800–1900,* 2nd ed. (Columbus, Ohio1998).

——. *Punch: The Lively Youth of a British Institution 1841–51* (Columbus, Ohio, 1997).

——. *The Shows of London* (Cambridge, Mass., 1978).

Anderson, Michael. "India, 1858–1930: The Illusion of Free Labor." In *Masters, Servants, and Magistrates in Britain and the Empire, 1562–1955,* edited by Douglas Hay and Paul Craven, 422–54 (Chapel Hill, N.C., 2004).

Ansdell, Douglas B. A. "William Lloyd Garrison's Ambivalent Approach to Labour Reform." *Journal of American Studies* 24 (1990): 402–7.

Anstey, Roger T. *Britain and the Congo in the Nineteenth Century* (Oxford, 1962).

——."Capitalism and Slavery—A Critique." *Economic History Review,* 2nd ser., 21 (1968): 307–20.

Asiegbu, Johnson U. J. "The Dynamics of Freedom: A Study of Liberated African Emigration and British Antislavery Policy." *Journal of Black Studies* 7 (1976): 95–106.

——. *Slavery and the Politics of Liberation: A Study of Liberated African Emigration and British Anti-Slavery Policy* (London, 1969).

Auerbach, Jeffery A. *The Great Exhibition of 1851: A Nation on Display* (New Haven, Conn., 1999).

Austen, Ralph A., and Woodruff D. Smith. "Images of Africa and British Slave-Trade Abolition: The Transition to an Imperialist Ideology, 1787–1807." *African Historical Studies* 2 (1969): 69–83.

Baer, Gabriel. "Slavery in Nineteenth Century Egypt." *Journal of African History* 8 (1967): 417–41.

Baker, Colin. "Tax Collection in Malawi: an Administrative History, 1891–1972." *International Journal of African Historical Studies* 8 (1975): 40–62.

Bartley, Paula. *Prostitution: Prevention and Reform in England, 1860–1914* (London, 2000).

Beachey, R. W. *The Slave Trade of Eastern Africa* (London, 1976).

Bebbington, D. W. "Review of G. I. T. Machin, *Politics and the Churches in Great Britain* (Oxford, 1977), and Robert Currie, Alan Gilbert, and Lee Horsley, *Churches and Churchgoers: Patterns of Church Growth in the British Isles since 1700* (Oxford, 1977)." *HJ* 21 (1978): 1013–16.

Beckert, Sven. "Emancipation and Empire: Reconstructing the Worldwide Web of Cotton Production in the Age of the American Civil War." *American Historical Review* 109 (2004): 1405–38.

Bell, Duncan. *The Idea of Greater Britain: Empire and the Future of World Order, 1860–1900* (Princeton, 2007).

Bellows, Donald. "A Study of British Conservative Reaction to the American Civil War." *Journal of Southern History* 51 (1985): 505–26.

Bender, Thomas, ed. *The Antislavery Debate: Capitalism and Abolitionism as a Problem in Historical Interpretation* (Berkeley, 1992).

Berger, Max. "American Slavery as Seen by British Visitors, 1836–1860." *Journal of Negro History* 30 (1945): 181–201.

Berlin, Isaiah. *Two Concepts of Liberty* (Oxford, 1958).

Berry, Sara. "Hegemony on a Shoestring: Indirect Rule and Access to Agricultural Land." *Africa* 62 (1992): 327–55.

Bethell, Leslie. *The Abolition of the Brazilian Slave Trade: Britain, Brazil and the Slave Trade Question 1807–1869* (Cambridge, 1970).

——. "Britain, Portugal and the Suppression of the Brazilian Slave Trade: The Origins of Lord Palmerston's Act of 1839." *EHR* 80 (1965): 761–84.

——. "The Independence of Brazil and the Abolition of the Brazilian Slave Trade: Anglo-Brazilian Relations, 1822–1826." *Journal of Latin American Studies* 1 (1969): 115–47.

——. "The Mixed Commissions for Suppression of the Slave Trade in the Nineteenth Century." *Journal of African History* 7 (1966): 79–93.

Bisset, Alexis. "Wilson Armistead and the Leeds Anti-Slavery Association" (BA thesis, Leeds University, 2007).

Blackett, R. J. M. *Beating against the Barriers: The Lives of Six Nineteenth-Century Afro-Americans* (Ithaca, N.Y., 1989).

——. *Building an Anti-Slavery Wall: Black Americans in the Atlantic Abolitionist Movement, 1830–1860* (Baton Rouge, La., 1983).

——. "Cracks in the Antislavery Wall: Frederick Douglass's Second Visit to England (1859–60) and the Coming of the Civil War." In *Liberating Sojourn: Frederick Douglass & Transatlantic Reform*, edited by Alan J. Rice and Martin Crawford, 187–206 (Athens, Ga., 1999).

——. *Divided Hearts: Britain and the American Civil War* (Baton Rouge, La., 2001).

Boritt, Gabor S. "Punch Lincoln: Some Thoughts on Cartoons in the Magazine." *Journal of the Abraham Lincoln Association* 15 (1994): 1–22.

Bosschep, Chris R. Vanden. *Carlyle and the Search for Authority* (Columbus, Ohio, 1991).

Boulukos, George. *The Grateful Slave: The Emergence of Race in Eighteenth-Century British and American Culture* (Cambridge, 2008).

Bradbury, Richard. "Frederick Douglass and the Chartists." In *Liberating Sojourn: Frederick Douglass & Transatlantic Reform*, edited by Alan J. Rice and Martin Crawford, 169–86 (Athens, Ga., 1999).

Brantlinger, Patrick. *Rule of Darkness: British Literature and Imperialism, 1830–1914* (Ithaca, N.Y., 1988).

Bratton, J. S. "English Ethiopians: British Audiences and Black-Face Acts, 1835–65." *Yearbook of English Studies* 11 (1981): 127–42.

Brauer, Kinley J. "The Slavery Problem in the Diplomacy of the American Civil War." *Pacific Historical Review* 46 (1977): 439–69.

Brent, Richard. *Liberal Anglican Politics: Whiggery, Religion and Reform 1830–1841* (Oxford, 1987).

Bridges, Roy. "Prelude to the Partition of East Africa." In *Imperialism, Decolonisation and Africa*, edited by Roy Bridges, 65–113 (Basingstoke, Hampshire, 2000).

Brown, Christopher Leslie. *Moral Capital: Foundations of British Abolitionism* (Chapel Hill, N.C., 2006).

Brown, Laurence. "Inter-colonial Migration and the Refashioning of Indentured Labour: Arthur Gordon in Trinidad, Mauritius and Fiji (1866–1880)." In *Colonial Lives across the British Empire: Imperial Careering in the Long Nineteenth Century*, edited by David Lambert and Alan Lester, 204–27 (Cambridge, 2006).

Brown, Robert T. "Fernando Po and the Anti-Sierra Leonean Campaign: 1826–1834." *International Journal of African Studies* 6 (1973): 249–64.

Burbank, Jane, and Frederick Cooper. *Empires in World History: Power and the Politics of Difference* (Princeton, 2010).

Burns, Arthur, and Joanna Innes, eds. *Rethinking the Age of Reform: Britain 1780–1850* (Cambridge, 2003).

Burton, Antoinette. "New Narratives of Imperial Politics in the Nineteenth Century." In *At Home with the Empire: Metropolitan Culture and the Imperial World*, edited by Catherine Hall and Sonya O. Rose, 212–29 (Cambridge, 2006).

——. "States of Injury: Josephine Butler on Slavery, Citizenship, and the Boer War." *Social Politics* 5 (1998): 338–61

Butt, John. "'Bleak House' in the Context of 1851." *Nineteenth-Century Fiction* 10 (1955): 1–21.

Buxton, Sydney. *Finance and Politics: An Historical Study 1763–1885*, 2 vols. (London, 1888).
Cairns, H. Alan. *Prelude to Imperialism: British Reactions to Central African Society 1840–1890* (London, 1965).
Campbell, Duncan Andrew. *English Public Opinion and the American Civil* War (Woodbridge, Suffolk, 2003).
——. "Palmerston and the American Civil War." In *Palmerston Studies II*, edited by David Brown and Miles Taylor, 144–67 (Southampton, 2007).
*Canadian Dictionary of National Biography [DCB/DBS]*, John English and Réal Bélanger, eds. (2003–present) [http://www.biographi.ca].
Canney, Donald L. *Africa Squadron: The U.S. Navy and the Slave Trade, 1842–1861* (Washington, D.C., 2006).
Carey, Brycchan. *British Abolitionism and the Rhetoric of Sensibility: Writing, Sentiment, and Slavery, 1760–1807* (Basingstoke, Hampshire, 2005).
Chamberlain, M. E. "Clement Hill's Memorandum and the British Interest in East Africa." *EHR* 87 (1972): 533–47.
Chase, Malcolm. *Chartism: A New History* (Manchester, 2007).
Claeys, Gregory. "The 'Left' and the Critique of Empire, c. 1865–1900: Three Roots of Humanitarian Foreign Policy." In *Victorian Visions of Global Order: Empire and International Relations in Nineteenth-Century Political Thought*, edited by Duncan Bell, 239–66 (Cambridge, 2007).
Cole, G. D. H. *Chartist Portraits* (London, 1941).
Coleman, Deidre. *Romantic Colonization and British Anti-Slavery* (Cambridge, 2005).
Coleman, Willi. "'Like Hot Lead to Pour on the Americans...': Sarah Redmond Parker—From Salem, Mass., to the British Isles." In *Women's Rights and Transatlantic Antislavery in the Era of Emancipation*, edited by Kathryn Kish Sklar and James Brewer Stewart, 173–88 (New Haven, Conn., 2007).
Colley, Linda. *Britons: Forging the Nation 1707–1837*, rev. ed. (New Haven, Conn., 2009 [1992]).
Collinge, J. M. *Office-Holders in Modern Britain: Volume 8: Foreign Office Officials 1782–1870* (London, 1979).
Comaroff, Jean, and John Comaroff. *Of Revelation and Revolution*, 2 vols. (Chicago, Ill., 1991–97).
Conrad, Robert. "Neither Slave nor Free: The Emancipados of Brazil, 1818–1868." *Hispanic American Review* 53 (1973): 50–70.
Cooper, Frederick. "Conditions Analogous to Slavery: Imperialism and Free Labor Ideology in Africa." In *Beyond Slavery: Explorations of Race, Labor, and Citizenship in Postemancipation Societies*, edited by Frederick Cooper, Thomas C. Holt, and Rebecca J. Scott, 107–49 (Chapel Hill, N.C., 2000).
——. "From Free Labor to Family Allowances: Labor and African Society in Colonial Discourse." *American Ethnologist* 16 (1989): 745–65.
——. *From Slaves to Squatters: Plantation Labour and Agriculture in Zanzibar and Coastal Kenya, 1890–1925* (New Haven, Conn., 1980).
——. "Networks, Moral Discourse, and History." In *Intervention and Transnationalism in Africa: Global-Local Networks of Power*, edited by Thomas Callaghy, Ronald Kassimir, and Robert Latham, 23–46 (Cambridge, 2001).
——. *Plantation Slavery on the East Coast of Africa* (Portsmouth, N.H., 1997).
Coupland, Reginald. *The Exploitation of East Africa, 1856–1890: The Slave Trade and the Scramble* (London, 1939).
Craton, Michael. *Sinews of Empire* (London, 1974).
Crawford, Martin. *The Anglo-American Crisis of the Mid-Nineteenth Century: The Times and America, 1850–62* (Athens, Ga., 1962).
Crofts, Daniel W. *A Secession Crisis Enigma: William Henry Hulbert and "The Diary of a Public Man"* (Baton Rouge, La., 2010).
Crook, D. P. "Portents of War: English Opinion on Secession." *Journal of American Studies* 4 (1971): 163–79.
Crowder, Michael. *West Africa under Colonial Rule* (London, 1968).
Cunliffe, Marcus. "America at the Great Exhibition of 1851." *American Quarterly* 3 (1951): 115–26.

——. *Chattel Slavery and Wage Slavery: The Anglo-American Context 1830–60* (Athens, Ga., 1979).

Curthoys, Mark. *Governments, Labour, and the Law in Mid-Victorian Britain: The Trade Union Legislation of the 1870s* (Oxford, 2004).

Curtin, Philip D. "The British Sugar Duties and West Indian Prosperity." *Journal of Economic History* 14 (1954): 157–64.

——. *The Image of Africa* (London, 1965).

Darwin, John. *The Empire Project: The Rise and Fall of the British World-System* (Cambridge, 2009).

——. "Imperialism and the Victorians: The Dynamics of Territorial Expansion." *EHR* 112 (1997): 614–42.

Davis, David Brion. "Declaring Equality: Sisterhood and Slavery." In *Women's Rights and Transatlantic Antislavery in the Era of Emancipation,* edited by Kathryn Kish Sklar and James Brewer Stewart, 3–18 (New Haven, Conn., 2007).

——. "The Emergence of Immediatism in British and American Antislavery Thought." *Mississippi Valley Historical Review* 49 (1962): 209–30.

——. *Inhuman Bondage: The Rise and Fall of Slavery in the New World* (Oxford, 2006).

——. *In the Image of God: Religion, Moral Values, and Our Heritage of Slavery* (New Haven, Conn., 2001).

——. *The Problem of Slavery in the Age of Revolution 1770–1823* (New York, 1999 [Ithaca, N.Y., 1975]).

——. "Review: Antislavery or Abolition?" *Reviews in American History* 1 (1973): 95–99.

——. *Slavery and Human Progress* (New York, 1984).

Desmond, Adrian, and James Moore. *Darwin's Sacred Cause: How a Hatred of Slavery Shaped Darwin's Views on Human Evolution* (Boston, 2009).

Dickie, John. *The British Consul: Heir to a Great Tradition* (London, 1997).

Dierksheide, Christa. "'Capable of Improvement': Commerce, Christianity, and the Idea of an Independent Africa, *c.* 1740–1810." (Unpublished paper, International Seminar on the History of the Atlantic World, Harvard University, 2006).

Dike, K. Onwuka. *Trade and Politics in the Niger Delta* (Oxford, 1966 [1956]).

Dimock, Elizabeth. "Women, Missions and Modernity: From Anti-Slavery to Missionary Zeal, 1780s to 1840s." *Itinerario* 34 (2010): 53–66.

Dooling, Wayne. *Slavery, Emancipation and Colonial Rule in South Africa* (Athens, Ohio, 2007).

Dorsey, Joseph C. *Slave Traffic in the Age of Abolition: Puerto Rico, West Africa and the Non-Hispanic Caribbean, 1815–59* (Gainesville, Fla., 2003).

Doyle, Mary Ellen. "Joseph Henson's Narrative: Before and After." *Negro American Literature Forum* 8 (1974): 176–83.

Draper, Nicholas. *The Price of Emancipation: Slave-Ownership, Compensation and British Society at the End of Slavery* (Cambridge, 2010).

Drescher, Seymour. *Abolition: A History of Slavery and Antislavery* (Cambridge, 2009)

——. "Brazilian Abolition in Comparative Perspective." In *The Abolition of Slavery and the Aftermath of Emancipation in Brazil,* edited by Rebecca J. Scott, 23–54 (Durham, N.C., 1995).

——. *Capitalism and Antislavery: British Popular Mobilization in Comparative Perspective* (New York, 1987).

——. "Cart Whip and Billy Roller: Antislavery and Reform Symbolism in Industrializing Britain." *Journal of Social History* 15 (1981): 3–24.

——. "The Ending of the Slave Trade and the Evolution of European Scientific Racism." *Social Science History* 14 (1990): 415–50.

——. "John Brown's Body in Europe." *Journal of American History* 80 (1993): 499–524.

——. *The Mighty Experiment: Free Labour versus Slavery in British Emancipation* (Oxford, 2004).

——. "Whose Abolition? Popular Pressure and the Ending of the British Slave Trade." *Past and Present* 143 (1994): 136–66.

——. "Women's Mobilization in the Era of Slave Emancipation: Some Anglo-French Comparisons." In *Women's Rights and Transatlantic Antislavery in the Era of Emancipation,* edited by Kathryn Kish Sklar and James Brewer Stewart, 98–120 (New Haven, Conn., 2007).

Driver, Cecil. *Tory Radical: The Life of Richard Oastler* (New York, 1946).

Driver, Felix. "Henry Morton Stanley and His Critics: Geography, Exploration and Empire." *Past & Present* 133 (1991): 134–166.

Dumett, Raymond. "Joseph Chamberlain, Imperial Finance and Railway Policy in British West Africa in the Late Nineteenth Century." *EHR* 90 (1975): 287–321.

——. "Pressure Groups, Bureaucracy, and the Decision-making Process: The Case of Slavery Abolition and Colonial Expansion in the Gold Coast, 1874." *JICH* 9 (1981): 193–215.

Dumett, Raymond, and Marion Johnson. "Britain and the Suppression of Slavery in the Gold Coast Colony, Ashanti, and the Northern Territories." In *The End of Slavery in Africa*, edited by Suzanne Miers and Richard Roberts, 71–116 (London, 1988).

Elbourne, Elizabeth. *Blood Ground: Colonialism, Missions, and the Contest for Christianity in the Cape Colony and Britain, 1799–1853* (Montreal, 2002).

Ellison, Mary. *Support for Secession: Lancashire and the Civil War* (Chicago, 1972)

Eltis, David. "Abolitionist Perceptions of Society after Slavery." In *Slavery and British Society, 1776–1846*, edited by James Walvin, 195–213 (Baton Rouge, La., 1982).

——. *Economic Growth and the Ending of the Transatlantic Slave Trade* (New York, 1987)

Emery, F. V. "Geography and Imperialism: The Role of Sir Bartle Frere." *Geographical Journal* 150 (1984): 342–50.

Emmer, Pieter. "'A Spirit of Independence' or Lack of Education for the Market? Freedmen and Asian Indentured Labourers in the Post-Emancipation Caribbean, 1834–1917." *Slavery and Abolition* 21 (2000): 150–68.

Engerman, Stanley L. "Servants to Slaves: Contract Labour and European Expansion." In *Colonialism and Migration: Indentured Labour before and after Slavery*, edited by Pieter Emmer, 263–94 (Dordrecht, Netherlands, 1986).

——. "Slavery, Freedom, and Sen." *Feminist Economics* 9 (2003): 185–211.

Enkvist, Niks Erik. "The Octoroon and English Opinions of Slavery." *American Quarterly* 8 (1956): 166–70.

Erdem, Yusuf. "Slavery in the Ottoman Empire and Its Demise" (DPhil thesis, Oxford University, 1993)

Etemad, Bouda. "Economic Relations between Europe and black Africa, c.1780–1936: A Quantitative Analysis." In *From Slave Trade to Empire: Europe and the Colonisation of Black Africa, 1780s–1880s*, edited by Olivier Pétré-Grenouilleau, 69–81 (Abingdon, Oxfordshire, 2004).

Etherington, Norman. "Frederic Elton and the South African Factor in the Making of Britain's East African Empire." *JICH* 2 (1981): 255–74.

Falola, Toyin. *Colonialism and Violence in Nigeria* (Bloomington, Ind., 2009).

——. "The End of Slavery among the Yoruba." *Slavery and Abolition* 19 (1998): 232–49.

Falola, Toyin, and Matthew M. Heaton. *A History of Nigeria* (Cambridge, 2008).

Farrison, William. *William Wells Brown: Author and Reformer* (Chicago, Ill., 1969).

Fehrenbacher, Don. *The Slaveholding Republic: An Account of the United States Government's Relationship with Slavery* (New York, 2001).

Fieldhouse, D. K. *Economics and Empire 1830–1914* (London, 1973).

Finn, Margot. "Slaves out of Context: Domestic Slavery and the Anglo-Indian Family, c. 1780–1830." *Transactions of the Royal Historical Society* 19 (2009): 181–203.

Fisch, Audrey. *American Slaves in Victorian England* (Cambridge, 2000).

——. "'Exhibiting Uncle Tom in Some Shape or Other': The Commodification and Reception of *Uncle Tom's Cabin* in England." *Nineteenth-Century Contexts* 17 (1993): 145–58.

Fisher, Humphrey J. "Review of Johnson U.J. Asiegbu, Slavery and the Politics of Liberation (London, 1969)." *Bulletin of the School of Oriental and African Studies* 34 (1971): 188–90.

Fladeland, Betty. *Men and Brothers: Anglo-American Antislavery Cooperation* (Chicago, Ill., 1972).

——. "'Our Cause being One and the Same': Abolitionists and Chartism." In *Slavery and British Society 1776–1846*, edited by James Walvin, 69–99 (London, 1982).

Flint, John. "African Historians and African History." *Past and Present* 10 (1956): 96–101.

Fogel, Robert W. "The Origin and History of Economic Issues in the American Slavery Debate." In *Without Consent or Contract: The Rise and Fall of American Slavery; Evidence and Methods,* edited by Robert W. Fogel, Ralph A. Galantine, and Richard L. Manning, 161–63 (New York, 1992).

Follett, Richard R. "After Emancipation: Thomas Fowell Buxton and Evangelical Politics in the 1830s." *PH* 27 (2008): 119–29.

Foner, Eric. *Free Soil, Free Labor, Free Men: The Ideology of the Republican Party before the Civil War* (Oxford, 1970).

Foner, Philip. *British Labor and the American Civil War* (New York, 1981).

Franzmann, Tom L. "Antislavery and Political Economy in the Early Victorian House of Commons: A Research Note on 'Capitalist Hegemony'." *Journal of Social History* 27 (1994): 579–93.

Freeden, Michael. *Ideologies and Political Theory: A Conceptual Approach* (Oxford, 1996).

———. "Ideology and Political Theory." *Journal of Political Ideologies* 11 (2006): 3–22.

Fulton, Richard D. "The London *Times* and the Anglo-American Boarding Dispute of 1858." *Nineteenth-Century Contexts* 17 (1993): 133–44.

Galbraith, John S. *Crown and Charter: The Early Years of the British South Africa Company* (Berkeley, 1974).

———. *Mackinnon and East Africa 1878–1895: A Study in the "New Imperialism"* (Cambridge, 1972).

———. *Reluctant Empire: British Policy on the South African Frontier, 1834–1854* (Berkeley, 1963).

Galeson, David W. "The Rise and Fall of Indentured Servitude in the Americas: An Economic Analysis." *Journal of Economic History* 44 (1984): 1–26.

Gallagher, John. "Fowell Buxton and the New African Policy, 1838–1842." *Cambridge Historical Journal* 10 (1950): 36–58.

Gallagher, John, and Ronald Robinson. "The Imperialism of Free Trade." *Economic History Review,* 2nd ser., 6 (1953): 1–15.

Gavin, R. J. "The Bartle Frere Mission to Zanzibar, 1873." *HJ* 5 (1962): 122–48.

Geiss, Imanuel. "Free Trade, Internationalization of the Congo Basin, and the Principle of Effective Occupation." In *Bismarck, Europe, and Africa: The Berlin Africa Conference 1884–1885 and the Onset of Partition,* edited by Stig Förster, Wolfgang J. Mommsen, and Ronald Robinson, 263–80 (Oxford, 1988).

Gleadle, Kathryn. *The Early Feminists: Radical Unitarians and the Emergence of the Women's Rights Movement* (Basingstoke, Hampshire, 1995).

Goldman, Lawrence. "'A Total Misconception': Lincoln, the Civil War, and the British." In *The Global Lincoln,* edited by Richard Carwardine and Jay Sexton, 107–22 (New York, 2011).

Gordon, David M. "The Abolition of the Slave Trade and the Transformation of the South-Central African Interior during the Nineteenth Century." *William and Mary Quarterly,* 3rd ser., 66 (2009): 915–38.

Gossman, Norbert J. "William Cuffay: London's Black Chartist." *Phylon* 44 (1983): 56–65.

Grant, Kevin. *A Civilised Savagery: Britain and the New Slaveries in Africa, 1884–1926* (New York, 2005).

Green, Abigail. "The British Empire and the Jews." *Past and Present* 199 (May 2008): 175–205.

Green, William A. *British Slave Emancipation: The Sugar Colonies and the Great Experiment 1830–1865* (Oxford, 1976).

———. "The West Indies and British West African Policy in the Nineteenth Century—A Corrective Comment." *Journal of African History* 15 (1974): 247–59.

Griffiths, Tudor. "Bishop Alfred Tucker and the Establishment of a British Protectorate in Uganda 1890–94." *Journal of Religion in Africa* 31 (2001): 92–114.

Grogan, Lady. *Reginald Bosworth Smith: A Memoir* (London, 1909).

Gross, Izhak. "Parliament and the Abolition of Negro Apprenticeship, 1835–1838." *EHR* 96 (1981): 560–76.

Hall, Catherine. *Civilising Subjects: Metropole and Colony in the English Imagination 1830–67* (Oxford, 2002).

———. "The Economy of Intellectual Prestige: Thomas Carlyle, John Stuart Mill, and the Case of Governor Eyre." *Cultural Critique* 12 (1989): 167–93.

Hall, Catherine, and Sonya O. Rose, eds. *At Home with the Empire: Metropolitan Culture and the Imperial World* (Cambridge, 2006).

Hamand, Wendy F. "'No Voice from England': Mrs. Stowe, Mr. Lincoln, and the British in the Civil War." *New England Quarterly* 61 (1988): 3–24.

Hamilton, Keith. "Zealots and Helots: The Slave Trade Department of the Nineteenth-Century Foreign Office." In *Slavery, Diplomacy and Empire: Britain and the Suppression of the Slave Trade, 1807–1975*, edited by Keith Hamilton and Patrick Salmon, 20–41 (Eastbourne, Sussex, 2009).

Hamilton, Keith, and Patrick Salmon, eds. *Slavery, Diplomacy and Empire: Britain and the Suppression of the Slave Trade, 1807–1975* (Eastbourne, Sussex, 2009).

Hammond, Richard J. "Economic Imperialism: Sidelights on a Stereotype." *Journal of Economic History* 21 (1961): 582–98.

Hargey, Taj. "Festina Lente: Slavery Policy and Practice in the Anglo-Egyptian Sudan." *Slavery and Abolition* 19 (1998): 250–72.

Hargreaves, John D. *West Africa Partitioned*, 2 vols. (Basingstoke, Hampshire 1985).

Harrison, Royden. *Before the Socialists: Studies in Labour and Politics, 1861–1881* (London, 1965).

Harwood, Thomas F. "British Evangelical Abolitionism and American Churches in the 1830s." *Journal of Southern History* 28 (1962): 287–306.

Haskell, Thomas. "Capitalism and the Origins of Humanitarian Sensibility, I." In *The Antislavery Debate: Capitalism and Abolitionism as a Problem in Historical Explanation*, edited by Thomas Bender, 107–35 (Berkeley, 1992).

Heartfield, James. *The Aborigines' Protection Society: Humanitarian Imperialism in Australia, New Zealand, Fiji, Canada, South Africa, and the Congo, 1836–1909* (London, 2011).

Helly, Dorothy O. "'Informed' Opinion on Tropical Africa in Great Britain, 1860–1890." *African Affairs* 68 (1969): 195–217.

——. *Livingstone's Legacy: Horace Waller and Victorian Mythmaking* (Athens, Ohio, 1987).

Herbert, Christopher. *War of No Pity: The Indian Mutiny and Victorian Trauma* (Princeton, 2008).

Heuman, Gad. "The British West Indies." In *The Oxford History of the British Empire*, edited by Andrew Porter and Alain Lowe, 3:470–93 (5 vols., Oxford, 1999).

——. *The Killing Time: The Morant Bay Rebellion in Jamaica* (London, 1994).

Heuman, Gad, and David V. Trotman, eds. *Contesting Freedom: Control and Resistance in the Post-Emancipation Caribbean* (Warwick, 2005).

Hogendorn, Jan S., and Paul E. Lovejoy. "Keeping Slaves in Place: The Secret Debate on the Slavery Question in Northern Nigeria, 1900–1904." In *The Atlantic Slave Trade: Effects on Economies, Societies, and Peoples in Africa, the Americas, and Europe*, edited by Joseph E. Inikori and Stanley L. Engerman, 49–76 (Durham, N.C., 1992).

Hollis, Patricia. "Anti-Slavery and British Working-Class Radicalism in the Years of Reform." In *Anti-slavery, Religion and Reform*, edited by Christine Bolt and Seymour Drescher, 294–315 (Folkestone, Kent, 1980).

Holt, Thomas C. "The Essence of the Contract: The Articulation of Race, Gender, and Political Economy in British Emancipation Policy, 1838–1866." In *Beyond Slavery: Explorations of Race, Labor, and Citizenship in Postemancipation Societies*, edited by Frederick Cooper, Thomas C. Holt, and Rebecca J. Scott, 33–59 (Chapel Hill, N.C., 2000).

——. *The Problem of Freedom: Race, Labor, and Politics in Jamaica and Britain, 1832–1938* (Baltimore, Md., 1992).

Hopkins, Anthony G. "The 'New International Economic Order' in the Nineteenth Century: Britain's First Development Plan for Africa." In *From Slave Trade to Legitimate Commerce*, edited by Robin Laws, 240–64 (Cambridge, 1995).

——. "Property Rights and Empire Building: Britain's Annexation of Lagos, 1861." *Journal of Economic History* 40 (1980): 777–98.

Hopper, Matthew S. "Globalization and the Economics of African Slavery in Arabia in the Age of Empire." *Journal of African Development* 12 (2010): 125–46.

——. "Imperialism and the Dilemma of Slavery in Eastern Arabia and the Gulf, 1873–1939." *Itinerario* 30 (2006): 76–94.

Howe, Anthony. "Two Faces of British Power: Cobden versus Palmerston." In *Palmerston Studies II*, edited by David Brown and Miles Taylor, 168–92 (Southampton, 2007).

Howell, Philip, and David Lambert. "Sir John Pope Hennessy and Colonial Government." In *Colonial Lives across the British Empire: Imperial Careering in the Long Nineteenth Century*, edited by David Lambert and Alan Lester, 228–56 (Cambridge, 2006).

Huston, James L. "Abolitionists, Political Economists, and Capitalism." *Journal of the Early Republic* 20 (2000): 487–521.

Huzzey, Richard. "British Liberties, American Emancipation and the Democracy of Race." In *The American Experiment and the Idea of Democracy in British Culture, 1776–1914*, edited by Ella Dzelzainis and Ruth Livesey (forthcoming).

———. "Free Trade, Free Labour and Slave Sugar in Victorian Britain." *HJ* 53 (2010): 359–79.

———. "Gladstone and the Suppression of the Slave Trade." In *William Gladstone: New Studies and Perspectives*, edited by Ruth Clayton Windscheffel, Roland Quinault, and Roger Swift (forthcoming, Ashgate, 2012).

Hynes, William G. *The Economics of Empire: Britain, Africa and the New Imperialism, 1870–95* (London, 1979).

Igbafe, Philip A. "The Fall of Benin: A Reassessment." *Journal of African History* 11 (1970): 385–400.

Innes, Joanna, and Arthur Burns. Introduction to *Rethinking the Age of Reform: Britain 1780–1850*, edited by Arthur Burns and Joanna Innes, 1–70 (Cambridge, 2003).

Jervey, Edward D., and C. Harold Huber. "The Creole Affair." *Journal of Negro History* 65 (1980): 196–211.

Johnston, Alex. *The Life and Letters of Sir Harry Johnston* (London, 1929).

Jones, Howard. *Blue and Grey Diplomacy: A History of Union and Confederate Foreign Relations* (Chapel Hill, N.C., 2010).

Jones, Peter. "Palmerston and the Slave Trade" (unpublished article, 2007).

Jones, Ray. *The Nineteenth Century Foreign Office* (London, 1971).

Jones, William Devereux. "The British Conservatives and the American Civil War." *American Historical Review* 58 (1953): 527–43.

Judge, David. "Public Petitions and the House of Commons." *Parliamentary Affairs* 31 (1978): 391–405.

Kale, Madhavi. *Fragments of Empire: Capital, Slavery, and Indian Indentured Labor in the British Caribbean* (Philadelphia, 1998).

Kalinga, Owen J. M. "The Karonga War: Commercial Rivalry and Politics of Survival." *Journal of African History* 21 (1980): 209–18.

Kayao&gbreve;lu, Turan. *Legal Imperialism: Sovereignty and Extraterritoriality in Japan, the Ottoman Empire, and China* (Cambridge, 2010).

Keene, Edward. "A Case Study of the Construction of International Hierarchy: British Treaty-Making against the Slave Trade in the Early Nineteenth Century." *International Organization* 61 (2007): 311–39.

Kidd, Colin. *The Forging of Races: Race and Scripture in the Protestant Atlantic World, 1600–2000* (Cambridge, 2006).

Kielstra, Paul Michael. *The Politics of Slave Trade Suppression in Britain and France* (Basingstoke, Hampshire, 2000).

Kinealy, Christine. *Daniel O'Connell and the Anti-Slavery Movement: "The Saddest People the Sun Sees"* (London, 2010).

Kinney, Michelle Anders. "'Doubly Foreign': British Consuls in the Antebellum South, 1830–1860" (PhD diss., University of Texas at Arlington, 2010).

Kirk, Neville. "In Defence of Class: A Critique of Recent Revisionist Writing upon the Nineteenth-Century English Working Class." *International Review of Social History* 32 (1987): 2–47.

Kitson Clark, G. "The Repeal of the Corn Laws and the Politics of the Forties." *Economic History Review*, n.s., 4 (1951): 1–13.

Laidlaw, Zoë. *Colonial Connections, 1815–45: Patronage, the Information Revolution and Colonial Government* (Manchester, 2005).

———. "Heathens, Slaves and Aborigines: Thomas Hodgkin's Critique of Missions and Anti-Slavery." *History Workshop Journal* 64 (2007): 133–61.

Lamb, Andrew. *A Life on the Ocean Wave: The Story of Henry Russell* (Croydon, 2007).
Landry, Henry E. "Slavery and the Slave Trade in Atlantic Diplomacy, 1850–1861." *Journal of Southern History* 27 (1961): 184–207.
Laqua, Daniel. "The Tensions of Internationalism: Transnational Anti-Slavery in the 1880s and 1890s." *International History Review* 33 (2011): 705–26.
Larsen, Timothy. *Friends of Religious Equality: Nonconformist Politics in Mid-Victorian England* (Woodbridge, Suffolk, 1999).
Laurence, K. O. *Immigration into the West Indies in the 19th Century* (St. Lawrence, Barbados, 1971).
Law, Robin. "Abolition and Imperialism: International Law and the British Suppression of the Atlantic Slave Trade." In *Abolitionism and Imperialism in Britain, Africa, and the Atlantic,* edited by Derek R. Peterson, 150–74 (Athens, Ohio, 2010).
——. ed., *From Slave Trade to "Legitimate" Commerce* (Cambridge, 1995).
——. *The Oyo Empire, c.1600–c.1836: A West African Imperialism in the Era of the Atlantic Slave Trade* (Oxford, 1977).
——. "The White Slaver and the African Prince: European and American Depictions of Pre-Colonial Dahomey." In *Images of Africa,* edited by Martin Gray and Robin Law, 22–41 (Stirling, 1990).
Lee, Julia Sun-Joo. *The American Slave Narrative and the Victorian Novel* (Oxford, 2010).
Lester, Alan. *Imperial Networks: Creating Identities in Nineteenth-Century South Africa and Britain* (London, 2001).
Lloyd, Christopher. *The Navy and the Slave Trade: The Suppression of the African Slave Trade in the Nineteenth Century* (London, 1949).
Logan, Deborah A. *Harriet Martineau, Victorian Imperialism, and the Civilizing Mission* (Farnham, Surrey, 2010).
Lorimer, Douglas A. *Colour, Class and the Victorians: English Attitudes to the Negro in the Mid Nineteenth Century* (Leicester, 1978).
——. "From Victorian Values to White Virtues: Assimilation and Exclusion in British Racial Discourse, c. 1870–1914." In *Rediscovering the British World,* edited by Phillip Buckner and R. Douglas Francis, 109–34 (Calgary, Alberta, 2005).
——. "The Role of Anti-Slavery Sentiment in English Reactions to the American Civil War." *HJ* 19 (1976): 405–20.
Louis, William. Roger. *Ends of British Imperialism: The Scramble for Empire, Suez, and Decolonization* (London, 2006).
Lovejoy, Paul. "Slavery in the Context of Ideology." In *The Ideology of Slavery in Africa,* edited by Paul Lovejoy, 11–38 (Beverly Hills, Calif., 1981).
——. *Transformations in Slavery: A History of Slavery in Africa,* 2nd ed. (Cambridge, 2000 [1983]).
Lovejoy, Paul, and Jan S. Hogendorn. "The Reform of Slavery in Early Colonial Northern Nigeria." In *The End of Slavery in Africa,* edited by Suzanne Miers and Richard Roberts, 391–414 (Madison, Wis., 1988).
——. *Slow Death for Slavery: The Course of Abolition in Northern Nigeria, 1897–1936* (Cambridge, 1993).
Low, D. A. *Buganda in Modern History* (London, 1971).
——. *Fabrication of Empire: The British and the Uganda Kingdoms* (Cambridge, 2009).
Lynn, Martin. "'The Imperialism of Free Trade' and the Case of West Africa, c.1830–1870." *JICH* 15 (1986): 22–40.
Madden, A. F. "The Attitude of the Evangelicals to the Empire and Imperial Problems, 1820–50." (DPhil. thesis, Oxford University, 1950).
Magee, Gary B., and Andrew S. Thompson. *Empire and Globalisation: Networks of People, Goods and Capital in the British World, c. 1850–1914* (Cambridge, 2010).
Mandler, Peter. *The English National Character: The History of an Idea from Edmund Burke to Tony Blair* (New Haven, Conn., 2006).
Mann, Kristin. *Slavery and the Birth of an African City: Lagos, 1760–1900* (Bloomington, Ind., 2007).
Manning, Patrick. "Slavery and Slave Trade in West Africa." In *Themes in West Africa's History,* edited by Emmanuel Kwaku Akyeampong, 99–117 (Athens, Ohio, 2006).

Mantena, Karuna. *Alibis of Empire: Henry Maine and the Ends of Liberal Imperialism* (Princeton, 2010).

Martinez-Fernandez, Luis. *Fighting Slavery in the Caribbean: The Life and Times of a British Family in Nineteenth-Century Havana* (Armonk, N.Y., 1998).

Mason, John Edwin. *Social Death and Resurrection: Slavery and Emancipation in South Africa* (Charlottesville, Va., 2008).

Mason, Matthew. "The Battle of the Slaveholding Liberators: Great Britain, the United States, and Slavery in the Early Nineteenth Century." *William and Mary Quarterly*, 3rd ser., 59 (2002): 665–96.

———. "Keeping Up Appearances: The International Politics of Slave Trade Abolition in the Nineteenth-Century Atlantic World." *William and Mary Quarterly*, 3rd ser., 66 (2009): 809–32.

Mathieson, W. L. *Great Britain and the Slave Trade* (London, 1929).

Matthew, H. C. G. *The Liberal Imperialists: The Ideas and Politics of a Post-Gladstonian Élite* (Oxford, 1973).

Maurer, Oscar. "'Punch' on Slavery and the Civil War in America 1841–1865." *Victorian Studies* 1 (1957): 5–28.

Mays, Kelly J. "Slaves in Heaven, Laborers in Hell: Chartist Poets' Ambivalent Identification with the (Black) Slave." *Victorian Poetry* 39 (2001): 137–63.

Mbaeyi, Paul Mmegha. *British Military and Naval Forces in West African History, 1807–1874* (New York, 1978).

McKinstry, Leo. *Rosebery: Statesman in Turmoil* (London, 2005).

McSheffrey, Gerald. "Slavery, Indenture, Legitimate Trade and the Impact of Abolition in the Gold Coast, 1874–1901: A Reappraisal." *Journal of African History* 24 (1983): 349–63.

Meer, Sarah. "Competing Representations: Douglass, the Ethiopian Serenaders, and Ethnic Exhibition in London." In *Liberating Sojourn: Frederick Douglass & Transatlantic Reform*, edited by Alan J. Rice and Martin Crawford, 141–65 (Athens, Ga., 1999).

———. *Uncle Tom Mania: Slavery, Minstrelsy and Transatlantic Culture in the 1850s* (Athens, Ga., 2005).

Metcalf, Thomas R. *Imperial Connections: India in the Indian Ocean Arena, 1860–1920* (Berkeley, 1998).

Midgley, Clare. "Bringing the Empire Home: Women Activists in Imperial Britain, 1790s–1930s." In *At Home with the Empire: Metropolitan Culture and the Imperial World*, edited by Catherine Hall and Sonya O. Rose, 230–50 (Cambridge, 2006).

———. "British Abolition and Feminism in Transatlantic Perspective." In *Women's Rights and Transatlantic Antislavery in the Era of Emancipation*, edited by Kathryn Kish Sklar and James Brewer Stewart, 121–39 (New Haven, Conn., 2007).

———. *Feminism and Empire: Women Activists in Imperial Britain, 1790–1865* (Abingdon, Oxfordshire, 2007).

———. *Women against Slavery: The British Campaigns, 1780–1870* (London, 1992).

Miers, Suzanne. *Britain and the Ending of the Slave Trade* (London, 1975).

———. "Slavery and the Slave Trade as International Issues, 1890–1939." *Slavery & Abolition* 19 (1998): 16–37.

Miers, Suzanne, and Martin A. Klein. *Slavery and Colonial Rule in Africa* (London, 1999).

Miers, Suzanne, and Richard Roberts. Introduction to *The End of Slavery in Africa*, edited by Suzanne Miers and Richard Roberts, 3–70 (London, 1988).

Mitchell, Brian R. *British Historical Statistics*, 2nd ed. (Cambridge, 1988).

Mitchell, Sally. *Francis Power Cobbe: Victorian Feminist, Journalist, Reformer* (Charlottesville, Va., 2004).

Mitton, Steven Heath. "The Free World Confronted: The Problem of Slavery and Progress in American Foreign Relations, 1833–1844." (PhD diss., Louisiana State University, 2005).

Mohapatra, Prabhu P. "Assam and the West Indies, 1860–1920: Immobilizing Plantation Labor." In *Masters, Servants, and Magistrates in Britain and the Empire, 1562–1955*, edited by Douglas Hay and Paul Craven, 455–80 (Chapel Hill, 2004).

Morrell, W. P. *British Colonial Policy in the Age of Russell and Peel* (Oxford, 1930).

Morrow, John. *Thomas Carlyle* (London, 2006).

Mulligan, William. "British Anti-Slave Trade and Anti-Slavery Policy in East Africa, Arabia, and Turkey in the Late Nineteenth Century." In *Humanitarian Intervention: A History,* edited by Brendan Simms and D. J. B. Trim (Cambridge, 2011), 257–280.
——. "The Fugitive Slave Circulars, 1875–76." *JICH* 37 (2009): 183–205.
Munro, Doug. "The Labor Trade in Melanesians to Queensland: An Historiographic Essay." *Journal of Social History* 28 (1995): 609–25.
Munro, J. Forbes. "Shipping Subsidies and Railway Guarantees: William Mackinnon, Eastern Africa and the Indian Ocean, 1860–93." *Journal of African History* 28 (1987): 209–30.
Murphy, Angela. *American Slavery, Irish Freedom: Abolition, Immigrant Citizenship, and the Transatlantic Movement for Irish Repeal* (Baton Rouge, La., 2010).
Murray, Alexander L. "The Extradition of Fugitive Slaves: A Re-evaluation." *Canadian Historical Review* 43 (1962): 298–314.
Murray, David R. *Odious Commerce: Britain, Spain and the Abolition of the Cuban Slave Trade* (Cambridge, 1980).
Needell, Jeffrey. "The Abolition of the Brazilian Slave Trade in 1850: Historiography, Slave Agency and Statesmanship." *Journal of Latin American Studies* 33 (2001): 681–711.
Newbury, Colin. "Great Britain and the Partition of Africa, 1870–1914." In *Oxford History of the British Empire,* edited by Andrew Porter, 3:624–50 (5 vols., Oxford, 1999).
——. *The Western Slave Coast and Its Rulers* (Oxford, 1961)
Newman, Judie. "Stowe's Sunny Memories of Highland Slavery." In *Special Relationships: Anglo-American Affinities and Antagonisms 1854–1936,* edited by Janet Beer and Bridget Bennett, 28–42 (Manchester, 2002).
Nippel, Wilfried. "Marx, Weber, and Classical Slavery." *Classics Ireland* 12 (2005): 31–49.
Northrup, David. *Indentured Labour in the Age of Imperialism, 1834–1922* (Cambridge, 1995).
Nowatzki, Robert. *Representing African Americans in Transatlantic Abolitionism and Blackface Minstrelsy* (Baton Rouge, La., 2010).
Nuermberger, Ruth Ketring. *The Free Produce Movement: A Quaker Protest against Slavery* (New York, 1942).
Nussbaum, Martha. *Creating Capabilities: The Human Development Approach* (Cambridge, Ma., 2011).
Nwokegi, G. Ugo. "The Slave Emancipation Problematic: Igbo Society and the Colonial Equation." *Comparative Studies in Society and History* 40 (1998): 318–55.
Nworah, Kenneth D. "The Aborigines' Protection Society, 1889–1909: A Pressure-Group in Colonial Policy." *Canadian Journal of African Studies* 5 (1971): 79–91.
Nwulia, Moses. *Britain and Slavery in East Africa* (Washington, D.C., 1975).
Offen, Karen. "How (and Why) the Analogy of Marriage with Slavery Provided the Springboard for Women's Rights Demands in France, 1640–1848." In *Women's Rights and Transatlantic Antislavery in the Era of Emancipation,* edited by Kathryn Kish Sklar and James Brewer Stewart, 57–81 (New Haven, 2007).
Oldfield, J. R. *Chords of Freedom: Commemoration, Ritual and British Transatlantic Slavery* (Manchester, 2007).
——. "Palmerston and Anti-Slavery." In *Palmerston Studies II,* edited by David Brown and Miles Taylor, 24–38 (Southampton, 2007).
——. *Popular Politics and British Anti-Slavery 1787–1807* (London, 1998 [Manchester, 1995]).
Oliver, Roland. Sir *Harry Johnston and the Scramble for Africa* (London, 1964).
Opare-Akurang, Kwabena. "The Administration of the Abolition Laws, African Responses, and Post-Proclamation Slavery in the Gold Coast, 1874–1940." *Slavery and Abolition* 19 (1998): 149–66.
Otte, T. G. "'Avenge England's Dishonour': By-elections, Parliament and the Politics of Foreign Policy in 1898." *EHR* 121 (2006): 385–428.
——. "'A Course of Unceasing Remonstrance': British Diplomacy and the Suppression of the Slave Trade in the East." In *Slavery, Diplomacy and Empire: Britain and the Suppression of the Slave Trade, 1807–1975,* edited by Keith Hamilton and Patrick Salmon, 93–124 (Eastbourne, Sussex, 2009).

——. "The Foreign Office, 1856–1914." In *Imperial Defence: The Old World Order 1856–1956*, edited by Greg Kennedy, 9–29 (Abingdon, Oxfordshire, 2008).

*Oxford Dictionary of National Biography [ODNB]*, edited by Lawrence Goldman (Oxford, 2004–present) [http://www.oxforddnb.com].

Parnaby, O. W. *Britain and the Labor Trade in the Southwest Pacific* (Durham, N.C., 1964).

Perbi, Akosa Admoa. *A History of Indigenous Slavery in Ghana* (Accra, Ghana, 2004).

Perham, Margery. *Lugard: The Years of Adventure, 1858–1898* (London, 1956).

Perraton, H. D. "British Attitudes towards East and West Africa, 1880–1914." *Race & Class* 8 (1967): 223–46.

Perreau-Saussine, Amanda. "British Acts of State in English Courts." *British Yearbook of International Law* 78 (2008): 176–254.

Persky, Joseph. "Wage Slavery." *History of Political Economy* 30 (1998): 627–51.

Petty, Alasdair. "Send Back the Money: Douglass and the Free Church of Scotland." In *Liberating Sojourn: Frederick Douglass & Transatlantic Reform*, edited by Alan J. Rice and Martin Crawford, 31–55 (Athens, Ga., 1999).

Phillips, Anne. *The Enigma of Colonialism: British Policy in West Africa* (London, 1989).

Pickering, Michael. "Mock Blacks and Racial Mockery: The 'Nigger' Minstrel and British Imperialism." In *Acts of Supremacy: The British Empire and the Stage, 1790–1930*, edited by J. S Bratton, Richard Allen Cave, Brendan Gregory, Heidi J. Holder, and Michael Pickering, 179–236 (Manchester, 1991).

Pilgrim, Elsie. "Anti-Slavery Sentiment in Great Britain 1841–1854: Its Nature and Its Decline, with Special Reference to Its Influence upon British Policy towards the Former Slave Colonies" (PhD thesis, Cambridge University, 1952).

Pitts, Jennifer. "Boundaries of International Law." In *Victorian Visions of Global Order: Empire and International Relations in Nineteenth-Century Political Thought*, edited by Duncan Bell, 67–88 (Cambridge, 2007).

Platt, D. C. M. *Finance, Trade, and Politics in British Foreign Policy 1815–1914* (Oxford, 1968).

Pollock, John. *Gordon: The Man behind the Legend* (London, 1993).

Porter, Andrew. "Church History, History of Christianity, Religious History: Some Reflections on British Missionary Enterprise since the Late Eighteenth Century." *Church History* 71 (2002): 555–84.

——. "'Commerce and Christianity': Providence Theory, the Missionary Movement, and the Imperialism of Free Trade, 1842–1860." *HJ* 26 (1983): 71–94.

——. "'Commerce and Christianity': The Rise and Fall of a Nineteenth-Century Missionary Slogan." *HJ* 28 (1985): 597–621.

——. *Religion versus Empire? British Protestant Missionaries and Overseas Expansion, 1700–1914* (Manchester, 2004).

——. "Trusteeship, Anti-Slavery and Humanitarianism." In *The Oxford History of the British Empire*, edited by Andrew Porter, 3:198–221 (5 vols., Oxford, 1999).

Porter, Bernard. *The Absent-Minded Imperialists: Empire, Society and Culture in Britain* (Oxford, 2004).

——. "Review Article: Imperialism and the Scramble." *JICH* 9 (1980): 76–81.

Prakash, Gyan. *Bonded Histories: Genealogies of Labor Servitude in Colonial India* (Cambridge, 2002 [1992]).

Prochaska, F. K. "Charity Bazaars in Nineteenth-Century England." *Journal of British Studies* 16 (1977): 62–84.

Quarles, Benjamin. "Ministers without Portfolio." *Journal of Negro History* 39 (1954): 27–42.

——. "Sources of Abolitionist Income." *Mississippi Valley Historical Review* 32 (1945): 36–76.

Querishi, Sadiah. "Robert Gordon Latham, Displayed Peoples, and the Natural History of Race, 1854–1866." *HJ* 54 (2011): 143–66.

Ratcliffe, Barrie M. "Commerce and Empire: Manchester Merchants and West Africa, 1873–1895." *JICH* 7 (1979): 293–320.

——. "Cotton Imperialism: Manchester Merchants and Cotton Cultivation in West Africa in the Mid-Nineteenth Century." *African Economic History* 11 (1982): 87–113.

Rediker, Marcus. *The Slave Ship: A Human History* (London, 2007).

Reynolds, K. D. *Aristocratic Women and Political Society in Victorian Britain* (Oxford, 1998).

Rice, C. Duncan. "'Humanity Sold for Sugar!' The British Abolitionist Response to Free Trade in Slave-Grown Sugar." *HJ* 13 (1970): 402–18.

——. "Literary Sources and British Attitudes to Slavery." In *Anti-Slavery, Religion and Reform*, edited by Christine Bolt and Seymour Drescher, 319–34 (Folkestone, Kent, 1980).

——. "The Missionary Context of the British Anti-Slavery Movement." In *Slavery and British Society 1776–1846*, edited by James Walvin, 150–63 (London, 1982).

——. *The Rise and Fall of Black Slavery* (London, 1975).

——. *The Scots Abolitionists* (Baton Rouge, La., 1981).

Richardson, David. "Background to Annexation: Anglo-African Credit Relations in the Bight of Biafra, 1700–1891." In *From Slave Trade to Empire: Europe and the Colonisation of Black Africa, 1780s–1880s*, edited by Olivier Pétré-Grenouilleau, 47–68 (Abingdon, Oxfordshire, 2004).

Robinson, Ronald, John Gallagher, and Alison Denny. *Africa and the Victorians: The Official Mind of Imperialism*, 2nd ed. (London, 1981).

Roeckell, Leila M. "Bonds over Bondage: British Opposition to the Annexation of Texas." *Journal of the Early Republic* 19 (1999): 257–78.

Rose, Jonathan. *The Intellectual Life of the British Working Classes* (New Haven, Conn., 2002).

Rothman, Adam. "Review of Seymour Drescher, *The Mighty Experiment* (Oxford, 2002)." *Journal of Interdisciplinary History* 24 (2004): 634–36.

Rugemar, Edward Bartlett. *The Problem of Freedom: The Caribbean Roots of the American Civil War* (Baton Rouge, La., 2008).

Runkle, Gerald. "Karl Marx and the American Civil War." *Comparative Studies in Society and History* 6 (1964): 117–41.

Schuler, Monica. *"Alas, Alas, Kongo": A Social History of Indentured African Immigration into Jamaica, 1841–1865* (Baltimore, Md., 1980).

Schulyer, Robert Livingston. "The Abolition of British Imperial Preference, 1846–1860." *Political Science Quarterly* 33 (1918): 77–92.

Schwartz, Suzanne. "Commerce, Civilization and Christianity: The Development of the Sierra Leone Company." In *Liverpool and Transatlantic Slavery*, edited by David Richardson, Suzanne Schwarz, and Anthony J. Tibbles, 252–76 (Liverpool, 2007).

Searle, G. R. *Morality and the Market in Victorian Britain* (Oxford, 1998).

Sell, Alan. *Philosophy, Dissent and Nonconformity* (Cambridge, 2004).

Semmel, Bernard. *Jamaican Blood and Victorian Conscience: The Governor Eyre Controversy*, 2nd ed. (Westport, Conn., 1972).

——. *Liberalism and Naval Strategy: Ideology, Interest, and Sea Power during the Pax Britannica* (Boston, 1986).

Sen, Amartya. *Development as Freedom* (Oxford, 1999).

Sewell, William H. "Ideologies and Social Revolutions: Reflections on the French Case." *Journal of Modern History* 57 (1985): 57–85.

Sexton, Jay. *Debtor Diplomacy: Finance and American Foreign Relations in the Civil War Era 1837–1873* (Oxford, 2005).

Shaikh, Farida. "Judicial Diplomacy: British Officials and the Mixed Commission Courts." In *Slavery, Diplomacy and Empire: Britain and the Suppression of the Slave Trade, 1807–1975*, edited by Keith Hamilton and Patrick Salmon, 42–64 (Eastbourne, Sussex, 2009).

Shepperson, George. "Harriet Beecher Stowe and Scotland, 1852–53." *Scottish Historical Review* 32 (1953): 40–46.

Sherwood, Marika. *After Abolition: Britain and the Slave Trade since 1807* (London, 2007).

Shlomowitz, Ralph. "Markets for Indentured and Time-Expired Melanesian Labour in Queensland, 1863–1906: An Economic Analysis." *Journal of Pacific History* 16 (1981): 70–91.

Sikainga, Ahmad Alawad. *Slaves into Workers: Emancipation and Labor in Colonial Sudan* (Austin, Tex., 1996).

Sinha, Manisha. *The Counter-revolution of Slavery: Politics and Ideology in Antebellum South Carolina* (Chapel Hill, N.C., 2000).

Sklar, Kathryn Kish. "'Women Who Speak for an Entire Nation': American and British Women Compared at the World Anti-Slavery Convention, London, 1840." In *The Abolitionist Sisterhood: Women's Political Culture in Antebellum America,* edited by John Fagin Yellin and John C. Van Horne, 301–34 (Ithaca, N.Y., 1994).

Sklar, Kathryn Kish, and James Brewer Stewart, eds. *Women's Rights and Transatlantic Antislavery in the Era of Emancipation* (New Haven, Conn., 2007).

"Slave Voyages Database," ed. David Eltis (Atlanta, Ga., 2008–present) [www.slavevoyages. org].

Smallwood, Stephanie. *Saltwater Slavery: A Middle Passage from Africa to American Diaspora* (Cambridge, Mass., 2007).

Smith, James Patterson. "The Liberals, Race, and Political Reform in the British West Indies, 1866–1874." *Journal of Negro History* 79 (1994): 131–46.

Smith, Robert. *The Lagos Consulate, 1851–1861* (London, 1978).

——. "The Lagos Consulate, 1851–1861: An Outline." *Journal of African History* 15 (1974): 393–416.

Stanley, Brian. *The Bible and the Flag: Protestant Missions and British Imperialism in the Nineteenth and Twentieth Centuries* (Leicester, 1990).

Steinfeld, Robert J. *Coercion, Contract, and Free Labor in the Nineteenth Century* (Cambridge, 2001).

Stepan, Nancy. *The Idea of Race in Science: Great Britain, 1800–1960* (London, 1982).

Stevenson, Louise L. "Virtue Displayed: The Tie-Ins of Uncle Tom's Cabin." [http:///www. iath.virginia.edu/utc/interpret/exhibits/stevenson/steveson.html].

Stone, Harry. "Charles Dickens and Harriet Beecher Stowe." *Nineteenth-century Fiction* 12 (1957): 188–202.

Stråth, Bo. "Ideology and History." *Journal of Political Ideologies* 11 (2006): 23–42.

Summerson, H. R. T. *"An Ancient Squires Family": The History of the Aglionbys, c. 1130–2002* (Carlisle, 2007).

Swaminathan, Srividhya. *Debating the Slave Trade: Rhetoric of British National Identity, 1759–1815* (Farnham, Surrey, 2009).

Temperley, Harold. "Lord Granville's Unpublished Memorandum on Foreign Policy, 1852." *Cambridge Historical Journal* 2 (1928): 298–302.

Temperley, Howard. "Anti-Slavery as Cultural Imperialism." In *Anti-Slavery, Religion and Reform,* edited by Christine Bolt and Seymour Drescher, 335–50 (Folkestone, Kent, 1980).

——. *British Anti-Slavery 1833–1870* (London, 1972).

——. "The Delegalization of Slavery in British India." *Slavery and Abolition* 21 (2000): 169–87.

——. "The Ideology of Antislavery." In *The Abolition of the Atlantic Slave Trade: Origins and Effects in Europe, Africa, and the Americas,* edited by David Eltis and James Walvin, 21–35 (Madison, Wis., 1981).

——. "The O'Connell Stevenson Contretemps: A Reflection of the Anglo-American Slavery Issue." *Journal of Negro History* 47 (1962): 217–33.

——. *White Dreams, Black Africa* (New Haven, Conn., 1991).

Teukolsky, Rachel. *The Literate Eye: Victorian Art Writing and Modern Aesthetics* (Oxford, 2009).

Thompson, Andrew S. *The Empire Strikes Back? The Impact of Imperialism on Britain from the Mid-Nineteenth Century* (Harlow, Essex, 2005).

——. *Imperial Britain: The Empire in British Politics, c. 1880–1932* (Harlow, Essex, 2000).

Thompson, E. P. *Customs in Common: Studies in Traditional Popular Culture* (New York, 1993).

Thornton, John. *Africa and Africans in the Making of the Atlantic World, 1400–1800,* 2nd ed. (Cambridge, 1998).

Tinker, Hugh. *A New System of Slavery: The Export of Indian Labour Overseas 1830–1920,* 2nd ed. (London, 1993 [Oxford, 1974]).

Toledano, Ehud R. *As if Silent and Absent: Bonds of Enslavement in the Islamic Middle East* (New Haven, 2007).

Tooze, Adam. *The Wages of Destruction: The Making and Breaking of the Nazi Economy* (London, 2006).

Trentmann, Frank. "Before 'Fair Trade': Empire, Free Trade, and the Moral Economies of Food in the Modern World." *Environment and Planning D: Society and Space* 25 (2007): 1079–1102.

——. "Political Culture and Political Economy: Interest, Ideology and Free Trade." *Review of International Political Economy* 5 (1998): 217–51.

Turley, David. "Anti-Slavery Activists and Officials: 'Influence,' Lobbying and the Slave Trade, 1807–1850." In *Slavery, Diplomacy and Empire: Britain and the Suppression of the Slave Trade, 1807–1975,* edited by Keith Hamilton and Patrick Salmon, 81–90 (Eastbourne, Sussex, 2009).

——. "British Antislavery Reassessed." In *Re-thinking the Age of Reform,* edited by Joanna Innes and Arthur Burns, 182–99 (Cambridge, 2003).

——. *The Culture of English Anti-Slavery, 1780–1860* (London, 1991).

——. "'Free Air' and Fugitive Slaves: British Abolitionists versus Government over American Fugitives 1834–61." In *Anti-Slavery, Religion and Reform,* edited by Caroline Bolt and Seymour Drescher, 163–82 (Folkestone, Kent, 1980).

Turner, Michael. "The Limits of Abolition: Government, Saints and the 'African Question,' c.1780–1820." *EHR* 112 (1997): 319–57.

Tyrrell, Alexander. *Joseph Sturge and the Moral Radical Party in Early Victorian Britain* (London, 1987).

——. "Making the Millennium: The Mid-Nineteenth Century Peace Movement." *HJ* 21 (1978): 75–95.

——. "The 'Moral Radical Party' and the Anglo-Jamaican Campaign for the Abolition of the Negro Apprenticeship System." *EHR* 99 (1984): 481–502.

Uba, C. N. "Suppression of the Slave Trade in the Nigerian Emirates." *Journal of African History* 32 (1991): 447–70.

Van Alstyne, Richard W. "The British Right of Search and the African Slave Trade." *Journal of Modern History* 2 (1930): 37–47.

Van Dijk, Teun A. "Ideology and Discourse Analysis." *Journal of Political Ideologies* 11 (2006): 115–40.

Walkowitz, Judith. *Prostitution and Victorian Society: Women, Class and the State* (Cambridge, 1980).

Walls, Andrew F. "The Legacy of Thomas Fowell Buxton." *International Bulletin of Missionary Research* 15 (1991): 74–77.

Waters, Hazel. *Racism on the Victorian Stage: Representations of Slavery and the Black Character* (Cambridge, 2007).

Williams, Eric. *British Historians and the West Indies* (London, 1966 [1964]).

——. "Laissez Faire, Sugar and Slavery." *Political Science Quarterly* 58 (1943): 67–85.

Wilson, Forrest. *Crusader in Crinoline: The Life of Harriet Beecher Stowe* (Philadelphia, 1941).

Winks, Robin W. *Blacks in Canada,* 2nd ed. (London, 1997).

Wolffe, John. "Lord Palmerston and Religion: A Reappraisal." *EHR* 120 (2005): 907–36.

Wood, Marcus. *Blind Memory: Visual Representations of Slavery in England and America, 1760–1865* (Manchester, 2000).

——. *Slavery, Empathy and Pornography* (Oxford, 2002).

Wright, J. L. "Nothing Else But Slaves: Britain and the Central Saharan Slave Trade in the Nineteenth Century." (PhD thesis, School of Oriental and African Studies, University of London, 1998).

Žižek, Slavoj. *The Parallax View* (Boston, Mass., 2006).

Zwanenberg, R. M. A. "Anti-Slavery, the Ideology of 19th Century Imperialism in East Africa." Typescript conference paper, Historical Association of Kenya Annual Conference 1972 (Sterling Memorial Library, Yale University, call number SML DT32.5.V35 1972).

Zweynert, Joachim. "Interests versus Culture in the Theory of Institutional Change?" *Journal of Institutional Economics* 5 (2009): 339–60.

# Index

138; and delegalization of slavery, 188, 190; and foreign slaveries, 71; and fugitive slave policy, 71; and Lagos, 253n123; and Ottoman Empire, 62; and Zanzibar, 151, 190

Xhosa people, 211

Yancey, William, 23

Zambesi River, 150
Zanzibar, 150–154, *153*, 155–156, 158, 159–160, 163, 169, 174, 188–193, 197n198, 261n75
Žižek, Slavoj, 213